Revolution Interrupted

Revolution Interrupted

*Farmers, Students, Law,
and Violence in
Northern Thailand*

Tyrell Haberkorn

THE UNIVERSITY OF WISCONSIN PRESS

Publication of this volume has been made possible, in part, through support from the **Association for Asian Studies, Inc.**

The University of Wisconsin Press
1930 Monroe Street, 3rd Floor
Madison, Wisconsin 53711-2059
uwpress.wisc.edu

3 Henrietta Street
London WC2E 8LU, England
eurospanbookstore.com

Copublished with Silkworm Books. Customers in Thailand and Southeast
Asia should order from Silkworm Books (www.silkwormbooks.com).

Printed in the United States of America

Library of Congress Cataloging-in-Publication Data
Haberkorn, Tyrell.
Revolution interrupted: farmers, students, law, and violence
in northern Thailand / Tyrell Haberkorn.
p.   cm. — (New perspectives in Southeast Asian studies)
Includes bibliographical references and index.
ISBN 978-0-299-28184-7 (pbk.: alk. paper) — ISBN 978-0-299-28183-0 (e-book)
1. Thailand, Northern—Politics and government. 2. Thailand—Politics and
government—1945–1988. 3. Tenant farmers—Thailand, Northern—Political activity. 4. Political
violence—Thailand, Northern. I. Title. II. Series: New perspectives in Southeast Asian studies.
DS588.N56H33   2011
959.3—dc22
2010038909

For my mother and my father

Contents

Foreword		ix
THONGCHAI WINICHAKUL		
Preface		xi
Note on Language, Translation, and Dates		xvii
List of Abbreviations		xix
Map of Chiang Mai and Thailand		2
Introduction: When Revolution Is Interrupted		3
1.	Breaking the Backbone of the Nation	29
2.	From the Rice Fields to the Cities	53
3.	From the Classrooms to the Rice Fields	81
4.	Violence and Its Denials	105
5.	A State in Disarray	129
	Conclusion: Resuming Revolution?	149
	Appendix: Leaders of the FFT Victimized by Violence, 1974–1979	159
Notes		165
Bibliography		201
Index		219

Foreword

THONGCHAI WINICHAKUL

At the detention building inside the compound of the School for Police Recruits in Bangkok in 1976–77, I was not surprised to find many of my fellow student leaders from the 6 October massacre at Thammasat University, when police and paramilitary forces had killed dozens and arrested hundreds for daring to resist the royalist military rule. But many more people were in the compound, too, for mysterious reasons. They were among the five thousand "dangers to society" arbitrarily detained with no charges or trials.

One of them was a school teacher, as nice and soft-mannered as a model Thai teacher can be. When she talked about her boss and opponents at school who probably reported her low-level political activities to the police, she did not swear, scold, or say a single foul word about them. As sad as she was, she had a little smile and could even laugh at her own fate. I do not remember when she was released, probably after a full term of "vocational training" for the "dangerous" people like her.

Around mid-1977, two brothers were put in a cell near the one that my friends and I had occupied for months. The elder brother was a successful farmer active in local politics at the district level in a northeastern province. He was not part of the Farmers Federation that Tyrell Haberkorn discusses in this book. The younger brother was a farm boy who studied at an open university in Bangkok. Neither of them knew why they were arrested, who reported them to the police, about what activities, or why they ended up at the same place with the alleged communists and enemies of the nation like us. The elder brother was worried; he insisted many times that he was not a communist.

There were many more. In this difficult time and unlikely place, we became good friends. Although it would have been better had we met under other conditions, I miss those people. This book brings back to me many memories of the time when our lives intersected.

I also remember reading in the news about all of those who were assassinated during these same years. I knew some of them personally, not merely as names without faces or as statistics. It was a dark age in modern Thai history, followed by a time when people were urged to forget for the sake of reconciliation, in order for the country to move on. In recent years, the 6 October massacre has been mentioned in public more often, although always cautiously and in limited fashion, usually with carefully chosen words. Yet the assassinations and the arbitrary detention of those "dangers to society," who are the main subjects of this book, have been overlooked.

In the name of reconciliation, the names and stories of these people have been swept under the rug. Their real lives and souls may never be recognized again, even to their children in some cases. Justice was also buried. For reconciliation "Thai-style" is the sacrifice of justice and the suspension of the rule of law that could incriminate the ruling elite and their networks—a group that has been in power since the mid-1970s, despite changes of government, parliaments, and generations. Reconciliation Thai-style is like the father who tells his children to go to bed and get some sleep after brutally punishing them for disobedience. The crime was a family matter. Good children are not supposed to cry for being abused.

Until it happens again, and again—most recently in 2010 while this book was in the final stages. And again, reconciliation without justice is expected. Soon the lost lives and souls will become faceless names, then eventually statistics. Then their stories will be silenced too.

Haberkorn writes to prevent the fading of life to oblivion, recounting stories that bring the forgotten back to life. She does so as only a good scholar can do, with deftness, sophistication, and insight. And with passion, too. This is not a simplistic commemorative salutation to the victims. Far from it. The best way to remember the forgotten is, as this book does, through careful research and nuanced interpretations to explain what happened to these people and how Thai society has dealt with their lives, souls, and stories. It is not an obituary, but a look into Thai society, face to face and eyes to eyes, to understand the other side of the Thai smiles. Haberkorn shows why farmers and students rose to challenges, why they were silenced, and why there were assassinations and arbitrary detentions. Not only does this book give voices to the silenced, but it also raises questions vital to Thai society and history.

I hope that one day we have enough courage to confront those questions.

Preface

In her poem "Cartographies of Silence," Adrienne Rich cautions her readers against failing to recognize the full, active nature of silence. Silence "is a presence / it has a history a form / Do not confuse it / with any kind of absence."[1] The poem traces the fracturing of romance and the growing divide between two people who once cared deeply for one another. Leaving the divide unspoken does not make it disappear but rather makes its edges more pronounced and threatening. Although Adrienne Rich is writing about love, her words succinctly capture one of the dynamics animating Thai political life and history.

Since the transformation from absolute to constitutional monarchy on 24 June 1932, governance in Thailand has depended on the silence of marginalized people. This category has included, but is not limited to, farmers, workers, the rural and urban poor, ethnic minority groups, dissidents, and women. Through actions explicit and implicit by those inside and outside the state apparatus with access to power and influence, members of these groups have variously been excluded from the political process, denied legal subjectivity, and given limited access to the possible benefits of development and progress. It is not simply that those with power have not listened to the voices of marginalized people, but rather that political life in Thailand has often required and sustained their exclusion.

This book is about a series of challenges to this foundational exclusion made by northern tenant farmers and their student allies in the wake of the 14 October 1973 movement. I trace how the members of the Farmers' Federation of Thailand (FFT) made concrete demands for laws, policies, and actions that would change the material conditions of their lives, while they simultaneously challenged the very form of the political decision-making structure. As soon as farmers began protesting in front of the provincial hall in Chiang Mai, counterprotestors admonished them to get out of the city so that the civil servants could enter the building without having to walk through the protests.[2] One implication of this statement is that farmers are meant to be out of sight in the countryside, producing rice for the people in the city to eat, but they are not meant to claim the city as a space in which they, too, can speak and demand rights. The gravity of the farmers' challenge can be read, I argue, in the violence with which their demands for legal reform were met.

What makes marginalized people a presence, rather than an absence, is that

they have consistently challenged their exclusion from rule through organizing, writing, appealing, and protesting, even when they have faced repression,
violence, and death. To posit this as a history is not to argue that there is a
unifying narrative linking all movements by marginalized people for a greater
stake in governance in Thailand in one trajectory. It would be intellectually and
politically irresponsible to argue, for example, that the peasant rebellions of the
nineteenth century led to the struggles of the FFT in the 1970s and the protests
of the United Democratic Front against Dictatorship (UDD) for reform of the
political system in the wake of the 19 September 2006 coup.

Instead, what can become visible are threads of the challenge to the exclusion of marginalized people from governance and political life more broadly.
When the red-shirted members of the UDD occupied the glitzy shopping area
of Ratchaprasong in Bangkok in April and May 2010, one of the claims made
by their detractors was that they were "hillbillies" (*khon bannok*) who should
go home.[3] Many members of the UDD are from the north and northeast, and
this claim can be read as a demand of people in the city who wanted to be able
to access their shopping malls again. But like the admonition that the tenant
farmers in Chiang Mai should return to the rice fields, the demand that the
UDD supporters leave the city is less about the daily conveniences and luxuries
desired by the people in the city and actually about the very question of who
is meant to participate in rule. The farmers of the FFT and the members of
the UDD were meant to follow the decisions made by those with power and
remain enveloped in silence, not claim themselves as people who can change
the shape of the decision-making structure. These resonant moments reflect the
gap between those who can participate in governance and those who cannot,
which has remained unbridged in Thailand since 1932. As in the disintegrating
relationship in Rich's poem, leaving this divide unspoken and unaddressed will
not cause it to cease to matter. Instead, this divide has the potential to become
more pronounced and disruptive politically, socially, and economically, unless
those with power are willing to share it with the majority of citizens who are
excluded from political life.

For activists and scholars concerned with injustice, the challenge is to learn
how to listen to the voices that are made silent in Thai political and social life.
Simultaneously, we must work to recognize and trace the ways in which marginalized people have both been excluded from political life and challenged
this exclusion. At the close of "Cartographies of Silence," Rich references a moment of possibility against silence and writes, "what in fact I keep choosing /
are these words, these whispers, conversations / from which time after time
the truth breaks moist and green."[4] This book comes at the end of ten years of
research and writing about progressive activism and state and parastate violence
in Thailand. During these ten years, I read and listened to whispers and conversations about solidarity and struggle, which made me feel as though another
world was possible. I also read and listened to stories of violence and sorrow

that chilled me to the bone. In the pages that follow, I have tried to honor these stories, while remembering that they are not my own.

At Cornell University, my dissertation committee generously offered advice, criticism, and boundless encouragement at every stage of the process, from a collection of thoughts to the book proposal. My chair, Andrew Willford, asked unanswerable questions at every moment of imagining, researching, and writing the dissertation. His generosity—as a scholar, teacher, and person—is unparalleled. Through real-time and e-mail conversations about Thai politics and literature, Thak Chaloemtiarana relentlessly reminded me to remain hopeful. Shelley Feldman's advice to hold the writing close to me, especially when it is difficult, has carried me through many long days and nights. Tamara Loos's enthusiasm about my academic and activist work has been life giving. Viranjini Munasinghe pushed me to ask broad questions, even as I stubbornly tried to write an area studies monograph.

Between 2003 and 2005, I was affiliated with the Department of History in the Faculty of Humanities at Chiang Mai University. During that time, Attachak Sattayanurak wrote me countless letters of introduction, listened to my ramblings about the recent Thai past, and gave me indispensable advice. The students and faculty in the department, especially Saichon Sattayanurak, taught me to write about how the past resonates in the present. The National Research Council of Thailand granted me permission to conduct research and helped me gain access to the National Archives in Bangkok as well as the Chiang Mai branch. The Thai-U.S. Educational Foundation (Fulbright) supported my research and helped me with many administrative concerns.

The research for this book has been supported by many sources at different stages. Dissertation research was supported by a Fulbright-Hays Doctoral Dissertation Research Abroad grant, an Alice Hanson Cook Award from the Department of Feminist, Gender, and Sexuality Studies at Cornell University, and grants from the Department of Anthropology, the Graduate School and the Southeast Asia Program at Cornell University. Follow-up research was funded by a Freeman Foundation Asia faculty grant at Colgate University and a grant from the Department of Political and Social Change at the Australian National University.

Without the people who shared their stories of struggle with me, this book would not exist. I was invited to commemorations and reunions, where I listened and listened. Many of those people are not mentioned by name here or in the body of the book so that their anonymity will be protected. It is a great pleasure, therefore, to name those who can be named here. Pa Wi at Suan Anya and Sinsawat Yodbangtoey at the Pridi Banomyong Institute shared their recollections of Ajarn Angun Malik with me and introduced me to others who did the same. Chompunoot Tosinthiti shared her recollections of the 1970s in Chiang Mai and introduced me to many other people who did the same.

The librarians at the Kroch Library at Cornell University, the Chiang Mai University Library, the Thai Information Center at Chulalongkorn University, the Thai National Archives, the Thammasat University Archives, and the National Library of Australia were unfailingly helpful. In particular, Daoruang Naewthong at the Thammasat University Archives and the late Ajarn David Wyatt at the Kroch Library helped me try to locate materials that did and did not exist. Until his death in November 2006, Ajarn Wyatt pushed me to keep writing, without hesitation, because history matters.

During seven years of graduate school, the Southeast Asia Program (SEAP) at Cornell was an intense and unparalleled intellectual community. I wrote my dissertation ensconced in an office at the Kahin Center, surrounded by the SEAPniks: Nina Hien, Jane Ferguson, Doreen Lee, Rick Ruth, and Samson Lim. Their questions, laughter, and shared commitment to critical studies of Southeast Asia made writing (and life) a joy. While I was completing the book manuscript, SEAP generously allowed me to come back as a visiting fellow for one magical North American summer. For making this possible, and their help in many endeavors, I am grateful to Nancy Loncto and Wendy Treat in Uris Hall.

I began revising the manuscript while teaching in the Peace and Conflict Studies Program (PCON) at Colgate University. Daniel Monk, Xan Karn, Andrew Rotter, Padma Kaimal, Tim Byrnes, and Nancy Ries taught me how to cross-country ski and become a teacher and colleague. The PCONistas inspired me tremendously, especially Kara Cooperrider and Cortney Ahern. Amy Feinstein made living, and running, on the quiet roads of Hamilton sparkle and shine.

I finished the manuscript in the southern hemisphere, as a member of the Department of Political and Social Change at the Australian National University. Ed Aspinall and all my colleagues have made Canberra an exciting and life-giving place to think, write, and teach. When I have tired of revising, Nattakant Akarapongpisak, Prajak Kongkirati, and Andrew Walker have been a few doors down the hall, ready to talk about injustice, human rights, and Thai politics and to then urge me to go back to writing. Alison Ley offered expert advice on the preparation of the manuscript. Across campus Craig Reynolds challenged me to sharpen my thinking and critiqued my reading of Jit Phumisak vis-à-vis the farmers' struggle. Conversations with Ana Dragojlovic made me want to write and write and write.

In addition to my dissertation committee, I am fortunate to have had many unofficial advisers throughout this process. In particular, Virada Somswasdi, Kasian Tejapira, Kanoksak Kaewthep, Coeli Barry, Thanet Aphornsuvan, Michael Montesano, Peter Bell, and Anna Marie Smith have all offered comments at different points. Chalong Soontravanich invited me to present an early version of my research in the Department of History at Chulalongkorn University. David Hayes of *openDemocracy* and Tom Fenton of *Critical Asian Studies* have pushed me to become a better writer. Ngampit Jagacinski was first my Thai-language professor and then became my friend. Her unflagging support has been crucial to the completion of this book.

Gwen Walker at the University of Wisconsin Press was enthusiastically critical from our first meeting and her questions have pushed me to become a more thoughtful writer and a riskier thinker. Janet Opdyke's copyediting smoothed my prose, and Sheila McMahon patiently guided me through the editing and publication process. I thank Peter Vandergeest and Paul Cohen for their meticulous reviews; they challenged me to rethink my ideas and their implications. Without Thongchai Winichakul's support and encouragement, this book would not exist, and without his example I would be a different kind of scholar. I am grateful for his difficult questions and careful readings of the manuscript.

An earlier version of the argument developed in the book appeared in "An Unfinished Past: The 1974 Land Rent Control Act and Assassination in Northern Thailand," *Critical Asian Studies* 41, no. 1 (March 2009). An earlier version of parts of chapter 3 appeared in an article published in a Thai women's studies journal, "At the Limits of Imagination: Ajarn Angun Malik and the Meanings of Politics," *Stance: The Thai Feminist Review* 1, no. 1 (August 2007).

I am grateful to Nij Tontisirin at Cornell University who made the beautiful map of Thailand for this book. I also gratefully acknowledge permission from Matichon Publishing to reprint the photograph on the cover, which was originally published in *Prachachat Weekly* 2, no. 93 (28 August 2518 [1975]): 7.

For friendship and solidarity, I would like to thank Arnika Fuhrmann, Patrick Pierce, Ginger Norwood, Kevin Hewison, Cisco Bradley, Pranom Somwong, Alexandra Denes, Worrasit Tantinipankul, Tracy Johnson, Namhee Lee, Viengrat Nethipo, elin slavick, Catherine Lutz, and Marion Traub-Werner. P'Po, Rasada Manurasada, Pornpen Khongkachonkiet, Peter Kornbluh, James Graham, and Nick Cheesman have shown me how scholarship can, and must, be put to use for justice in an unjust world. Jim Glassman and Thitiya Phaobtong have shared *sai oua* and a relentless commitment to challenging oppression. Erick White has helped me with phantasmagoric translations. Parissara Liewkeat has long been both my fiercest critic and my strongest supporter. As a writer and a friend, Jennifer Solomon has pushed me to first articulate, and then live, what I want and what I mean. Tze May Loo has given me movement in the form of contingency. For sharing spotted cows and an acute commitment to the possible, I am grateful to Gayatri Menon. Doreen Lee read the whole manuscript multiple times. Since meeting her on the first day of graduate school in August 2000, she has been my first reader and comrade in all things, from writing against violence to photocopying revolution.

My older sisters and brothers—Elizabeth Haberkorn, Susan Snyder, and B.J. Haberkorn, and their partners—have unfailingly supported my work materially and emotionally. My nieces and nephews remind me that another world must be, and is, possible. Kathy Kelleher and Richard and Genevieve Tyrell followed the progress of this book with constant encouragement.

My parents, William Edward and Sheila Kelleher Haberkorn, surprised me by offering to proofread the entire first draft. While they argued with one another on the finer points of grammar, they were both very dissatisfied with the ending and the continued failure to hold the assassins of the farmer leaders accountable. I could not agree more. This book is dedicated to them, with love and gratitude, for teaching me to struggle in the service of both knowledge and justice.

Note on Language, Translation, and Dates

All translations in this book are mine unless otherwise indicated. I quote extensively from translations of difficult-to-locate periodical, archival, leftist, and other sources. While the original Thai text is not present in the book, those readers interested can find 70 to 80 percent of the quotations in the footnotes to my dissertation: Tyrell Haberkorn, "States of Transgression: Politics, Violence, and Agrarian Transformation in Northern Thailand," PhD diss., Cornell University, 2007.

The Thai words in this book have been transliterated into roman characters, with two exceptions: the appendix, which lists the members of the Farmers' Federation of Thailand victimized by violence; and bibliographic information for Thai-language sources. The farmers' names remain in the original Thai as a reminder of the specificity of their lives. The bibliographic information remains in the original Thai to allow readers to locate my sources more easily.

For the transliterated words, I have followed the guidelines of the Royal Institute outlined in "Principles of Romanization for Thai Script by Transcription Method," with three exceptions. If one follows the guidelines, the word for "lord" and the first part of the word for "farmer" are to be spelled identically, in spite of the fact that in their Thai form they begin with a different consonant. In order to avoid confusion, I have transliterated "lord" as *jao* and "farmer" as *chao na*. I have transliterated "professor" as *ajarn*, rather than *ajan*, due to personal preference. With respect to individual names, if there is already a transliteration familiar through general use, I have used it instead of following the Royal Institute guidelines.

Finally, in Thailand, dates are calculated in terms of the Buddhist era (BE), which is common era (CE) plus 543 years. This means, for example, that 1973 CE is 2516 BE. Although I use CE dates in the main body of my text, when citing Thai-language sources, I first specify the BE publication date and then include the CE date in brackets immediately following.

Abbreviations

BE	Buddhist era
CE	common era
CIA	Central Intelligence Agency
CMU	Chiang Mai University
CPT	Communist Party of Thailand
ESC	Eastern Student Center
FFT	Farmers' Federation of Thailand
FIST	Federation of Independent Students of Thailand
GNP	gross national product
ID	identification
ISOC	Internal Security Operations Command
KGB	Committee for State Security
LRCA	Land Rent Control Act
MP	member of parliament
NARC	National Administrative Reform Council
NSC	Northern Student Center
NSCT	National Student Center of Thailand
OIA	Official Information Act
PAD	People's Alliance for Democracy
PCON	Peace and Conflict Studies Program, Colgate University
PDG	People for Democracy Group
SAP	Social Action Party
SEAP	Southeast Asia Program, Cornell University
SPT	Socialist Party of Thailand
TCP	Thai Communist Party
UDD	United Democratic Front against Dictatorship
UNESCO	United Nations Educational, Scientific, and Cultural Organization
VDA	Volunteer Development Assembly

Revolution Interrupted

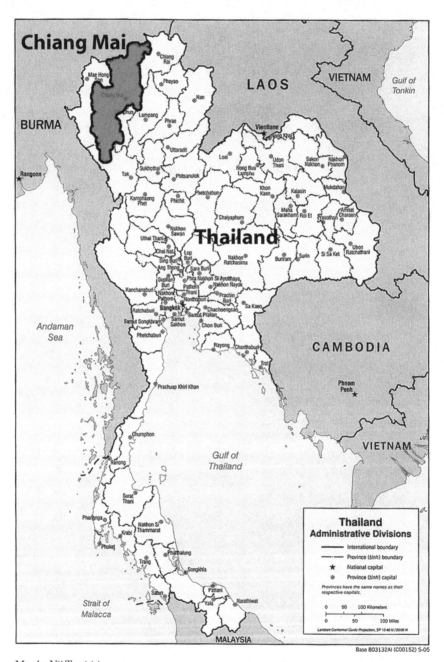

Map by Nij Tontisirin

Introduction

When Revolution Is Interrupted

It is the peoples' charge that the government and Thai law are capitalist and tools of the capitalists. The farmers have not been helped and have not received justice. They don't know who to turn to now.

> Anonymous editorialist, *Thai Niu*, 12 August 2517 [1974]

I am objecting to a model which concentrates attention upon one dramatic episode—*the* Revolution—to which all that goes before and after must be related; and which insists upon an ideal type of this Revolution against which all others may be judged.

> E. P. Thompson, *The Poverty of Theory and Other Essays*

In mid-August 1974, farmers from seven central Thai provinces threatened to renounce their citizenship and burn their state-issued identity cards. In the months following the end of nearly forty years of dictatorship and the democratic opening inaugurated by the events of 14 October 1973, farmers were one of several politicized groups that took to the streets in Thailand. For months they had beseeched the prime minister to take action to reduce their debt and secure a fair price for rice. Their appeals were ignored; the deputy prime minister refused even to meet with them. With nowhere else to turn, they turned to themselves. Unafraid of creditors and other capitalists, they hoped to win for themselves a new life without oppression. The farmers announced their intention to cease paying taxes and to end their recognition of the Thai state leadership as their own. Instead, they planned to set up an autonomous, liberated zone (*khet plotploy*). By September 1974, the farmers were standing firm in their threat to secede. If the state used force against them, the farmers promised to respond in kind.[1]

With this threat of force, the Thai prime minister, Sanya Thammasak, finally took notice of the farmers. Neither he nor the deputy prime minister, Prakob Hutasingh, wanted to believe the threats were real. In contrast, Police Director General Prachuab Suntharangkul saw in them a real and imminent danger. He cautioned that "the phrase 'liberated area' is one that Communists use, perhaps suggesting that the farmers have been incited by the Communists."[2] He ordered the police to investigate the farmers' meaning in using the phrase. If the farmers violated the law, he would order their immediate arrest.

In threatening to create an autonomous zone, the farmers were placing themselves at the head of a long trajectory of revolt. This tradition of revolt included peasant rebellions in the nineteenth century, and, in the latter half of the twentieth, came to be linked to Cold War fears of an imminent communist takeover. Unlike their predecessors, however, a few days after Police Director General Prachuab gave the order to investigate the possible revolt, the farmers withdrew their threat in favor of continued protest.[3] The specter of revolution seemed to drift out of the Thai picture.

Police Director General Prachuab's concern about the renegade farmers, which echoed the broader panic of Thai and U.S. counterinsurgency specialists, must be seen against the backdrop of communist transitions to power in neighboring Vietnam, Cambodia, and Laos in 1975. Despite the fears of elites inside and outside the Thai state, Thailand remained, in the geopolitical language of the day, a "domino" that continued to stand even as its eastern and northern neighbors "fell." Dissident Thai farmers did not, in Lenin's articulation of Marx's idea of revolution, "*shatter, break up, blow up* . . . the whole state machinery."[4] The open space of politics created by the 14 October 1973 movement for democracy was destroyed less than three years later by a massacre of unarmed progressive students and activists at Thammasat University on the morning of 6 October 1976. A coup followed on the evening of the massacre. The administration of the Thai state was handed back to the military and bureaucratic elite, and the monarchy was left intact. Although the Communist Party of Thailand (CPT) continued to fight a war against the Thai state that it had begun in 1965, by the mid-1980s the CPT had been dissolved. Many of the cadres not killed by Thai military forces during the war surrendered and resumed their lives outside the maquis.

Yet to conclude from this series of statements that there was no revolution in mid-1970s Thailand would be to misapprehend both recent Thai history and the meaning of revolution. The triumphant counterinsurgency specialists who congratulated themselves on the successful protection of Thailand from communist revolution were correct, but only partially. There was no *communist* revolution in Thailand. But what if the twentieth-century "revolution" is divided from the term *communist*? What if the vanguard of revolution was not the Communist Party, or what if there was in fact no vanguard at all? What if, as Greg Grandin suggests in his book about liberation and counterinsurgency in Guatemala, the Cold War was "not only between the United States and the Soviet Union but between different views of the shape that social citizenship would take" caused by the experience of the "dramatic torsion between the anticipation of development and equality and the reality of exclusion and exploitation"?[5] What if revolution can take the classic form of the capture of state power by the masses but can also constitute, in the words of Michael Walzer, the "conscious attempts to establish a new moral or material world and to impose, or evoke, radically new patterns of day-to-day conduct"?[6] Even if these attempts are repressed, and even if revolution is interrupted, in James Scott's terms, "a memory of resistance and courage that may lie in wait for the future" remains.[7] By considering revolution in these terms, it is possible to make a new assessment of the desires for change and imagination for the future, whether realized or not, that animate struggles for social and political transformation. This approach will also help to demystify domination not only by tracking the daily resistances to it but also by illuminating the blueprints for different ways of life and models of government that threatened to overturn oppression of the many by the few. How, then, might one understand how progressive movements and the violence that represses them are bound together and mutually constituted? Put differently, what might counterrevolution—and its histories—look like? To be clear, my intention is not to argue that any and all movements for social and political transformation are revolutionary but rather to question the overly swift and simplistic depictions of revolution and, by implication, counterrevolution that have tended to prevail.

This book pairs a rethinking of revolution with a disquieting paradox drawn from the height of the Cold War in Thailand. This paradox, which took place on the terrain of land tenancy, is that farmers became a greater threat to landlords by meeting them as equals on the shared terrain of the legal system than they would have had they attempted to destroy them through armed insurgency. When farmers picked up the law as their tool of organizing and liberation, they individually faced assassination and Thai society collectively faced a series of events that climaxed in chaos and national crisis.

The focus of a short-lived struggle in 1951, by the mid-1970s tenancy reached a breaking point. During these three decades, high rents, severe land shortages, and broad and growing economic inequity struck at the ability of farmers to feed themselves; paying rent proved unsustainable for farmers who could not retain enough grain for their families. In the aftermath of the 14 October 1973 movement, landless and tenant farmers organized into the first national, autonomous Thai farmers' organization, the Farmers' Federation of Thailand (FFT). Federation activists in Chiang Mai and Lamphun provinces in northern Thailand led a struggle to pass a law that standardized and lowered the level of rent on rice land, the Land Rent Control Act (LRCA) of December 1974. Farmers, working with sympathetic students and lawyers, transgressed the boundaries of class and space to organize to spread information from village to village, and to make the provisions of the LRCA a reality. Their work was met first with anxiety on the part of some landowners and state officials (including disbelief when farmers cited the new law) and then with the harassment of activists. Then major FFT leaders were targeted one by one across the country. Between March 1974 and September 1979, thirty-three were assassinated, eight were seriously injured, and five were "disappeared."[8] At the height of the violence, between March and August 1975, twenty-one FFT leaders were killed. The assassinations were particularly concentrated in Chiang Mai province, where eight FFT leaders were assassinated in the two months between June and August 1975, including the northern president and national vice president, Intha Sribunruang, on 30 July 1975.[9] Even before the 6 October 1976 massacre and coup returned Thailand to dictatorship, the assassinations of FFT leaders created pervasive fear throughout the countryside and put an end to the FFT's efforts at legal organizing.

Only in one case was an arrest made, and the suspected assassin was released before he was prosecuted. Over thirty years later, the assassins remain unnamed and, in the view of many former farmer and student activists with whom I spoke, unnameable. This means that it is impossible to ask those who pulled the trigger who, or what, led them to do so. In the absence of definitive knowledge about what fueled the murderous rage behind the assassinations, some inferences may nevertheless be made. The evidence surrounding the FFT's activities in the months preceding the killings suggests that landholding and state elites were profoundly unsettled and displaced by the efforts to pass and implement the LRCA.

This book takes the stance, which some may find surprising or even heretical, that northern farmers became revolutionary when they chose *not* to resolve their grievances with the Thai state by setting up an autonomous, liberated zone as the central farmers threatened to do. Instead, they became revolutionaries when they made themselves not only the objects but also the subjects, of the law, and forced landowners and the state to become accountable to them. Although a possible communist future was a frightening prospect to the landed, bureaucratic, and other elites, the more concrete reality of their loss of control over political and legal subjectivity was an even greater danger. This—not the occupation of Bangkok by CPT forces or the seizure of land in the Chiang Mai suburbs by CPT cadres—was the revolution interrupted in the mid-1970s.

It is by being mindfully heretical in my analysis that I am able to bridge politics and scholarship and connect people's lives to the production of knowledge in which their actions gather meaning and historical significance. The violence with which the farmers' actions were met indicates that their opponents were caught off guard by the farmers' new legal subjecthood. Yet in choosing the law as their terrain of struggle rather than extraparliamentary insurgency, as their ancestors and the CPT had done, the farmers carried out a revolution that was also unexpected by scholars. Cynthia Enloe urges scholars to be surprised, by which she means "to have one's current explanatory notions, and thus one's predictive assumptions, thrown into confusion."[10] She writes against a cynical form of knowing that only notices the ways in which the status quo remains unchanged and instead insists that observing how the status quo is produced, and contested in the process, is essential. In failing to apprehend the import of the farmers' actions, scholars have obscured the multiple sites in which the established order in Thailand was first unmade and then reconsolidated during the 1970s. Writing against the rise of fascism in Germany in the late 1930s, Walter Benjamin insisted, "The current amazement that the things we are experiencing are 'still' possible in the twentieth century is not philosophical. This amazement is not the beginning of knowledge—unless it is the knowledge that the view of history which gives rise to it is untenable."[11] It is not the content of the violence against farmers and other dissidents in Thailand in the 1970s that surprises and disturbs me but rather the persistent and collective silence about it over thirty years later. In the context of continuous and always shifting repression against those who challenge the established order, this silence threatens to become deafening. Considering this struggle as an interrupted revolution offers a way to understand this silence, and to suggest a way it can be broken. To interrupt is to stop, break, or hinder speech, movement, or another process. The temporal nature of interruption means that the process, in this case the transformation of Thai social and political life, can begin again.

What appears at first glance to be a parliamentary and ultimately unsuccessful struggle in a peripheral location is reinterpreted in this book as a revolutionary change felt from margin to center and center to margin. The remainder of this introduction is devoted to creating an analytic framework in which this reinterpretation becomes meaningful. I outline in more detail the redefinition of the idea of *revolution* that my argument demands. Simultaneously, I explore the political, geographic, and historical conditions of revolution's emergence in northern Thailand in the mid-1970s. I begin with the conditions of land tenancy in Chiang Mai province.

Tenancy and Lingering Feudalism

Land tenancy—the practice by which a farmer plants, grows, and harvests a crop on land owned by someone else in exchange for payment in cash or kind—formally emerged in Thailand during the reign of King Chulalongkorn (1868–1910), long before the end of absolute monarchy in 1932. Under Chulalongkorn, a land tenure law was instituted that required landowners either to use their land or forfeit ownership. In consequence, renting out land became a necessary, and profitable, enterprise for landowners.[12] In the mid-1970s, slightly forty years after the official end of feudalism with the transition to a constitutional monarchy, the tenancy struggle exposed the vestiges of feudalism and became the vehicle through which marginalized farmers challenged their exclusion from politics. Nationally, nearly 80 percent of Thailand's population was rural in the 1970s.[13] While the fact that the overwhelming majority of Thai citizens live in the countryside provides a clear reason for focusing on farmers' lives, one of the operative conclusions of this book is that the effects of the tenancy struggles were soon felt outside the rural areas in which they began.

The explosiveness of tenancy as a political issue in the mid-1970s can be partially explained by the material conditions faced by farmers. Where rates of tenancy and other such conditions fail adequately to account for farmers' actions, the entrenched histories of inequality in rural Thailand may offer another partial explanation. Yet even taken together, these factors cannot wholly explain why tenancy became so contentious during the height of the Cold War in Thailand. The lacunae left by both of these partial explanations provide space for the entrance of politics, historically and analytically.

As the economist Krirkkiat Phipatseritham argued, the aggregate data for land tenancy in Thailand in the mid-1970s did not indicate an urgent problem.[14] In comparison to the exploitative and entrenched tenancy practices in the Philippines, prerevolutionary tenancy systems in China and Vietnam, and vastly unequal land distribution and absentee landlordism in Brazil, the system of tenancy in Thailand may seem relatively benign.[15] In particular, the rate of tenancy in the northern region, of which Chiang Mai is one constituent province, may not seem unduly high. In 1973, 12.25 percent of all agricultural land in Thailand was tenant occupied, or 13,834,225 *rai* out of 112,943,669.[16] In the central region, 39.27 percent of agricultural land was tenant occupied, or 7,982,733 *rai* out of 27,274,496. In the northern region, 15.74 percent of agricultural land was tenant occupied, or 3,652,068 *rai* out of 23,189,043. In the southern region, 4.42 percent of agricultural land was tenant occupied, or 605,151 *rai* out of 13,684,941. In the northeastern region, 3.27 percent of agricultural land was tenant occupied, or 1,594,273 *rai* out of 48,796,089.[17] The aridity of the northeastern region and the preference for growing crops other than rice in the southern region meant that tenancy rates were lower in those areas. The region with the highest rate of tenancy has historically been the central region, largely due to the expansion of landownership under Chulalongkorn and land acquired through canal excavation in the Rangsit Plains during the same era.[18]

Yet a closer examination of Chiang Mai province, in terms of both tenancy and other material conditions in the 1970s and earlier, unsettles the picture of relatively low rates of tenancy in northern Thailand. Chiang Mai, now part of northern Thailand, was established as the capital of the Lanna kingdom by King Mengrai in 1292 CE.[19] Chiang Mai province is located 750 kilometers north of Bangkok in the Ping River basin. Although the Lanna kingdom was colonized by Siam in 1892 CE, Chiang Mai has remained a significant regional center up to the present. The basin is comprised primarily of very fertile, highly productive, and thus valuable rice paddy land. The area of Chiang Mai province is 20,107 square kilometers and comprises 3.92 percent of Thailand's total area.

Within Chiang Mai province, there are nineteen districts, including the urban district of Muang, which comprises Chiang Mai city. In the 1970s, these nineteen districts were comprised of 179 subdistricts, which were further subdivided into 1,462 villages.[20] In 1976, the total population of Chiang Mai province was 1,100,325; the population of Chiang Mai city was 104,519.[21] In other words, over 90 percent of the population of Chiang Mai province resided in rural areas.

Since the time of the Lanna kingdom, the few wealthy landowners and the many laboring residents of Chiang Mai and neighboring Lamphun and Lampang provinces have been tied together in a variety of intimate patron-client relationships. During the feudal era, these relationships were largely between lords and serfs, while after the end of the Lanna kingdom the relationships evolved into those between landlords and tenant farmers. While relations were sometimes smooth, rebellions and other forms of noncompliance by northern peasants in the eighteenth and nineteenth centuries marked a significant challenge to what may have appeared to be the impervious power of the lords.[22]

In 1973, Chiang Mai had the highest rate of tenancy within the northern region, with 35.13 percent of the agricultural land occupied by tenants or 353,221 *rai* out of 1,005,468.[23] In 1973, with 54,225 tenant households, Chiang Mai province also had the largest total number of tenant agricultural households of any province in the country.[24] Rather than reflecting a sharp increase in tenancy in Chiang Mai province, the conditions in the mid-1970s were instead indicative of entrenched high rates of tenancy combined with already high rental prices, which were slowly creeping even higher. Data collected by Carle C. Zimmerman during 1930 for his *Siam Rural Economic Survey, 1930–1931*, just before the transition from absolute to constitutional monarchy, suggests that farmers in Chiang Mai in the 1930s faced conditions similar to those faced by farmers in the 1970s.[25] Even allowing for the explanatory limitations of the survey, given its small scale, Zimmerman found that the largest landowners in the country resided in Chiang Mai, with one landowner in Sankampaeng owning 1,027 *rai*; the next-largest landowner, who resided in the central region, possessed less than one-third of that amount, with holdings of 302 *rai*.[26] Zimmerman also found that Chiang Mai had the highest rates of landlessness and tenancy in the north in 1930.

Northern rental practices also led to particularly high rental prices. Rents in the central region often amounted to one-third of the harvest, usually paid as a set amount of rice or cash, while the wealthy landowners of Chiang Mai other northern provinces typically demanded half the harvest for themselves.[27] Drawing on research conducted in Sanpatong district of Chiang Mai province, Paul Cohen found that between 1952 and 1955 the rate of rent increased from a lower fixed amount to a fifty-fifty split. By 1967–68, dividing the rice harvest evenly had become the dominant practice, but some landlords in the same villages were demanding up to 60 percent.[28]

In addition to high rental rates, tenant farmers also faced insecurity of tenure from year to year. The majority of landlords, whether neighbors, family members, or absentee investors, preferred verbal to written contracts.[29] One of the difficulties of studying land tenancy practices is that landlord-tenant relations differ depending on the classes and locations of both parties and the connections between them. In one 1975 study, sociologists from the National Research Council of Thailand reported that in Chiang Mai province 53.41 percent of all tenant farmers rented land from family members, 27.27 percent rented land from other residents of the same region, and 19.32 percent rented from absentee landlords.[30] Unlike the central region, where the majority of landlords were absentee, the relative proximity of landlords in Chiang Mai made contention over tenancy highly visible, local, and intimate.[31] The argument in this book is not that every landlord-tenant relationship became a site of contention and political transformation; they did not. Instead, I offer an explanation of how and why changing the terms of this relationship became the basis for reimagining Thai society, and the trigger for the brutal repression of those who did so.

The broader agricultural context in which the tenancy struggle acquired significance was one of long-standing difficulties faced by farmers. Agriculture as a whole comprised 50.1 percent of the gross national product (GNP) in 1950 and only 32.2 percent in 1975.[32] Rice fell from 33 percent of exports in 1965 to 19 percent in 1974 to only 12.9 percent in 1975.[33] In addition, rice farmers were paid notoriously low amounts by mills for their crop. The government instituted a price guarantee in 1968, but most rice mills refused to pay it.[34] Between 1969 and 1973, in every region except the south, the percentage of rural households living on incomes of less than 6,000 baht per year increased; in the north, the percentage grew from 51.9 percent to 63.6 percent.[35] In the mid-1970s, 80 percent of farmers were in debt and owed, on average, around 4,000 baht; farmers paid interest rates of 10 to 14 percent, with rates in the north higher than elsewhere in the country.[36]

While activists and government officials hoped that land reform, initially conceived in the 1930s and made an official policy in 1975, would change the conditions faced by landless and tenant farmers by putting an end to the concentration of land in the hands of the few, it completely failed to do so. In his National Economic Plan of 1933, the first to be developed after the transition from absolute to constitutional monarchy in 1932, People's Party member Pridi Banomyong called for the nationalization of all land in Thailand. However, the plan never amounted to more than a proposal and resulted in Pridi being accused of being a communist.[37] Field Marshal Phibun Songkhram passed the Land Code of 1954, which limited landownership to 50 *rai*; however, this limit was per person, not per family, so large landholders could evade the code by formally placing their land in the name of their children and other relatives.[38] Although the dictatorial triumvirate of Thanom Kittikachorn, Praphat Jarusathien, and Narong Kittikachorn investigated the possibility of land reform in 1971, they did not take any concrete action.[39]

Yet when the Land Reform Act was passed on 17 January 1975, rather than being the radical measure of land redistribution it might have been, it functioned as a stalling, "preemptive measure" designed precisely to avoid significant redistribution of resources.[40] Technically, the act allowed the government to appropriate, with compensation, any landholding greater than 50 *rai*. However, a number of exceptions limited this: if one possessed animals, one could own 100 *rai*; if one worked the land oneself, one could own 1,000 *rai*; or if one engaged in "modern farming methods," one could own more than 1,000 *rai*, at least for a time.[41] The terms of the act aside, it simply was not implemented on more than a marginal basis: during the four years of land reform (1975–79), while 2,216,340 *rai* of private and crown land were selected for land reform, only 4 percent, or 88,868 *rai*, was actually put under the program, and this was primarily land donated by the crown.[42] Those farmers who did obtain land were awarded a "temporary land development contract," not ownership per se.[43] Critics noted that the program failed due to opposition from landlords, a lack of financial support from the state, and a general unwillingness on the part of government officials to implement it.[44]

Although, given the redistributive impulse of land reform, one might have expected revolutionary action to emerge from it rather than a land tenancy struggle, it was the latter that occurred. In contrast to land reform, which was spearheaded by the state with the full support of the monarchy, the land tenancy struggle was originated by the farmers themselves. Although the rule of lords theoretically ended with the country's transformation from an absolute to a constitutional monarchy on 24 June 1932, in the mid-1970s, tenant farmers in Chiang Mai began to feel as though little had changed from the feudal era. The tenant farmers' movement arose due to a variety of factors, including material conditions, the political context of the time, and the changing consciousness of the farmers. An attempt at legal land reform in 1951 had been crushed by landlord influence within provincial governments. When the events of the 14 October 1973 movement for democracy ushered in a period of open politics, farmers were ready for change.

Politicizing Tenancy

On 5 October 1973, Thirayuth Bunmi, the former secretary-general of the National Student Center of Thailand (NSCT), along with other supporters, held a press conference on Sanam Luang, across from Thammasat University, calling for an end to the dictatorship and the promulgation of a new constitution. At the press conference, Thirayuth released the names of 100 prominent academic and government figures who had signed a petition in support of a constitution. While marching through Bangkok, on 6 October 1973, 11 members of the group calling for a constitution were arrested; they were denied the rights to receive visitors and to post bail. By 8 October 1973, the number of detained people had risen to 13; on the evening of the eighth, students at Thammasat University decided to call off exams until further notice and take to the streets. The protests at Thammasat University grew until hundreds of thousands of people were in the streets in Bangkok, Chiang Mai, and provinces across the country, calling for the release of those arrested and echoing their demands. In Bangkok, the protests erupted into violence between unarmed protestors and state forces early on the morning of 14 October 1973. That evening, King Bhumipol made a public announcement and named Sanya Thammasak, the rector of Thammasat University, as the new prime minister. Despite the removal of the dictators Thanom Kittikachorn, Praphat Jarusathien, and Narong Kittikachorn and the appointment of Sanya, the fighting did not die down until late on the fifteenth. At least 77 people were killed and 856 wounded between the fourteenth and the early hours of the fifteenth.[45]

The nearly three years between 14 October 1973 and 6 October 1976 was a period of incredible political possibility and change in Thailand. Groups whose political action had been restricted under the dictatorship, including those of students and workers, as well as farmers, organized and protested in unprecedented numbers. Progressive activists in and outside the streets imagined, wrote about, and worked toward a different, more just Thai society. People crossed lines of space and class to act together to challenge injustices. Yet growing polarization between the "right" and "left," as well as fears that Thailand would follow its eastern and northern neighbors in adopting communism, led to a violent backlash from both state and parastate actors. Throughout 1975 and 1976, progressive students, journalists, socialists, and workers, in addition to farmers, were subjected to growing harassment, intimidation, threats, and assassinations. On the morning of 6 October 1976, right-wing state and parastate forces brutally massacred unarmed students at Thammasat University in Bangkok.[46] By the evening, the twelfth military coup since 1932 returned Thailand to dictatorship and ended the period of open politics.

Thirty years later, various issues surrounding this period of political possibility, its imagination of a different, more just future for the mass of Thai society, and its demise remain unresolved and understudied. With a few significant exceptions, existing English- and Thai-language analysis primarily addresses two areas: students and their experience in Bangkok around the two principal dates, 14 October 1973 and 6 October 1976; and the failure of the Maoist-Leninist CPT to capture state power.[47] As Thongchai Winichakul has argued, the massacre at Thammasat University on the morning of 6 October 1976 is an event that continues to be characterized by silence and ambiguity for those who survived the event as well as present-day Thai society.[48] Yet much of the 1973–76 period remains shrouded in silence because there is not even the minimal circulation of information needed to produce ambiguity.

On initial consideration, one might ask if 14 October 1973 can be considered a revolution. The dictatorship was ended and a civilian assumed the position of prime minister after days of protests in the streets. However, although the civilian government after 14 October 1973 decriminalized dissidence and therefore contributed to creating the space in which farmers were able to transform their lives and Thai society, the event itself did not comprise a revolution. The uncomplicated explanation for this is that the three dictators left the country at the request of the king. The voice that they responded to was not that of the people, no matter how one conceives of the "people," the Thai monarchy, or the relationship between them. The more compelling explanation, and the one I develop in this book, is that tenant farmers both fomented revolutionary political transformation and changed the very forms and locations of politics in Thailand. Material demands and changing circumstances intersected to make tenancy explosively contentious in Chiang Mai in the mid-1970s. In order to reduce the amount of rice they paid as rent, farmers discovered that they also had to challenge the form of their relationships with landlords; the sheer act of challenging landlords without being silenced or ignored was new. Similarly, landlords came to feel as though they were losing much more than grains of rice when farmers challenged them. Together with other participants in the conflict, including local and national state authorities and students and other allies of the farmers, farmers and landlords politicized physical spaces often portrayed as being removed from politics. Farmers spread information about the 1974 Land Rent Control Act in village temple meeting halls. Landlords refused to follow the law and to accept the share of the harvest offered to them at the edge of the rice fields. During the events leading up to 14 October, student activists made the city streets sites of political education and dissent. Farmers pushed this idea even further, politicizing the land itself.

It is likely clear by now that the idea of politics I rely on in my analysis is rather different from the usual meaning of the term. For example, the most recent edition of the *Royal Institute Dictionary*, which is positioned as the official lexicon of the Thai language, offers this definition of *politics* (*kanmuang*):

> Work related to the state or the nation, for example, the study of politics consists of the study of the state, the organization of the state, and the workings of the state; (2) Administration of the nation, particularly related to the policy of administration, for example, international politics consists of the workings of international policy; (3) Management or supervision of civil administration, for example, political positions have the duty of management (Cabinet) or the supervision (Parliament) of the national administration. (Spoken) To have a hidden point, for actions to have a hidden motive, for example, to pretend to be sick.[49]

If one uses this definition, then the farmers' actions, or their contention with the landowners, might not seem political at all. Many, but not all, scholars have adhered to a similar idea of politics in their academic work.[50]

The absence from most accounts of Thai activist history and politics of many of the stories I engage with in this book forces us—as Thai and foreign scholars, critics, and activists—to develop new categories and strategies of analysis. While this argument is one I develop throughout this book, I offer a few preliminary guidelines here. In short, I first call for a radical opening of studies of politics to include subjects, actions, and sources not always considered as falling within its sphere. I then draw on Gramscian ideas of hegemony to propose a broad framework in which these various forms of politics become socially and historically significant. Finally, I elaborate the form of relations among the subjects who populate these fields of politics.

While my ultimate goal is to challenge the definition of *politics* described above, here I want to suggest that the study of provincial administration or international politics, for example, is more complicated than the idea indicated by the Royal Institute definition. In that definition, only *states* and the bureaucrats who populate them are considered to be political actors in their own right. In her groundbreaking feminist critiques of international relations, Cynthia Enloe has repeatedly urged scholars to examine the voices and experiences *behind* the broad relationships and conflicts that define global politics.[51] In *The Curious Feminist: Searching for Women in a New Age of Empire*, Enloe critiques the failure of scholars in the field of international relations to engage those who populate "margins, silences, and bottom rungs" and examine why and how they remain located as such.[52] At the core of her analysis is the question of power and the failure of such analyses to comprehend "the actual amount and the amazing variety of power that are required to keep the voices on the margins from having the right language and enough volume to be heard at the center in ways that might send shivers up and down the ladder."[53] By studying the voices and experiences that have been made marginal, scholars are able to understand the layers of power, negotiation, and contention that comprise what may appear to be the seamless workings of diplomacy and international relations.

Yet it is not only important to broaden our conception of political actors to include people located on the margins. Even if we understand politics as the rule (or the appearance of rule) by a state and the various forms of resistance to it, I propose that we operate under the assumption that the actions that comprise rule and resistance far exceed state administration and protests in the streets. *Politics* is both of those things, but it is also the actions off the streets that make those in the streets possible. *Politics* is also the desire and will to imagine a different, more just society and the courage to take the risks necessary to bring it about.[54] For example, I argue that the collective actions taken by the farmers and students who animate my analysis here represented the imagination of a different future. The risks taken to imagine this future and the deadly costs they incurred in attempting to implement it were explicitly political.

These various forms of politics become meaningful, and therefore consequential, as struggles for hegemony. Antonio Gramsci casts hegemony as a form of "leadership," explaining that a "social group dominates antagonistic

groups ... [and] leads kindred and allied groups. A social group can, and indeed must, already exercise 'leadership' before winning governmental power
(this indeed is one of the principal conditions for the winning of such power)."[55]
Gramsci is clear that the resistant group's struggle is not only to resist the hegemony of the dominant group but to produce it as well.

In the chapters that follow, I track these struggles as they developed between
progressive activists and the Thai state and between farmers and landowners in
Chiang Mai. In each moment of contention between these groups, the struggle
is never only about the specific demand at issue but is simultaneously about
determining the very terms on which that demand is made and answered. For
example, the struggles for rent relief in Chiang Mai province were at once about
the amount of rice to be paid as rent and about who had the right to define
and enforce the terms of land rental. As farmers began to educate one another
about their legal rights, and to urge landowners to follow the dictates of the new
Land Rent Control Act in 1974 and 1975, landowners lost rice (in comparison to
prior years), but they also lost their position as the sole determinants of *deciding*
how much rice would be paid by farmers as rent. Raymond Williams elaborates
Gramsci's idea of hegemony in terms of how one formulates one's conception
of the world and the positions of oneself and others within it. Hegemony "is not
limited to matters of direct political control but seeks to describe ... a particular
way of seeing the world and human nature and relationships. ... [T]he ways of
seeing the world and ourselves and others are not just intellectual but political
facts, expressed over a range from institutions to relationships and consciousness."[56] As I will demonstrate, how landowners and farmers came to perceive
one another became deadly political by late 1975. The farmers' struggles moved
from the merely political to the revolutionary when it began to appear they
were winning the contest for hegemony.

Making Revolution

To write about revolution at the beginning of the twenty-first century raises the
question of what one means by the term. There is no single, tidy definition that
can encompass all of the actions in support of social and political phenomena
identified as revolutionary. Williams traces the proliferation of meanings of the
term since its emergence in the English language in the fourteenth century
and argues that common to many of its uses, social, political, and otherwise, is
the idea of revolution as "not so much the steady and continuous movement of
a wheel as the particular isolation of a top and bottom point which were, as a
matter of course, certain to change places."[57] When Marx and Engels published
The Communist Manifesto in 1848, they defined revolution as occurring when
"the violent overthrow of the bourgeoisie lays the foundation for the sway of
the proletariat."[58] Since then, successive generations of socialist, communist,
and other radical thinkers and activists have argued and fought over how to

foment revolution and then how to fulfill it without betraying its promises. By the close of the twentieth century, with the collapse of many states founded on Marxian, Maoist, or Leninist ideas, there are still no definitive answers to these questions. The indiscriminate ravages of Cold War counterinsurgency also mean that there are many fewer possible answers available to examine. Not only were overtly communist and socialist movements targeted, but radical democratic movements, liberation theology movements, and, pertinent to my concerns, tenancy movements were also destroyed as subversive. Thailand was not the only country where revolution was interrupted.

Scholars working inside and outside Marxian frames have offered a nearly endless series of definitions of *revolution*, variously emphasizing the temporality of revolution, the decision-making process of a revolutionary leadership, or new forms of revolutionary action. This polyvalence can seem to threaten to preclude the possibility of analytic clarity. In this vein, Eugen Weber, in a review article spanning Lenin, Proudhon, and Arno Mayer, wrote in the early 1970s, "We know too much nowadays to explain very much. We certainly know too little to explain anything thoroughly. But as long as our notions of historical change continue to turn on terms as imprecise as revolution and counter-revolution, they remain blocked, and focused on problems already left behind."[59] Yet even Weber's admonition comes at the end of an essay in which he also argues for the multiplication of new categories of revolution, suggesting that "We should abandon the notion of one revolution, identified with only one direction of theme; replace the question: 'what is revolution?' by the question: 'what kind of revolution is it?'"[60] The issue here is not to name each and every struggle and movement a "revolution" but rather to consider how received, and at times doctrinaire, ideas of revolution and "the party" mask other forms of social and political revolt.

Understanding the processes by which people choose to challenge the status quo, to imagine a different future, and to take risks to make it real—even when history and the present warn them of the potential consequences—is difficult because it demands that scholars develop units of analysis capable of apprehending the changing shapes, forms, and sites of these challenges. Yet as an activist scholar who knows that my academic production exists within, not aside from, the same world filled with oppression that I research, to make the attempt is relentlessly compelling. Weber's ambivalence about revolution as a unit of analysis reveals its difficulty *and* its promise. As long as those who rule constantly refine their methods of oppression, the oppressed will have to dream up new strategies for ending injustice. There is unlikely to be a quick end either to oppression or attempts to overturn it through revolution in the service of different, more just futures.

In the remainder of this section, I offer a working description of the kind of revolution that Thai tenant farmers fomented in the mid-1970s. Before turning to the specificities of the mid-1970s, however, I examine the two ways in which any discussion of revolution in Thailand is particularly troubled. The first is the contested status and legacies of 24 June 1932, the transition from absolute to constitutional monarchy. Reflecting on his participation in the People's Party, the small group that planned the events, Pridi Banomyong explained that lacking a word for *revolution* in Thai, group members "used the ordinary words 'change the system of government in which the king is above the law to the system of government in which the king is under the law.'"[61] Although the transformation of absolute to constitutional monarchy is discussed and written about as a "revolution" by some, many others, including scholars and early Thai communists and radicals, have instead seen it as a coup d'état that left the elite secure in their positions and strengthened the military, doing nothing to change the lives of ordinary people.[62] For dissident northern tenant farmers in 1951 and progressive students in 1973, the desire to make the unfilled promises of 1932 real was a strong motivation for action.

The second tension inherent to revolution in Thailand is linguistic. Following the events of 1932, Prince Wan chose to translate *revolution* as *patiwat*, which Kasian Tejapira notes was "literally 'turning or rolling back,' with the conservative connotation of 'restoration,' instead of denoting the radical break with the past or the progressive and qualitative change of affairs of the English original."[63] In response, in the aftermath of World War II, Pridi instead "coined the word *aphiwat*, literally 'super-evolution.'"[64] *Patiwat* remains the word in use today, and *aphiwat* cannot be found in either the *Royal Institute Dictionary* or the *Matichon Dictionary of the Thai Language*, which, as I take up more fully in chapter 1, presents itself as an alternative to the canonical lexicon offered by the Royal Institute.

When the northern tenant farmers of the FFT and their student and lawyer allies became involved in struggling to change their lives and Thai society, they did not name it *revolution*, *patiwat*, or *aphiwat*. I choose to do so in this book because only thus can the connections among their actions and the backlash to them be understood. Unlike the Indonesian Revolution of the late 1940s, the tenant farmers did not declare independence and oust a colonial regime. Unlike the Cuban Revolution of 1959, the property of the landed aristocracy in Thailand was not seized and collectivized. The monarchy remained untouched. What are often seen as the typical hallmarks of revolution were thus absent from the Thai situation; yet, as Philip Corrigan and Derek Sayer argue in their study of British state formation, revolution "is not just about changing deeds of ownership or capturing 'power,' but *making* new ways of relating, new social identities—a new moral order, a new kind of civilization, a different socialization."[65]

This—the transformation in relations between farmers and landlords, farmers and students, and farmers and government officials, and among farmers themselves—was the revolution in northern Thailand in the mid-1970s. In order to effect this transformation, farmers and their student allies drew on their own lived experience and the writings of local Marxian radicals of an earlier generation, as well as New Left, socialist, and other progressive thinkers from around the world, first to imagine and then to create a more just future. Students, farmers, and workers allied themselves in solidarity with one another in what was known as the "three links" (*sam prasan*), as well as in many other contingent alliances. In Chiang Mai, students from Chiang Mai University (CMU), Teachers' College, and other regional schools organized themselves into a student solidarity group called the Farmer Project (Khrongkan Chao Na), which worked with the farmers of the FFT. What kept either students or farmers from becoming a vanguard was their appreciation of their different experiences and position in Thai society and what this meant they could learn from one another. Working together, they transformed their own lives and began to foment changes in the landlord-tenant and state-citizen relations structuring Thai society.

These transformations, and the reactions to them, were built on a series of transgressions. To transgress is to violate a limit or boundary. For Georges Bataille, what is transgressive is determined by what is forbidden at any given moment, in the sense that "there is no prohibition that cannot be transgressed."[66] Drawing largely on Mikhail Bakhtin's analysis of Rabelais and the carnivalesque, Peter Stallybrass and Allon White regard transgression as encompassing practices that contradict, invert, or function as alternatives to the status quo.[67] At the most basic level, the actions of farmers and students can be understood as crossing boundaries and their opponents' criticism and backlash as an attempt to maintain, or perhaps draw even sharper, boundaries. Through these processes of crossing, maintaining, and rebuilding boundaries, farmers, students, landowners, and state officials transformed their position in society as subjects.

In the chapters that follow, I trace the operations and effects of transgression in three spheres. First, I trace how students and farmers transgressed their origins in order to become politicized subjects and to work together. Second, I argue that the combined organizing actions of farmers and students amounted to a transgression of the existing rural relations of power that governed interactions among farmers, landowners, and state officials. Paradoxically, by working *within* the terms of the system, farmers and students launched a challenge more destabilizing than an attempt to smash the system directly would have been. Finally, I trace the forms of violence that greeted farmer-student organizing as transgressions that both revealed the transformations that had already taken place and made impossible any return to the *status quo*. Counterrevolution interrupted the tenant farmers' struggle but could not erase its effects.

The collaboration between farmers and students at this time was marked by two kinds of transgression—those of class boundaries and space. My conception of class is informed by Marxian and feminist analyses of capitalism as a process rather than a totality.[68] By focusing on capitalism as a process rather than a closed structure, the concept of class becomes fluid. This creates "the possibility of energetic and unconfined class identities, where the compelling question is not 'What is my class belonging?' but 'What is my class becoming?'"[69] In turn, given that class is an identity that is continually shifting, class then "becomes legible as a potential effect of politics, rather than merely its origin or ground. Commonality and community may be seen as produced, not simply expressed, through political mobilization."[70] I want to be clear that not all students were from a middle- or upper-class background. Many were, but many were not. Instead, resonant with J. K. Gibson-Graham's analysis, due to their access to higher education, students possessed the possibility of a middle- or upper-class future, no matter what their class origins. Rather than treating class as the primary marker of identity, I examine how it interacts with another aspect of identity, namely, geographic location.[71]

As I consider how farmers and students transgressed the boundaries between rural and urban spaces, or between the village and the city, I question these categories and the "seemingly unproblematic division of space" that underlies them.[72] Rather than taking these categories as fixed and natural, I am mindful that the division of space is constantly made and remade. Within this context, I cast the movement of farmers into city streets and students into villages as actions that challenged the existing divisions and relations between rural and urban spaces. News reports about farmer protests in the streets of Bangkok and Chiang Mai starkly reflected the anxieties produced by these crossings. What made this anxiety different from the fears of CPT cadres marching into the cities is that they were completely lawful. Had CPT cadres marched into Bangkok wearing fatigues and carrying automatic weapons, Thai military and security forces could have immediately mobilized against them as insurgents who wanted to destroy the nation. Instead, when farmers entered the cities to protest, they were only exercising their rights as full citizens. The responses to their actions, however, indicate that in reality their rights of citizenship were never intended to be as full as those enjoyed by the landlords. Yet to mobilize against them would have been to acknowledge openly the disenfranchisement at the core of Thai society, and the continued de facto exclusion of the majority of citizens from legal and national subjectivity after 1932 and even after 1973.

The Interruption of Counterrevolution

In 1951, landowners were able to prevent the decree of the 1950 Land Rent Control Act in Chiang Mai province by contradicting the farmers' claims to hunger and impoverishment. By 1974, however, landowners could not silence the farmers' call for land rent relief. In 1951, the farmers were subject to laws but were unable to affect their content or bring about implementation. By 1974, they were presenting themselves as subjects who should play a part in drafting laws, as well as active agents of the latter's implementation. Against the backdrop of the failure of farmers to achieve a similar transformation in 1951, their success in 1974 challenged land rent practices, as well as landowners' positions as elites, decision makers, and patrons in the northern countryside.

Katherine Bowie presents compelling evidence that the idea of peasants and lords coexisting happily in nineteenth-century Lanna is a myth.[73] Yet even in the 1950s and 1970s, the landlords, who were the descendants of these lords (figuratively and sometimes literally), believed this myth.[74] They viewed themselves as kind patrons who took care of the farmers, their figurative fathers and older brothers. This is not to say that landlords did not appreciate the benefits they accrued but that they believed they acted in a just, and even generous, manner toward the farmers. Many farmers disagreed and instead saw in the lords' actions only greed and dehumanizing injustice. The landlords were greatly unnerved by the outward expression of the farmers' disagreement, that is, their movement to pass and then implement rent-control measures. In order to understand how landlords might become alarmed, let us consider the relationship between farmers and landlords as a dialectical one in which each was constituted in relation to the other. The landlords retained their power and position in no small part due to the rice and other support they received from tenant farmers. If the rice was withdrawn, and, even more significantly, if the farmers ceased to recognize the landlords as those with the power to determine the terms of tenancy relationships, then in what sense were they still landlords? Furthermore, if the farmers claimed that they were not beneficently provided for by the landlords, could the landlords continue to perceive themselves this way? The farmers' actions constituted a withdrawal from their once interdependent relationship, while simultaneously calling into question its ostensible justification.[75] For a brief time, farmers and landlords seemed to be on a path toward becoming equal in the eyes of the law, each a partner in a contractual relationship overseen by the state.

By using the *law*, which had previously been the province of the landowners, the farmers' actions amounted to a transgression of existing rural relations of power. Transgression does not destroy but instead, as Mary Beth Tierney-Tello writes in her analysis of experimental fiction written by women living under Latin American dictatorships, it "can be seen as part of the quest to disarticulate dominant conventions and authoritarian modes."[76] By arguing that the previously informal, unregulated landlord-tenant relationships needed to be subject to legal regulation, farmers exposed what they regarded as the injustice of the status quo.

By choosing the law as their weapon of disarticulation, the farmers' attack on landowners was particularly acute. To claim, as I do in this book, that law became a site and tool of revolution is a surprising enough assertion to warrant a brief explanation. Following Sally Merry, I understand law as "both a system of meaning and an institutional structure backed by the political power of the state."[77] Yet in mid-1970s Thailand, the law contained multiple systems of meaning, and the state was not the only power backing its institutional structure. While the legal text at the center of this book is the 1974 Land Rent Control Act, this law became significant in "a society characterized by a multiplicity of legal orders, each with its own basis of legitimacy and coercive force, each formally severed from the other."[78] David Engel characterizes the act as the method by which "the government injected itself directly into the contractual relationship between landlords and tenants."[79] Yet this injection was textual only, as became clear in the months after the passage of the act when government officials refused to spread information about the new law, let alone ensure its enforcement.

These are the parameters of meaning, power, and constraint within which tenant farmers chose to use the law, rather than taking up a more traditional form of revolt or any of James Scott's "weapons of the weak," in order to change their lives and Thai society.[80] At best, law may be an instrument of reform, which is how, according to its former cadres, the CPT viewed the 1974 Land Rent Control Act. Foreshadowing the harsh Marxian criticisms of his analysis of the law in *Whigs and Hunters: The Origin of the Black Act*, E. P. Thompson noted that according to established Marxian thinking, "The revolutionary can have no interest in law, unless as a phenomenon of ruling-class power and hypocrisy; it should be his aim simply to overthrow it."[81] At worst, in the eyes of its critics, law may appear to be a mere tool of the master. As the poet Audre Lorde wrote in another context, "*For the master's tools will never dismantle the master's house.* They may allow us to temporarily beat him at his own game, but they will never enable us to bring about genuine change."[82] For Lorde, even when the master's tools are in the hands of the oppressed, an indelible mark of domination remains.

Yet it was precisely choosing the master's tool, and then taking it from the master and transforming it, that constituted revolution in mid-1970s Thailand. A well-known Thai phrase reads, "The class that writes the laws, certainly writes the laws for [i.e. in the interests of] that class" (*chonchan dai khian kotmai ko nae sai phua chonchan nan*). This phrase reflects the longstanding control over the law by elites. For elites to write the laws for themselves was to position themselves as the subjects of law and everyone else as its objects. While landowners felt the law slipping through their fingers, farmers turned the law into a potent tool of liberation. Antonio Gramsci explains that in a time of revolution, "Structure ceases to be an external force which crushes man, assimilates him to itself and makes him passive; and is transformed into a means of freedom, an instrument to create a new ethico-political form and a source of new initiatives."[83] In the hands of the tenant farmers of the FFT and their allies, law worked and was transformed in this fashion. As the violent backlash to the farmers' use of it indicates, law can become revolutionary and capable of destroying the established order when it falls into unexpected hands.

If the ruling class no longer leads, but dominates through coercion, then what emerges is a "crisis of authority" or what Gramsci also refers to as a "crisis of hegemony."[84] I propose that we should understand the period of assassinations of FFT leaders in 1975 as this kind of crisis. In a crisis of authority, Gramsci argues, "the great masses have become detached from their traditional ideologies, and no longer believe what they used to believe previously, etc. The crisis consists precisely in the fact that *the old is dying and the new cannot be born; in this interregnum a great variety of morbid symptoms appear.*"[85] Within the new context of increased participation and activism following 14 October 1973, northern farmers were no longer willing to submit to the previous terms of land tenancy or to acquiesce in their old positions as compliant or quietly dissenting subjects. By going out into the streets to protest, organizing with allied students, and becoming legal educators of one another, they directly challenged the power of the ruling class and their state allies. Similar challenges were launched by workers, teachers, students, and other progressive groups. Their challenges to the old system and their imagination of a better future were met with a violent backlash from conservative forces. The morbid symptoms that appeared were harassment, intimidation, and assassination of progressive activists. These actions signaled the importance of the progressive transformation being wrought, as right-wing landowners and their state and parastate allies simultaneously attempted to halt its advance. I regard these morbid symptoms as indicators of the instability of landlord-tenant relations, urban-rural relations, and the Thai state. By privileging these moments, the fragility of Thai social relations and the fluidity of revolution and counterrevolution then in progress are revealed.

The action that finally interrupted the farmers' struggle came over a year before the 6 October 1976 massacre. The assassinations of the farmers reached their height at the end of July 1975. In response to calls from activists for state action to end the assassinations, inaction and then a seemingly bizarre series of protests and counterprotests ensued. As the counterprotests by right-wing groups and then the police grew, the law came to be the object in question. At the height of counterrevolution, uniformed and drunken police sacked the prime minister's house in the middle of the night. Their demand? The restoration of sacredness and meaning to the law. In the remaining months of 1975 and 1976, the FFT's organizing largely retreated underground. Although the 1974 Land Rent Control Act remained on the books, it has not been used since 1975 and is in essence a dead letter today.

There is an additional, speculative point I wish to make about transgression and violence. Had the farmers called for the destruction of the entire land rental system—and simply refused to pay rent—the landowners could have simply used their relationships with state officials to force the farmers to pay. Instead, the farmers' legal activism transgressed the existing system of rural relations of power by exposing it. Although over thirty years have passed, no one has been held accountable for the assassinations of the farmers. Surviving farmer and student activists believe that elite right-wing and landholding forces were behind them. While I cannot prove that the landlords and their state, parastate, and right-wing allies were behind the killings of the farmers, it is not impossible that they were. If the landowners did order the killings, however, this would represent a final, complete transgression of their own perceived role as beneficent patrons.

Finally, there is another unsettling question that haunts this book. As Thailand is often overlooked in studies of state violence in Southeast Asia, given the scale of the state murders of millions of people under Suharto in Indonesia and the Khmer Rouge in Cambodia, this book also suggests that a different set of questions about violence must be asked. How did the targeted killing of thirty-three farmer leaders shut down a movement of over one million people? What about this violence has led the assassins to remain unnamed, and unnameable, over thirty years later?

Danger and the Methodology of Anonymity

This book is based on field research that I carried out in Chiang Mai and Bangkok between 2001 and 2008, as well as extensive research in Kroch Library at Cornell University.[86] I draw on a wide range of sources, including oral histories, notes from events I attended, cremation volumes, newspapers and other published material, and documents from provincial and national government archives, university archives, and activist archives. Opting for a different approach than that of many anthropological works, I have treated interviews as a supplement to textual materials rather than the other way around. The primary sources consulted were thousands of pages of Thai-language newspapers, journals, cremation volumes, and other published materials, as well as state and activist archival unpublished materials.

Each kind of source demanded particular methodological considerations. The contentious, unresolved nature of the histories of progressive activism and state and parastate violence in Thailand necessarily complicated these considerations. Here I discuss the analytic and ethical concerns behind these considerations, and explain my approach to citation and the choice of sources.

First, the possession of progressive or leftist documents was grounds for arrest following the 6 October 1976 massacre. By 9 October 1976, it was reported that over one million books and documents had been seized from bookstores and university campuses in Bangkok alone.[87] Nearly every former activist I met remembered the books and periodicals they once possessed but were forced to discard, burn, or otherwise destroy. S., a former CMU student and Farmer Project activist, told me about how she buried her copies of a Thai translation of a collection of stories by Maxim Gorky and a book of Vietnamese short stories, along with other items, behind her parents' house following 6 October.[88] S. then spent five years in the jungle with the CPT. By the time she returned, the cumulative yearly flooding had saturated the ground so many times that she could not locate the books she had buried years earlier. Likewise, the offices of the Northern Student Center and the FFT were destroyed in October 1976; today there are no surviving public copies of *Thai Farmer* (*Chao Na Thai*), the FFT's newspaper. This does not mean that *nothing* written from a progressive perspective survived. Much did survive and can now be found in various libraries, as well as in many private collections, but it does mean that what survived is only a fraction of what once existed.

Of particular importance among the nineteen periodicals used, I drew on many Chiang Mai–based newspapers from a range of perspectives, from very conservative and pro-landowner papers (*Thai Niu* and *Thin Thai*) to Chiang Mai University student publications (*Su Sarn Muanchon* and *Walanchathat*) and progressive and left-leaning papers that were published for short periods (*Sieng Mai* and *Sieng Chonabot*). In the introduction to the second edition of *Capitalism and Confrontation in Sumatra*, Ann Stoler explains that lacking archival documents written from a peasant perspective about the Dutch colonial period in Indonesia, she intended "to write a history from the bottom up by reading upper class sources upside down."[89] Similarly, the relative lack of sources from a farmer or student perspective meant that I had to read between or even against the lines of conservative newspapers, government periodicals, and government archival documents to aid in my reconstruction of farmer-student solidarity.[90] Given the anxiety that farmer-student solidarity provoked among landholding and other elements in Chiang Mai, it is not surprising that conservative papers such as *Thai Niu* and *Thin Thai* meticulously documented the actions of farmer and student organizations. To be clear, I do not treat conservative, state, or the available printed sources from a progressive perspective, such as *Athipat*, the newspaper of the National Student Center of Thailand, as objective sources of information. Instead, I attend to the dissonance often present among various sources and ask what the discrepancies between them can tell us about how social change is understood by different actors.

Conducting interviews with former activists, students, farmers, teachers, and other people challenged me to think about methodology, responsibility, and dissonance in another way. I conducted, in total, twenty-six lengthy oral history interviews, nineteen with former student activists and seven with former farmer activists. In addition, I spoke informally, over a period of five years, with over a hundred former activists at political rallies, Communist Party of Thailand and other reunions, study groups, and other events. This included approximately seventy former student activists and approximately thirty former farmer activists. There are two reasons why I interviewed more former students than former farmers. The primary reason is that many of the most significant farmer leaders in the north were assassinated whereas a greater number of students survived. In addition, former students are at the forefront of the emerging network of those who want to document their own past, and therefore they were both more accessible and more willing to speak with me. In every interview, I was forced to confront what is at stake, and for whom, in tracing the histories included in this book. While I cannot entirely eliminate the danger involved in making these histories public, I can at least limit the risks to individuals. During the process of research and at the moment of this writing, I have taken specific steps to protect those involved. I did not audio-record any of the interviews I conducted but immediately took copious notes following each conversation. Additionally, I guaranteed anonymity to each person I interviewed. In the pages that follow, I do not identify anyone I spoke with by name or current occupation. Instead, I identify people with a Roman alphabet letter, such as S., and by describing what they were doing between 1973 and 1976. When using published sources or referring to people who are no longer alive, I use their real names.

I waited until the end of my period of field research to ask people for individual interviews. Many of the people I interviewed I knew well by the time we sat down for a formal conversation. Leading up to that point I was vetted many times and through multiple channels. Before anyone spoke with me, he or she wanted to ascertain that I was who I claimed to be and not an agent of the U.S. government or another malevolent force.[91] Each interview was predicated, from the beginning, on my not recording the conversation and not using the interviewee's name. Even with these precautions, more than one conversation was carried out in whispers or in a secluded place. Many people spoke of the pain caused by the actions they had taken, and for which they worry they could suffer further. Others are still actively engaged in opposing the state or capitalism and are under direct threat today. I do not doubt that many of the people I interviewed would have refused to speak to me if I had wanted to record our conversations.

In *The Other Side of Silence: Voices from the Partition of India*, Urvashi Butalia explains that "there is no simple way in which one can march in and attempt to break that silence, irresponsibly and unproblematically. . . . How much of what people spoke about, or of what they did not say, could I put down in print?"[92] While completing this book, I faced, and continue to face, similar questions. Many of the stories I listened to and learned about are absent from the book in detailed form and will remain written only in my notes. Many of these are the most shattering and dramatic stories of the violence that interrupted the revolution and the possibility of a different future in northern Thailand in the mid-1970s. Yet, even though everyone with whom I spoke knew that I was an academic writing about past- and present-day struggles, I determined that I would not write about every story to which I listened.

The deliberate decision to provide a double-layered anonymity, in which names and current occupations are left unspecified, is important for another, perhaps less individual, reason. In the prefatory note to her memoir *Reading Lolita in Tehran*, Azar Nafisi describes the extensive lengths she went to in order to mask the identities of the female students who populated her underground literature course. This was to protect them from persecution at the hands of the Iranian state, "but also from those who read such narratives to discover who's who and who did what to whom, thriving on and filling their own emptiness through others' secrets."[93] It is nearly impossible to have a discussion today about the recent radical past without someone bemoaning the former student activists who have become politicians or successful businesspeople or have taken up other occupations the speaker deems to contradict the activist's radical youth. While I think the expression of those sentiments is not insignificant, it has no place in this book. First, it simply falls outside the realm of my project. Second, and to my mind far more importantly, such an activity verges on contempt. I listened to people's stories and here attempt to transmit them. But they are not mine to record and name; that right belongs to those who lived them.

I offer one final note on what some readers may see as a glaring omission: I did not interview landlord-capitalists or government officials. When I began my research, I made a self-conscious decision to learn about the stories and struggles of the students and farmers. As I began to learn more about the tenancy struggle and the unsolved assassinations, this then became a practical choice as well. As I have argued throughout this introduction, this book is about a recent history that is still deeply contentious. My intentions were constantly called into question, and whom I knew and whom I spoke with were often matters of interest to former students and farmers. I was marked as "safe" by former farmer and student activists because I placed myself explicitly in alliance with them; had I attempted to make connections with landowners and government officials, I feared that my relationships with former farmer and student activists would have been imperiled. Within this context, my decision to write from the perspective of the farmer-student alliances was at once both practical and political.

Chronology and Outline

As will be clear from the following guide to chapters, this book is primarily about a very short period of time in Thai history: from 1973 until 1976. There are threads extending back to 1950 and following 6 October 1976 to the present. When thinking about different ways of organizing the argument, I was initially resistant to adhering to a chronology. I worried that in doing so I would necessarily impose linearity on a story that is anything but linear. However, by largely adhering to a chronology, I aim to facilitate my analysis of contention, contradiction, and other critical themes.

A popular Thai phrase states "Farmers are the backbone of the nation" (*chao na pen kraduk san lang khong chat*). Drawing on close readings of newspaper articles and dictionaries, chapter 1 is about the origins, shifting meanings, and manipulation of this phrase. As the prevention of hunger and the production of rice came to be seen as crucial in the defense of the Thai nation against communism at the dawn of the Cold War, farmers were steadily marginalized as political or even human subjects in state and elite discourses. At the center of this chapter is an examination of provincial archival records about the failure to decree the 1950 Land Rent Control Act, the precursor to the 1974 act, in Chiang Mai province. While the law was passed at a national level in October 1950, its use in each individual province required an additional decree. I analyze the contempt of the landlords, the dissidence of the farmers, and the conflictual positions of different state actors in order to historicize the struggles and violence discussed in the next chapters and to create an interpretive framework within which these struggles and violence become meaningful.

Chapter 2 is about the establishment of the FFT and the revitalization of the struggle for rent control in Chiang Mai in 1974. Bridging the gap between 1951 and 1974 is a reading of the farmers' actions through *The Real Face of Thai Feudalism Today*, by Jit Phumisak. Initially published in 1958, *The Real Face* was quickly banned and then reprinted after 14 October 1973. Like Jit's writing, which exposed the problematic constitution of the monkhood, monarchy, and military as the most important institutions in Thailand, the farmers' action challenged dominant ideas of politics and proper political subjects.[94] By joining with one another and bringing their protests from the countryside into the city streets, farmers fundamentally transformed themselves into a new kind of dissenting political subject and exposed their earlier exclusion. Drawing on a range of newspapers, cremation volumes, and commemorative accounts written by former activists, this chapter examines the protests leading up to the revival of the movement for land rent control in November 1974.

Chapter 2 is an examination of how the farmers of the FFT provoked concern by leaving the countryside for the cities and by claiming a shared status with state and landholding elites. In contrast, chapter 3 draws on oral histories and written texts to trace how members of two groups—students and teachers—caused a panic by refusing their elite status and leaving cities for the countryside to join with the farmers in their struggle. Adapting a formulation of Paulo Freire's, here I use the term *pedagogy of solidarity* to refer to the knowledge built through the shared struggle across class and space boundaries of farmers, students, and teachers.[95] What binds students and teachers together in analytically significant ways is that they refused the usual vanguard position assumed by middle-class intellectuals and instead chose to learn from their farmer colleagues. For example, when students skipped class in order to work with farmers in Chiang Mai and neighboring Lamphun and Lampang provinces, they did so in order to learn not only about another way of life but also how to be responsible as political actors in a new era.

The sum total of the individual and collective actions around land rent control and other issues in the north in 1974 and 1975 effected a revolutionary transformation at once material and social. Chapter 4 examines the Gramscian symptoms of crisis that appeared in the form of criticism, harassment, intimidation, and ultimately assassination of farmers by a likely, though unconfirmed, combination of landholding, state, parastate, and right-wing actors in the 1970s.

In response to the mystery of the farmers' assassins, this chapter offers one version of the events leading up to and surrounding the assassinations. In particular, I focus on the life of the northern FFT president, Intha Sribunruang. Intha was at the forefront of the fight to implement the 1974 Land Rent Control Act in Chiang Mai and the neighboring provinces. By tracing his murder as an act of violence that tore through his family, this chapter highlights how the political became devastatingly personal.

Following Intha's assassination, what had been only the scattered morbid symptoms of counterrevolution escalated into a national crisis. Chapter 5 is about the rapid series of events that followed calls for government officials to find the assassins, including the arrests of farmers and students on trumped-up charges, protests, their release, and counterprotests. This chapter draws on extensive northern and national newspaper coverage and activist archival documents to analyze how various government officials continually denied the claims of activists, obfuscated their own roles, and contradicted one another during this series of events. Counterrevolution, in my analysis, climaxed in the vandalism and sacking of Prime Minister Kukrit Pramoj's house in Bangkok by drunken, uniformed police officers calling for the return of rule by law, or the implementation of the written law in a manner with which they agreed, rather than rule by the mob, or the implementation of the law in a manner with which they did not agree. Rather than viewing the apparent fragmentation of the Thai state as a temporary aberration, this chapter argues that the chaos inside the state made the preceding violence possible.

In the conclusion, I reflect on the histories and possible futures of the tenant farmers' struggle from the point of view of the present situation. Although the ability of violence to silence and shape history is of concern throughout the book, this chapter considers the constrictions imposed on the political participation of certain actors and the continued resonance of the violence of the 1970s in the present. The temporality of interruption means that not only can revolution begin again but it is constantly beginning again. I examine a series of actions that possibly share the tenancy struggle's radical potential to imagine a more just society. The book ends with speculation, a possible dream, about what the present and future might have looked like if the revolution had not been interrupted so violently in 1975.

1

Breaking the Backbone
of the Nation

We could argue that it is always the specter of an open rebellion by the
peasantry which haunts the consciousness of the dominant classes in
agrarian societies and shapes and modifies their forms of exercise of
domination.

Partha Chatterjee, *The Nation and Its Fragments*

Housed in the former headquarters of the Railway Labour Union, the Thai
Labour Museum is only a short distance from the hotels, banks, and gleaming
high-rises on Petchburi Road in Bangkok.[1] The permanent exhibits at the museum narrate the struggles of Thai workers from the feudal era to the present
day. While many of the displays focus on workers as urban dwellers and producers, one of the Cold War era posters caught my eye. The poster was a Thai
government creation included in a display about workers' lives in the 1950s. It
was divided into two panels of equal size. Emblazoned across the top was the
text "Communist or Freedom." On the left, the communist side, was an image
of many people working in a parched field with neither rice nor buffalo. Under-
neath, the viewer was told, "In Communist countries, citizens do not have the
right to own land. Everyone is forced to work as though they are buffalo." On
the right, the side of freedom, life was brighter. Four farmers worked with one
plump buffalo to harvest abundant rice. A wooden house on stilts was on the
edge of the frame. Written across the bottom was the assertion, "Thai farmers
love and zealously guard their land. They own it."

For the class of farmers wealthy enough to own their rice fields, landownership may have served as a powerful preemptive reason against joining the communist insurgency.[2] Yet not all Thai farmers in the 1950s were able to purchase land. Instead, some farmers rented land and shared the rice harvest with

landowners as rental payment. Other farmers hired out their labor to landowners for a cash or rice wage; they often did so before the rice-planting season began and therefore sold their labor for a relatively low wage. Looking for a solution to their chronic poverty and hunger, tenant farmers in Chiang Mai demanded land rent relief in 1951. The tenant farmers organized and called for the decree of the 1950 LRCA in Chiang Mai province. The act, which standardized and lowered land rent prices, did not immediately apply anywhere in the country; instead the use of the law in a particular province had to be mandated by royal decree. Although their struggle aroused fears of communism in some quarters, at the heart of it was a call for the fuller realization of participatory, democratic politics. The farmers cited 1932 and the transformation of Thailand from an absolute to a constitutional monarchy as inaugurating a new era and offered a logic for the changes in tenancy practices they sought. Ironically, given accusations by landowners and some state actors that their demands for land rent control were "communist," the farmers did not receive support from Thai communist forces, either in 1951 or when the struggle resurfaced in 1974. Land rent relief, particularly relief defined by passage of and adherence to a legal act, did not comprise revolutionary structural change in their eyes.

In contrast, I argue that in struggling for land rent control, the farmers fomented fundamental change in multiple registers. The tenant farmers' demands in 1951 and later in the 1970s for the legal regulation of land rental practices first threatened and then unseated centuries of patron-client relationships in Chiang Mai. The anxiety expressed by landowners indicated concern about the spread of communism (and their own potential loss of land), but it also reflected a significantly different vision of the rural balance of power than that of the dissenting tenant farmers. In this chapter, I trace the contention over the 1950 LRCA in Chiang Mai as a precursor to the movement for land rent relief in Chiang Mai in 1974. My analysis here historicizes the struggles and violence that I discuss in the remainder of the book and also contributes to creating an interpretive framework within which the contention in the 1970s becomes meaningful.

Grasping the significance of the farmers' actions about land rent control demands an analysis of farmers as a specific kind of political subject. By developing an optic that accounts for this farmer political subject, in this chapter I also extend and challenge earlier work about agrarian life and resistance. Yet the case of land tenancy demands not only an idea of farmers as complex, political subjects but also a similarly nuanced conception of landowners. To this end, I argue that landowners were panicked about the 1950 LRCA for reasons that exceeded the fear of material loss. They were anxious because the farmers' claims challenged their public, and self-, image as generous individuals who took care of the people who worked their rice fields. Financial losses could be recovered, but image, as events in the 1950s and later in the 1970s acutely illustrated, was far more fleeting.

Foregrounding Land Rent Control

In the 1950s, land rent prices were uneven across central and northern Thailand. Further, the prices were rising with each passing year as cultivable land grew scarcer. As the author of an editorial published in the *Bangkok Post* in 1951 commented, land rents were often "ruinously high."[3] Farmers in many areas had to give the landowners 50 percent or more of the rice harvest as rental payment.

In an attempt to address this, on 12 October 1950 Prime Minister Phibun Songkhram signed the LRCA, which lowered and standardized rice paddy land rents to between 5 and 25 percent of the yearly rice harvest.[4] The act affected broadcasted rice paddy land less than 100 *rai* and transplanted paddy land less than 50 *rai* in area.[5] Under the new act, the amount of rent charged for a given area was determined by the yearly yield. Land with a greater yield commanded a proportionately higher rent, while land with a lower yield commanded a lower rent. For example, for rice paddy with a yearly yield of more than 40 *thang* per *rai*, a landowner could charge up to 10 *thang* per *rai*, or 25 percent; for rice paddy with a yearly yield of less than 20 *thang* per *rai*, a landowner could charge up to only 1 *thang* per *rai*, or 5 percent.[6] For tenant farmers subject to often high, uncertain rents, the act proposed an alternative, stable system of land rent pricing.

The act also offered rent adjustments for low yields and unforeseen problems. If weather or other natural disasters reduced a tenant's yield to less than a full crop, the act stipulated that the *tenant* could reduce the amount of rice he or she paid as rent. If the yield was less than one-tenth of the usual crop, then the tenant did not have to pay rent. In addition, the act specified that land rent could only be collected after the harvest, rather than before the planting season, as was preferred by some landowners.

Finally, the act delimited the parameters of the relationship between the landlord and the tenant. It exempted the tenant from paying tea money or offering other services to the landlord.[7] Under the law, landlords were barred from forcing the tenant to pay a higher rent than that specified under the act. Land leases could only be canceled for a specific set of reasons, including failure of the tenant to pay rent during the prior year and subletting by the tenant without the prior permission of the landlord. If a landlord planned to cancel a contract, he or she was required to give the tenant appropriate notice and could not do so in the middle of the rice-planting season. Disagreements between landlords and tenants were to be mediated by the local district officers.

In letter, the LRCA promised a significant reduction in land rents. By positing both the landlord and the tenant farmer as decision-making partners in a contractual relationship, the act also recast landlord-tenant relations. If it were fully implemented and enforced, tenants would cease, at least in letter, to be at the complete mercy of landlords.

After the signing of the LRCA, the Ministry of Interior was responsible for determining for which provinces the act should be decreed. On 4 May 1951, a royal decree covering the eighteen provinces of central Thailand was issued.[8] Regionally, central Thailand had a higher rate of tenancy than northern Thailand.[9] Among northern provinces, Chiang Mai has been exceptional, with a rate close to that of the provinces of central Thailand due to a number of factors, chief among them the rich, fertile land in the Ping River basin. The Chiang Mai provincial government reported that in 1951, 59.5 percent of total rice land was owner operated (this included owners who paid a wage to laborers to work the land), 31.6 percent was occupied by tenant farmers, and the remaining 8.9 percent was occupied by part-time owners.[10]

On learning of the decree of the 1950 LRCA in central Thailand, tenant farmers in Chiang Mai hoped for its decree in northern Thailand. A group of self-identified poor farmers from Saraphi district wrote a letter in support of the decree of the act and sent it to their member of parliament (MP), Thongdee Isarachiwin. In the letter, which is held in the Chiang Mai branch of the National Archives, the farmers argued that the high and arbitrary rates of land rent charged in Chiang Mai were "an antiquated tradition actually dating from the time of absolute monarchy, but not appropriate in the present period of democracy."[11] The landowners did not share the farmers' opinion.

The Lanna kingdom ended when it was colonized and incorporated into Siam in 1892.[12] On 24 June 1932, the People's Party launched the transformation from an absolute to a constitutional monarchy. When a provisional constitution was announced a few months later, it formally placed the Thai nation in the hands of its citizens. The constitution began with the phrase "The supreme power in the country belongs to the people."[13] Yet making this real in practice was difficult. In August 1951, when the Chiang Mai provincial government invited the largest landowners in the province to comment on the proposed decree of the 1950 LRCA, six of the twenty-two invitees still retained the title "lord" (*jao*).[14] When asked their opinion about the situation of the tenant farmers, the landowners denied the farmers' claims of poverty and hunger. Despite an insistence otherwise, as reflected by the archival file, the provincial government based its recommendations to the Ministry of Interior primarily on the opinions of the landowners. As a result, the 1950 LRCA was never implemented outside of the eighteen provinces of central Thailand.[15] In Chiang Mai, the landowners were able to use their influence within the provincial meeting room to ensure that the analysis and demands of the farmers went unheard and unheeded.

Given the nondecree of the 1950 LRCA in Chiang Mai, the first question must be: why study this act? Even, or perhaps especially, due to the lack of decree of the 1950 act, I argue that an analysis of the contention surrounding it reveals a struggle at once material and strikingly social and ontological. When influential landowners fought against the decree in the north, they clearly acted in defense of their substantial financial interests. When farmers struggled for the decree in Chiang Mai province, they did so, as they explicitly state, because their stomachs were empty. Yet, read differently, the contention surrounding the 1950 act can also be understood as a fight to publicly decide what was considered "the truth" (*khwamching*) about the condition of farmers' lives. The challenges put forward by the farmers in the 1950s, and later in the 1970s, threatened not only to limit the substantial financial gains landowners derived from unjust land rent practices but also to transform the very social and political order that underpinned landowners' position as elites and the farmers' position as subject to the landowners' decisions. This transformation acted to question the assumed benign nature of patrons' (landlords') relationships with clients (tenants). As significant as was their fear of loss of power within the rural order, the critical assessment of landlords as less than generous patrons also threatened their self-conception as beneficent fathers, uncles, and older brothers to tenant farmers.

Yet there is another register in which analysis of this struggle is important, that of historiography. Kanoksak Kaewthep's work on the FFT represents the most in-depth academic engagement with twentieth-century Thai farmers' movements.[16] While I address the FFT and Kanoksak's work more fully in subsequent chapters, his assessment of farmers' activism in the period prior to the 14 October 1973 movement bears on my project here.

Kanoksak summarizes the period before 1973 as one in which, although farmers were active, they primarily "complained" (*rong rian*) to the government. Farmers lacked a societywide, sustained, and coordinated movement. They responded locally to individual problems but did so without linking with farmers in other localities or creating a long-term plan.[17] In Kanoksak's view, the midcentury organizing by farmers also faced the concomitant lack of a politicized consciousness. He writes that "the U.S. imperialist's indirect control over Thailand was not very obvious to the people. Consequently it was not possible for people's political class consciousness to develop. There was no viable political environment in which people could gain their political experiences."[18] Taken together, what do Kanoksak's critiques of the structural limitations and undeveloped consciousness of the farmers in the 1950s mean? Can political consciousness only develop when struggle is carried out at a national level, or is it possible, indeed necessary, for it to arise within other scales? As I argue throughout this book, even when a shift in political consciousness can be identified through the emergence of a nationwide movement, the locus of change can be elsewhere. The locus of change is at the edge of a rice field when one farmer tells his neighbor about the new LRCA he heard was decreed in the central region. The locus of change is the raised platform in the middle of a rice field or the village temple compound where a group of farmers gather to plan the content of a protest letter. Political consciousness is born when a small group of people come together to talk about injustice in their lives, when people who are not oppressed listen to oppressed people and realize that their lives are bound up with those of others, and when either of these groups risks sharing its nascent knowledge with others.

Despite his analysis of the limitations of organizing in the 1950s, Kanoksak does not dismiss it as insignificant. Instead he cites the continual oppression of farmers and failures prior to 1973 as the foundation on which the FFT was established in November 1974.[19] In his assessment of the FFT, he argues that it was groundbreaking because it was the first autonomous, national organization created by farmers for farmers.

Although I agree with Kanoksak's assessment of the FFT's significance, the evidence present in the Chiang Mai provincial archives makes it possible to reconsider his analysis of the earlier farmers as lacking political consciousness and engaged primarily in complaint. While certainly the Saraphi farmers' letter can be read as a complaint to the government, it also goes beyond complaint to offer a vision for a different political system. By critiquing political decision-making structures and identifying themselves as political actors with the authority to speak about land rent conditions in Chiang Mai, the Saraphi farmers reflected a politicized consciousness. They challenged established authority and offered a reformulation of it through their actions.

This chapter takes the letter of the Saraphi farmers held in the Chiang Mai archives as a point of inspiration and departure. Their dissent in 1951 makes claims to either a completely subdued rural population or seamless rule by landowners impossible to sustain. Further, given the claims about farmers' lives made in the 1950s by different state institutions, bureaucrats, politicians, and editorialists, the Saraphi farmers' analysis stands as a critical counterclaim.

Conceptually, this chapter can be divided into three parts. In the first part I consider how various representations of farmers locate them as having a politically important existence but fail to imagine the farmers themselves as capable of political action. I trace this lacuna across counterinsurgency rhetoric about hunger, dictionary definitions, and an editorial about the oppression of farmers. In the second part I unpack the contents of the archival file on the 1950 LRCA. Beginning with a closer examination of the Saraphi farmers' letter, I reconstruct the chain of events that ultimately led to the nonimplementation of the LRCA in Chiang Mai. I argue that in the midst of the competing representations of farmers' lives discussed here, the case of the Saraphi farmers forces a reexamination of both the histories and possible futures of farmer dissent. Finally, in the third section I consider the excesses and limitations of both the archival file and my analysis.

The Hunger of Politics

In 1951, when the Saraphi farmers demanded the decree of the 1950 LRCA in the north, their request was denied. Simultaneously, their claims to hunger and impoverishment, which underlined their desire for the decree, were denied as well. The major landowners and Chiang Mai bureaucrats repeatedly insisted that the farmers were not angry and not troubled (*mai duat ron*). On initial reflection, one might be tempted to take this denial as an attempt by the land-lords to preserve their vision of northern Thai tradition (*prapheni*). While this is part of the story, their concern about the troubles of the farmers acquires an additional meaning when read together with the rising panic over the spread of communism at the time. With the establishment of the People's Repub-lic of China on 1 October 1949, Thailand wanted to ensure that communism remained outside its borders. Perhaps ironic, or perhaps prescient, given the vanguard position of farmers in Maoist visions of revolution, farmers emerged in the 1950s as key protectors capable of halting the spread of communism in Thailand.

The representations of farmers in government documents, Thai- and English-language newspaper accounts, and the *Royal Institute Dictionary* share one characteristic: *farmers are important to politics, but they are not (imagined to be) political.* Farmers were viewed as a tool of counterinsurgency because avoid-ing hunger and famine was seen as a critical part of preventing communism. As growers of rice, the staple grain in Thailand, farmers could prevent hunger. As long as people were not hungry, the official line went, they would not want to topple the existing system. This is the context of politics in which the Saraphi farmers' dissenting actions acquired subversive meaning.

On 4 September 1950, the South and Southeast Asian rice-importing coun-tries (Singapore, the Federation of Malaya, India, Ceylon, Indonesia, North Borneo, Hong Kong, and Sarawak), along with the United States and Great Britain, convened an "informal" conference on rice in Singapore.[20] Singapore's English-language daily paper, the *Straits Times*, reported that the purpose of the meeting was "to exchange information in regard to the estimated rice require-ments of the participants, the estimated availability and how best to meet the deficit."[21] While the *Straits Times'* reporting on the outcome of the conference was slim, the English-language daily *Bangkok Post* reported on it extensively. At the time, Thailand was one of the primary rice-producing nations that would be selling rice to the assembled importing nations.

According to an article in the *Bangkok Post*, equal distribution of rice across the region was important in order to "prevent any great number of people in the deficit countries going hungry and, therefore, becom[ing] more susceptible to subversive propaganda."[22] If one's belly is full, one does not (cannot? will not?) dream of a different life or another future. By preventing hunger, communism could be prevented. In the assessment of the *Bangkok Post* reporter, one of the outcomes of the meeting was to recognize "the importance of Thai rice as an anti-communist weapon" in the struggle.[23] At the close of the conference, the *Bangkok Post* ran a front-page headline that read "Anti-Communist Success Said Dependent on Rice."[24] Not only would bellies full of Thai rice be a great protection against the spread of communism but "the delegates were agreed that the supply of rice and the price have great political significance."[25] The consumers of rice were clearly addressed here, but what about the growers of rice? What about the farmers?

One answer to this question came over a year later in a *Bangkok Post* editorial titled "On Land Reform."[26] The editorial was about a conference on land tenure convened by the United Nations Educational, Scientific, and Cultural Organization (UNESCO) and held from 8 October to 20 November 1951 in Madison, Wisconsin.[27] The author predicted that when the Thai delegates returned they would

> bring back with them suggestions for land reform which should be organized into a national blueprint for a system of land tenure incorporating the best features of landownership and tenancy methods of free countries in all parts of the world. This is the best answer to Communist claims about land reform. Soviet propagandists have dangled promises of great changes to impoverished and hungry people in other lands.... [T]he peasants of Eastern Europe, like the peasants of Russia, have learned that Soviet "collectivization," or land reforms imposed from the top, brings worse oppression than before. Confiscation of property and liquidation of landowners as practiced in Russia, Eastern Europe and now in China have not done anything to improve the lot of the farmer. All that "collectivization" has accomplished is to make a tool out of man for the state.[28]

I quote at length from the *Bangkok Post* editorial because the author raises many pertinent questions about hunger, poverty, and the fears of a communist future. Again, hungry people were cast as susceptible to propaganda. But perhaps more striking is the comment that collectivization has made "a tool out of man for the state." Yet won't the farmers who grow enough rice to fill bellies across Thailand and the rest of Southeast Asia *also* be made into tools for the (anticommunist) state? The problem was not service for the state but service for a particular kind of state.

In his influential work on peasant rebellion in colonial India, Ranajit Guha critiques historians who have failed to discern a politics populated by nonelite actors.[29] Most important, this failure means that existing writing about peasant revolt has been unable to imagine revolt as an intentional undertaking by peasants. Rather than viewing peasant insurgency as constituted by peasants' desire for change, "[I]nsurgency is regarded as *external* to the peasant's consciousness and Cause is made to stand in as a phantom surrogate for Reason, the logic of that consciousness."[30] Metaphors of natural disaster are used to describe peasant uprisings or they are explained within a framework of cause and effect. Guha notes that these causes—which include hunger—are often "factors of economic and political deprivation which do not relate at all to the peasant's consciousness or do so negatively—triggering off rebellion as a sort of reflex action ... that is, as an instinctive and almost mindless response to physical suffering ... or as a passive reaction to some initiative of his super-ordinate enemy."[31] However, Guha argues that this kind of analysis not only fails to perceive the peasant as an agent of politics but also fails to adequately assess the consequences of rebellion for peasants. Dismissing the argument that peasant rebellions were spontaneous, he states that they were anything but be-cause peasants "had far too much at stake and would not launch into it except as a deliberate, even if desperate, way out of an intolerable condition of existence. Insurgency, in other words, was a motivated and conscious undertaking on the part of the rural masses."[32] Not only was rebellion an action that might result in incarceration, other punishment, or death, but it simultaneously threatened to shift the ontology of the peasants' (and the lords') world(s). As Guha explains, "To rebel was indeed to destroy many of those familiar signs which he had learned to read and manipulate in order to extract a meaning out of the harsh world around him and live with it. The risk in 'turning things upside down' under these conditions was indeed so grave that he could hardly afford to en-gage in such a project in a state of absent-mindedness."[33] The task for historians of colonial India, therefore, is to research and write about peasants "as an entity whose will and reason constituted the praxis called rebellion."[34]

Although I do not address Thai peasant revolt here, rebellion was a frequent occurrence in the nineteenth century.[35] Rather, Guha's analysis of the historiog-raphy of colonial India is resonant with both the representations of farmers in 1950s Thailand and my own methodological concerns. As noted above, it was believed that communism could be prevented as long as no one was hungry. Within this logic, only those with empty bellies might want communism. The role of farmers was precisely to fill those bellies and prevent the nation, and even the region, from being devoured by a communist future. What happens when farmers themselves are hungry, when their bellies are empty, and they want something *other than* communism? Can they be understood? Are they imaginable? Perhaps they were not for the various architects and protectors of the Thai nation-state. Inspired by Guha, I trace both the unimagineability of politicized farmers and their irrefutable vision of a different, more just future—a future that may, or may not, have been communist.

Definitions, of Backbones and Farmers

In newspaper and other discussions of the roles of farmers in anticommunist counterinsurgency in the 1950s, a particular image of the farmer was being pro-duced. This image was not created accidentally but was as important as literally appropriating the labor of the farmers as a crucial counterinsurgency tool. You see, farmers had to solve the problem of hunger without ever being hungry themselves. *This* demands a particular kind of actor.

In the letter to their MP arguing for the decree of the 1950 LRCA in Chiang Mai, one of the ways in which the Saraphi farmers identify themselves is as "the backbone of the nation" (*kraduk san lang khong chat*). This was the basis on which they made their claim for the decree. Yet the phrase was not coined, or even only used, by the farmers.

While I have not yet located the first occurrence of the phrase, here I explore two moments of its use. First, I trace the emergence of the phrase over three editions of the official, state-endorsed dictionary of the Thai language, the *Royal Institute Dictionary*.[36] Then I turn to a newspaper editorial from *Prachathipatai*, a pro-Phibun Thai-language paper, titled, in an ironic play on words, "The Backbone of the Farmers" (*kraduk san lang khong chao na*). I offer my analysis as a partial genealogy of the phrase, one attentive not only to the position of farmers vis-à-vis the nation but also to the imagined subjectivity of the farmers.

The Royal Institute was established on 31 March 1933, only nine months after Siam was transformed from an absolute to a constitutional monarchy.[37] In 1934, the newly established institute was tasked with the editing of a comprehensive dictionary of the Thai language. Prior to the establishment of the Royal Institute, the Department of Religion had published a dictionary in 1927, but as the introduction to the first edition of the new dictionary noted, it was not comprehensive and was deemed to be too greatly focused on Pali and Sanskrit words.[38] Instead, what was needed after the promulgation of Siam's first constitution was a book that would include all of the *Thai* words in use at the time.[39] The dictionary was thus cast as a lexicon in the service of the newly changed nation.

Sixteen years elapsed from the inception of the dictionary project until the Royal Institute published the first edition in 1950. While an investigation into the contentious discussions that may have gone into the compilation of the first edition is far beyond the scope of my analysis, given the newness of the institute, and the nation, the length of time involved is perhaps not surprising.[40] Following the publication of the first edition, the institute maintained a committee of scholars to review proposed words and disseminated the new words in succeeding editions of the dictionary.

Anthony Diller notes that while the *Royal Institute Dictionary* has not been without its critics, it is considered the definitive dictionary of the Thai language.[41] Indeed, many abbreviated Thai dictionaries include a note stating that they are based on the *Royal Institute Dictionary*.[42] The *Royal Institute Dictionary* is positioned as the official, authoritative arbiter of the meaning, pronunciation, and history of each word in the Thai language. To determine the meaning of a word is always a significant act. Meaning making is certainly not the exclusive province of a dictionary, but the significance of the *Royal Institute Dictionary* as the official codification of the Thai language cannot be denied. Following the publication of the initial edition in 1950, revisions were issued in 1982 and 1999.[43] When I arrived in Thailand in December 2003 to begin my dissertation research, it was the first book I purchased.

Curious about how the official dictionary defined "farmer" (*chao na*), I looked it up. There is no specific entry for "farmer." However, a few months later, I found the file on the 1950 LRCA in the Chiang Mai provincial archives. When I came across the phrase "backbone of the nation" (*kraduk san lang khong chat*) in the Saraphi farmers' letter, I didn't know how to translate it. Although I knew the meaning of the root word, "bone" (*kraduk*), I was confused as to why farmers would refer to themselves as a kind of bone. As I continued my research into the farmers' movement of the 1970s, I heard the phrase over and over again. That was months ahead, however, and my first instinct was to open the dictionary.

I picked up my new edition of the *Royal Institute Dictionary* and turned to the root word, "bone" (*kraduk*). Not only is "backbone" (*kraduk san lang*) listed as a subentry for "bone," but the very phrase that sent me to the dictionary was present as well. The backbone is defined as "the bone that is in the middle of the back of the body, characterized by interconnected joints that form a line beginning from the top of the behind. The backbone protects the spinal cord from danger. It is therefore an important part, the part that is the supporting strength. *For example, farmers are the backbone of the nation.*"[44] Farmers are not only present in the dictionary; they are defined as the exemplary backbone.

Curious as to whether farmers and backbones were rendered similarly in the earlier editions, I then examined the 1950 and 1982 editions of the dictionary. The 1950 entry for "bone" is very short and does not include a subentry for "backbone." However, in 1982 there is a subentry for "backbone of the nation." It is defined as "the most important part of the nation, usually referring to farmers."[45]

A specific articulation of farmers to the Thai nation emerges over the course of the three editions of the *Royal Institute Dictionary*. Yet, as one considers the various definitions along with the history of farmers' lives in Thailand, a dissonance emerges. If farmers are the backbone of the nation, the nation's supporting strength, then why, at so many moments in the second half of the twentieth century, have they been ignored, denied, and harassed by various state officials and bodies?

One's backbone connects the base of the skull to the pelvis. Without a backbone, the body cannot stand upright and collapses. Yet the backbone is rigidly held in place, in part due to its structural position. On second thought, perhaps the official dictionary definition and state (in)action do not necessarily stand in contradiction to one another.

Fracturing the Backbone of the Nation

On 21 June 1951 the first half of a two-part opinion essay titled "The Backbone of the Farmers" (*kraduk san lang khong chao na*) was published in *Prachathipatai* newspaper. Assuming the penname Mister Bumbam, the author bemoaned the tragic situation of farmers. Mister Bumbam offered a three-part typology of farmers, ranging from the least oppressed to the most oppressed. He detailed the capricious, harsh, and arbitrary treatment meted out to tenant farmers and laborers at the hands of some landlords.

Throughout his essay, Mister Bumbam urged his audience to understand the plight of the farmers. Despite his admirable and striking critique of the oppression felt by farmers, he did not appear to imagine them to be part of his audience. His audience ate rice but did not grow rice. This became even more apparent by the close of the second part of his essay when he turned to the issue of solutions to the problems at hand. In contrast to his fiery critique, he implored the landlords to be kinder and various government ministries to take equally tepid steps to address the injustices experienced by the farmers. His solutions were strangely out of step with his critique of the status quo.

Mister Bumbam began his piece by making a claim about the knowledge of his readers, commenting, "All of us Thai people should know very well who we are talking about when we say the backbone of the country."[46] Although the phrase "farmers are the backbone of the nation" does not appear in the 1950 edition of the *Royal Institute Dictionary*, Mister Bumbam's comment indicates that it was already in circulation in 1951.

He then wrote not about the collapse of the backbone but about its fracture. He asked, "If our backbone is broken or cracked, then what is it like? But the backbone of the country is already cracking."[47] This was significant because the farmers grew the rice eaten by his readers, their families, their neighbors, and the nation. The importance of farmers was not confined to Thailand, he insisted, but extended to the whole world.

In Mister Bumbam's view, not only were farmers the backbone of the nation but they were comparable to "a very large rice cooking pot." The Japanese did not seize Thailand during World War II because "they were afraid if they seized Thailand, the very large rice cooking pot would shatter. They would all starve."[48] In his assessment, Thai farmers not only kept the bellies of the citizens full, but they safeguarded the sovereignty of the nation as well. During World War II, the threat of hunger restrained the Japanese forces. Resonantly, in the 1950s, preventing hunger was seen as a way to stop the spread of communism.

The opening of the essay is important because Mister Bumbam framed the rest of his discussion by appealing to the bellies of his readers. He next turned to a description of the three kinds of farmers in order to show the points at which the backbone was cracking. The three kinds of farmers were: (1) "prosperous farmers" (*chao na wathana*), who owned and farmed their own land; (2) "fed-up farmers" (*chao na pha kan ueam*), who rented land to farm; and (3) "farmers soaked in sweat for the haves" (*chao na ap ngua phua khon mi*), who had neither their own land nor the ability to rent land. If his readers did not want to go hungry, he indicated, then they must pay attention to the wretched (*na anat*) lives of the farmers.

Of the three groups of farmers, the first, "prosperous farmers," was clearly the most comfortable. Prosperous farmers "don't have to worry about anything."[49] They owned agricultural equipment, buffaloes, cows, cars, and houses. During the planting and harvest seasons, the farmer and his family worked their land and hired laborers if they needed help. Once the harvest was over, this kind of farmer tended to save his rice rather than selling it because he tended to not have debts. Mister Bumbam noted that this kind of farmer was able to feed and take care of his family. In summary, he said that the prosperous farmers live "freely and extremely happily."[50]

The second group, "fed-up farmers," was in a far less desirable situation. Unlike the prosperous farmers, who owned their own land and tools, these farmers rented everything. If anything happened to their rented buffaloes, they had to inform the owner immediately. In the case of a drought or a flood, they were still required to make rental payments on the land and animals. They were often forced to go into debt in order to do so. If a farmer could not make the rental payments on time, he or she was required to pay an additional amount as a late fine. Mister Bumbam indicated the greed of some landlords when he noted that they demanded full payment from the farmer "whether he has food to eat or not, no matter if his wife starves."[51] While Mister Bumbam did not directly address the 1950 LRCA in his essay, I contend that if it had been implemented and enforced to the letter, it might have helped improve the lives of some of the fed-up farmers.

The name of the third group of farmers in Mr. Bumbam's typology, "the farmers soaked in sweat for the haves," is particularly acute. He began this section by explaining that this name for the farmers "means that the haves are parasites on this group of farmers similar to *Loranthus viscum*, which kills the farmers in cold blood."[52] These farmers were unable even to rent and had to hire themselves out to work on other people's land. They worked, ate, and lived from day to day. They were often compelled to sell their labor before the planting season commenced because they needed rice or money. As they had to sell their labor ahead of time, they were forced to accept lower wages than they would receive if they contracted their labor after the season began. In Mister Bumbam's stark terms, these farmers were "pressed, picked, impoverished." Their livelihood was "uncertain."[53] After describing the three groups of farmers, Mister Bumbam despaired of the survival of the Thai nation. If the government did not take steps to support the second and third groups, then Thailand could not survive. This was due to the vast majority of Thai people being farmers "ever since the time of our grandparents and great-grandparents."[54] In this moment he *almost* addressed farmers but fell short. Yet, at least for a brief moment, farmers were acknowledged as something other than producers of rice.

Even if farmers were not only producers of rice to fill nonfarmers' bellies, they remained, in Mister Bumbam's worldview, incapable of making changes in their own lives. Despite his emphasis on the wretched conditions of their lives, he did not call on farmers to organize, protest, or even write a letter of complaint. Instead, he addressed landlords and various parts of the government.

According to Mister Bumbam, if landlords were unable to work their own land, then they should hire a manager who would oppress the farmers as little as possible. He called on the ministries of Agriculture, Education, and Interior to take action. The Ministry of Agriculture should distribute more agricultural equipment for communal use. The Ministry of Interior should address the issues of land tenancy, landlessness, the price of rice, and the status of the canals and water. The Ministry of Education should expand its agricultural education programs so that children in rural areas could gain relevant agricultural expertise.

These solutions, Mister Bumbam wrote, even if implemented fully, would necessarily fall short of addressing the problems he described. The sweat of the farmers could not be dried by the occasional kindnesses of a few sympathetic landowners. What was needed was a call for justice and structural change, not amelioration.

Riding Expensive Bicycles: Hunger and Democracy against Contempt

Less than two weeks after Mister Bumbam's series of articles was published, the Saraphi farmers made such a call in the letter they wrote to their MP requesting the decree of the 1950 LRCA in Chiang Mai province. Critical for my purpose of demonstrating how land tenancy became an acutely intimate site of contention, the archival file of which the letter is one part documents the contestation between landlords and tenant farmers. Contained within the file are letters written by farmers from Saraphi and Doi Saket, Thongdee Isarachiwin, the provincial government, and the Ministry of Interior, in addition to transcripts of meetings held at the provincial hall. There are no records of face-to-face meetings, but through the farmers' letters and landlord contributions to meetings they counter each other's formulations of their lives and the world. Chiang Mai provincial officials and Thongdee are present as interlocutors to this contestation.

The documents in this file are important in a number of registers. At the most basic level, like the newspaper articles and the dictionary, the file is a site of representations of farmers. Significantly, the letters by the Saraphi and Doi Saket farmers are a much different kind of representation than the others: the letters are *representations of farmers by farmers*. While the Doi Saket letter is short, the Saraphi letter, which I address in detail here, goes beyond self-representation to represent democracy. I recognize that the letters have histories of production that I cannot trace—that is, I cannot know for certain that the person who penned the letter also planted rice with his own hands in 1951.

Finally, although the act was never decreed, the anxiety precipitated by the

Saraphi farmers' letter reveals the tenuousness of the position of the landowners. The letter can be read as diagnostic of the possibilities of the power of a united rural opposition. Twenty years later, both the power of the united rural opposition and the anxiety of the landholding elites were irrepressible.

On 19 March 1951, five months after the enactment of the LRCA, the Ministry of Interior in Bangkok sent an urgent letter to each province asking whether or not it was appropriate to decree the law in the province.[55] The Chiang Mai government responded within a month (on 19 April 1951) and cited traditional Lanna land rent practices as the reason why the act would be inappropriate for use in Chiang Mai. The tradition cited encompassed both the amount of land rent and the relations between landowners and tenants. Traditionally, landowners and tenants split the rice harvest in half or according to some proportion agreed on by the two parties. In the eyes of the Chiang Mai government, however, more important than the amount of land rent exchanged was the interdependence between the landowners and tenants. The 1950 act threatened to destroy the tradition by which generous landowners provided for tenant farmers whatever they could not provide for themselves. The author of the letter explained, "If it so happens that farmers are lacking work animals or capital, even including clothing to wear, the landowners will charitably provide them to the farmers. They are interdependent. . . . [I]f this act is decreed here, it will likely give the landowners an opportunity to cease their charity and disengage from this interdependent relationship."[56] This comment raises the question of the nature not only of tradition but of interdependence (*kan thoi thi thoi asai kan lae kan*). While the landlords claimed their actions were generous charity, for farmers this was neither sufficient nor without oppressive obligations.[57] Writing in the context of changing patron-client links in Southeast Asia during the colonial era, James C. Scott argues that in exchange for a minimum of physical safety and material subsistence clients will support patrons. When these terms cease being met, clients will withdraw their support.[58] In this moment, what were farmers expected to do in order to continue receiving the charity of the landowners? In other words, what was their contribution to this interdependence? While it is not stated directly, it would appear to be unquestioning adherence to a system of land rent that they regarded as unjust. The farmers argued that they could no longer survive within this system. Survival was a problem both material and political.

When farmers in Saraphi and Doi Saket districts learned of the Chiang Mai government's recommendation against the decree, they wrote to Thongdee Isarachiwin, their MP, to ask for his help in reversing the decision. The 3 July 1951 letter, signed by eighteen farmers from Yangnung and Nongfung subdistricts in Saraphi district, was particularly striking for its position in calling for justice.[59] Calling on Thongdee as self-identified "impoverished farmers" (*chao na phu yak chon*), the farmers in Saraphi refuted tradition and defined the meaning of democracy. As mentioned earlier, the Saraphi farmers wrote that the traditional relationship cited by the Chiang Mai government was "an antiquated tradition actually dating from the time of absolute monarchy, but not appropriate during the present democratic period."[60] In one case, they noted that a landlord had demanded two-thirds of the harvest as rent. Out of 360 *thang* of rice, a landlord took 220 *thang*; the remaining 140 *thang* was not enough rice for a family to eat for one year. If one were to place the Saraphi farmers within Mister Bumbam's typology, given the amount of rent they paid they would have fallen between the second and third groups of farmers. While they were able to rent land to farm, like the "fed-up farmers," the amount of rent charged ensured that their own rice supply would remain tenuous, like the "farmers soaked in sweat for the haves."

Rather than relying on the possible charity of the landowners, the Saraphi farmers wanted the LRCA to be decreed in Chiang Mai so that they would have enough rice to fill the stomachs of their families for all twelve months of the year. In addition, they criticized their exclusion from the provincial-level discussions about the law and asked to be consulted by the district commit-tee.[61] In this moment, the Saraphi farmers interrupted the influence of the landowners by noting the absence of tenant farmers from the decision-making process thus far. More important, by insisting that they be consulted regarding decisions that would affect them, the Saraphi farmers enacted the democracy they wished to live within.

The Saraphi farmers set in motion a chain of actions that nonetheless ended with the passive refusal to decree the LRCA in Chiang Mai. On 30 July 1951 Thongdee Isarachiwin wrote a letter conveying the concerns and demands of the farmers to Phibun Songkhram, the prime minister. Thongdee charac-terized the reason for his involvement as resulting from the disproportionate persecution and oppression experienced by Chiang Mai farmers at the hands of landowners. He tied this directly to the lack of involvement of the state in aiding Chiang Mai farmers, who he noted "have been oppressed by the wealthy for over one hundred years. They should receive the same justice as the farmer brothers and sisters in central Thailand."[62] Thongdee's sincerity was questioned by the Chiang Mai government, the landowners, and an editorial writer in the *Siam Rat* newspaper.[63] They argued that his motivation to advocate for the tenant farmers was purely vote related. Yet each of these sources also argued that the farmers who wanted the decree of the act in Chiang Mai were an insignificant minority of farmers. If Thongdee was simply interested in garner-ing votes, wouldn't it make more sense to choose the majority group? Either these farmers *were* the (unacknowledged) majority and/or the accusation of vote buying was untrue!

Following Thongdee's letter, in a letter dated 30 August 1951, the Ministry of Interior in Bangkok requested a reevaluation of the possible decree of the LRCA from the Chiang Mai government. The Chiang Mai government and the Ministry of Interior exchanged letters for the next five years, ending with a letter dated 19 December 1956 from the Ministry of Interior requesting the final recommendations regarding the possible decree of the 1950 act.[64] Although the Chiang Mai government never responded to this request (or did not archive it), the 1950 LRCA was never decreed in Chiang Mai or in any province outside the initial eighteen decreed in central Thailand.

The archival file therefore documents the nondecree, the nonevent, of the 1950 LRCA in Chiang Mai. Writing about her research in the Dutch colonial archives regarding how the Dutch addressed what they perceived as the threat of the *inlandsche kinderen*, the children of European men and Indonesian women, Ann Laura Stoler foregrounds the noneventful as a site of analysis. She does not, as one might expect, focus on "the concrete and discrete events that made up social reform (which policies were carried out and which not)."[65] Instead, drawing on archives as processes, sites, and technologies of contested knowledge, Stoler examines the proposals and incomplete, unrealized projects of the Dutch to educate, train, and otherwise discipline the *inlandsche kinderen*. By focusing on the noneventful—what was not realized but imagined, proposed, discussed, and attempted by the Dutch—Stoler is able to consider "deep anxieties about a Dutch national past and of an Indies colonial future, of a colonial utopia obliquely addressed."[66]

Informed by Stoler's work, I read the documents of nonimplementation of the act as critical documents not only of the refusal (by landowners and government officials) of the Saraphi farmers' vision of democracy but also as diagnostic of an emerging tension concerning the maintenance of the rural order. In this case, not only were farmers' demands for lower land rents denied, but their claims to knowing the truth about their own lives were silenced as well.

Given the characterizations of farmers as passive—yet important—national-political beings in the *Royal Institute Dictionary*, the fight against communism, and Mister Bumbam's analysis of the struggle against their own oppression, their active presence here is at once surprising, and important. The indignation and ferocity with which the landlords responded to the farmers' claims about their own lives underscore the nature of the political passivity constitutive of the other representations of the farmers.

While the report of the reevaluation of land rent in Chiang Mai sent to the Ministry of Interior stated that all the different sectors were consulted, my reading of the report, as well as the contents of the archival file, suggests that the primary source of the reevaluation was a one-hundred-minute meeting with seventeen major landholders in Chiang Mai on 9 August 1951.[67] The meeting began with an apology from the government official, Udom Bunprasop, who led the meeting. He explained that the Chiang Mai government had already informed the Ministry of Interior that the act was inappropriate for use in Chiang Mai. However, due to the letter from Thongdee in support of the farmers' demands, the Ministry of Interior wanted a more thorough evaluation.[68] Udom claimed that he was "only the middle man, the servant of every side."[69]

The landowners made no such pretense to impartiality. They spoke with certainty and unironic contradiction about their own lives and those of tenant farmers. The lack of contention in the meeting is surprising; from the transcript of the meeting the seventeen individuals almost seemed to speak with one voice. The landowners repeatedly insisted that their landholdings were small; even the landowner who owned 100 *rai* noted that it was *only* 100 *rai*.[70] Despite their status as small landholders, they noted their generosity in giving animals and clothes to their tenants. If the LRCA was decreed in Chiang Mai, the landowners lamented, they and their families would be devastated.

One of the first comments made during the meeting was an explicit denial of the impoverishment cited by the Saraphi farmers: "The tenant farmers in Chiang Mai have a lot. They are not poor. . . . They have thousands of baht."[71] Another landowner, Worasak Nimmanan, offered the observation, "[E]veryone renting land has a permanent house already, they aren't troubled, and they aren't really poor."[72] He further argued that if the act was decreed, his family would face personal ruin as even half the rice harvest would not be enough to eat for twelve months. In Worasak's assessment, most landowners had other occupations already, and he would be forced to find yet another job for "the money to buy household items and pay my children's school fees, [for] my family is quite large."[73]

While the Saraphi farmers argued that they needed the LRCA to be decreed so that they would have enough rice to eat, Jao (Lord) Pong-in, another landowner, denied that lack of rice was an issue for tenant farmers. Instead he argued that they rented in order to engage in "large-scale production, not for eating . . . [and thus they] rent to expand their business."[74] Individually, Worasak and Jao Pong-in each denied the claims the Saraphi farmers made to hunger and lack of rice. Considered together, their comments constituted a dissimulating reversal whereby tenant farmers became agricultural industrialists and landowners became hungry workers.

Kraisri Nimmanhemin's comments during the meeting reflected a particularly sharp dismissal of the farmers' claims. Kraisri began his speech by noting the similarity between the tenant farmers and the (capitalist) landowners; the tenant farmers "are not workers, but another kind of capitalist."[75] In case this was not enough to disavow the claim made by the farmers to a position of impoverishment and disadvantage vis-à-vis the landowners, Kraisri offered concrete evidence. He explained, "I ask you to observe how they make merit, how they dress, what kinds of things they use. For example, they ride expensive types of bicycles, such as the Raleigh and the Humber. People in the cities don't ride this type, [but] everyone in the country does."[76] As long as tenant farmers could donate money to the temple, purchase their own clothes, and purchase a sturdy bicycle, then, he seemed to suggest, land rents did not need to be standardized or lowered. What had to be visible in order to constitute impoverishment? If documented landlessness and claims to hunger did not suffice, what would?[77]

Kraisri's comment about the bicycles used by tenant farmers became evidence in the reevaluation of the 1950 LRCA written by the Chiang Mai provincial government. This report was sent to the Ministry of Interior in Bangkok on 29 September 1951.[78] In addition to the bicycles and clothes cited by Kraisri, the report claimed that the farmers also had substantial savings.[79] Despite the note by Udom Bunprasop to the effect that he had to be very careful to interrogate the veracity of each claim to truth or troubles, his reliance on the landowners' statements indicates whose version of reality he chose to support. He argued that the decree was unnecessary because the majority of the tenant farmers were not really poor and were not really troubled. Further, citing the fear of the tenant farmers and making an implicit reference to the influence held by the landowners, the author concluded that the act should not be decreed. If land rent control was decreed, then perhaps landowners would refuse to rent land altogether and tenant farmers would be forced to work as laborers.

As I read the transcript of the meeting of landowners, I was struck by what I read as the landowners' self-interested comments. Their exaggerated claims to their own impoverishment and dismissal of the hunger of farmers can be read as a valiant attempt to ensure the shelving of the 1950 LRCA for Chiang Mai and therefore their continued financial success. In this moment, landowners were faced not only with the potential diminishment of their material wealth but also the loss of their social (and self-) image as generous patrons. Preventing this loss required a struggle that was at once political and epistemological. I suggest that we also should read this as an equally valiant attempt by the landholding elite to retain their position not only as, in Marx and Engels's term, "the ruling material force of society," but also as "its ruling intellectual force."[80] Their attempt was successful, for a time.

Missing Letters and Archival Oversights

Almost a month before the Chiang Mai provincial government submitted its report to the Ministry of Interior, Thongdee Isarachiwin sent an additional urgent letter to both Prime Minister Phibun Songkhram and the Ministry of Interior. In the letter, Thongdee criticized the conduct of Udom Bunprasop, the Chiang Mai official in charge of the review of the possible decree of the LRCA. Thongdee accused Udom of violating government directives related to the review by unabashedly aligning himself with the landlords. Thongdee urged Phibun to set up a committee to investigate Udom's behavior and transgressions of the rules of conduct for civil servants. This letter was not included in the archival file but was printed in full in the Thai-language daily newspaper *Kittisak*.[81] I offer a closer examination of the letter in order to illustrate the specific ways in which Udom's claim to be "only the middleman, the servant of every side," was insincere.

Thongdee began his letter by explaining that, in accordance with Ministry of Interior's instructions, Udom met with farmers in seven districts in Chiang Mai—Sanpatong, Sankhampaeng, Mae Rim, Mae Thang, Chiang Mai city, Sansai, and Saraphi—between 15 and 22 August 1951. In contrast to the 9 August meeting with the landowners, if invitations were issued or minutes taken, they were not preserved in the archival file. Thongdee noted that every time Udom addressed the tenant farmers, rather than telling them about the government policy for farmers, a policy described by Thongdee as one that recognized that "farmers are the backbone of the nation," Udom violated the government's policy. Thongdee accused Udom of using outright threats to intimidate the farmers. Udom allegedly insisted that splitting the rice harvest in half was a long-standing tradition among Chiang Mai people and should not be changed. If the LRCA was decreed, he threatened, it would give the owners an opportunity to fail to fulfill their obligations to the farmers. Most of the owners would choose to work the land themselves. This would be very difficult for the farmers. When the landowners refused to rent their land to the tenant farmers, the civil servants and district officers would not be able to help them.[82] Rather than attempt dissimulation in the style of the landlords, Udom opted for direct fearmongering.

In addition, Thongdee alleged that Udom had permitted the landlords to attend the meetings and bully the tenant farmers. In case Udom's threats of a dismal (and hungry) future were not enough to intimidate the farmers, the presence of landlords and their supporters constituted an additional pressure. Thongdee offered specific details, noting that Udom "let the wealthy landowners use megaphones to insult and yell that this is a horrible law, that it is a law that will bring trouble to the country, that it is a communist law, etc."[83]

The accusation that the law was "communist" gives us reason to pause. In this instance there is not enough information to discern what Thongdee or the people using the term as an accusation meant. Did they mean Maoist revolution? If so, was it a form of regime change with farmers as the vanguard? In the sense that Udom insisted that the decree of the LRCA would give the landowners a crack through which to refuse to rent their land, might the decree also create a crack through which farmers could continue to advocate for justice?

Most striking, however, is Thongdee's use of the ever-present phrase "farmers are the backbone of the nation." Thongdee summarized Udom's actions as "[H]e cheers on the capitalists who have expansive, wide holdings of land, so that they can plow over the backs of the impoverished farmers, who are forever going to be the backbone of the nation."[84] In Thongdee's formulation, the farmers were not the backbone of the nation because they grew the rice everyone eats. They were the backbone of the nation because the landlords' wealth was built on their backs, literally. In this moment, Thongdee critiqued not only Udom but also what he perceived as the deeply classed formulation of the Thai nation.

Undecideability: Excesses of Communism

In this chapter, I have engaged many references to something called "communism." Farmers, as growers of rice to feed the citizens of the nation, were defined as a strategic tool to be used against the spread of communism. Underlying this vision seems to be the persistent idea that people with full bellies are less interested in critiquing the current regime or dreaming of a different possibility. Within this formulation, there was no space in which farmers themselves might be hungry, and therefore communist. This lacuna may have reflected an underlying vision of the Thai nation in which farmers were less than citizens. Or, as I argue that farmers were consistently represented as being implicated in politics without themselves being political actors, it may follow that the possibility of a communist farmer simply would have been of no concern. Therefore, their hunger would have been of no concern as well.

As is pointedly obvious in the previous section, however, nearly every formulation of communism I have engaged thus far has been either wholly undefined or vaguely defined. While Thongdee noted that landowners in Chiang Mai used the accusation that the LRCA was a "communist" law as a tool to intimidate farmers, the meaning of *communist*, as understood by either the landlords or Thongdee himself, remains unclear.

Two days after Thongdee's letter was published in *Kittisak*, an editorial about the possible decree of the 1950 LRCA in Chiang Mai was published in *Siam Rat*, another Bangkok daily.[85] In contrast to many of the other formulations, the author of the *Siam Rat* editorial offered a very specific vision of communism. Significantly, the author's formulation also provides another lens through which to the view the issue of the landowners' fear and anxiety.

While the author of the *Siam Rat* editorial dismissed the need for the decree, he offered a note of warning. The author cautioned that careful explanation and understanding were necessary because, "Who benefits between the landowners and the land tenants is clear. However, if this hasn't yet become trouble, hasn't yet become grave, then we shouldn't touch the relationship. Because doing so might create feelings of enemies between different classes. This would be an opening that would allow the entry of communism."[86] This is a strikingly astute passage. While advocating against the decree of the LRCA, the author did not deny that the landlords were the clear beneficiaries of the relationship. The author seemed to suggest that discussion about class difference should be avoided. Drawing the next logical conjecture, he seemed to indicate that in so doing communism could be avoided. To make a practice of not speaking about class differences is to attempt to render them unnameable. The editorialist himself leaves class differences unarticulated, noting that it is clear who, between landowners and tenants, benefits from the status quo without ever naming landowners as the beneficiaries.

The rhetorical form of his editorial is intriguing, for even as he refuses to explicitly name class differences and what they mean concretely, his readers could draw the same conclusions from his analysis that I have. While the admonition to leave the clear differences among classes unsaid seems naive, perhaps it was meant as a request, or even a plea. The author was clearly aware that class consciousness would likely emerge from such an engagement. As evidenced by the Saraphi farmers' letter, class consciousness *did* arise from the recognition of inequality between their lives and those of the landowners and then led to the proposal of a future in which this inequality was addressed. On the surface, the editorialist seems to write in the service of overtly repressing the acknowledgment of class in Thai society. Yet I wonder if there is another way in which this editorial can be read. Is it possible that in calling on the public to leave class differences unnamed, while simultaneously indicating (i.e., all but naming) them, the author subverted his own purpose?

Here the *Siam Rat* editorialist suggests that at its most dangerous, class consciousness might lead to a desire for communism. As long as farmers (and their potential allies) did not become class conscious, the nation would remain free of communism. Even if every belly were filled, that might not be enough to ward off the development of class consciousness.[87] Further, as emerges again in my discussion of the struggle to pass and implement the 1974 LRCA, communism was not the *only*, or the most dangerous, possible outcome of the development of class consciousness by rural tenant farmers and their allies. Landowning and other conservative forces often cited communism, which they seemed to understand as the complete eradication of their way of life, as their deepest fear. Yet taking democratic politics to its fullest extent, a situation in which landowners and tenant farmers would meet each other on the same footing of the law (at least on paper), represented a threat perhaps less total but more immediately real. Communism could be explicitly opposed and vilified, but in the period of open politics following 14 October 1973, legal land rent reform was more difficult to dismiss.

Classification and Historiographic Quandaries: Defining Claims to Legitimacy

In this chapter I have privileged the 1951 letter from the Saraphi farmers as an indication of farmers as political actors against various other representations of them as, paradoxically, implicated in politics without the possibility of acting within them. The contention between landowners and tenant farmers in Chiang Mai province was significant because it revealed the ways in which the struggle over the 1950 LRCA was at once about the amount of rice paid as rent and about who had the power to name the truth about farmers' lives. While the Saraphi farmers lost the struggle to decree the act, the presence of their letter in the Chiang Mai provincial archives suggests that they did not fully concede the ontological struggle.

Yet, the Saraphi farmers' letter presents difficulties of interpretation. In one sense, one might argue that their struggle was unsuccessful because the act was not decreed for use in Chiang Mai. At the same time, their letter provoked contention that revealed, and may have fractured further, the fragile power of the landowners. Analytically, how does one classify this? How does one assess and place the Saraphi farmers within a genealogy of manifestations of farmers' political consciousness and action in Thailand?

While I noted the resonances between aspects of revolt noted by Guha and the changes wrought by the Saraphi farmers, the farmers were clearly not engaged in revolt. As Kanoksak notes, their action was not on the scale or of the order of the organized, national, autonomous FFT. The farmers were not using Scott's "weapons of the weak" to chip away at the system of domination.[88] In fact, they were challenging the system of domination using its own terms and strategies. In writing and submitting a letter in which they demanded that they, as "the backbone of the nation," be consulted about legislative decisions that affected their lives, they challenged the 1951 government to be democratic. By offering a definition of democracy through their actions, the farmers enacted the future that they wished to see.

A formulation of Andrew Turton's may be helpful. Although it was developed to account for post-1976 farmer organizing, it is relevant here as well. He characterizes one of the results of new forms of organizing as the emergence of *claims to legitimacy*. He explained that "new forms of knowledge about, and appropriate to, conditions of livelihood are produced and disseminated; there is a new assertion of dignity and human worth, a new self-confidence and boldness."[89] The Saraphi farmers' letter can be understood as a claim to legitimacy. In their letter the farmers offer a vision of their lives—as filled with hunger, difficulty, and hope for a different future—that is at odds with every other representation of them in circulation at the time. Even though their claim to legitimacy was contested by the landowners, and the landowners' (illegitimate) claim was successful in preventing the decree of the 1950 LRCA, the anxiety precipitated by the farmers' letter revealed the tenuousness of the position of the landowners. The letter can also be read as diagnostic of the possibilities of the power of a united rural opposition. Twenty years later, both the power of the united rural opposition and the anxiety of the landholding elites returned, stronger than before.

Postscript: Dissenting Dictionaries

Matichon Press issued a short dictionary in 2000 titled *Dictionary outside the Royal Institute* (or perhaps *Dictionary beyond the Royal Institute*) (*Photchananuk-rom Nok Ratchabandit*).[90] This dictionary was published in a full-length version, *Matichon Dictionary of the Thai Language*, in 2004. While noting that the *Royal Institute Dictionary* was the foundational dictionary (*photchananukrom lak*), the compilers explained that while the purpose of the Royal Institute's volume was to "'set' the rules of usage," their project was to "'reflect' usage."[91] The full-length *Matichon Dictionary* offers a point of comparison, perhaps offering a hint as to the sincerity of the definition in the *Royal Institute Dictionary*. Under "bone," the subentry definition for "backbone" ends with an illustrative example: "[T]he government *says* that farmers are the backbone of the nation."[92] Exactly.

2

From the Rice Fields to the Cities

Today's Thai farmers are not the same as the farmers of yesteryear, because we have firmly come together.

Sign held during farmer protest in Chiang Mai

Ongoing power struggles among the members of the ruling triumvirate—Field Marshal Phibun Songkhram, Police General Phao Sriyanond, and Field Marshal Sarit Thanarat—created the space for some forms of dissent in the decade following the end of World War II.[1] Pushing through the cracks and fissures of repressive rule, the Chiang Mai farmers who called for the decree of the 1950 LRCA in 1951 attempted to expand this space. When Field Marshal Sarit staged a coup, declared martial law, and named himself sole premier in October 1958, this possibility of open dissidence disappeared. During Field Marshal Sarit's premiership and then that of Field Marshal Thanom Kittikachorn, who seized power after Sarit's death in 1963, there were severe restrictions on protest, speech, and life generally. Under these restrictions, repressive state action and damaging inaction were more likely to pass without direct criticism from those affected than they might have during another time.

The tenancy problem, which was steadily growing in the north, was one key area of state inaction. Other than an unanswered query from the Ministry of Interior in Bangkok about whether it would be appropriate to decree the 1950 LRCA in 1956, the national and provincial governments were silent on land tenancy issues in Chiang Mai for nearly twenty years. This inaction was one more level of state disavowal of the Chiang Mai farmers' calls for the decree of the 1950 LRCA. In the meantime, farmers' living and working conditions plunged deeper and deeper into crisis. Land rents continued to be exorbitant across the north, sometimes climbing even as high as two-thirds of the rice harvest.[2] Compounding these problems was a general shortage of land, particularly lowlands suitable for wet-rice cultivation. While rice yields in the Ping River valley in Chiang Mai and Lamphun were on average over fifty *thang* per *rai*, higher than most in the country, there simply was not enough land to go around.

Even those farmers who possessed land increasingly possessed less. In 1963, the average amount of land held by farmers nationally was 21.7 *rai*; the average amount held in the north was 16.1 *rai*. By 1973, the average amount of land held by farmers in the north had dropped to 8.8 *rai*; 27 percent of farmers possessed less than 5.0 *rai*. Another estimate indicated that approximately one-third of northern farmers owned all of their land, one-third were part owners, and one-third were tenant farmers. This did not account for those farmers who were completely landless, meaning farmers who neither possessed nor were able to rent land.[3] A number of factors precipitated the growing land shortage in the north, including the shrinking of the once-expanding land frontier, population growth, disinheritance (as already small parcels of land were subdivided among siblings), and indebtedness.[4]

The difficulties and suffering experienced by farmers in Chiang Mai were mirrored in different ways across the country. One progressive newsweekly identified the most significant problems faced by farmers in late 1973 as access to land and loss of land to "capitalist landowners" (*nai thun jao khong thi din*), followed by low market prices for crops and high land rent prices.[5] Farmers in the northeast, who had the lowest average per capita income of all Thai farmers, faced a significant shortage of cultivable land and a lack of sufficient irrigation to cope with the arid environment.[6] Southern farmers experienced low market prices for their rubber and the increasing growth of commercial plantations.[7] Although farmers in the central region had the highest average per family income, they also had the highest rate of indebtedness.[8] Many farmers and other impoverished people were forced to use moneylenders who operated outside the official banking system. While these lenders were willing to lend to individuals with no credit history, they often did so at exorbitant rates. As a result, a farmer might borrow a principle sum of 2,000 baht from a nonbank moneylender and watch it skyrocket to 20,000 baht in a few months. Many farmers who owned land and gave their land title as a guarantee lost their land in this manner. Unfortunately, because farmers agreed to these terms, they often possessed no legal recourse.[9]

Left to their own devices, bureaucrats may have remained indefinitely silent about tenancy issues in the north and crises elsewhere. Yet in the changed context engendered by the events of 14 October 1973, farmers were unwilling to accept state inaction. Beginning in March 1974, farmers took to the streets and addressed their demands for redress and justice simultaneously to the Thai public and various parts of the Thai state. Through a series of protests that began on a small scale and were then held simultaneously in provincial capitals and Bangkok, active, progressive farmers grew into an increasingly critical mass. By joining with one another and bringing their protests from the countryside into the city streets, farmers fundamentally transformed themselves into a new kind of dissenting political subject not present in Thailand before. By bringing themselves and their issues to Sanam Luang in the heart of Bangkok, the farmers made their struggle a visibly public one.[10] As the farmers and the government traded lists of demands and responses over the months between March and November 1974, the farmers became increasingly politically savvy and the government's promises increasingly difficult to keep. The farmers' largest protest began on 19 November 1974 with the establishment of the FFT. Not only was the FFT the first autonomous, national farmers' organization in Thailand, but the November 1974 protest was also the point at which the farmers were able to secure the most concrete promises from the central state.[11]

While some farmers from Chiang Mai traveled to Bangkok to join the protests there, many remained to fill the streets of the old city and camp out on the steps of the provincial building. Their primary concern was tenancy relief, and they quickly revived the call for the decree of the 1950 LRCA for Chiang Mai and neighboring Lamphun province. This call grew louder as the harvest season approached in late 1974, and it was included in the list of demands that the fledgling FFT submitted to the prime minister on 19 November. In response, rather than decreeing the 1950 act for the northern provinces, the government decided to promulgate a new LRCA immediately applicable to the entire country in December 1974. While the transformative possibilities engendered by the passage of the 1974 LRCA soon exceeded the text of the law, embedded in its provisions was a radical reconfiguration of rural relations of power. This reconfiguration was produced not only by the form of the law but also by the actions taken by farmers. Within the first six months after its inception, the FFT had become a significant political and social force whose presence could be felt in villages and cities across the country. In contrast to the earlier struggle to decree the 1950 act, which was thwarted before a larger movement or discussion began, the tenancy struggle in 1974 was a catalyst that launched and foreshadowed broader changes.

The possibility—and danger—of the transformations fomented through the farmers' protests is most sharply refracted against the analysis of a work published between the two tenancy struggles: Jit Phumisak's *The Real Face of Thai Feudalism Today* (*Chom Na Khong Saktina Thai Nai Patchuban*).[12] *The Real Face* was published in 1957, then rapidly banned after Field Marshall Sarit took power in 1958. Jit wrote what Craig Reynolds, who translated *The Real Face* in 1989, has called "a Gramscian study before Gramsci" about how feudalism, or *saktina*, and capitalism functioned in Thailand both before and after 1932.[13] His primary example of feudalism, which Jit argued persisted after its official end with the abolition of the absolute monarchy in 1932, was the relationship between a landlord and a tenant. While Jit did not cite the 1951 struggles of the

Saraphi and Doi Saket farmers, his text speaks directly to their experience of poverty and denial. Similarly, Jit's analysis of how the relations of production inform social and political life in arenas outside economic life eerily prefigured the resistance the farmers' met in their material and economic struggles to secure land rent relief in the form of law in 1974.

Yet the relevance of *The Real Face of Thai Feudalism Today* to understanding the significance and power of the farmers' movement exceeds Jit's choice of examples. Through his writing, Jit disarticulated the "web of meanings . . . articulated in law, in public ceremony, and in symbolism (whether it be monumental sculpture or the plan of the capital or the ubiquity of monasteries)," which both secure the state's legitimacy and "inextricably associate the military, the monarchy, and the Buddhist monkhood as a triad that stands for 'Thailand.'"[14] This exposure, undoing, and refusal to abide by dominant (and dominating) meanings made *The Real Face* and Jit himself threatening and even seditious.[15] In a resonant fashion, once farmers chose to place their hope with each other and the shared project of organizing rather than waiting for state officials to take action, they began to be perceived as dangerous by their critics within and outside the Thai state.

Dismantling Feudalism

The outpouring of progressive dissidents into the streets during the three years between October 1973 and 1976 was accompanied by a simultaneous boom in progressive publishing. Books written by Thai communists, socialists, and other radicals originally published in the 1940s and 1950s and banned under repressive regimes were brought out of hiding and reprinted. The works of poets and novelists and other thinkers writing in the service of social justice outside Thailand were rapidly translated, including the writing of Frantz Fanon and Paolo Freire in addition to Mao Tse-tung and V. I. Lenin.[16] Students, CPT intellectuals, and activists of all sorts within Thailand wrote their own tracts, variously published by the many new presses or the student or other relevant organizations themselves. What many volumes published and circulated during this period shared, no matter the specific context or issue addressed, was either a critique of the status quo or an attempt to articulate what a different future should, or should not, look like. In this respect, one can see how *Looking Ahead* (*Lae Pai Khang Na*), a set of two novels describing the broken promises of the 1932 transition from absolute to constitutional monarchy written by Kulap Saipradit while in jail during the 1950s and published together in 1975, might sit on a shelf next to a translation of Paulo Freire's *Pedagogy of the Oppressed*.[17] Kulap critiqued the form of society and social relations; Freire offered strategies for unbinding and remaking relations between oppressors and the oppressed in society.

Many books were published in paperback "pocketbook" form, for ease of carrying as well as to keep the prices accessibly low.[18] Literally hundreds of books, as well as many new newspapers and other periodicals, emerged after 14 October 1973, only to be seized by state authorities or destroyed by their owners before this could happen after the 6 October 1976 massacre and coup. Intrigued by how to think about the relationship between the writings about ending injustice and the actions taken to do so, or what Paulo Freire calls *praxis*, I asked everyone I met who was active during the 1973–76 period what books he or she read.[19] Without fail, one of the two or three books each person mentioned was *The Real Face of Thai Feudalism Today* by Jit Phumisak. The other volumes varied, but Jit always made the list. *The Real Face* was initially published in the yearbook of the Faculty of Law at Thammasat University in 1957, under the name Somsamai Srisudravarna, and then reprinted numerous times beginning in 1974.[20] The reasons given for reading (or buying and intending to read) *The Real Face* shed some light on why Jit was so popular: he had joined the CPT struggle and was then killed by state forces, he wrote about farmers, a friend said he was brilliant, and he was a *Thai* Marxist. Yet Jit went beyond the description of injustice in Thailand; in *The Real Face*, he epistemologically subverted injustice. For farmers and students active around tenancy in the north, Jit's analysis of feudalism, law, and knowledge was particularly salient.

Jit's primary concern in *The Real Face* was to analyze feudalism by examining the relations of production. He did so by considering the relationship between a landowner, Bamrung, and his wife, Si, and asking, "Who is the labor boss and who is the laborer? Who owns the land and the other means of production, and who rents the land and the means of production? Whose labor works the fields?"[21] The answers have a clear meaning: "If, when production is in progress, nobleman Bamrung is the owner of the land and lies around the house wiggling his feet—be they tiny or big—and woman Si rents the land, tills the field, plants the rice, harvests the rice, and gives nobleman Bamrung half of it as rent according to the half-share rent system," then Bamrung is a "saktina Land-Lord" and Si is a "poor peasant."[22] What makes Bamrung the oppressor of Si is that he profits from her labor without working himself. Jit's subversion began with his choice of a familial relationship—especially the intimate, private one between a husband and a wife—as capable of illustrating feudalism. When the farmers from Saraphi district called for the decree of the 1950 LRCA in 1951, they claimed exploitation at the hands of the landlords. The landlords responded by saying that they viewed themselves as the older brothers of the farmers and therefore were not their oppressors. Had Jit been present in the meeting room at the provincial building during this discussion, he might have said, "So, you are the older brothers of the farmers? And you are content to watch your younger brothers starve as long as your own bellies are full?"

The reality, as the Saraphi farmers learned in 1951 and the farmers of the FFT learned over twenty years later, is that feudalism reaches beyond the register of the material. Although *saktina*, the Thai word for *feudal*, literally means "power over the rice fields," Jit theorized the ways in which this power was felt outside the fields. Jit wrote, "'[S]aktina' is a social system, and this social system typically includes three elements: the economic, the political, and the cultural."[23] One of the primary tools for retaining control over these three connected spheres was the law.[24] Not only was the oppressor class content to use the law as a tool, but under absolute monarchy, "the saktina went so far as to forbid the People from studying law. What was considered to be the law and what the saktina permitted to be studied—indeed required to be studied—were the texts setting out the regulations for royal pages, instructions for the royal palace which the slaves, retainers, and the People had to observe correctly."[25] Peasant knowledge of the law—let alone subjecthood within or use of it—was dangerous. While Jit made it clear that he was describing feudal practices before and after the 1932 transformation from absolute to constitutional monarchy, one wonders if he could have imagined that law in the hands of oppressed farmers would still be so destabilizing in 1974. The experiences of the northern farmers in 1974 illustrate how disbelief at their adoption of the law turned to fear—of loss and change—on the part of landowners and bureaucrats. Jit Phumisak's history stretched—and stretches—into the present.

Not unlike many other writers who raised their pens in the tradition of revolution—or wished to begin one—Jit offered an analysis of pervasive injustice without being entirely explicit about a solution. He outlined what can be read as a possible revolutionary program of action and another fragmentary suggestion. Commenting on peasant rebellions of the nineteenth century, Jit wrote, "[W]e can see that the peasant disturbances did no more than serve as a ladder to political power for other classes to step on.... In no way can the saktina yoke really be removed until the establishment of the peasant state is made possible."[26] Shortly thereafter, he wrote that in order to cast off the yoke of feudalism, peasants must join with workers, as the workers have "considerable foresight and a high level of political consciousness and because it is uncompromising in its attitude, the peasantry will be able to destroy completely the decayed remnants of the saktina which have continued to exploit it, and thus make true gains from their own revolutionary struggle."[27] Workers would populate the new revolutionary state as leaders and "eliminate the exploiters once and for all and ... take control of political institutions as instruments for safeguarding and collectively redistributing the profits to the masses who are the owners of the means of production."[28] For Jit, this meant that peasants would form cooperatives and "be able to consolidate themselves into units, to organize themselves systematically, and genuinely to destroy the decayed remnants of the saktina!"[29] By radically changing how production is organized and carried out, feudalism would be eliminated. The creation of the peasant state would bring with it a new set of practices, leadership, and morality.

Yet nothing can change in the fields without a change in thinking about who works the fields and who reaps the benefits of that labor. The chronicle of the changes, and consolidations, of this thinking is history. Jit argued that, like the law, the feudal lords controlled the writing of history because "the subject of history tells of the experience of human social struggle, and this history is like an example of the social struggle, for life in future generations ... which will open the way to correct action. Because the saktina are fully aware of this point, they thus reach in to take hold of historical study in order to use this subject for their own class interests."[30] The one who controls the past also controls the future; the imagination and construction of a different future involves wresting the imagination of the past out of the hands of the oppressors. Craig Reynolds argues that one of the reasons *The Real Face* was so compelling is because it resonated with processes beginning to come to the fore: "The Thai people, struggling to meet the material needs of their existence, sought to become the masters of their own fate, to make their own history, to become the subject of history rather than its passive object."[31] Jit Phumisak criticized the writing of history while also rewriting and presenting anew the chronicle of who worked the fields and who consumed the product of that work in the Thai past. His analysis exposed how the exclusion of the experiences of peasant and other marginalized subjects in Thai history presented the power of the lords as seamless and benign; what is at issue is not only that this was a flawed representation but also that this helped the lords consolidate and strengthen their control. Resonantly, northern tenant farmers used the law to change the way the product of their labor was distributed; their actions were significant not only because they used the law to change the relations of production but also because they were never meant to be the agents doing so. The reaction to the farmers' movement for legal reform and then their use of the tenancy law to change their lives makes it clear that in the 1970s poor rural people were still excluded from Thai legal subjecthood. The feudal lords, and their mid-twentieth-century descendants, worked relentlessly to keep control over both history and the law because they knew that the struggle for the land was also a struggle over meaning and meaning making.

Demonstrations and the Accusation of Chaos

In October 1974, Inson Buakiew, a prominent member of the Socialist Party of Thailand (SPT) and MP from Chiang Mai, observed that there were two kinds of responses to the nearly incessant protests and strikes in the first half of 1974: conservative and progressive. The conservatives (*phuak anurak niyom*) viewed the protests as indicating, "Everyday our homeland is exceedingly chaotic. This kind of feeling causes them to feel uneasy and to think all the time that if it is like this, it is better to give all the power to a military dictatorship, to deal with everything decisively and tidily."[32] In contrast, he argued that the progressives (*phuak kaeo na*) "have the consciousness of enthusiasts of democracy. When they read news about the strikes and protests of different groups, they feel very satisfied that there is haggling between different interest groups emerging in society."[33] Inson saw this consciousness as a direct outcome of the sacrifices of life and death made during the events of 14 October 1973. While the feelings and actions of many individuals during this period exceeded the formulation of two opposing groups postulated by Inson, public debate was often posed in these two binary frames. Over the course of 1974, the farmers' stance toward the government shifted from one of a beseeching subject to one of a demanding subject. This change was matched by a transformation of farmers from being organized in relatively isolated, province- or district-based groups to membership in a nationwide organization with many allies. Either one fully supported dissenting politics or was wholly against it. Very little space was left for those located variously in between. This lack of a middle ground had grave consequences over the next months and years. Even before physical violence began, as the farmers protested and traded lists of demands with the state, the language used by each signaled the changes of perception and position taking place. But it was not only their words but also the substance of the farmers' calls for radical action, and the fantastical and ultimately failed promises the central government made throughout 1974, that were new in the Thai political landscape.[34] These radical calls and empty promises indicated the growing strength of the farmers' movement and the fragility of the state's authority.

On 1 March 1974, the first large-scale farmer protest took place when approximately a thousand farmers from the central region assembled on Sanam Luang in Bangkok. Citing the increasing price of the basic necessities for living and agricultural production, the farmers called on the government to guarantee the price of paddy rice and consider ways to help them. The farmers went home, and two months passed without any concrete action. In May 1974, hundreds of farmers from the central region returned to Bangkok. Citing rampant cheating at the hands of landlords and problems of indebtedness, they appealed again to the government for help.[35]

In response, Prime Minister Sanya Thammasak's government created the Committee to Investigate the Problems of Indebted Farmers to examine the situation in the central provinces of Ang Thong, Phichit, Phitsanulok, Phetchabun, and Kamphaeng Phet. The committee was not empowered to take any restorative action. The farmers continued pressuring the government for action. Documentation of their suffering would not suffice.

In response, on 4 June, Prime Minister Sanya's government decreed Article 17 in order to give the committee the power to take action to redress the farmers' grievances. Initially included in the 1959 Constitution under the dictatorial government of Field Marshal Sarit Thanarat, and included in the constitutions of subsequent military dictatorships, Article 17 provided for absolute, unchecked power. The new Constitution had not yet been promulgated, and the Constitution containing the version of Article 17 deployed by Sanya to help the farmers remained from Field Marshal Thanom Kittikachorn's regime.[36] Article 17 made it possible and legal for the government to make any

order or take action if it was deemed "appropriate to prevent, repress or suppress any act subverting the security of the Kingdom, the Throne, national
economy or affairs of State, or any act disturbing or threatening public order
or good morals, or any act destroying national resources or deteriorating public
health and sanitation."[37] In short, the decree of Article 17 permitted any action by state actors and had the power to make such an action unpunishable.
Under Field Marshal Sarit, Article 17 was a dreaded measure used to legitimize
the assassinations of hooligans, suspected communists, and other dissenting or
criminal actors, among other things.[38] In another political moment, Article 17
might have been used to quash the protests of the farmers. Therefore, what did
it mean that it was pressed into service seemingly *for* the farmers? There are
many ways that this may have been understood in relation to the farmers' demands. The protection of national security and the maintenance of order were
at the core of Article 17. A generous reading may be that farmers' continued
subsistence was seen as essential to the national economy. It is also possible, recalling my discussion of hunger and counterinsurgency in chapter 1, that empty
farmer bellies raised concerns about dangers to national security and possible
subversion. Similarly, there may have been concern that if the farmers continued protesting, then a threat to the maintenance of public order might arise. In
this respect, the decree of Article 17 may have been a preemptive action taken
to avert this possibility.

In theory, the decree of Article 17 in this case meant that the committee was
"empowered to reallocate land and investigate grievances of landless farmers"
and "given unprecedented authority to arrest and detain uncooperative land
owners."[39] Yet arresting uncooperative landlords would require more than the
decree of Article 17. In practice, Article 17 failed to change the farmers' situation. At the most basic level, the committee was overwhelmed with complaints:
10,999 petitions in the first month (June) and after that over 14,000 per month,
for a total of 53,650 by September 1974. The committee was able to settle only
1,635 of these before the 6 October 1976 coup.[40] Today the remaining petitions
are still uninvestigated, and unresolved.

Given the ineffectualness of the committee under Article 17, one interpretation might be that the article was decreed for symbolic reasons. David Morell
and Chai-anan Samudavanija argue that the absolute measure was deployed
out of "fear that the situation would get out of control. Conflicts between
local land owners and the farmer-student groups were becoming heated. After
decades of apparent rural political passivity, suddenly conflicts seemed to be
erupting everywhere at once."[41] Yet, if the measure was designed to pacify the
farmers and their supporters, two farmer accounts from June 1974 suggest that
it did not. Shortly after the decree of Article 17, *Athipat*, the weekly newspaper
of the NSCT, carried a photograph of a male farmer plowing a rice field with a
buffalo; the caption under the photo read, "What is Article 17? I don't know. I
only know that right now the government is trying to use it as an instrument to

help us. I don't know if it will help us or not. I only know that there are a lot of bad civil servants, and a lot of capitalists thick with money."[42] Similarly, another farmer protesting in late June explained that Article 17 would not work because of ingrained tensions ordering relations among civil servants, landowners, and farmers; he commented, "The farmers who ask for help are in distress because we are poor. In the past when we have asked for help from civil servants they have not wanted to help because we have nothing with which to reciprocate. But when the capitalists seek them out, they will help because the capitalists are wealthy, they give them ducks and chickens to eat."[43] The farmers' accounts reflect the growing distrust many farmers felt toward the state, as well as their keen understanding of the relationships among some state officials, capitalists, landowners, and themselves. The alliance between some bureaucrats and capitalists was conceived here as starkly material. As the farmers' movement developed over the next months, the material and ideological came to increasingly intersect.

Given the failure of Article 17 to change their lives, the farmers continued to protest. At the end of June 1974, approximately 10,000 farmers from eleven provinces traveled to Bangkok to protest. From 24 to 29 June, they remained assembled at Sanam Luang.[44] *Thai Rat* heralded the beginning of the protests with the headline "The Backbone of the Nation Cries Out."[45] During this protest, a group comprised of farmer representatives from each of the provinces present was appointed to meet with the government. At this time, they submitted six demands to the prime minister's office, demanding that the government:

1. Allocate land that troubled farmers could rent in order to subsist for that year and arrange for farmers who once owned land to use their original land.
2. Establish a committee to investigate the loss of land by farmers. If the evidence indicates that the farmers were cheated by capitalists, the government should seize the land and return it to the original owners.[46]
3. Investigate the payment of interest in excess of the amount stipulated by the interest rate law. In cases in which there has been overpayment, the government should return it to each farmer involved. In addition, the government should rent and buy land from capitalists, which farmers would be allowed to rent and buy from the government at fair prices.
4. Allocate permanent land for landless farmers but not unusable land.

Capitalists were called on to:

5. Stop seizing land and transferring ownership of it, including all the land seized since the beginning of the protests.
6. Drop all legal cases against farmers filed since Article 17 went into effect.[47]

Once they submitted their demands, the farmers vowed to remain at Sanam Luang until the government responded. They were joined and supported this time by a range of groups, including the NSCT, the Federation of Independent Students of Thailand (FIST), the People for Democracy Group (PDG), and the Hotel and Hostel Workers Union.[48] On the second day of the protests, *Thai Rat* proclaimed that the farmers on Sanam Luang were "struggling for [their] life."[49] On the third day, *Thai Rat*'s language shifted, with a headline reading "Farmers from 11 Provinces Entered Bangkok and Took Over Sanam Luang to Make 6 Demands."[50] What constituted the farmers *taking over* Sanam Luang was their sheer presence filling the open space. This change turned into an explicit criticism of the farmers on the fifth day of the protests, in which a headline reading "Deputy PM [Prime Minister] Explains That the 'Chaotic' Farmers Declare That They Are Not Satisfied" was emblazoned in large letters across the front page of the newspaper.[51]

In the course of five days, the protesting farmers went from being "the backbone of the nation" to "chaotic" in the pages of one widely read centrist national newspaper. Over the next two years, the accusation of "creating chaos and unrest" (*khwam wun wai*) emerged as a frequently used justification for various kinds of violence. Here its use signaled the boundary between acceptable and unacceptable dissent. This protest marked the shift from farmers petitioning, or crying to the government for help, to farmers demanding that the government take action. This shift itself indicated the social and political opening created by the transition from an authoritarian bureaucracy to a more democratic form of rule. In the eyes of Prakob Hutasingh, the deputy prime minister, and perhaps others, this was going too far.

Yet no matter how individual ministers may have felt about the farmers, the government responded. Prime Minister Sanya's government responded to the farmers' six demands with an executive order on 29 June. The executive order addressed the farmers' demands point by point:

1. The government will allocate land for troubled farmers in time for this year's planting season. The government will return land that was originally theirs. However, if that land is currently being used by someone else who has obtained it honestly and justly, it is not just to take it from them. In this case, the government will arrange for adjacent land for the farmers or will buy land and arrange for farmers to lease to buy it in 1974. The Bank for Agriculture and Agricultural Cooperatives will provide help.

2. For farmers who have been cheated out of their land by capitalists, the committee established by Soh. Soh Roh 33/2517 (the Committee to Investigate the Problems of Indebted Farmers) will investigate and report the results of the investigation and action to the prime minister. This is not limited to farmers who were cheated during the agricultural year 1973 but applies to prior years as well.

3. In the investigation following section 5 of the aforementioned order, if farmers have been forced to pay interest in excess of that stipulated by the law, whether

it is a monetary amount or in the form of agricultural products, the government will examine and return the lost land to the farmers or have the capitalists pay the appropriate reparations.

4. If the landowners have changed, or tried to change, or transferred ownership of land that is under dispute during this investigation, the committee will be able to issue an order to halt that action and propose that the prime minister examine and direct further action.

5. The government will allocate permanent land to landless farmers in the form of cooperatives. The government will not allocate land that is already being farmed.

6. The government will halt ongoing disputes between farmers who have misunderstood and think they have a right to and are using land belonging to other people. The government will not arrest or bring charges against the farmers. For those farmers already being prosecuted, the government will halt the prosecution.[52]

The executive order was remarkable as an indication of the prime minister's intention to resolve the farmers' problems. Yet, implementation of its stated promises was fraught with difficulty. To begin with, although the Bangkok-based prime minister's office made the promises, they had to be carried out by provincial, district, subdistrict, and village officials who "were reluctant to carry out such unprecedented orders; and either overtly or covertly . . . refused to do so."[53] Recalling the critiques of the farmers regarding the ineffectiveness of Article 17 in the hands of civil servants, it is also possible that officials may have received enticements from landowners and capitalists that deepened their reluctance.

In addition, the prime minister's office and the (expanded, as of this order) Committee to Investigate the Problems of Indebted Farmers lacked the authority to back up the promises made. This functioned to make the theoretical promises empty in practice. For example, although the third item promised that farmers who had lost their land because they were charged excessive interest would be compensated, there was no stipulation of who would determine the amount and form of compensation. The fifth item, which promised the distribution of land to landless farmers, could not be implemented without an official land reform policy, and land reform legislation was not passed until 1975.[54] Absent a comprehensive land reform program, which the policy enacted in 1975 was not, how could the prime minister possibly find land for every farmer who needed it? As regards the unjust transfer of landownership mentioned in the fourth item, "the government in fact had no legal authority to stop citizens from transferring their land ownership rights to others. To do this, a special act of the National Assembly would be required."[55]

Given the emptiness of the promises, why did the Sanya government make them? David Morell and Chai-anan Samudavanija argue that the prime minister "yielded to the farmers' demands out of fear that the students, farmers, and workers would join forces to create more trouble."[56] What was the content of this *trouble*, and why would the Sanya government have been afraid? Perhaps the influx of *chaotic* actors into the city of Bangkok, bringing chaos (as described by the deputy prime minister), was considered trouble. Perhaps the sheer joining together of farmers, students, and workers across boundaries separating cities and rural areas and lines separating classes constituted trouble. Perhaps the fear of loss of support from landowners and other capitalists, and the ducks and chickens they provided to fill the bellies of willing civil servants, constituted trouble. But perhaps it was not their own empty bellies that were a cause for concern but those of disenfranchised, troubled rural people. The fear of what they might do, when hungry, when hopeless, when angry, when united with students and workers, seemed never far from the minds of state officials, landowners, and other conservative forces.

Fear of Liberation and the Establishment of the FFT

State officials were not the only ones who made promises they did not keep. Farmers made threats that they did not carry out to completion. On 9 August 1974, farmers from nine provinces returned to Bangkok. Critical of the lack of concrete changes in their situation since the 29 June executive order, they held a public debate at Sanam Luang. At its conclusion, they held up their citizen identification (ID) cards and proclaimed, "This is the last time that we have come to ask for help from the government. If we don't receive justice, we will turn in our citizen ID cards and resign our citizenship."[57] In response, Deputy Prime Minister Prakob Hutasingh accused the farmers of being selfish and falling prey to instigators.[58] Prakob was unwilling to believe, or at the very least publicly concede, that the farmers could plan such a drastic action. This threat, and the farmers' decision to continue protesting rather than carry it out, is the story with which this book began. The farmers threatened to set up a "liberated area of their own and refuse to pay taxes."[59] This claim by the farmers was a powerful threat and, unlike the promises made by the Prime Minister's Office, not entirely empty. Though unrealized, the claim and the responses it provoked reveal and refract anxieties about the body of the Thai nation, the specter of communism, and the return of farmer revolt. Instead of renouncing their citizenship, over the next months farmers struggled to become full legal subjects, an ultimately more destabilizing proposition.

The protests by farmers and their allies continued to grow in size and range over the next few months and culminated in a large, extended protest between 19 and 29 November 1974. In Bangkok, approximately twelve hundred farmers representing twenty-three provinces assembled on Sanam Luang. Heralding the farmers' arrival in Bangkok, one daily newspaper reported, "Farmers enter the beautiful city in successive groups: '[We] cannot depend on anyone else.'"[60] On 19 November, the assembled representatives in Bangkok declared the formation of the FFT.

That same day, the fledgling FFT submitted a list to the government, demanding that it:

1. Allocate land to landless farmers in time for this year's rice-growing season.
2. Create a committee to investigate the loss of land by farmers who have been cheated by capitalists. In the event of a legal case between farmers and capitalists, the government should arrange for collateral for farmers who lack sufficient resources.
3. Allocate permanent land to landless farmers.
4. Pass a law limiting the amount of land that can be owned by one person. In Isan, this should be no more than 100 *rai*. In other regions, it should be no more than 50 *rai*.
5. Decree the 1950 LRCA and set the rental period at six years. As for the new LRCA, the farmers will compose a draft for government review.
6. Pay farmers' debts to creditors in full and allow farmers to redeem their land, through purchase, rent, or lease to buy, at a just price.
7. Provide proof of ownership to farmers who have occupied public land for at least ten years.
8. Cancel government projects that have led to losses or trouble for farmers and with which the majority of troubled farmers do not agree, for example, a plan to build a dam in Udon Thani province.
9. Guarantee that the price of paddy rice will not fall to less than three thousand baht per *kwian*.[61]

As the farmers waited for a response from the government, the size of the protests grew. By 28 November, tens of thousands of fliers had been passed out across Bangkok, calling for support of the farmers' demands.[62] On 29 November, the protests swelled to over eighty thousand people, as the farmers were joined by Buddhist monks and nuns, students, workers, and others.[63] This was the first time that monks had ever joined a political protest *as monks*.[64] Their presence on Sanam Luang caused a small uproar, and by early December there were protests both critical of the monks and in support of them.

At 10:49 a.m. on the twenty-ninth, the government replied to the demands of the FFT with the following eight-point response.

1. The provinces will allocate land that landless farmers can use during the 1975 rice-planting season.
2. The provinces will make public the results of investigations into land issues and whether or not capitalists have acquired land in just ways. If the results of the investigation raise doubts, a group composed of an equal number of farm-

ers, students, and civil servants will consider whether or not it is appropriate to launch a new investigation.

3. Permanent land will be allocated to landless farmers in the form of cooperatives.

4. Collateral for farmers who do not have sufficient resources will be arranged. In the case of accusations of trespassing by farmers, the state will appoint lawyers for the farmers and will help determine a value that is appropriate for the situation.

5. If the Parliament does not pass the new LRCA proposed by the government by December 1974, the government will decree the 1950 LRCA in Chiang Mai and Lamphun provinces before the end of December.

6. The government will help repurchase land that farmers pawned or mortgaged to capitalists if the capitalists are willing to sell it. Help will be provided by the Bank for Agriculture and Agricultural Cooperatives in an amount not exceeding forty thousand baht per case.

7. The government will revoke the land title and Noh. Soh. 3 for land in Dong Rai Fon, Dong Phayayang, Saraburi district, Chainat province, where an investigation has revealed that powerful people produced documents of rights to public land. Further, the government will give this land to the farmers who farmed it before. It will also give farmers documents of rights and the harvest from the crops they planted.[65]

8. The government will consider canceling projects that cause the majority of citizens trouble. If the government is unable to stop the project, the state will pay compensation for affected land at a just price. For compensation already paid, if the majority of the compensation was not just, the state will provide more. If farmers are unable to find new land, the state will find adjacent land for them.[66]

Following the government's reply to their demands, the farmers and their supporters left Sanam Luang and dispersed. Although the government responded positively to many of the farmers' demands, what may seem initially like concessions emerge as less so on closer examination. Morell and Chai-anan assert that the government was already in contact with the Lawyers' Association of Thailand to arrange legal counsel for farmers. They further note that the first demand, that land be provided to landless farmers in time for the 1974 rice-planting season, was the only one the government could not resolve.[67] Rice is typically planted between May and August and harvested between October and January. Therefore the government literally could not meet the demand for the 1974 calendar year.

In my assessment, the most important outcome of the protests was not the government response but the establishment of the FFT. This time, the farmers came to Bangkok not to plead with the prime minister for help but to harness their collective power. Addressing the formation of the FFT, Phinit

Jarusombat, the vice secretary of the NSCT, explained that the farmers united because the government failed to understand their problems and did not "pay attention to them or think about ways to help them at all. This is because the government doesn't understand the real lives of the farmers, the people who carry the sickle."[68] By protesting and continually bearing witness to their own lives and asserting their sole right to do so, farmers expanded the space of politics and the range of actors who could be political subjects. The FFT was established with Chai Wangtrakul, a farmer from the central region, as the president and six regional vice presidents, including Intha Sribunruang as the northern vice president, Daeng Hundee as the northeastern vice president, Wichai Phikulkhaw as the central vice president, and Chamrat Muangyam as the eastern vice president.[69] The FFT was organized to parallel the state administrative structure, with regional, provincial, district, subdistrict, and village levels. At each level, the governing structures were composed of member-elected representatives.[70] Members were required to pay a four-baht yearly membership fee; this fee was used to fund the FFT's activities.[71]

In addition to paying the membership fee, members were encouraged to attend FFT protests and other activities whenever possible.[72] By supporting each others' struggles and being visible in the streets of Bangkok and in front of provincial offices across the country, leaders and members of the FFT hoped to improve the lives of Thai farmers. Their specific goals were "1. To protect the farmers' interests; 2. To mitigate the farmers' troubles and hardships; 3. To educate the farmers in the Land Rent Control Act of 1974."[73]

Before assassinations of major leaders and the 6 October 1976 coup halted its work, the FFT raised the issues of various kinds of farmers from all different regions. As for the composition of the FFT, one estimate suggests that 60 percent were poor farmers, including many tenants; 20 percent were landless farm workers; and 20 percent were slightly more affluent farmers, some perhaps owning a small amount of land.[74] Andrew Turton divides the concerns taken up by the FFT into urgent problems, including "grants of land for the coming planting season, price regulation, reduction of farm rents, suspension of court cases involving farmers, release of those arrested for trespass, and help for flood victims," as well as well as long-term issues, including "land reform and permanent provision of land to the landless, and a solution to the problems of indebtedness and high interest rates."[75] Turton then clarifies the significance of this range of actions by asserting that the FFT "spoke for the rural poor, the landless, those with smallholdings, tenants, and in a wider sense for all those who experienced injustice and denial of democratic freedoms. In other words, it claimed to speak for the majority of the rural population."[76] Ascertaining whether or not the FFT really spoke for "the majority of the rural population" is impossible, but the organizing of the next year and the memory of this by those involved and their descendants indicate that the FFT had an important effect on rural peoples' lives, consciousness, and concrete political power.

The sheer size of the FFT also indicates the breadth of its significance. Between November 1974 and the October 1976 coup, it established a presence in forty-one of Thailand's seventy-two provinces. During this period, the FFT was estimated to have had 1.5 million members nationwide.[77] It grew particularly rapidly in the three northern provinces of Chiang Mai, Lamphun, and Lampang and was headquartered in Chiang Mai. In Chiang Mai province alone, it had branches in every district and was reported to have had over 100,000 members.[78] From its beginnings in the early months of 1974, the struggle over land rent and the growth of the farmers' movement were mutually constitutive in the north.

Beyond the Edge of Hope in Chiang Mai

Approximately one month after the first set of farmer demands was issued in Bangkok, and amid growing protests across the country, on 20 July 1974, the deputy minister of interior, Police Lieutenant General Chumphon Lohachalah, sent each governor and district officer an urgent document urging them to solve the troubles (*duat ron*) of the farmers locally. In his words, "[L]ocal problems should be dispensed with and solved, they shouldn't be solved by the center giving orders."[79] Although Chumphon's words may be read as an early call for decentralization before structural adjustment made it in vogue, they must also be read as a request to keep the farmers out of Bangkok. After all, if farmers' problems could be resolved by district or provincial officials, then they might not feel compelled to travel to the capital. The presence of farmers in the city represented a crisis that had to be addressed. In addition, their presence enacted and represented a growing displacement. What was displaced was the former status quo, in which farmers, as the backbone of the nation, performed an important political role as producers of food in 1950s era counterinsurgency rhetoric. Despite their essential role, within this rhetoric, farmers were not imagined to be political themselves. By 1974, their presence in the streets confirmed their irrefutable status as political, and politicized, public actors.

The next day, *Thai Niu*, a conservative, in Inson Buakhiew's terms, Chiang Mai daily newspaper, ran an editorial in response to a communiqué from the Ministry of Interior. The unnamed author began by cautioning that, although the problems between farmers and capitalists in other provinces were also present in Chiang Mai, the severity of drought in the north might further deepen the tensions. The author noted that even though they did not have enough water, the farmers had not started protesting—*yet*. The author urged state officials to help the farmers because "farmers who have lost hope might protest for their livelihood, [and] this could arise one of these days."[80] What was at stake for this author was not the sheer presence of farmers en masse in the city but the *meaning* of that presence. In addition, in this moment, hunger again became political. While in the 1950s preventing hunger was an important anticommunist measure, here hunger was posed as the possible catalyst of protest. Yet it is not only hunger that is critical here, but hope. *Hope* and the possibility of *help* from the government were continuously intertwined in the language used by farmers as well as those writing about them. Farmers hoped that the state would help them. When farmers lost hope, then they protested. Or so the narrative went. Yet not unlike the use of natural causes to explain farmer revolt, the emphasis on *hope* is problematic. Like natural disasters, the reference to losing hope in government action as the reason why farmers protested places the impetus for farmers' actions with someone other than the farmers themselves. In other words, it elides the possibility that farmers chose to protest because they saw it as a productive way to attain their demands. This elision and the emphasis on *hope* and *fear* also negates the idea of farmers as *political* actors.

The editorial author asked the governor and district officers to inspect all rice-growing areas immediately and provide every kind of help possible to the farmers. They should use all of their power and resources because, the editorialist warned, "It is uncertain how much longer they can endure. It is certain that now they are troubled. The severe farmer threat has come to many areas already. They are waiting, to see how the homeland is going to come help them. And when, or if, they will be abandoned to march in the city."[81] For this writer, farmers were perpetually waiting, or so he or she hoped. It was not only farmers who were locked into a particular kind of role, but, as the reference to "abandonment" indicates, those within the state or outside it who might come to their aid were also meant to perform in a particular fashion. In this case, the word used by the author for "city" was *muang*, which could refer to Chiang Mai city, not only Bangkok. The "farmer threat" was not specified further, but it seems to have been constituted by the presence of protesting farmers in the city. Although the editorial began with a discussion of the threat the drought posed to farmers' lives, it closed with the rewriting of *farmers* as the threat. The object of this threat was left unstated.

A few months later, the farmers marched in Chiang Mai city. On the morning of 5 November 1974, a group of farmers assembled in Sanpakoi subdistrict and marched to Tha Pae gate in Chiang Mai city. By the afternoon, they had been joined by farmers from every district in Chiang Mai and Lamphun provinces. The farmers called for the decree of the 1950 LRCA in Chiang Mai and Lamphun. The headline of an article describing the protests noted that the farmers were "call[ing] for government to deal with the capitalists."[82] Farmers "came to protest together to call for the government to decree the Land Rent Control Act because every day they suffer at the hands of the capitalists until they cannot take it anymore."[83] The farmers justified their demand by noting that the act had been in use in the central provinces for over twenty years. Why could it not be used in Chiang Mai and Lamphun as well?

Two days later, *Thai Niu* ran an unsigned editorial about the farmers' protest titled "The Lament of the Farmers."[84] The author began by recapping the actions of the farmers and then noted that they had been forced to protest; the government could not help them because "the capitalist side stood firm."[85] Sidestepping the issue of the at times cozy relations between some state officials and some landowners, the author noted, "The homeland couldn't help them, since there was no law from which to derive power."[86] For this reason, the farmers organized and decided to call for use of the 1950 LRCA in Chiang Mai and Lamphun. The logic behind this was "to give the civil servants of the homeland an instrument to use and a way for the tenant farmers to appeal to landowners, in order to create some justice."[87] The law was imagined as a lever that could be used to force a change, at least officially, in the relationships between landlords and tenant farmers, as well as their interlocutors, civil servants. Over the next year, the implementation of land rent control measures in Chiang Mai first exceeded, and eventually fell short of, the official changes engendered by the LRCA.

On returning to the unsigned editorial, one is greeted with two surprising, almost conflicting concluding statements. First the author commented that the 1950 LRCA was "behind the times already. It has many provisions that are not appropriate for the situation of the current government."[88] According to the author, this was the apparent reason why the Ministry of Agriculture and Cooperatives was in the process of drafting a new law, with provisions, the editorial asserted, that "will not allow the landowners to take too much advantage of the farmers. The price of the rent will be determined by the tenant farmers, the landowners, and the local officials together." Over the next month, there was slippage between the 1950 act as "behind the times" and the farmers as such. As for the phrase "appropriate for the situation of the current government," I suggest one must ask *who* was the government? What constituted a law *appropriate* for the government?

The editorial closed by insisting that the farmers must protest in larger numbers in order to achieve their goals because only a large-scale protest would force the government to take action. Simultaneously, the editorialist issued a warning about the effects that might follow from such protests, commenting that the actions of the farmers "should indicate to all *rice eaters* that they should know that *people who grow rice* are troubled and do not receive justice. They are joining together to make demands. If there are no people who listen to what they say and help them it is certain that the beseeching voice will not simply stop there."[89] For the first time in the commentary on the 1974 protests, "rice eaters" are mentioned as a category of individuals. In Mister Bumbam's 1951 editorial on the difficulties faced by farmers, he implored his rice-eating readers to pay attention to the difficult lives of the farmers so that they would continue growing enough rice for others to eat.[90] In 1974 rice eaters were again being asked to comprehend the injustices faced by farmers. In 1974, as in 1951, although farmers grew rice, critics seemed to forget, or at least forgot to mention, that they also needed to eat rice in order to survive.

Legal Debates in the Streets

Despite the wishes of conservative editorialists and government officials, continued farmer protests in Chiang Mai city appeared inevitable in 1974. On 15 November, Chiang Mai and Lamphun farmers threatened a protest of thirty thousand people in Bangkok if the government did not decree the 1950 LRCA. In response, Deputy Minister of Interior Atthasit Sitthisunthorn urgently called the governor of Chiang Mai, Asa Meksawan, and the governor of Lamphun, Bunlom Phuchongsakul, to Bangkok. He wanted to explain to them in person how to "bring the policy of the state back to explain to the farmers to wait for the new law, one that will have better results."[91] The farmers wanted the new law to be in effect before the harvest season (October to January) was finished, that is, before the landowners came to collect the rent. Farmers were continuously asked to wait—first for the government to help them, and then for the new law. Yet, how could the deputy prime minister's assurance that the new law would be better help the farmers if the landlords came calling before it was passed?

The farmers were not satisfied with this assurance from afar and went to Bangkok themselves in an attempt to meet with the prime minister and his deputy. They met instead with Suthi Akatkrit, one of the state officials on the Committee to Investigate the Problems of Indebted Farmers. Suthi again told them that the 1950 act had provisions "inappropriate" for the present moment. They should wait for the new law because they would "get better results than from the old law."[92] Again, *what* was inappropriate about the 1950 act was left unspecified.

When appealing to the farmers to be patient and wait for the kindnesses of the government did not work, one editorial writer tried practical fact. But his or her numbers were not quite right. The editorial, titled "Farmers and Old and New Laws," began by explaining that the terms of engagement had changed and "representatives of the Chiang Mai and Lamphun farmers are standing firm in the demand to the government, to ask them to follow their desires," rather than the landlords standing firm in their position.[93] The threat by representatives of the farmers that thirty thousand farmers would protest to demand the decree of the 1950 act had caused the government to become "worried and anxious."[94] The author then castigated the farmers for wasting time and money traveling to Bangkok rather than waiting for the two governors to return. The author urged the farmers to wait for the new, better law. However, he or she made a blatantly erroneous claim. Writing about the 1950 act, he or she noted, "[I]f we speak truly, the 2493 [1950] Law has provisions for controlling the price of rent for large areas, 100 *rai* and bigger."[95] But the opposite was true: the 1950 act applied to broadcasted paddy land consisting of *less* than 100 *rai* and transplanted paddy land of *less* than 50 *rai*.[96] Perhaps the writer read the 1950 act in error. Perhaps the reversal was intentional. Most, if not all, of the tenant farmers who were protesting rented well under 50 or 100 *rai*; the terms of the 1950 act, therefore, were sufficient. The writer concluded the editorial with the following plea: "When the governors of the two provinces receive the policy to bring it back they will see the different parts of the old and new laws. It will make the farmers understand clearly that they should not become panic stricken and incite the people who don't really know and then ask them to go and waste time and money without any benefit."[97] Without any benefit to whom? By uniting, the farmers appealed to one another. By protesting, they appealed to the Thai public. Through these actions, and by bringing their troubles from the rice fields into the city and the streets of the capital, Thai farmers created a new page in history.

The author also urged the farmers to "restrain themselves."[98] Restrain themselves from what? The farmers were protesting, not looting. Yet clearly some observers felt threatened by the outpouring of farmers into the streets and their demands for justice. Further, what was meant by the phrase "people who do not really know"? Farmers *did* know about the laws and their right to protest. More than anything, this editorial revealed the anxiety and panic felt by the farmers' critics; in an attempt to cast the farmers as panic stricken, the fears of others were revealed. Less than two weeks later, the government promised either decree of the 1950 act or the promulgation of a new one in time for the 1974 rice-harvesting season.

On returning from Bangkok, the farmer representatives conveyed the government's advice to wait for the new law to their colleagues in Chiang Mai and Lamphun. Dissatisfied with state inaction and the admonition to wait, farmers "threatened to burn and abandon the rice in the fields in many districts, if the state officials and the government don't help with the disputes over land rent between the farmers and the landowners."[99] Approximately fifty farmers went to the provincial office to meet with Asa Meksawan, the Chiang Mai governor. They warned that without immediate help from the government they "would have to burn the rice in the fields, although the burning would be in the fields of the wealthy capitalists," not all fields.[100] When Asa was contacted for his perspective on the meeting, he confirmed that fifty farmers met with him on 20 November at the provincial hall. He commented, "Manop Manochai, the leader of the farmers, said that they might proceed in any which way. But in the instance of them going to burn the rice in the fields, I don't believe that it is possible, and I didn't hear anyone say that."[101] Like the threat of the farmers in Bangkok to turn in their citizen ID cards, the threat of the Chiang Mai farmers to burn the unharvested rice was a serious one. Given that a portion of the rice would belong to them under the terms of tenancy once it was harvested, it was also a radical one. The farmers were placing their own bellies on the line. Yet like the threat to turn in the citizen ID cards, the burning of the rice in the fields never came to pass.

Instead, the farmers decided to continue protesting. As the FFT was established in Bangkok on 19 November 1974, simultaneous protests began in

Chiang Mai. There, approximately two thousand farmers massed at the provincial building.[102] On the morning of 22 November, thousands of farmers from different districts flooded into Chiang Mai city in trucks and buses.[103] In total, over three thousand farmers assembled in front of the provincial office and vowed to remain there until they received a response to the nine demands presented to the government in Bangkok. As long as the demands of those waiting on Sanam Luang in Bangkok were not met, they would not disperse either.[104] In addition to signs and placards, they brought cooked and uncooked rice, fish, and blankets.[105] The farmers were prepared to wait.

Using megaphones, the farmers appealed to everyone in the streets around them to join their call for the immediate decree of the 1950 LRCA in Chiang Mai and Lamphun. Although they supported all nine demands shared by the FFT, their primary concern was land rent relief. Those who spoke "called for sympathy with the farmers," claiming, "[We] grow rice with our own hands, and are taken advantage of by capitalists all the time, until we have become like slaves who cannot raise our heads, from the time of our grandfathers to the time of our children."[106] The posters carried by the farmers similarly appealed to those around them to join the demonstrations. One poster carried by a group of farmers from Mae Taeng district in Chiang Mai province simply read, "The struggle of the farmers will grow, will win."[107] When the government failed to take action, farmers turned to their fellow citizens for sympathy and support.

In the middle of the protest, *Thai Niu* ran another article criticizing the demand for the decree of the 1950 act. Marut Bunnag, the president of the Lawyers' Society of Thailand, again stressed that the terms of the 1950 act were no longer appropriate for Thailand in 1974. Reiterating earlier critiques, but (again) without explaining them fully, he said, "It is behind the times to use [it] now. It won't create any benefits for the farmers."[108] Marut also said, "The anxious worry of the farmers is a main problem of the country. If we don't hurry to solve it and make it go away, there will be a movement that will cause many difficulties and will not have an end."[109] Although Marut asserted that the farmers' demands were out of step with the times, he also foresaw that their struggle might extend indefinitely if their demands were not met.

In late November, the official stance of at least one part of the state administration shifted sharply. What was initially worry turned to anger toward farmers, who were perceived as ungrateful. Rather than admitting the government's failure to help the farmers, the minister of interior accused the farmers of being selfish and said, "It is not right. The government has given the best assistance within the limits of the law, which has to consider justice without favoring any side."[110] Whether it was the threat of the farmers to burn the rice in the fields, their sheer presence on Sanam Luang and in front of the Chiang Mai provincial office, or something else altogether, the minister's rebuke was telling. There were no reports or evidence of the farmers carrying out destructive or violent actions; at worst there was only the threat to burn the rice in the fields of wealthy Chiang Mai landowners. The "selfishness" cited by the minister of interior must have referred to the speeches and demonstrations in the streets. In the minds of some, farmers were expected to be grateful, quiet, and hidden (or at least in the fields outside the city). What seemed selfish to the minister of interior was not the farmers' protests qua protests but the gap between the farmers' protests and the expectation that they would not protest.

This sentiment was reinforced the next day, when an angry letter was sent to the protesting Chiang Mai farmers. On 28 November, farmers in Chiang Mai and Bangkok burned puppets of deputy prime minister Prakob Hutasingh. He had been appointed the president of the internal government committee to help the farmers, and puppets of him were burned as a criticism of his ineffectiveness.[111] On the same day the protesting farmers in Chiang Mai received a threatening letter signed by someone, or a group, writing under the name *phan muang* (which can be translated as either "encircle the city" or "a thousand cities"). The letter declared that the protesters would be bombed. The author cautioned, "You cannot come to assemble and occupy the area of the provincial hall, because we cannot work. It's better if you please go occupy the rice fields and look for support there. If you don't believe this, there will be an awful event. Watch out for death. . . . Old people will die because of children."[112] Although the author of the letter used a pseudonym, the reference to not being able to work because the farmers were occupying the area around the provincial office suggests that he or she might have been a state official. Again, given the explicit suggestion that the farmers should return to the rice fields, the tension seems to have been caused by the presence of farmers in the city. Who are the "children" to whom the author refers? Are they the leaders of the FFT or the university students who joined their protests? Most of the leaders of the FFT "were married men with families aged between 30 and 45, with a few of over 60."[113] Rather than young, most were middle-aged. Another possible reading is that *children* was used in a metaphorical sense, a reference to persons who were not yet considered full citizens. Instead of dispersing in fear after receiving the letter, the farmers vowed to fight even harder. They continued to protest in front of the provincial office and posted fliers criticizing the government, one of which read, "Brothers and sisters, dear farmers, have you seen help from the government already or not yet? The state has not agreed to help solve the problems of the farmers. Why have tyrants been allowed to trample on Thai soil again?"[114] In the opinion of the minister of interior, the farmers were selfish because they refused to wait for help from the government and protested in the streets instead. The farmers, for their part, identified the lack of action or help from the government, and the abuses this facilitated, as tyrannical. Jit Phumisak would have approved of the farmers' analysis!

When the government responded on 29 November to the nine demands of the FFT, the farmers in Chiang Mai dispersed along with their colleagues in Bangkok. Their primary concern, land rent relief, was addressed in the fifth response: If the Parliament does not pass the (new) Land Rent Control Act proposed by the government by December 1974, the government will decree the 1950 Land Rent Control Act in Chiang Mai and Lamphun provinces before the end of December. On 16 December 1974, the government promulgated the new LRCA.[115] For the farmers in Chiang Mai and Lamphun primarily targeted by this action, the passage of the act was another beginning, not the end, of a much more protracted struggle with landowners and state officials.

Possible Justice between Two Acts

In contrast to the 1950 LRCA, which required a royal decree for each province in which it was going to be applied, the 1974 LRCA applied immediately to the entire country from the day it was passed. The 1974 act was more extensive and differed significantly from the 1950 act in terms of its application, rates and terms of rent, and terms of enforcement. The 1950 act envisioned land rental as a relationship between tenants and landlords, with the rare interference of the district officer, who was called in only if a dispute arose regarding a contract or other tenancy matters. In the case of a dispute, the 1950 act stipulated that the tenant and the landowner were both to contact the local district office, and the district officer would have the final word on the dispute. Either party could appeal the ruling but had to do so within sixty days.

In contrast, the 1974 act stipulated the establishment of provincial and district committees to oversee its implementation and administration and mediate any disputes arising from it. The provincial committees were to be headed by the governor and include as members the public prosecutor, the agricultural officer, the land officer, one director from each of the other authorities of the province, five tenant farmers, and three landowners appointed by the governor. The provincial committees were charged with determining rules for setting the maximum rice land rental rate and yield for use by the district committees in each province, determining if any kinds of agricultural crops needed to be banned in the interests of economics or land or water conservation, compiling yearly data on land rent in the province, assigning the beginning date of the season for the cultivation of rice in each area, and serving as the arbiter of appeals made by tenants or landowners under the act.

The district committees were to be headed by the district officer and include as members the district agricultural officer, the district land officer, the headmen from each subdistrict where there was land tenancy, the chief officer of the district authorities, five tenant farmers, and three landowners appointed by the district officer. The district committees were responsible for determining the maximum rice land rental rate for the district, examining and arbitrating disputes brought by either tenant farmers or landowners, and any other duties determined by either the act or the provincial committee. By involving tenant farmers directly in the administration of the law as members of the provincial and district committees, farmers were positioned as subjects of the law, not only subject to the law.

Both the 1950 and 1974 LRCAs specified that land rent could only be collected after the harvest, rather than before the planting season as some landowners preferred. Regarding the amounts of land rent required, the 1950 act standardized rice paddy land rents to between 5 and 25 percent of the yearly rice harvest. Under the act, the amount of rent charged for a given area was determined by the yearly yield. Land with a greater yield commanded a proportionately higher rent, while land with a lower yield commanded a lower rent. For example, for rice paddy with a yearly yield of more than 40 *thang* per *rai*, a landowner could charge up to 10 *thang* per *rai*, or 25 percent; for rice paddy with a yearly yield of less than 20 *thang* per *rai*, a landowner could charge up to only 1 *thang* per *rai*, or 5 percent.[116] The act also offered rent adjustments for low yields and unforeseen problems. If weather or other natural disasters reduced a tenant's yield to less than a full crop, the act stipulated that the *tenant* could reduce the amount of rice he or she paid as rent. If the yield was less than one-tenth of the usual crop, the tenant did not have to pay rent at all.

In contrast to the standardized rent ceilings of 5 to 25 percent of the harvest stipulated in the 1950 act, under the 1974 act the district committees were to take into account the quality of the land in their district when determining the rental rate. In addition, before determining the final rental amount, the tenant was to deduct not less than one-third of the yield in order to cover cultivation expenses. Then, after this deduction, the rental rate could not be more than one-half of the remaining crop. In the case of damaging weather or other natural disasters, it was up to the district committee to determine the amount of rent to be paid. In Chiang Mai, the amount set by the 1974 act had the potential to be far less than the amounts landowners had been able to command in prior years. However, until each district committee determined the appropriate rental rate under the 1974 act, the maximum rates stipulated by the 1950 act were to be used. This amount was also often far less than one out of three parts of the yield, which was the basic suggestion for the determination of the rental rates in the 1974 act. As became clear in the following months, and as I discuss in chapter 4, this caused some concern and anger on the part of many landowners.

The 1950 act fixed the rental period at less than five years; the only recourse farmers might have to arbitrarily canceled rental contracts was the district officer. In contrast, the 1974 act fixed the rental period at six years; this was intended to counteract the arbitrary cancellation of rental contracts at the whim of landowners. Under the 1974 act, the contract could only be canceled by the landowner if the tenant did not pay rent for two consecutive years or committed a variety of other dishonest or harmful acts.[117] If the landowner intended to terminate the contract, then he or she was required to write a letter to the tenant explaining the reasons and send a copy to the chairperson of the district committee. Once the tenant received the letter, he or she had thirty days to protest the termination to the district committee.[118]

For northern farmers, the passage of the 1974 LRCA was the product of a struggle for relief from high land rent prices that dated back to 1951. While their concerns in 1951 were dismissed within the walls of the provincial office, their demands in 1974 could not be so easily refused. The terms of the acts are different in two primary areas: who is involved in land rent relations and the actual price of land rent. Under the 1950 act, the landlord and tenant were the two main parties involved; only in the case of a problem might the district officer interfere. The 1974 act, on the other hand, stipulated the proliferation of committees to oversee and monitor it. Whether or not this was a good thing, for either farmers or landowners, depended largely on the actions of the civil servants and other members of the committees. I have already mentioned the differences in land rental prices, and I rather suspect that the knowledge that the 1950 rates would almost certainly be lower than the 1974 rates may have been behind some of the admonitions to the farmers to wait for the 1974 act. Similarly, this may have been why the farmers were so eager for the decree of the 1950 act and the deferral of a new act.

Threatening Language

Perhaps the most important change contained in the 1974 LRCA was that tenant farmers were stipulated as one of the groups to be placed on the district and provincial committees created by the act. Not only were they included in the committees but a greater number of tenant farmers than landowners (five as opposed to three) were to populate each committee. The district committees, not all of which were off the ground before the 6 October 1976 massacre created another seismic shift, were intended to mediate the relationships among landlords, tenant farmers, and government officials. In 1951, tenant farmers and landlords never sat down together at the same table to make decisions about how to address tenancy in Chiang Mai; the significant (i.e., decision-making) conversations were between landlords and provincial officials. Of note, also recall that, although the outcomes of their conversations negatively impacted the lives of the farmers, the archival record does not indicate that landlords and provincial officials actively plotted against farmers for their own gain. Instead, although it seems at odds with the solutions they proposed, the landlords appear to have kept the farmers' interests in mind and perceived their own relationship to the farmers as one of "family members." The landlords perceived themselves as the fathers, uncles, and older brothers of farmers; the farmers' demands for the decree of the 1950 LRCA in Chiang Mai challenged their material wealth but also stood as a critique of the form of interdependence practiced by the landlords. At the very least, the farmers' demands indicated that the landlords were failing as wealthy, almost familial patrons; perceived in a more radical form, the farmers who called for the decree of the act indicated that the system the landowners claimed was interdependent was instead a system of exploitation and oppression. Six years before its initial publication, the Saraphi farmers performed Jit Phumisak's analysis of feudalism old and new.

By the 1970s, the status of this system was becoming less ambiguous. The committee rooms populated by the 1974 LRCA were not the only places where rapid transformation could be felt. In the months leading up to the act's promulgation in December 1974, landless and tenant farmers became a visible presence in the streets. They camped out on Sanam Luang in Bangkok and in front of the provincial hall in Chiang Mai. Their presence was heralded by the worries of various state officials and pundits; among other things, the farmers were warned that protesting in the streets was not an efficient way to reach their goals. When appeals to economy did not work, then outright intimidation and name-calling were employed.

The public presence of the farmers in the streets and the visible tensions caused by this were indications of the significant reconfigurations of power that were taking place in rural spaces and articulated across rural and urban spaces. Yet there was a far more subtle register in which transformations could be perceived as well. This register was the use of words, which is nearly always a careful act. The word in question is *capitalist* (*nai thun*).

In 1951, the farmers from Saraphi and Doi Saket used the term *landlord* (*jao khong thi din*) to refer to the people who owned the land on which they grew rice. The power of the farmers' critique at that time was in their insistence that they be included in making the policy decisions that affected their lives. Their use of the term *landlord* allowed for a continued perception of a relationship of interdependence.

By June 1974, farmers and their supporters were using the term *capitalist*, often in combination or interchangeably with *landlord*. In the lists of demands submitted to Prime Minister Sanya Thammasak, *capitalists* were presented as those who cheated farmers out of land, charged exploitative interest rates, and otherwise stood in the way of justice. In their responses to the farmers' demands, the Sanya government adopted the same usage.

The Royal Institute defines *capitalist* as "a person who owns the capital to use for manufacturing products, a person who invests in production, or gives capital to others for production."[119] Yet how it was used by the farmers, and even the Sanya government in response, far exceeded this definition. In the farmers' usage, *capitalists* were those who owned land, provided credit, and lent money. Initially, the farmers cast doubt on the means and intentions behind these three actions. Later the most radical elements of the progressive forces called into question the sheer ethics of land possession and personal profit. Not only did the use of the word *capitalist* at this time signal the social and political transformation that was under way, but it also contributed to it. Once labeled as such, and lumped in with creditors, landowners were forced to confront a new image of themselves, or perhaps an image of their new selves. Some responded by feeling injured. Some responded with fear and anger. The areas controlled by feudal lords and in need of revolutionary action that Jit identified—law and history—might be understood as *public* aspects of politics. But as feminists remind us, the *personal* is also political. In this case, the personal fear and anger felt by landlords became political.

3

From the Classrooms
to the Rice Fields

1974, 1975, those were good years. It was my second year of university, but
I rarely sat in a classroom. I spent all my time out in the villages, living
and learning with the farmers.

> M., a former Chiang Mai University student,
> on how her life changed after 14 October 1973

During the three years before the 6 October 1976 massacre, M. was one of thousands of people whose life became oriented around political action and work
for justice. One very wet afternoon in the middle of the rainy season we met to
drink glass after glass of tea and talk about her experience as a student activist
in Chiang Mai. We sat on the porch of a house that once belonged to another
woman who cared about justice, Ajarn (Professor) Angun Malik. Ajarn Angun
taught in the Faculty of Humanities at CMU from 1968 to 1977. Through her
example and her actions, she offered material support and many other kinds of
encouragement to student and farmer activists. In 1974, she opened her house
and garden, Suan Anya, to the farmers of the newly formed FFT and the
students of the Farmer Project, who worked with the FFT. When a house
occupied by members of the Farmer Project was raided and students and farmers were arrested on alleged possession of weapons and seditious documents
in May 1976, Ajarn Angun put up the title for Suan Anya as bond for their
release.[1] When she died in 1991, she left Suan Anya to her former students.[2]
M. studied with Ajarn Angun between 1974 and 1976 and later became the
caretaker of Suan Anya.

M. was born into a farming family in Khon Kaen in northeastern Thailand.
In the early 1970s, she was sent to live with her aunt in Bangkok to complete
secondary school. She lived in Thonburi, on the opposite side of the Chao

Phraya River from Thammasat University. When we met, she gave me a copy of a mimeographed essay she wrote on the twentieth anniversary of the 6 October 1976 massacre. The essay located the beginning of her political consciousness with the events of 14 October 1973. Led by a friend from school, on 13 October, she joined a group of forty to fifty secondary students who began walking from their school at Wat Suwannaram, in Bangkok Noi. They crossed the railway tracks and Pinklao Bridge before joining the demonstration at Thammasat University. Her group marched with university students and citizens from Ratchadamnoen Avenue to Chitralada Palace. In the early morning of 14 October 1973, before state forces attacked the demonstrators, she hopped on a bus to go home to take a shower. She planned to return to the protest in a few hours. A few minutes after boarding the bus, she heard gunshots. When she arrived at her aunt's apartment near Siriraj Hospital, she listened to the news and knew that there was fighting between protestors and police and soldiers, close to where she had been a few hours ago. Over the next days, she learned of the injuries and deaths.[3]

M. finished secondary school in early 1974. At that point, she chose to leave Bangkok and go north to continue her education at CMU. She entered the Faculty of Humanities and majored in English. She chose English because she liked languages and literature. When I asked her which authors were most influential in her life at that time, she immediately cited Kulap Saipradit and Jit Phumisak. She remembered that she was frequently late to the meetings of the Women's Group, which she described as "like an early feminist group," during her first year because she often went to the Huay Kaew waterfall near the CMU campus to read Kulap's novels after classes ended for the day.[4] She laughed as she relayed the story to me—she grew so absorbed in his writing about a possible socialist future that she forgot the time and was late to the feminist meetings about injustice in the present.

Yet as M. narrated it, by far the most important and influential (for the rest of her life) experience during her years at CMU was her involvement with the Farmer Project (Khrongkan Chao Na). The Farmer Project was a group of high school and university students who worked in alliance with the FFT in Chiang Mai, Lamphun, and Lampang provinces. After she mentioned being involved, I asked if the project was part of the Northern Student Center (NSC) or a separate organization at CMU. Neither, she said; the project was a special group outside the structure of either of these. The organizers of the Farmer Project divided each province into different areas. With a few other students, M. was responsible for Hang Chatr district, in the western part of Lampang province.

She spoke of swapping her university uniform of a black skirt and pressed white shirt for the uniform of student activists of the time: jeans, a T-shirt or indigo-dyed cotton farmer's shirt, a pair of flip-flops, and a woven *yam* (satchel) bag. While the university uniform is often worn by students outside of classes to reference their status as university students and future professionals, the clothing of student activists in the 1970s seemed to reflect their ambivalence about this immediate conferral of status. While significant as a visible indication of their dissidence, as emerges again and again, even within this story, changing clothing was not enough to strip students of their status.

Thus dressed like the many other student activists she joined, M. left the classroom to organize with tenant and landless farmers to demand justice from landowners and Thai state officials. Many professors, including Ajarn Angun, allowed her and other students to miss class and awarded grade points for her and others' work "helping society." When she missed math classes, her friends in the Women's Group tutored her and helped her pass the exams.

When she was in villages in Hang Chatr district of Lampang province, M. explained, the farmers fed and "treated" them and they "didn't have to use money" (*lieng mai tong sia ngun*). When I asked what it was like to be a female activist, surrounded by male activists in the NSC, she commented that when she was in the villages with the farmers, "It was like I was a district officer" (*pen baep pen nai amphur*). If the meetings the activists held were large, then all the residents of the village attended; if the meeting was only a small, planning session, she explained to me, then only the (male) leaders attended. She commented that even though she was a woman she was treated well because she was a university student. Her explanation is significant in multiple registers. It reveals the profound gendering of the categories of both *university student* and *district officer*. She was aware that she was respected and taken seriously because her position as a university student carried with it an assumption of male power. The lack of farming women at the small planning meetings indicates that this ability to assume male power was only accessible to particular women. Although students may have changed out of their pressed uniforms into jeans and shirts as a sign of solidarity with the farmers, their classed status was not shed nearly as easily. Like the meanings of clothes that could not be shed, a student being treated "like a district officer" reveals the complications of solidarity. Students and farmers did not magically cast off their old positions and hierarchies the moment that they began working together. Instead, as they learned how to struggle together, they began to do so. To their opponents, the sheer act of students and farmers joining hands seemed like a dangerous challenge to their power.

M. reflected on that period and commented, "Ay, *nong*, then I knew my life had value, I knew the work was important.... Those years were so happy. I went everywhere, to every village where farmers were organizing across the north." She paused for a moment, and so I asked, "And then what happened, *phi*?"[5]

M. looked at me and said, "By the middle of 1975, by 1976, even before 6 October, everything was changing. Farmers were being assassinated. It was dangerous everywhere. I even carried a small pistol, even though I never used it. I didn't know how to use it."

What is striking about this fragment of M.'s life story is the palpable excitement and sense of possibility that she felt. When she reflected on her experience organizing with farmers in the mid-1970s, she recalled the concrete nature of their work together around land rent control and other issues, as well as the joys of sharing meals and life across their different identities. The friendship and camaraderie built between students and farmers transcended their class origins and imagined class futures. For her, and many farmers, workers, slum dwellers, teachers, and others, the three years between October 1973 and October 1976 were marked by transformations that far exceeded the significance encapsulated in the 14 October 1973 event. As individual change became social, it simultaneously became political.

Through their work with the Farmer Project, M. and her fellow activists learned how to work across differences of class and space in order to struggle together with farmers. Adapting a formulation of Paulo Freire's, I use the term *pedagogy of solidarity* to refer to the knowledge built through the farmers' and students' shared struggle and its implications. By pedagogy, I mean the negotiation and production of meaning through teaching and learning.[6] By solidarity, I mean the practice of acting in alliance with another in pursuit of a shared vision or project. The *pedagogy of solidarity*, therefore, also signals the process by which the farmer-student alliances not only changed the lives of the individuals involved but also challenged the prevailing political and social order.

In his well-known book *Pedagogy of the Oppressed*, Freire drew on his experience as a literacy educator in the slums of Brazilian cities to offer a vision and methodology of liberation through radical humanization. At the heart of Freire's analysis is a recognition that everyone—whether one is a privileged university student or an impoverished, illiterate slum dweller or a tenant farmer—suffers from oppression. It is only when all people, those who are oppressed and those who oppress, or benefit from oppression, realize that their lives are bound together that liberation can begin. The process of liberation "cannot be purely intellectual but must involve action; nor can it be limited to mere activism, but must include serious reflection: only then will it be a praxis."[7] Action and reflection both come in multiple, often intertwined forms. When farmers camped out on Sanam Luang and in front of the Chiang Mai provincial building to demand a new LRCA repeatedly throughout 1974, they were engaged in action. In the months between each protest, as they discussed and assessed their progress and organized the next demonstration, they were engaged in reflection. Differences of space and time not only demarcate the line between action and reflection but also bring them together as praxis. Action and reflection worked cyclically to continually inform the next steps of the growing farmers' movement; the movement was a praxis.

The emergence of the pedagogy of solidarity occurred within a broader context of the radicalization of education in 1970s Thailand. The intertwining of education and progressive politics led to the extension of teaching and learning outside classroom walls in numerous ways, particularly the expansion of student rural development projects. Two of the primary predecessors to the Farmer Project were the Volunteer Development Assembly (VDA), a student volunteer development program at CMU active from the late 1960s, and the official Return to Rural Areas Program supported by the Sanya government in 1974. While both the VDA and the Return to Rural Areas Program were critiqued for their lack of a concrete impact on rural peoples' lives, they created a foundation and point of departure, literally and imaginatively, for later student solidarity with farmers. Against this backdrop, the work of the students in the Farmer Project stands out as one in which students struggled to work side by side with farmers toward a shared goal rather than above them. As students left the classroom to struggle with the farmers in 1974 and 1975, they learned not only about another way of life but how to be responsibly political in a new era. By *responsibly* political I refer to the process by which students came to understand that their actions with farmers could be helpful, and at times dangerous, for farmers.[8] Through their work together, students and farmers shifted the meanings of *politics* and *the political.* Not unlike who determines the rightful owners of particular spaces or who can use a particular tool, who determines what constitutes politics and who can participate in it are questions shot through with power, domination, and potential revolution.

The Politics of Education: New Roles for Students after 14 October 1973

Despite the importance of 14 October 1973 as a "political as well as an intellectual revolution," it was by no means the *beginning* of progressive student and intellectual political consciousness.[9] Thanet Aphornsuvan and Prajak Kongkirati, to give two examples, have painstakingly traced the varied developments of the (often urban) student and intellectual progressive movements since the 1932 revolution.[10] Although they were restricted or surveilled under various dictatorial regimes, students at Thammasat and other Bangkok universities published magazines and books, organized, and at times protested. In Chiang Mai, Nisit Jirasophon and others involved in student organizing at CMU actively questioned and critiqued Thai society and political institutions throughout the late 1960s and early 1970s.[11]

As part of these efforts, in October 1970 a group of six young men published a collection of short stories under the name Young Men in the Flats at the Edge of the Mountain (*chao num thi rap rim doi*).[12] Throughout the stories the authors expressed their dissatisfaction with the present moment and imagined a range of solutions: one called for a return to the past, another called for a simpler way of living, and others looked toward a different future. Common across the six stories was a pervasive questioning of Thai society, the university, their peers, and most of all themselves. *Who am I? What is my role in what is going on around me?* Commenting on the stories in an introduction to the book, the historian Nidhi Eoseewong (then a young lecturer) wrote, "They are perhaps a small ripple, without meaning at all. If they are six people, I think that they are very interesting people. If they are one thousand people, I think we have to be interested."[13]

In the changed atmosphere created by the events of 14 October 1973, this small ripple grew and morphed into a series of formidable waves. Therefore, while it would be a grave error to locate these events as either the beginning or the peak of progressive political and social consciousness and change in Thailand, their effect on what was imaginable, possible, and permissible was undeniable. Between October 1973 and October 1976, the students and other intellectuals (including professors, former students, and writers) intensified their questioning and critique of various forms of injustice in Thai society— and their own roles in perpetuating or eliminating it. Out of this recognition, they wrote and translated hundreds of books; overhauled existing political, social, and literary organizations and established new ones; protested endlessly; and allied themselves with other people and groups searching for justice. The changes in what kinds of relationships and actions could be dreamed and carried out were particularly evident in students' growing concern and passion for rural areas and the people who inhabited them—farmers.

In making this claim, I do not want to erroneously suggest that all students were urban. They were not, as the example of the life of the M., who was from Khon Kaen province, makes clear. However, universities *were* urban; even CMU, one of the relatively new regional universities, was firmly located within Chiang Mai city. Although in terms of physical distance the residents of Chiang Mai city may have been closer to rice fields than their Bangkok counterparts were, this does not mean that they had ever ventured into them. Similarly, resonant with how I have been explicit about the range of class positions experienced by farmers, I want to be clear that not all students were of the middle or upper classes. Many were, but many were not. Instead, despite their class origins, what students shared due to their access to higher education was the possibility of a middle- or upper-class future. Citing the effect of the expansion of universities, including the foundation of regional universities such as CMU, under the Sarit regime, Benedict Anderson noted that with more young people attending universities, "It was possible to *imagine* within the confines of a single household a successful dry-cleaner father and an embryonic cabinet secretary son."[14] This path was not one that every student chose, however. Instead, many chose to work with farmers, simultaneously imagining a different, more just (if not more prestigious for themselves), shared future.

Although this movement soon expanded outside the university walls, it began inside them. In an introductory essay to a book published in 1975 by the Thammasat University Students' Association, *People of the New Generation*, Thak Chaloemtiarana called for equality within the university and for a university that served society. Thak explained that this could be accomplished through equality between professors and students: "Professors' academic duties and service must have meaning for society and the desires of students. This service is not to make the 'exalted title' of the professors go down into an inferior one. But it is to make the professors serve a function that has meaning for society and students. Students are not 'children.'"[15] In his essay, Thak called for a reorientation of both life within the university and the university's orientation toward, and within, Thai society. In the remainder of the book, students and professors alike contributed articles taking these ideas further. With titles such as "Ideas about the New Kind of Students," "How Can Women Join the Revolution?" "Education for the Masses," and "Power of the People," the authors each engaged specific questions relevant not only to university students but to those outside the university as well. Peppered with images of material hardship, poems about freedom, and photographs of recent protests, the articles may be read as an affirmation of Thak's call for greater participation in Thai society by university students and professors.

The book was not an anomaly but one of many publications filled with resonant questions. Cultural critics, professors-cum-translators, and socialist and CPT intellectuals interrogated the role of education and often, by extension, the roles of students and young people in Thai society. In articles with titles such as "Universities and the Role They Should Fill in the Present Society" and "Study for Life? Whose Life?" authors critiqued the status quo and attempted to find solutions to the problems they identified.[16] Their writing ranged from explicit criticism of the Ministry of Education to blueprints for revolutionary subjects. In a broad sense, their combined efforts may be seen as trying to shift education in Thailand from a narrow system of schools producing future elites and masters (not unlike Louis Althusser's Ideological State Apparatuses) to a Freirian idea of education as a shared process of liberation, and perhaps beyond.[17] Not irrelevant, Paulo Freire's manifesto, *Pedagogy of the Oppressed*, was translated into Thai in 1974—twice![18] While an exhaustive analysis of the various perspectives that emerged is beyond the scope of this book, examination of a few of them illustrates the depth of their critique of Thai society, as well as the lengths they walked, figuratively speaking, to imagine a different society.

The distance between real, lived experience and education as practiced in schools was paramount for some critics. In an essay titled "Who Does the Present System of Education Serve?" published in *Athipat*, the unnamed author argued that the current system of education only served to widen the gap between wealthy, educated people and workers. Critical of the Ministry of Education, the author called for reform of the primary and secondary school curricula and suggested, "If we analyze every book that we study, especially Thai literature and history, it is appropriate to discard and burn all of them. Don't use them further as textbooks because those books don't have any usefulness—they only cram the thinking of the masters into us."[19] Instead, the system of education "must touch the reality of society" and reflect the range of experience in society.[20] Resonantly, in a piece titled "Education and Democracy," Chaiyong Pornmuang challenged people to think about education as something that happens everywhere, not just within the school walls. He called for a national vision of education that could create people who believed in the value of themselves and had the ability to discuss social, political, economic, and other issues of import in their lives.[21] While Thak urged those within the university to bridge the gap between themselves and the rest of the people, these two authors called for the institutions themselves to change in order to close the gap.

In contrast, a CPT intellectual and another socialist writer both offered far more drastic criticisms and suggestions for change. Writing under the pen name Amnat Yutthawiwat, Phin Bua-on, a longtime CPT member and intellectual, published a book titled *Education Revolution: Following the Path of Socialism*.[22] He began his introduction with the following summary of the problem at hand: "Who is education arranged for, what kind of education is arranged, and how is education arranged? The heart of the history of the arrangement of education is the history of class struggle, the history of the struggle of ways of thinking, and the history of the struggle of the paths [of struggle?]."[23] Critiquing the current system of education in Thailand as one by and for the capitalist class, he analyzed education reforms in China and Tanzania in light of the state of education in Thailand and offered a set of possible changes. Appended to Amnat's writing was a collection of recent articles in *Athipat*, *Prachachat Weekly*, *Prachachat Daily*, *Sieng Mai*, and *Prachathipatai* critiquing the Ministry of Education, various curricula, the oppression of students in the classroom, and the system of education in general. Boxed text on the next to last page of the book proclaimed, "Youth must dare to destroy old things (that are backward and reactionary) and dare to create new things (that are progressive). Youths have the strength and the ability to destroy the old and create the new."[24]

An even more strident Marxist-Leninist take on young peoples' roles was coupled with essays about 14 October 1973, imperialism, and class structure in a collection published by the three regional student unions (the NSC, Northeastern Student Center, and Southern Student Center). In an essay titled "The Roles of Young People and Students in the Present Situation," an author writing under the name Niwet Tongkwao suggested the modifications students and young people should make to their behavior in order to be proper revolutionary subjects.[25] They must not separate themselves from the people, laboring people must be at the forefront of the struggle, there must be equality between women and men, they must be confident in collective work and methods, they must study in a scientific manner, they must oppose thinking like masters, and finally, they must oppose the kind of work in which one's goal cannot be seen.[26] Offered almost as a formula, there seems to be no space in which to question the construction of the proper revolutionary youth in Niwet's writing. For the students and farmers who worked together in Chiang Mai, there was neither a formula nor an already delimited path for revolutionary action. Instead they built a path, and created praxis, through their shared organizing and support of one another in the face of danger.

Leaving the City: Return, Politics, and Personal Change

Although there was a proliferation of writing about farmers and an upsurge in projects linking students with rural people in the relatively open political space following 14 October 1973, student interest in rural life and its problems began years before. Inspired variously by the need to *develop* the countryside (not least to prevent its inhabitants from becoming communists) and the examples of the lives of other young people, especially the work and death in 1971 of Komol Keemthong, many young people went on what may roughly be called "volunteer development camp" (*khai asa phathana*) trips to the countryside in the late 1960s and early 1970s. Komol Keemthong was a 1970 graduate of the Faculty of Education at Chulalongkorn University. Rather than accept a lucrative job in Bangkok on graduation, he chose to take up a position as a teacher in a remote village school in Surat Thani province in southern Thailand. Tragically, along with another teacher, Ratana Sakulthai, Komol was killed on 22 February 1971 during clashes between state and communist forces. In an article about the development of the student moment, Thanet Aphornsuvan recalled that while Komol was working in Surat Thani, on trips to Bangkok Komol would often tell his colleagues and friends about the difficulties faced by the villagers, who were caught between the communist forces and the Thai military. Surachai Phiphatsurisak, who was close to Komol, explained that "all the time that I was with Komol, I felt that he was the hope of all young people. . . . He believed that if the foundation was good, what went on top would also be good."[27] Komol's ideas about the need for students to respond to the gulf between poor and wealthy and rural and urban people in Thai society were very influential with many young people.[28] H., a former CMU student and activist, located his interest in social change as beginning during high school. Inspired by Komol, in 1972 a group of students from H.'s elite boys' high school in Bangkok organized a development camp in Pathumthani. They helped the villagers dig ponds and simultaneously learned about their lives. In addition to digging ponds, on trips of typically a few weeks duration, students built schools, constructed roads, and provided basic medical and dental care. The results of the programs were contradictory. On the one hand, many critiques resonate with John Dennis's analysis of the projects. Dennis concluded that students acted without taking villagers' needs and ideas seriously and that their programs were "often short-lived and unsatisfactory. Free medicine ran out soon after students departed; toilets built by students were left unused because the water supply was too scarce to flush them; new schoolhouses remained empty because the government could not provide teachers."[29] While long-term, concrete changes in villagers' living conditions may have been few, many students were affected as a result of their work and the relationships they built with rural people. As Kanoksak Kaewthep notes, these programs "gave the students particularly the progressive ones the opportunity to contact local people. Thus was laid the groundwork for their later activities among the grassroots."[30]

While an examination of every rural development project completed by students during this period is far beyond the scope of this book, examination of two specific programs both provides a context for understanding the transgressive nature of the Farmer Project and suggests questions that might be asked about its limitations. The CMU Volunteer Development Assembly, active between 1969 and 1971, was the forerunner, in terms of geographic location and an attempt to ask critical questions about rural-urban relations, of the later Farmer Project. The official, government-sponsored Return to Rural Areas Program, which ran during 1974, was a contemporary of the Farmer Project. Although the programs operated almost simultaneously, they were radically different. Each raises a series of questions about the relationships between students and villagers, the role(s) of the Thai state, and the possibilities and limits of the various projects. The work of the students of the Farmer Project, who worked with the FFT between 1974 and 1976 around land rent control, was both an extension and a refutation of these programs.

Contained Tensions: The CMU Volunteer Development Assembly

The VDA was established in 1966. Between 1966 and 1971, its members had, among other things, built a health station in the Samoeng subdistrict of Chiang Mai province, built a permanent wooden bridge in Mae Hong Son province, and built schools in many different places. Its work was funded by the CMU Students' Association and donations from state agencies, business associations, and foundations.[31] At any given time, it was able to support the work of eighty to one hundred volunteers. In 1971, the VDA published a book documenting its activities between 1969 and 1971. The way in which members of the VDA presented their work is as, if not more, relevant than their actual work for understanding their goals and the ideas behind their actions.

As a project of the CMU Students' Association, the VDA was officially sanctioned by the university and advised by a group of professors. The first lines of the introduction in the annual report for 1971 explained that its purpose was "to cooperate with one another to improve the conditions of existence of communities in the rural areas with the strength and abilities they already have. The target of the development camp is the better existence of the rural people, who are the majority of citizens in the country."[32] The remainder of the introduction was devoted to a further explication of the purposes and goals of the organization and a list of the rules adhered to by the members.

Following the introduction, the CMU Students' Association and the president of the university each contributed a short piece. The Students' Association placed the VDA within the broader context of extracurricular activities. Although the membership of the VDA was small in comparison to the entire university population, because the members came from many different faculties they were "able to bring knowledge and true determination to help impoverished rural people, who live in areas very far from progress."[33] Mary Beth Mills argues that along with *development* (*kan phathana*), *progress* (*khwam charoen*) has long been part of the modernizing strategy and rhetoric in Thailand.[34] Yet as the teleology of development has played out in Thailand, although the lives of some have improved, it has not been universal. The lives of others, largely poor, rural people, have been further marginalized, economically and politically.[35] Therefore, while the precise meaning of *progress* could be questioned here, what is primarily significant is that the student volunteers were seen as bringing the university, or at least the knowledge transmitted within its walls, to the villagers.

In his essay, the president of the university, Dr. Yongyut Sujjavanich, contrasted the consumer goods and materialism found in Bangkok with the relative backwardness and poverty found in the countryside. He insisted that the students of the VDA were doing very important work because they were fulfilling their responsibility to society and "especially to the rural areas that in the past were forgotten. The people there are Thai people, who dwell on Thai land that our ancestors preserved with their flesh and blood, and gave it as the legacy to all of us Thai people. It is appropriate already that we must help and tend to our brothers and sisters with care, and protect our land for us."[36] The use of the pronoun *our* created a palpable ambiguity in Dr. Yongyut's writing. In his marked insistence that rural people are also Thai people, one wonders who he envisioned as included among those to whom the land and country belonged. His comment is infused with a sense of urgency, almost an overdue need to attend to the forgotten rural people. The threat of communism may have made preserving the land even more important at that moment. In the second half of his essay, he explained that the volunteer development work also taught students about their own strengths and helped build community among them.

The remainder of the book is devoted to a meticulous accounting of the work of the VDA from 1969 to 1971. A summary of each trip made by the members is listed, including the date, location, number of students involved, and precise development work they undertook. We learn, for example, that between 3 and 23 March 1970, forty-eight male students, forty-five female students, and six advisers went to Rong Dah subdistrict, Wang Nua district, in Lampang province. Their primary projects included building a school and a dam. In the evaluation following the volunteer camp, both the male and female students were faulted for lacking group unity; the suggestion was made that older students should take the lead in making younger students feel welcome. In addition, between 10 and 30 March 1970, a group of volunteers went to Si Thoy subdistrict, and Pa Daed subdistrict, Mae Toy district, in Chiang Rai province. One of their primary projects was to offer basic health care; the number of aspirin tablets (a thousand), multivitamins (five thousand), and other medical and pharmaceutical supplies taken with them were meticulously listed.

I could continue conveying details for each of the trips undertaken by the VDA between 1969 and 1971. Yet, the pages interspersed between each major report section in the book are far more perplexing. There are four sets of three pages each. In my initial reading of the book, I almost missed them—flipping quickly past them because I imagined them simply as filler or dividing pages. Perhaps the in-between pages were intended as such, but they function as far more. Each set of three pages is comprised of the following: one page with a grainy drawing depicting an aspect of rural life, one page with a paragraph signed by someone calling himself or herself "the sacred hand of the countryside" (*bun mu chonabot*), and then an additional page. In one case, the additional page is filled with a reproduction of a poster advertising the camp, in another it contains an unsigned snippet of writing, and in the other two cases it contains signed pieces of writing. The poems and quotes interspersed between the development camp narratives function as a counternarrative, calling into question the camps and the university and state apparatuses behind them.

To begin, "the sacred hand" seems to address the students involved in the VDA, and young people more generally, in his or her writing. The most striking of the pieces is one that I read as a manifesto for Thailand's sovereignty in development. Referencing the recent increase in available agricultural machinery,[37] the author exclaims:

> To buy a tractor to use is not strange
> *But we must follow our own path*
> When we come to this point, we must ask
> *Is our Thai path our own, or not?*
> Who are we following?
> We have come [this way] how many tens of years?
> Would [they] listen?
> [*They*] *don't listen*
> The people who follow the [American] ass policy should resign first.[38]

This is a straightforward critique of development's mandates to follow a standard path set by someone else regardless of specific local conditions. The call for Thailand to follow its own path is not unusual. What is unusual and courageous is the presumed addressee of the writing and the criticism made in the final, small-printed line. The book was published in 1971, and Thanom Kittikachorn was prime minister until 17 November of that year, when he and Praphat Jarusathien staged a coup and installed themselves as military dictators. Thanom and Praphat both enjoyed close ties to the United States. It seems likely that the piece was written and the book published before the coup.

The other selections were even more thought provoking than the sacred hand's writing. The first was an excerpt from a speech given by King Bhumipol to police and army personnel in June 1971. In it he urged everyone to work together to protect the country. Everyone shared the duty to do so, and if anyone did not accept his or her duty, it could be dangerous. In his words, "If any such group does their duty weakheartedly, it will be a danger. It may cause the nation to break into pieces."[39] In light of the knowledge that Thanom and Praphat staged a coup in November, the king's June words are almost eerie in their foresight.

The second was a Thai translation of Mao Tse-tung's poem "Snow." The poem, written in February 1936, begins with a reference to the northern land. Although the north Mao referred to was northern China, one can see how the reference might have also made sense within the context of Chiang Mai and northern Thailand. Mao praised the beauty of the land during the cold season, when it was blanketed with the white of the snow. Then, in the second half, he referenced prior emperors of China, including Chin Shih-huang and Han Wu-ti, who, in his assessment, lacked poetry. The time of the emperors was past, and the new generation would soon come into its own.

> But only today . . .
> You people who have distant vision
> We must see the new
> From the people of the new generation.[40]

Read one way, Mao's poem may only be an homage to the beauty of the north, which could be imagined to be northern Thailand, and to the strength of the young people, or in this case the development volunteers. One English-language commentary on the poem notes that Mao wrote it in February 1936, four months after the Long March and two months after "the policy of a national united front of resistance against Japan was formally adopted and the creation of a 'People's Republic' envisaged," and that it must be understood in this context.[41] Returning to northern Thailand, and considering the juxtaposition with the earlier critique of development, the inclusion of Mao's poem is also a critique of the old leaders in Thailand, in this case the ruling leaders Thanom and Praphat.

I translate the final, unsigned snippet of writing contained on the in-between pages in full here:

> We hope very much that
> The heaping flames of ideals and purpose
> Such that all of us together have ignited
> Is ready to be ignited anew, and become better, and bigger.[42]

Left unspecified, the reader does not know what precisely constitutes these ideals. One place we might have learned more was the "rural life" issue of

Walanchathat, for which an advertisement was placed in the back of this book. *Walanchathat* was a CMU student publication published twice in 1971. Unlike other student publications at CMU at the time, such as *Su Sarn Muanchon*, a newspaper published under the direct support and advisement of the Department of Mass Communications in the Faculty of Humanities, *Walanchathat* was published by an independent group called the United Front of Chiang Mai University Students (Naeo Ruam Naksuksa Mahawithayalai Chiang Mai).[43] *Walanchathat*'s independence from the university bureaucracy (and the state, as public universities in Thailand are state institutions) was acutely reflected in the topics and perspectives explored between its covers.

Edited with the involvement of many of those who earlier wrote under the moniker Young Men in the Flats at the Edge of the Mountain, the first issue of *Walanchathat* was published in June 1971. Titled "Human and Society," the issue included articles about the student movement in Thailand, Marxian and Hegelian influences on the writing of history, the New Left, and Thailand's foreign relations policies, as well as politically inspired poems, including one dedicated to Komol Keemthong. In the second issue, released in September 1971 and titled "Green Danger" (*phai khiew*), the authors directly addressed those whose power was assured by their olive-colored uniforms and government-issued weapons: the Thai military. At times writing under pseudonyms, the authors of the articles in the "Green Danger" issue criticized the overarching role of the military in Thai political and social life. Issued in the period of time leading up to the November 1971 coup, and in circulation following the coup, the "Green Danger" issue of *Walanchathat* can be read as an immanent and courageous critique of the growth of the role of the military in politics.[44] Even though the most critical articles were written under pseudonyms, had the Special Branch police (Santiban) or other security forces wanted to learn of the authors' identities, they would likely have been able to do so.[45] As one of the members of the *Walanchathat* editorial group commented at the commemoration of Nisit Jirasophon's life and death in April 2005, they distributed the "Green Danger" issue even though there might have been consequences. Another person commented that he didn't know what would happen once the issue was printed—if the copies would be seized, if they would be arrested, or worse. In the words of one of the editors, after the "Green Danger" issue, *Walanchathat* became "very, very famous."[46] Unfortunately, this notoriety and the coup ensured that neither the "rural life" issue of *Walanchathat* nor any future issues were ever released.

Instead, as a provisional conclusion I offer the following speculation. Based on the majority of the material in the book published by the VDA, the ideals referenced may have been those of helping villagers improve and develop their lives. Yet, based on the in-between pages, they may have been critiques of the dominant form of development and hope for a new day. Or perhaps it was both.

A Narrow Conception of Politics: The
Return to Rural Areas Program

The VDA at Chiang Mai University was one of many small groups and clubs organized at various Thai universities to do small-scale development projects beginning in the late 1960s.[47] Following 14 October 1973, the Sanya Thammasak government founded and heavily supported an expansion and national institutionalization of this program. The new program was given the name Return to the Rural Areas Program (Khrongkan Klap Su Chonabot) and placed in a new Center for Democracy Propagation (Sun Songsoen Kan Phoei Phrae Prachathipatai) under the administration of the Bureau of Universities. The program was given a generous budget, and a committee of academics, students, and bureaucrats was appointed to oversee it. While many of the earlier programs, such as the VDA at CMU, were largely focused on material development, the Return to Rural Areas Program was instead focused primarily on *political education.* In the aftermath of the changes wrought by the end of dictatorship and the beginning of a kind of democracy, Sanya Thammasak "believed that the new constitution by itself would be inadequate to help the people understand their roles as public citizens. He contended that a massive political education program would greatly benefit the rural populace whose experience with self-government was so limited."[48]

The program began with an initial pilot launched in February 1974 covering fifty districts. In April 1974, it was expanded to cover the entire country. Supported by a budget of twelve million baht, approximately three thousand students traveled to 580 districts across the country.[49] All the participating students underwent initial training and then traveled to the countryside in mixed-gender groups of eight people. Like earlier programs, this one had mixed results, and many critics questioned whether it was relevant for the rural participants. For example, although they were only in the countryside for a few weeks, many students grew ill from eating the food and drinking the water.[50] Another critic noted that some of the students hoped to run for Parliament in the future and were using the program as an early campaigning opportunity. Simultaneously, local influential figures, and at times military or law enforcement figures, sometimes spread rumors that the student volunteers were communists or other agitators.[51] The logistics of so many students traveling to the countryside, as well as the potential problems when what were essentially three thousand strangers entered close-knit communities, were not insignificant.

Yet a far more significant problem was that of precisely what constituted the *political* education at the heart of the program. To begin, how can politics or political consciousness be taught? How can it be taught in a few weeks? On this topic, one critic made the observation that: "the hope that students are going to propagate democratic thinking successfully and rapidly, like snapping a finger . . . is something that is very hard to do. Because feelings and thinking about politics of the citizens in any country is not something that can be built in a short time. If anything, it is one kind of culture whose accumulation must take a long time."[52] At best a few weeks might allow for an introduction to an idea of politics. Even such an introduction, however, would be meaningless unless those holding state, landholding, and other forms of power changed *their* ideas about who could participate in politics.

Most striking, given the rapid growth of the farmers' movement throughout 1974, the idea of *politics* used by the Return to Rural Areas Program seemed divorced from issues of livelihood. One explanation may be that in fact it was the *farmers* who made livelihood, and the accompanying concerns of hunger and justice, *political* through their protests in the second half of 1974. In addition, one of the problems identified through the program was a lack of interest in politics by many rural inhabitants. Yet the Return to Rural Areas Program was almost concurrent with the beginning of the protests that eventually led to the establishment of the FFT. While there were many rural inhabitants who were not part of the FFT, it is still surprising that a lack of interest in politics could be identified as a problem.

On the conclusion of the Return to Rural Areas Program, the Bureau of Universities conducted two seminars to evaluate and write a comprehensive report about the program. The first seminar was held on 2–3 May 1974 at Chulalongkorn University and was attended by all of the professors who had served as advisers. The second, much larger meeting was held on 4–5 May 1974 at a Department of Police facility in Chonburi province and was attended by the student heads of each unit as well as the advisers. The bulk of the report was dedicated to a summary of the major problems found in rural areas. These problems were divided into three categories: politics and administration, economics, and social/education/health. Finally, the obstacles faced by the student volunteers and possible plans for future programs were detailed.

The problem of "interest in politics" (*khwam son chai thang kanmuang*) was listed as a subfield of politics and administration. Fourteen specific observations were made about this problem. The first was, "People in rural areas are interested in economic issues that are close to them, about their mouths, their stomachs, and their livelihood more than political issues."[53] Here economics and survival are directly counterposed to politics. Yet, as the tenancy struggle demonstrates, material survival was nearly always intertwined with politics, particularly for farmers and other rural people. Of the remaining observations, seven were concerned with some aspect of elections, including a general lack of knowledge about elections, critical attitudes toward MPs generally due to the misconduct of a few in the past, lack of experience in different voting methods, and dissatisfaction with vote buying. Although the preponderance of observations related to elections may reflect the frequent equation of democracy with elections in Thailand, surely politics is not only constituted by them? Of the remaining observations related to a lack of interest in politics, one cited a lack of understanding of the meaning of democracy. Another addressed the problem of the domino effect that occurred when a lack of interest in politics by local leaders led to a lack of interest among other people as well. Yet another identified as a problem poor people who were interested in communist ideas because they saw them as a way to improve their lives. Another observation reported that in some areas with at-large criminals, some citizens felt a dictatorship would more effectively discipline them. The final observation cited as a problem people who thought the administration of Thailand should be a mixture of socialism and democracy.[54]

Of the fourteen suggestions for future action to resolve these problems, ten dealt directly with the issue of elections. The remaining four offered strategies for disseminating information about *politics*: promoting the knowledge of people about their rights and responsibilities in a democracy; including a curriculum about politics and administration in schools at various levels; promoting education about politics and administration in various kinds of media in simple, easy to understand language; and promoting the peoples' interest in and understanding about different political systems.[55] While these strategies were exciting and could have led to a productive widening of the sphere of political participation in Thailand, it is clear that the definitions of *politics* and *the political* envisioned were very narrow.

Knowing that the primary form of rural political participation was conceived officially as voting, the alarm over farmers' protests in the cities acquires another level of meaning. Addressing the repeated comment that rural people lack political consciousness, Thanet Aphornsuvan asks how, then, to explain the many farmers who took to the streets and protested? For many of their opponents, he explains, the response was to label them as either causing chaos or being the instruments of another force.[56] Already in the early months of the farmers' protests and the establishment of the FFT, these strategies were used against the farmers. The accusations, which indicated that in the opinion of the speaker farmers were out of place in public politics, only continued to grow as farmers and their student allies made material life political over the next months and year.

The Pedagogy of Solidarity: Farmers and Students Teaching and Learning against the Grain

On a hot, sticky morning I met with L., a former FFT activist, in the garden of a sympathetic retired professor who often opens his house and garden in Chiang Mai to artists and activists as a safe (read free from the watchful eyes or intervention of the Santiban) space. This professor's actions recall Ajarn Angun Malik's in the 1970s. His gate is always open, and those aware of the space know that they are welcome.

L. picked up the package of carrot-flavored sesame candy that I had brought as a small thank-you gift. The candy was divided into six pieces in a translucent wrapper. We began by talking about the LRCA, and he used the candy to illustrate how the act changed the distribution of rice between landowners and tenants. Placing his finger along the edge of the second piece of candy, he explained that after the act was passed landowners could only take one-third of the rice.

"Did the act work, did landowners really take only one-third?" I asked. L. responded that the act had worked "in some places because the landowners were afraid of the Communist Party—but in some areas they weren't afraid. In other situations they tried to create fear and anxiety." They did so through the actions of right-wing groups, such as the Red Gaurs, right-wing students, and Nawaphon, which included wealthy farmers.[57] That the LRCA was the law was quite immaterial. Once it reached the districts, its implementation was inconsistent, varying from one locality to another. The irony of the landowners adhering to the terms of the act due to fear of the CPT is that, in L.'s assessment, the CPT was not involved in the land rent struggle because the party did not see it as leading to regime or structural change. Yet, as he pointed out to me, the land rent struggle was the most important struggle for the farmers, especially those in the north.

L. was a teenager during the 1970s, and his father and uncles were also involved in the FFT. As he talked about his life as a young FFT activist, I was struck by the energy with which he spoke—the sharpness with which he expressed his belief that another future might have been possible had the movement not been crushed by the string of assassinations of FFT leaders and the 6 October 1976 massacre. His longing for this unrealized future was most acute in his comparison of material life in the mid-1970s to the present moment.

"Na, *nong*, thirty years ago, in the fields there was rice, in the rivers there were fish," he said.[58]

Surprised, I said, "Really, *phi*?"

"Really. But now, there is not. Because the chemicals kill everything. There is a kind of snail that eats the rice—people want to kill the snails—but it kills everything. There are no more fish in the rice fields. People have to sell all their rice—or another product—for the market. Maybe they can sell it for a hundred thousand baht. But then you have to use that money to buy food, to pay school fees, to buy medicines, all with that amount of money. For a whole year. It's impossible."

Today, even if there were fish alive in the rice fields, the use of pesticides and other chemicals would make them dangerous to eat.[59] But it wasn't only the changes in the availability and safety of food that L. cited as important changes that had occurred in the intervening thirty years. He continued, "Another thing that is different is that the next generation of farmers has been able to study further. So now they work in the city as soldiers or police, or if they are women, they work as teachers. Now they have more money, more things, a bigger house."

I asked him if many of the younger generation were involved in the current struggles of the farmers over landlessness and community forestry.[60]

"Some, but not very many. They aren't farmers anymore, their parents are farmers," he said.

"Do you think their lives are better, because of your struggles?" I asked. After the 6 October 1976 massacre, L. fled to the jungle to join the CPT along with M. and many other student and farmer activists. He left the jungle in 1983, as the CPT was dissolving. In his view, it was often harder for the farmers to return from the jungle than it was for the students. Students were able, though with some difficulty, to reenter universities and continue studying. Then they graduated with a degree and could find work easily. When farmers returned they had to find a new piece of land to use. If they had a family, they had to find a piece of land large enough to support it.

L. laughed and said, "Is their life better? I am not sure. Perhaps more comfortable, perhaps easier. But better, I am not sure. I am not sure." L. seemed to compare his life to theirs—and despite the material difficulties and deprivation he faced in the FFT, later in the CPT, and after returning from the jungle, he assessed their lives of relative ease as somehow lacking. What constitutes this lack? Perhaps it is the possibility of a different future. Perhaps it is the shared life of struggle. Perhaps it is something else.

While students who worked with farmers often spoke about their experiences in the villages as a time of awakening and shared lives, I wondered if farmers perceived the experience similarly. Concerned with the dangers of romanticizing either farmer-student relationships or the farmers themselves, I continually attempted to ask questions about sources of tension and conflict among farmers and students.[61] In one of my attempts to address this, I asked L. if the students who came to the villages, with either the Return to Rural Areas Program or the Farmer Project, helped to buy the food they ate while in the villages. He seemed almost offended, or at least surprised by my question.

"Oh no, no," he said. "The students were like the children, the grandchildren, of the farmers. One day they ate at this house, and then the next day they ate and slept at another house." Further, he noted, when one of the FFT leaders had to flee to the jungle following repeated assassination attempts in 1975, he stayed with students in the city to avoid detection by state or right-wing forces for two or three months before he was able to go to the jungle. This formulation, which I heard from many former farmer activists, is a different take on the familial claim made by landowners. The foundation of the relationship between farmers and students, what made family possible, was a shared struggle for justice. This shared struggle bound them together, while the exploitation offered by landowners rent them apart.

A Politics of Life and Death

The passage of the new LRCA on 16 December 1974 was the *beginning* of a new phase of struggle, not the end of the struggle for land rent relief in Chiang Mai province. First, the specific provisions of the act combined with bureaucratic inefficiency inaugurated a brief liminal legal moment. The 1950 LRCA was never decreed outside of central Thailand and in fact was repealed in the first lines of the 1974 act. Yet, until the district and provincial committees determined the rental rates under the 1974 act, the rental rates from the 1950 act were in force. Second, although the 1974 act applied immediately to the entire country, farmers did not necessarily immediately learn about or benefit from it. Standing in their way was general bureaucratic slowness as well as intentional refusals by some civil servants and landowners to spread information about and adhere to the act. Both of these things—the liminal legal moment and the slowdowns in spreading information about the act—created situations in which landowners, farmers, and their allies found themselves in new and transformed positions.

These positions were also deeply political. My definition of *political* differs greatly from that used by the Return to Rural Areas Program. When I contend that they were in newly *political* positions, I mean that the relations among landowners, farmers, and their allies were constituted by and constitutive of contention whose meaning and effects exceeded each single relation between any two individuals. As the events of the year following the passage of the 1974 LRCA illustrated, this contention was not only about the price of land rent but also shot through with matters of life and death.

On 29 December 1974, just over ten days after the LRCA was signed, the governor of Chiang Mai province, Asa Meksawan, sent a copy of the new act to every district officer in Chiang Mai. He requested that they immediately distribute copies to every subdistrict and village headman in their districts. The important thing, he noted, was that the citizens in each district learn immediately about the act.[62] The provincial land rent committee was established in Chiang Mai on 3 March 1975. Elections for the district committees were held on 9 and 10 March 1975.[63] On 18 August 1975, a manual about implementation of the act, including additional guidelines created by the Ministry of Interior and the Ministry of Agriculture and Cooperatives, was sent to each district officer, who was then asked to share it with the district land rent committee and any district officials who might be involved.[64] Despite all of these measures, implementation of the LRCA in Chiang Mai was uneven. Some farmers knew about it the day it was passed, and others had to wait for many months to learn about their new rights.

Much to the consternation of landowners, some tenant farmers began using the rental rates stipulated by the 1950 act almost immediately. When landowners came to collect their rental payments in late December and early January, farmers refused to pay the high rates they requested. The FFT in Chiang Mai and Lamphun reported in mid-December that there had been "600 cases of successful resistance to 'landlords' bullying' and 100 cases of refusal to pay rents above the new legal maximum."[65] In response, the landowners adopted the tactics of the farmers and organized and took to the streets. On 7 January 1975, at 11:00 a.m., a group of approximately two hundred landowners from various districts in Chiang Mai marched to the provincial office to meet with Asa Meksawan. They were very angry and believed that the new terms of land rent were unfair and unjust (*mai pen tham*).

The tenant farmers were offering them 10 *thang* per *rai* as payment, which was the maximum rate stipulated by the 1950 act. Thon Chaichompoo, a landowner from Saraphi district who rented out 22 *rai* to tenants, was upset that his tenants were only offering this amount. He expected that they would pay the former amount, which he did not specify precisely but claimed was one out of three parts of the entire harvest. Asa Meksawan's response to the landowners and their representatives was to inform them that at this time, as the provincial and district committees were not yet set up, they could not yet follow the terms of the new act and were therefore compelled to follow the terms of the 1950 act. Addressing landowners, he said that he would "rather that you compromise with goodwill. If they have to cite the act, it will destroy the goodwill between you."[66]

In addition to those farmers who did not know about the LRCA, many were afraid to push landowners to adhere to it and face their potential anger. Part of the problem was that, although the LRCA contained specific provisions for its implementation and enforcement, many subdistrict and village heads simply chose not to cooperate and not to inform farmers of their new rights. Therefore, the farmers decided to organize and inform one another. In collaboration with students and lawyers, the FFT engaged in a massive legal rights education campaign.

Students supported the farmers' organizing efforts from an early stage by raising money for their protests, accompanying them to speak with government officials, and joining the farmers' protests on Sanam Luang in Bangkok and in front of the Chiang Mai provincial office. However, this support took a new form following the passage of the LRCA and the establishment of the Farmer Project.

Working with the FFT, the students of the Farmer Project spread information about the Land Rent Control Act and helped farmers use the committees established by the act to dispute unjust landlords. I argue that through these alliances students and farmers began learning from and teaching each other. In a Freirian sense, both students and farmers came to consciousness. For farmers who learned about the act, this knowledge marked the possibility of a more just tenant-landlord relation and also a new position as political subjects who could exercise rights. As students left the classrooms to struggle side by side with the farmers, they learned about the realities of injustice and another way of life. Through their work together, both farmers and students became aware of their positions vis-à-vis one another—and later, how these positions were implicated in danger.

In their early actions together, students remained in the role of teacher. One former activist with the NSC and the Farmer Project explained that following the passage of the 1974 act, "I and the other CMU students who were activists copied the bill by mimeograph. Then we distributed it to farmers in Lamphun—three thousand copies. Then in each district, the farmer leader spread the news. They set up a meeting and would invite the students to come to the meeting. They used the students to explain the bill to farmers in each district." Not only students but activist lawyers were deployed to decode the new act and what it meant for farmers' lives. Pradap Manurasada, a noted human rights lawyer, was one of these. Writing in his father's funeral book, one of his sons who attended CMU wrote, "I can remember a clear picture of my father sitting in a meeting with farmers, educating the farmers in Hang Dong—Mae Rim—Mae Taeng until it was nighttime in the middle of the rice field. It was good, there was a table, one chair, and a lamp. He explained the Land Rent Control Act, their rights, and the development of different laws."[67]

A colleague of Pradap's told me that while he was involved in advocating for farmers who launched cases under the LRCA, Pradap often traveled between Chiang Mai and Bangkok, where he lived. Pradap did not receive any money for the work, and in fact, he paid for his own food and lodging. The owner of a bus company that traveled the Chiang Mai–Bangkok route supported the movement and allowed him to ride for free.[68]

The dynamic between farmers and students shifted as a result of the work of the FFT and the Farmer Project. While the idea behind the Return to Rural Areas Program had been that students would teach rural people about democracy and politics, in this case students and farmers began learning from each other and teaching each other together. The rice fields were one literal site where farmers learned about their new rights. Once farmers understood their rights under the act, they could, at least in theory, demand fair rent prices. The rice fields, and the villages that bordered them, were also places where students learned the meaning of politics and political responsibility. Former student activists in Chiang Mai have commented to me that their lives were changed by going to work in the villages with the farmers. With support from like-minded professors who excused their nonattendance, activist students such as M. began learning from farmers rather than in the classrooms.

I want to be clear that this process was not seamless, and power was not necessarily shared equally. In a study completed nearly ten years after the 6 October 1976 coup forced the farmers and students to either disband or take their struggle underground, Andrew Turton raised many critiques of their collaboration. Chief among them was that the students took too strong a role in setting the agenda and strategies of the FFT.[69] While I am mindful of this concern, I am reluctant to wholeheartedly agree that it was students who radicalized farmers through their sharing of the writings of Mao Tse-tung and Che Guevara. First, students were not the only group of individuals who chose to join the CPT, even before the 6 October 1976 coup made it imperative for many. L., the young FFT activist I discussed earlier, commented that the CPT's idea of surrounding the cities with the countryside came more easily to the farmers than the students. More important, however, is that I assess the impact of working with farmers as a far more radicalizing event for students than the effects of students on farmers.

Commenting on the rising wave of violence against farmers in 1975, one farmer activist remarked that in the months before 6 October 1976 "it was a well-known fact that if you had students at your house who wore glasses, and officials or the headman came around, you had to hide them inside your house and not let them be seen." Resonantly, a former student activist explained, "I didn't make myself known in the village. Because I could leave, but the villagers couldn't leave. I didn't want to cause problems for the people. This was my responsibility to the people." His learning to be responsible involved an appraisal of his own mobility and status in contrast to those of the villagers. This is the pedagogy of solidarity: to learn how to be in alliance and how to struggle together with the knowledge of what this struggle means for the lives of all involved.

I began this chapter with a reflection on the ideas of the Brazilian educator Paulo Freire. While the Farmer Project was not a self-consciously Freirian movement, its emergence was simultaneous with the translation of Freire's *Pedagogy of the Oppressed* in Thailand. In the heady atmosphere of questioning the educational system following October 1973, interest in Freire's ideas emerged in Thailand. Only a few months separated the two Thai translations of *Pedagogy of the Oppressed*, one of which was published by the NSCT and the other by the FIST.[70] The publishers' introductions to both translations focus overwhelmingly on education as a possibly liberating and humanizing process.[71] In a note to the readers following the text of the FIST translation of Freire, the translator, Cho Khiewphumphuang, explained that in the world there are two kinds of people: the oppressed (*phu thuk kot khi*) and the oppressors (*phu kot khi*).[72] Cho further noted that people must choose to stand with either the oppressed or the oppressors, and the person who says he or she is "in the middle" (*khwam pen klang*) is lying.[73]

In *The Real Face of Thai Feudalism Today*, Jit Phumisak warned that peasants should not ally themselves with the middle class because the middle class will ultimately ally themselves with the feudal class.[74] While progressive students in the 1970s could be seen as middle class, or on their way to joining the middle class, the students of the Farmer Project had no interest in allying themselves with landholding, state, or other elites. In the eyes of elites, the students' realization that their lives were bound up with the lives of the farmers was precisely the problem. When student activists and farmers worked together to demand the rights promised by the 1974 LRCA, they learned to see the world in the two grave categories of oppressor and oppressed.[75] As their solidarity deepened throughout 1975 and stretched toward revolution, this education became implicated in the grave matters of life and death for farmers and students.

4

Violence and Its Denials

Rather than view violence, then, simply as a set of discrete events, which quite obviously it also can be, the perspective I am advancing seeks to unearth those entrenched processes of ordering the social world and making (or realizing) culture that themselves are forms of violence: violence that is multiple, mundane, and perhaps all the more fundamental because it is hidden or secret violence out of which images of people are shaped, experiences of groups are coerced, and agency itself is engendered.

Arthur Kleinman, "The Violences of Everyday Life"

When farmers and students came together in 1974 and 1975 to first pass and then implement the 1974 LRCA in the north, they catalyzed a political and social transformation. Farmers brought their demands to the city streets and became vocal advocates for their own rights. Students learned about rural life, the struggles of farmers for livelihood and justice, and their own places alongside farmers in those struggles. Working together, farmers and students effectively accomplished their goal of spreading information about the standardized and lowered amounts of land rent required under the new act. Yet, extending beyond their immediate action around land rent issues in 1974 and 1975, through their work together, farmers and students actively imagined and created the possibility of a different, shared future. At the center of their solidarity, and the acute possibilities for change it foreshadowed, was transgression.

In the short term, farmer-student organizing around land tenancy issues threatened to reduce the financial profits of the landowners. Far more significant, farmers and students together represented a force that could transform the very social and political order that underpinned landowners' elite and powerful positions. Their transgressions became revolutionary when the possibility of a different future began to emerge out of the risks and pleasures experienced by farmers and students coming together across often disparate class origins and futures and across rural and urban spaces to work for shared goals. As students and farmers passed out copies of the 1974 LRCA and challenged landlords to adhere to it, they were engaged in what Slavoj Žižek has called "revolutionary micropolitics" in the context of Russia. Žižek wrote of "the incredible explosion of grassroots democracy, of local committees sprouting up all around Russia's big cities and, ignoring the "legitimate" government, taking matters into their own hands" and "the untold story of the October Revolution, the obverse of the myth of the tiny group of ruthless dedicated revolutionaries which accomplished a *coup d'état*."[1] The goal of the revolution fomented by farmers and students was not a new state but instead a Thai future in which all individuals were full legal, national subjects.

The farmers' and students' organizing was soon met with a range of Gramscian symptoms of crisis, which manifested themselves as a series of violent acts. Farmers and their allies faced intimidation, harassment, arbitrary arrest, and ultimately assassination at the hands of state and parastate forces. In total, between March 1974 and September 1979, thirty-three farmer leaders were assassinated, eight were seriously injured, and five were disappeared.[2] At the height of the assassinations, between March and August 1975, twenty-one FFT leaders were killed.[3] The assassinations were particularly concentrated in Chiang Mai, where eight FFT leaders were assassinated in the two months between June and August 1975 alone.[4] The assassinations of farmers were committed openly and seemingly without fear of consequence. The symptoms of crisis began as a backlash and then escalated into counterrevolution by mid to late 1975. By early 1976, the FFT had largely disappeared from public sight and farmers and students had taken their struggles underground.

Thirty years after the assassinations of the FFT leaders, the assassins remain unnamed and at large. Only in the case of the July 1975 assassination of Intha Sribunruang, the northern president of the FFT and the primary force behind the implementation of the LRCA, was an arrest made. Under circumstances that remain unclear, the suspect was later released and never prosecuted. When I asked one former CMU activist in 2005 if he thought it would be possible to name the assassins in his, or my, lifetime, he didn't hesitate before replying with a definitive *no*. Speculation identifies a combination of elite landholding interests, as well as state and right-wing forces, as those behind the assassinations. The unnameability of the assassins is both constituted by and constitutive of the interruption that halted the revolution fomented by the tenant farmers and their allies.

In response to this unnameability, here I offer one version of the events surrounding the assassinations. I take as a starting premise that among the issues around which the FFT was active in the north, the struggle for land rent control was the most materially, socially, and politically contentious. At once, land rent control raised the ire of landowners and some of their state allies and offered farmers and their student allies tangible opportunities to change both their own lives and Thai society. Although the effects of the backlash soon grew wider, contention began intimately between tenants and landlords shortly after the passage of the LRCA on 16 December 1974. Hasawut Withitwichaikul, a Thammasat University law professor, commented that the act "created an opportunity in which landowners and tenants really had to confront each other face-to-face."[5] At once tense, these meetings were also rife with the possibility of betrayal by both farmers and landowners.

The heightened fears of communist revolution in Thailand following the fall of Saigon and Phnom Penh in April 1975 shifted the meanings of this betrayal, and farmers were publicly cast as only able to betray the nation. At the height of this anticommunist fervor, in early May 1975 the FFT returned to Bangkok to protest for what would be the last time. Shortly after the protest, the farmers vowed never to return to Bangkok and the assassinations of the FFT leaders intensified. Minus a few uneasy exceptions, state officials responded to the assassinations with indifference. The murder of Intha Sribunruang, which came at the height of the assassinations of FFT leaders in the north, shows very clearly how these assassinations functioned as part of a concerted attempt to subjugate dissenting views and actors. Intha was at the forefront of the fight to implement the 1974 LRCA in Chiang Mai and the neighboring provinces. As an act of violence that tore through his family, Intha's murder also highlights how the political became devastatingly personal. Within the context of a range of violence against farmer activists and other new political actors, the assassinations and concomitant state inaction not only was an interruption of the tenant farmers' revolution but was, and remains, a grave threat to parliamentary democracy.[6] Yet this is not only a story of unending, seamless repression. At each moment of indifference, denial, and dissimulation, progressive activists responded with calls for accountability and an end to violence. Their peaceful protests following Intha's death functioned to interrupt state, parastate, landholding, and other elite influence and violence.

Immediate Tensions of Implementation

Although the terms of the 1974 act stipulated that district committees were to set the amount of land rental payments, the process of determining the membership of these committees extended well into 1975. As a provisional solution until the committees set the new amount, the rates stipulated by the 1950 LRCA were to be used. The maximum allowed under the 1950 act was 10 *thang* of rice per *rai* of paddy land. In the Ping River basin (including many parts of Chiang Mai and Lamphun), which has very high rice yields, this could amount to even less than one-quarter of the total rice harvest.

One Chiang Mai landowner, Saengkaew Waelayen, noted that prior to the passage of the 1974 LRCA, his tenants were required to pay him 25 *thang*, or one-third of the total harvest of 75 *thang* of rice per *rai*. Following the passage of the act, his tenants refused to pay him this amount and offered him the legal maximum of 10 *thang* per *rai*. He was upset with this—not least, he said, because when he requested the previously agreed upon 25 *thang* he was "accused of wanting to fleece" the farmers.[7] Saengkaew's discomfort raises the question of *why* he was troubled by this accusation. Was it because he was being publicly confronted with it? Or was it because he did not want to see himself as someone who oppressed farmers for his own gain? If the latter, then his actions reveal the fear of loss of his status or self-perception as a benevolent patron as well as a full or overflowing rice barn.[8]

Eiakiew Chalermsuphakul, a landowner in Lamphun, faced a different situation. On 23 December 1974, one week after the LRCA was signed into law, he met with fifteen farmers who rented land from him to divide the year's harvest. When he sat down with his tenants, he demanded half the rice harvest. This group of farmers had rented from him for many years, and he expected the usual rental amount of one-half. But the farmers only offered one-third of the harvest (already above the 10-*thang* ceiling that they were now legally required to pay). Eiakiew and the farmers argued for many hours, but they were unable to come to an agreement.

Eiakiew began to feel displeased with the situation. He pulled out a gun and fired four shots. Luckily, the bullets did not hit anyone. Immediately, the farmers left the meeting and went to the police station to report his actions. Eiakiew was called to the police station, where he confessed that he had shot his gun four times into the ground. He was charged with three offenses: intimidating and frightening people, carrying a gun in a community, and discharging a gun in a community. He paid a fine of sixteen hundred baht and then left the police station.[9] Having failed to frighten the farmers, Eiakiew also found himself on the wrong side of the law.

In a newspaper report about the event, the inability to reach an agreement with the farmers was cited as the trigger for Eiakiew's anger. The LRCA brought with it not only standardized, reduced rental prices but also a legal basis from which farmers could hold landlords to the new prices. Nearly overnight, landlords lost their prerogative to set the terms of rice land rental. Land rent instead became a relation between two parties, who, even if not equal per se, met on shared terrain. This, perhaps, was part of what made Eiakiew Chalermsuphakul angry.

Yet not all landowners expressed their displeasure with the new land rent regime with the same criminal flair. Instead, many landowners simply refused to divide the rice. Leave the rice in the fields, some large landowners reportedly said, and let it rot. While large landowners could do this and still profit, it spelled hunger and suffering for tenant farmers and their families. Tenant farmers developed creative and courageous strategies to both hold landlords to account and expose the continuing inequalities present in Thai society.

In some cases, farmers used the forces of public scrutiny and electoral politics to pressure landowners to follow the dictates of the new act. This strategy worked particularly well with Worasak Nimmanan, who ran as a Democrat Party candidate for MP in the third zone of Chiang Mai province in the 26 January 1975 election.[10] Worasak had been one of the most outspoken opponents of the decree of the 1950 LRCA in Chiang Mai when the farmers from Saraphi and Doi Saket called for its decree in 1951. Notably, Worasak opposed the 1950 act because he claimed that if he received anything less than half the rice harvest from his tenants his family would starve.[11] His words, along with those of other major Chiang Mai landowners, were powerful enough to keep the 1950 act from being decreed. In 1975 the NSC identified Worasak as one of the two largest landowners in Chiang Mai province.[12] Despite his firm status as a wealthy landowner, by 1975 Worasak faced a dramatically different political landscape than that of the early 1950s.

One of the districts in which Worasak rented out land was Sanpatong. In late December 1974 he went to meet his tenants there to divide the rice harvest. At their first meeting, he was evasive with the farmers. He claimed to have no knowledge of the newly passed LRCA. He left Sanpatong without reaching an agreement with the farmers. However, he pledged to return on the first day of 1975 with new year's presents for the farmers and to properly divide the harvest. Despite his promise, 1 January 1975 came and went without Worasak's return to Sanpatong.[13]

Worasak finally returned to Sanpatong at 10:30 a.m. on the morning of 2 January. This time he did not claim ignorance of the new act; he simply refused to follow it. Instead, he tried to reach a compromise with the farmers. The farmers responded by requesting that he follow the law and adhere to the rental rates outlined in the new act. Tensions between Worasak and the farmers grew heated enough that the police were called to observe the meeting. Worasak again failed to reach an agreement with the farmers and again left Sanpatong without dividing the rice harvest. He told the farmers to leave the rice in the fields. When they came to plead and beseech him to divide the rice, then he would listen to them.

However, the farmers didn't see a need to implore Worasak to divide the rice. Instead, they told a Chiang Mai daily newspaper, *Thin Thai*, of the events that had transpired and his refusal to divide the rice harvest according to the law. The farmers said that with holdings of over 1,000 *rai*, Worasak's behavior was like that of other capitalists. The farmers believed that the delay in dividing the rice would be temporary. With the election coming up, Worasak couldn't afford to lose votes.[14] The farmers were right. As soon as their story was published in *Thin Thai*, Worasak Nimmanan sought out the editor of the paper in order to tell his version. First, he claimed that there were only 500 to 600 *rai* of land in Sanpatong for which he was responsible, not 1,000 *rai*. Further, of the 500 to 600 *rai*, only 80 belonged to him. The rest belonged to his wife's family; he simply administered it.

Then, in a tactic that reappeared again and again throughout 1975, Worasak claimed that those who claimed to speak for the farmers were not farmers in Sanpatong but were actually politicians. In 1951, Worasak had claimed that the farmers from Saraphi district who called for the decree of the 1950 LRCA in Chiang Mai were not *really* poor.[15] Instead, in 1975, he denied that the farmers who called on him to follow the law were farmers at all. Nevertheless, he said that he would be happy to accept the legally stipulated rent of 10 *thang* of rice per *rai* of paddy land cultivated. If the yield for any given *rai* was less than 40 *thang*, he would accept 6 *thang* as rental payment.[16] Despite his quick acquiescence, Worasak lost the election for MP to Songsuk Phakkhesem, a fellow Democrat, and Inson Buakhiew, who ran in the election as a Socialist Party candidate from Hang Dong district.

Perhaps Worasak was unconcerned about his relations with his tenants in Hang Dong (where he also owned rice paddy land) because it was apparent even before the election took place that Inson had widespread support in his home district. Whatever the reason, in January 1975, Worasak demanded that tenants on his land in Hang Dong district give him half the rice harvest, as per their usual arrangement, and refused to divide the rice unless they did so. Fearful of not receiving any rice at all, the farmers paid what he demanded. Yet in addition to bringing public pressure to bear against unjust landlords, if landlords did not follow the LRCA, farmers could, and did, sue them. Working with Pradap Manurasada, a progressive lawyer and the FFT's legal adviser, over thirty farmers filed a case against Worasak in July 1975.[17] As successive hearings were held throughout 1975, it appeared as though the court would decide in favor of the farmers. In November, Worasak agreed to pay 66,250 baht in restitution to the farmers in exchange for their dropping the case against him.[18] Shortly before the case was resolved, Silpachai Manorat, one of the tenant farmers who had sued Worasak, commented on his position as an MP and noted, "People who write the laws ought to enforce and follow the law."[19] While Silpachai's words may seem commonsensical, Worasak was just one state official who did not follow the dictates of the 1974 LRCA. In other cases, state officials actively obstructed its use rather than helping FFT activists spread information about the act.

Worasak's losses in 1975 were a far cry from his experience in the early 1950s. When he and other landowners were threatened by the possible decree of the 1950 LRCA, they simply denied the veracity of the protesting farmers' claims about their hunger and impoverishment to the provincial representative of the Ministry of Interior charged with making a recommendation about the decree. The farmers were not given a chance to refute Worasak's assertions. They likely did not even learn of the precise content of them, since the meeting between landowners and provincial officials was a closed meeting at the provincial hall by invitation only. The only accusation that the farmers heard from the land-owners about the undecreed act was that it was "a communist law."[20]

In 1950, Worasak exercised power behind closed doors to ensure that there was no change in the land rent regime. In 1975 the farmers brought their dis-agreement into full public view in the newspapers and the courts. Worasak was forced to respond to their accusations. At once a productive strategy for forcing Worasak to follow the law, the efficacy of the farmers' actions also indicated the breadth of social change that was occurring, of which the actual amount of land rent collected was only a material marker.[21]

May 1975: Warning Signs and Communist Dominos

As farmers left their villages to protest in the cities and students left university classrooms to work with farmers in the rice fields, rural-urban relations were dramatically reconfigured. The stories of how Saengkaew Waelayen, Eiakiew Chalermsuphakul, and Worasak Nimmanan dealt with their tenants' demands that they follow the 1974 LRCA indicate that rural relations themselves were undergoing transformation as well. As farmers took action to hold landowners accountable, they also radically challenged rural relations of power and author-ity. In his thesis, "The Role of the Thai Student Movement in Rural Conflict, 1973–1976," John Dennis argues that by urging rural people to take their issues first to provincial cities and then to Bangkok, the students transgressed "the logic and discipline of the administrative or patron-client axis of authority."[22] This transgression was one that was at once material and symbolic. Dennis further notes that "the student movement clearly underestimated the ability of provincial authorities to block Bangkok-approved rural reforms, but I would be hesitant to speculate to what extent this was prompted by the protection of actual material interests, rather than out of anger at the violation of traditional status relations."[23] Resonantly, it is clear that the cause of the contention sur-rounding the struggle to pass and implement the 1974 LRCA in Chiang Mai and the neighboring provinces far exceeded the disparity in the number of *thang* of rice landowners received as rent before and after the passage of the act. Prior to the act, the relationships between landlords and tenants were private, even intimate, relations in which the parameters were set largely, if not wholly, by the landlords. In the space of a few months, not only did farmers initiate contentious negotiations with the landlords, but they did so publicly. When their negotiations failed to come to resolution, farmers, at least initially, were willing to enlist the force of the state to pressure the landowners to adhere to the law. The contention over land rent was largely responsible for the backlash against the FFT and farmer-student solidarity because it brought farmers and their allies into direct conflict with landlords. To be clear, I am not arguing that land rent control was necessarily the most important or primary issue facing activists in the north; other important rural issues in the north at the time included mining, forestry, and the rights of agricultural laborers, for example. Instead, what I am suggesting is that the struggles to implement the 1974 LRCA were those in which existing relations of power, influence, authority, and even compassion were most forcefully challenged. Although Katherine Bowie has challenged the representation of beneficent landlords taking care of those who worked the land, the Chiang Mai landowners' responses to the proposed decree of the 1950 LRCA and Saengkaew Waelayen's comments in 1975 indicate that many landowners perceived themselves to be beneficent and kind.[24] In the struggle surrounding the passage and implementation of the 1974 LRCA, they came face to face with public accusations of themselves as capricious and greedy. These accusations were backed up with the many reports of landowners who refused to adhere to the new law, such as Eiakiew Chalermsuphakul and Worasak Nimmanan. At this moment, landowners' transgression of their own assumed moral code was revealed.

Complicating matters significantly were the political transitions that some of Thailand's neighbors underwent in 1975. The communist and genocidal Khmer Rouge seized the Cambodian capital Phnom Penh on 17 April 1975. Less than two weeks later, on 30 April 1975, Saigon fell to the Vietnam People's Army. The Pathet Lao established the Lao People's Democratic Republic on 2 December 1975. Although Ne Win was firmly entrenched as the military dictator of Burma and Malaysia's coalition government was successfully battling insurgency, the communist revolutions in neighboring countries made many nervous that Thailand would be the next country to become communist.

Amid reports in May 1975 that wealthy Thais were leaving the country, Buntheng Thongsawat, the minister of interior, insisted, "We will not become Communist. Instead of fleeing, the rich should remain behind, make sacrifices and help the government improve the economy of the country and the living conditions of the people."[25] Responding to the concerns of those inside and outside Thailand, in an interview in June 1975 Prime Minister Kukrit Pramoj refuted the possibility that Thailand would be the next "domino" to "fall" to communism, declaring, "I believe in the domino set. . . . But a domino set has limited pieces of dominoes. It doesn't cover the whole world. We [in Thailand] are not dominoes."[26] Despite the reassurances of Buntheng and Kukrit, for many in Thailand the fears of a communist future were palpable. One longtime resident of Chiang Mai told me that a relative sold land in Sanpatong district in 1975 due to concern that it would be seized by the communists. The landowner preferred to sell the land before that came to pass.

Within this context, tensions between progressive activists, including students and farmers, and various conservative forces, including some landowners and state officials, became pronounced. Katherine Bowie describes this period as one marked by "rapidly metamorphosing relations between the state and those who opposed it."[27] In Chiang Mai, students and farmers were accused of being "agitators" (*nak plukradom*) who "incited" (*yu yong*) the people.[28] In addition, rumors flew about the supposedly seditious actions of farmers, students, workers, and other activists. In June 1975 the provincial police commissioner, Police Lieutenant General Sanan Narindarasorasak, alleged that students were giving villagers in the north and northeast M16 automatic rifles and M79 grenade launchers along with training about how to use them to fight the government. The NSCT refuted his allegations and said that, although students had visited many villages, they did so in order to educate the villagers, not arm them.[29] As 1975 wore on, not only would spreading knowledge be conflated with providing weapons, but certain kinds of knowledge became perceived as dangerous. Farmers and students, particularly those active in the north, learned firsthand the material consequences of this perception.

Theorizing Assassination (When the Killers Remain Unnameable)

Facing a host of problems, not least lingering questions about the implementation of the 1974 LRCA during the December 1975–January 1976 harvest, in early May 1975 the FFT organized a large protest in Bangkok. Supported by the "three links" (*sam prasan*) of farmers, students, and workers, over two thousand farmers massed at Thammasat University and Sanam Luang. Concurrent protests took place in regional capitals.[30] They submitted eight demands to Prime Minister Kukrit Pramoj's government on 6 May, primary among them that the government ensure that farmers have land to use before the rice-planting season commenced. This was to be done by setting up a committee comprised of equal numbers of state, farmer, and student representatives to investigate landlords and force those who didn't adhere to the LRCA or otherwise caused problems for farmers to appear before the committee.[31] The Kukrit government rejected this and the other demands, explaining that the farmers had no authority to forcibly compel landlords or other capitalists to appear before a committee.[32] On hearing this, one of the regional vice presidents of the FFT, Vichai Pikulkhao, declared that the farmers would leave Bangkok and not return, or in his words, "We won't come back but will fight in the provinces, using our own methods."[33] When the farmers first left their villages to protest in the cities only a year before, it was because they had lost confidence in their ability to achieve change while remaining there. The decision to return to struggle at the village level was born of a similar exhaustion of hope.

Yet, while the farmers' demands in Bangkok may have failed, Andrew Turton notes that once the FFT shifted its organizing back to the villages, its actions became more radical and it "began to achieve the most by recruiting and politicizing villagers; holding meetings to inform farmers of their legal rights, especially under the Land Rent Control Act; denouncing corrupt officials for misappropriating development funds; denouncing and opposing landlords,

mine and tobacco factory owners, etc."[34] While northern farmers who protested in the streets of Chiang Mai city and Bangkok in 1974 were criticized
and belittled for bringing their issues to the cities, the response with which
their return to the villages was met was far more violent. The students' and
farmers' organizing was initially met with verbal harassment, as well as fliers
posted in some villages warning outsiders to keep out. Unsigned and posted
anonymously (and therefore untraceable), these fliers often contained vicious
and defaming language, referring to students and farmers as agitators or communists. Then, throughout 1975 and 1976, student and shared student-farmer
houses in Chiang Mai were both raided by the police and burned down in
unsolved cases of arson.[35]

The violence culminated in a series of assassinations of FFT leaders. While
the unresolved nature of the assassinations, and the lack of confessions by the
assassins, means that it is impossible to definitively know the reason for them,
many observers and critics show strong support for linking the assassinations
in the north to conflict over the LRCA. In an article written shortly after the
assassination of Intha Sribunruang, Katherine Bowie and Brian Phelan observed that the villages where FFT leaders were killed were those with both a
high rate of tenancy and many farmers who belonged to the FFT.[36] Kanoksak
Kaewthep cited the LRCA as a factor that obstructed "the exploitation of local
landlords and capitalists. As a result, severe conflict arose between the peasants
and the FFT on the one hand, and the landlords, capitalists, and local officials
who joined the landlords to protect their interests, on the other hand."[37] Intha
Sriwongwan, a northern FFT leader, asserted that the assassinations were carried out by hired gunmen and happened "because landlords were scared that
the farmers' activities would erode the stranglehold the landlords have on the
land tenure in the North."[38] The farmers were killed in broad daylight and often
in settings that indicated that their assassins did not fear apprehension. Intha
Sribunruang was assassinated in front of his house at the height of the killings
on 30 July 1975. Sawat Thatawan, another FFT leader, was killed on his way
home from Intha's funeral on 3 August 1975.

Sithon Yodkantha, who became the president of the northern branch of
the FFT following Intha's assassination, noted that the killings seemed to have
been strategically planned and carried out. Sithon compared the assassinations
to cutting off the arms and legs of people before killing them completely. At
first, village-level leaders and district committee members of the FFT were targeted. Then, once a significant number of minor leaders had been killed, Intha,
a major leader and intellectual of the movement, was assassinated.[39]

Although the assassinations remain unresolved and the assassins unnamed,
the various responses, and lack of response, to them provide another layer of insight about the importance and revolutionary potential of the tenancy struggle.
By examining the responses to the assassinations, I trace their personal, social,
and political effects. While my work cannot uncover the assassins, I interrogate

the conditions under which their identities and the larger forces behind them remain unknowable.

State (In)actions: Ignorance, Indifference, and Incompetence

As farmers were assassinated in increasing numbers in 1975, the FFT and its allies called on the Thai state to take action to investigate the murders and protect the farmers. In mid-July the NSCT published a declaration about the farmer assassinations on the front page of its newspaper, *Athipat*. It stated that the farmers in the north who had been killed and injured up to that point were largely local village leaders and members of the FFT, many of whom held leadership positions in the federation. They were people who had struggled fiercely for justice and were loved by their fellow villagers. Each assassination was carried out by someone from another place and was conducted in such a manner that it went well, so much so that each seemed to have been planned ahead of time. In nearly every case the police had claimed that there wasn't enough evidence to make an arrest. In the opinion of the *Athipat* staff, the police had failed to carry out their duties properly.[40] In late July the FFT submitted a letter to the Ministry of Interior, "asking it to provide security measures to the farmers who are fighting for justice" and for "the Government to reconsider the case and publicise the murders so that the Government will provide full protection to farmers who are fighting for justice."[41] Instead, rather than investigate the murders, most state officials claimed to be unable to take action, refused to take action, or outright denied the importance of the assassinations. In addition to the unknown identities of the assassins, the various Thai state denials of Intha's and other farmers' deaths are politically significant. The denials reveal a combination of indifference, incompetence, and active attempts to downplay the importance of the FFT's work.

When students asked Prime Minister Kukrit to intervene to stop the assassinations, he claimed ignorance and said that it was a matter better left to the police. Kukrit alleged he was like everyone else, only learning of each assassination when he read about it in the newspaper.[42] Asa Meksawan, the provincial governor of Chiang Mai, on the other hand, cited the sheer difficulty of the situation as the reason for inaction: "[P]olice have found it difficult to dig into these cases because they have not been able to obtain cooperation from witnesses. Police have to grope into the dark by themselves. It's like looking for a pin in the ocean."[43] Rather than absolving the police, the excuses for inaction Asa and Kukrit offered only served to make them look incompetent.

Despite Prime Minister Kukrit's assertion that dealing with the assassinations was the responsibility of the police, various sectors of the police were not eager to intervene. Deputy Minister of Interior Chumphon Lohachalah called for "cooperation from the people on this also, because the police are not deities, they can't know or manage everything."[44] He further claimed that the police were unable to protect the farmers because there were fewer police than farmers in the country.[45] But surely there were other viable options for protecting the farmers than assigning police to them in a one-to-one ratio, which seemed to be what Chumphon was suggesting.

Police General Phoj Phekanan, the head of the Department of Police, echoed and even expanded on Deputy Minister Chumphon's comments and denials of the ability of the police to protect the farmers. When asked in an interview what the police were doing to protect the farmers, General Phoj responded by saying, "Don't think that the police have abandoned [them] . . . but don't think that the police are like Narai with four arms, omniscient . . . or have enough police strength to protect all of the farmers. There are more farmers than police, I don't know how many. . . . [T]herefore, they [the farmers] must help."[46] When asked to clarify what he meant by "help," the police general said, "[T]he farmers must help by being the ears and eyes of the police."[47] Yet given police inaction, and even rumors of police involvement in the assassinations, farmers may have been wary of collaborating with them.

Then the interviewer asked Police General Phoj why it appeared that the police didn't seem to know or care about the fact that many of the assassinated farmers were leaders of the FFT. Phoj responded that he wished the farmer leaders had been officially registered or that he had been provided with a list of their names. He claimed that the police only learned about the leadership positions of the farmers when they were printed in the newspaper following the assassinations. If there had been a list, he might have "paid special attention."[48] Up to this point, the interview, which was published in the conservative Chiang Mai daily *Thai Niu*, had consisted exclusively of verbatim questions and answers. After this statement, the interviewer, Therd Tharaninthorn, wryly commented, "Hmm. You speak as if your police feel too far behind. But, for example, with Mr. Intha Sribunruang, all of the people in the city know that he was a top leader of the farmers. But for the police who feel that they are behind, he had to be killed and dead before they knew."[49] Therd surmised that either Police General Phoj did not think before he spoke or he had inadvertently revealed the indifference of the police to the farmer assassinations.[50]

Paradoxically, by denying the political nature of the assassinations so vehemently, some officials actually underlined the political importance they attached to the farmers' activism. They flatly denied the difference between the farmer assassinations and other murders during the same period.[51] As one example of this denial, Buntheng Thongsawat, minister of interior, made the following statement to Parliament: "These killings are like other murders occurring everywhere in the country. The government can't consider whether the person was important or not, or if the person was a farmer leader or not. We must view every life as important to protect."[52] Even in Buntheng's formulation, every life should be protected. Yet the record of blatant state inaction in the face of assassinations of farmer leaders indicates that some lives may have been deemed more important to protect than others.

While at least the Ministry of Interior acknowledged the assassinated leaders *as* leaders, an article in *Yuthakot*, the journal of the army, went one step further and indicated that at least one part of the military disputed this fact.[53] In a September 1975 article, Major Worawut Kosonyutthasorn referred to the assassinated FFT leaders as "people *who call themselves* leaders or representatives of farmers."[54] Then each assassination to date was listed, and the leadership position of each farmer was specifically denied. He described Intha Sribunruang as "the person who appointed himself the president of the Northern Farmers' Federation."[55] These were not political killings, Major Worawut claimed; rather "the people who died were simply ordinary villagers who have left this world."[56] He denied the significance of both the farmers' deaths specifically and the FFT broadly. By denying that the leaders of the FFT *were* leaders, he effectively denied the existence of the FFT as a political organization. When considered together with the harassment the FFT leaders had experienced when organizing to implement the LRCA, Major Worawut's comments acquire another layer of meaning. As live activists, Intha and other FFT leaders were inappropriately political and thought to be outside agitators. As dead activists, they became ordinary villagers. If sharing information about national laws had been considered appropriate or normal for rural villagers, perhaps the FFT activists would not have been killed.

Intha Sribunruang's Struggle for Justice

The life and work of Intha Sribunruang stand as an acute refutation of Major Worawut's argument. Intha Sribunruang was born in 1930 and was a resident of Baan Long village, in Pa Pong subdistrict, Saraphi district, Chiang Mai province. He was married and had five children—two sons and three daughters. Intha had completed four years of primary school and spent the years from the age of twelve to sixteen living as a Buddhist novice.[57] He was described as "generous, calm, thoughtful, careful, and he liked working for the collective good so much that he had been elected headman for five years."[58] At the time of his death in late July 1975, Intha possessed a small fruit garden and operated "a small shop, selling this and that," out of his house.[59] He no longer possessed rice paddy land of his own, as he had sold it order to pay his children's school fees.[60]

Intha was an organizer and leader long before the establishment of the FFT. He founded a village drama group, was elected village headman, served as a member of the subdistrict (*tambon*) committee, and led a government-sponsored district farmers' cooperative.[61] In an interview shortly after his assassination, Intha's wife, Ruankham, commented that even though he did not have a strong background in formal education, he read voraciously about the lives of workers and farmers and listened to the radio a lot. He first became involved in progressive politics when students were protesting the U.S. presence in Thailand in 1973.[62] When farmers across the nation were protesting in November 1974, Intha brought a delegation of farmers from Saraphi district to join the protests in Chiang Mai. He was selected as a representative join the protests in Bangkok. When the FFT was established on 19 November 1974, Intha was elected as one of the regional vice presidents.[63]

In the eight months between the passage of the LRCA in December 1974 and his assassination in July 1975, Intha traveled to every district in Chiang Mai province to talk to villagers about their rights under the newly passed law. This organizing work was critical, Intha explained, because many villagers did not know that the law existed. He further commented that they "do not yet really understand this Act, and its importance, or the benefits the Act affords them."[64] One editorial published after Intha's assassination described his work as "mediating and struggling for the capitalists to accept collecting rent from farmers following the new law ... because civil servants are not able to make all of the landowning capitalists accept the new law of the government."[65] Once the villagers understood their rights under the act, they could, at least in theory, demand fair rents. Simultaneously, the legal education organizing done by Intha is significant precisely because he did it as a farmer—not a professor, not an MP, not a student, not a development official. This in no way diminishes the significance of the alliance work done by students and lawyers; rather it highlights another shift resulting from the work of the FFT. In *Pedagogy of the Oppressed*, Paulo Freire explains that a liberatory process of education involves "co-intentional education," in which all students and teachers are "co-intent on reality, are both Subjects, not only in the task of unveiling that relation, and thereby coming to know it critically, but in the task of re-creating that knowledge. As they attain this knowledge of reality through common reflection and action, they discover themselves as its permanent re-creators."[66] The oppressed do not follow the lead of a vanguard, but through their participation come to embody leadership. The organizing among farmers, students, and lawyers around the 1974 LRCA may usefully be understood in this register. By becoming teachers of farmers and students—of legal knowledge, the meaning of rights, and the facts of rural life—Intha and other FFT activists expanded the possibility of what kinds of political action farmers could take and what kinds of futures might be possible in Thailand. Simultaneously, by joining with students, lawyers, and others through their organizing, they re-created the possibility of alliances among differently situated actors.

At times the subdistrict heads (*kamnan*) were not content to simply *fail to inform* villagers of the act but actively lied about the land rent situation in their subdistricts and harassed FFT members. Intha noted that he had been chased out of some villages, and in other villages he saw fliers posted telling the FFT to keep out of the area.[67] Instead of printing information about the new law, the radio and newspapers only reported that the FFT had "incited the masses."[68] Intha asked, "Was disseminating information about a national law the purview only of communist front organizations?"[69] Rather than forming and using the committees stipulated by the act to settle rent disputes between landowners and farmers, Intha commented that "in some areas the *kamnan* will keep around a gangster or a young policeman to become involved."[70] While this kind of intimidation contributed to creating a climate of fear, it was not enough to stop the farmers from demanding that landowners follow the new law.

In addition to his work spreading information about the LRCA, Intha was also the founder and editor of the FFT's newspaper, *Thai Farmer* (*Chao Na Thai*). The officers of the FFT and the newspaper were located on the grounds of CMU, in a building that once housed single faculty members. With the help of allied faculty, a spare room was taken over by the FFT. One former activist told me about the experience of screen printing the newspaper on the campus by hand. They used red ink for the front page. On the cover was an image of a farmer with a plow and the words "Rise up and struggle." Only two issues of the paper were printed before Intha was assassinated. In the first issue, an article titled "Introducing Thai Farmers" was printed. In it, farmers were urged to "pick up weapons of correct thought" and to understand the rules of struggle. As the article described the first rule of struggle:

> Righteousness will prevail over evil. To put it simply, it is that the oppressed, persecuted, bullied side is the side that has not received justice. When this side struggles against the oppressors, we must believe that the struggle of the farmers is built on a foundation of correctness and justice, such that in the end we will have to prevail. Because we believe that one day there will only be sympathy, there will be a wide range of people who join the struggle, not only farmers, but also students, civil servants, teachers, professors and other people who love justice, who sympathize with the farmers, and understand the benevolence of farmers who use their labor to take care of everyone in the country.[71]

In 1950, those who opposed the decree of the act cited as reasons the *interdependence* between the landlords and tenants and the benevolence of the landlords. Here the FFT offers a different understanding of interdependence, citing the farmers' labor—producing food (rice) for the nation—as a benevolent act. The sense of justice operative for the FFT grew out of an understanding of this interdependence between the farmers and the rest of the nation. The basic premise advanced here is that once their potential allies realized the oppression faced by the farmers, they would naturally choose to join the struggle. Many former student activists with whom I spoke offered a similar narrative of their own involvement. Many students were born into privileged families. Once they witnessed the lives of farmers, however, they began to come to consciousness about injustice. They felt compelled to join the farmers, even if solidarity was more difficult to build across differences of class and experience than the vision articulated by Intha in his article.

Intha continued by explaining that the power of the farmers came from their difference from the capitalists:

> Another weapon of thinking of the farmers is the behavior of the cornered gangster capitalists. This behavior is the killing of the farmer leaders. I say this because the cooperation and strengthening of the struggle of the farmers, especially on the issue of the Land Rent Control Act, has caused these big capitalist landowners and some civil servants who act like slaves who serve the capitalists, to lose their gains and reputations and to be condemned by the masses.... They therefore struggle desperately to find a way out. In this, they are not at all different from a rabid dog that is chased, beaten and cornered. He cannot find a way out and therefore he has no other way out other than finally turning to definitively destroy the other. We, all the farmer brothers and sisters, must comprehend this and see the real nature of the capitalists. This is their weak point. We must understand that the enemy of the farmer is in trouble. They are about to be destroyed and the farmers are close to victory.... We farmers have the great, powerful strength of the masses, we are a hundred thousand, we are a million. We came together and organized together, with a strength that is stronger and with a higher consciousness. We know that we will win in the end.[72]

Intha perceived the desperation of the landlords. Yet, even if the farmers were able to comprehend the suffering of the landlords, they could not use this to protect themselves.

In his last interview, in mid-July 1975, Intha offered a slightly different assessment of the assassinations of FFT leaders. He said that they were the result of "a conflict of interest with the landowners about the price of land rent. It's about the land, it's about money. Some people are killed not because it is about money. More likely it is a disagreement over the land. This plan is only to threaten and to harm the opposition's struggle."[73] Intha's comments here are astute. The assassinations were about "interference" with landowners. Yet they were not only about money and the price of land rent. The organizing of the FFT around the 1974 LRCA challenged the relations of land rent and also who determined and transformed those relations. While not revolutionary in the view of the CPT, the idea of the law as a tool in the hands of tenant and landless farmers threatened to overturn the rural status quo and remove landlords from their positions of unchallengeable power.

In his essay "Withdrawal Symptoms: Social and Cultural Aspects of the October 6 Coup," Benedict Anderson argues for an understanding of the 6 October 1976 massacre as a unique moment not only due to the public, moblike nature of the violence but also as the culmination of two years of right-wing violence against progressive activists. He attributes the open forms of violence to shifting class formations and ideological conflict. In particular, he cites the transgressive class behavior of middle-class students as a major cause of panic and alarm among conservative forces.[74] In chapter 3 I explored the transgressive class behavior of students who left the classroom to learn in the fields with the farmers. Here I stress a resonant thesis. Perhaps as alarming to the elites as students who did not aspire to join them were farmers—like Intha and other members of the FFT—who understood and used their legal rights. For years, farmers only experienced legal change as its objects. With the 1974 LRCA, farmers came into view as subjects of law and actors at the forefront of its implementation.

In other words, the assassinations were an attempt to return the farmers to their pre-October 1973 state of relative repression. In the afterword to his book *A Miracle, a Universe*, about political repression and its aftermath in Uruguay and Brazil, Lawrence Weschler describes both liberation and repression in terms of subject formation. He explains that liberation is a process in which "an entity which had been content to receive the action of other people's sentences now suddenly demands to initiate such actions on its own."[75] Repression is a similarly grammatical process, one in which "the authorities scramble to find some way of recapturing individuals (or polities) who have suddenly taken to behaving like subjects, so as to turn them back once again into mere objects."[76] The assassinations may be read as an attempt to recapture the farmers, who, in learning about their legal rights, had become new subjects altogether.

Not only were landlords no longer sure who held the power in their individual relationships with their tenants, but they were also being taken to court and accused of being greedy by farmers. Their methods were exposed in the press, and they were labeled as capitalists by nearly everyone. They were cornered, afraid, ashamed, and losing power. It is not surprising that they may have turned to violence. Whether, and how often, they resorted to violence, unfortunately, remains unknown.

Like many other progressive activists, Intha reported being threatened; he described the man who threatened him as a tough, big man with scars on his neck, face, and arms.[77] After Intha's death, his father, Jai Sribunruang, commented that Intha anticipated his assassination. Jai told a newspaper reporter that "Mr. Intha knew that he was going to be killed in advance. He even told his son that if a stranger came on a motorbike in front of the house, to tell him."[78] Yet Intha did not let his fear of being assassinated stop him from organizing and even noted that he took his son with him everywhere so that he would learn how to struggle for justice.

On the morning of 30 July 1975, Intha was home alone. His wife, an assistant nurse, was attending a training session in the village. She often ran the shop, but he offered to run it for her that morning so she could attend. His five children were all at school. He was wearing a white undershirt and a pair of black pants. At 9:45 a.m., two men pulled up in front of Intha's house on a red Yamaha motorbike. The driver remained on the bike while his passenger got off and asked Intha for some cigarettes. As Intha was handing him his change, he shot Intha point-blank in the head eleven times. The assassin used a .22 caliber pistol with a silencer. Intha died instantly.[79] His murder came only eleven days after he predicted a speedy end to the assassinations.

Tensions of Investigation

Intha's prominence and importance to the FFT engendered a range of seemingly contradictory actions on the part of various state actors and agencies. On the one hand, some actors were catalyzed to take action to apprehend his assassin, while others pursued a strategy of denial and dissimulation in line with the pattern following the assassinations of other farmer and activist leaders noted earlier. The tension between these two kinds of action illustrates the price of dissent paid by some state officials and perhaps hints at the intentions behind the murders of Intha and other FFT leaders.

Intha Sribunruang was the seventeenth farmer leader to be killed nationally since the killings began in March 1974 and the sixth to be killed in northern Thailand since June 1975. Intha's prominence as president of the northern branch of the FFT and the accumulated assassinations leading up to his death sparked protests and action across the country. His death affected many people, and one newspaper reported that it "sent a wave of shock and anger through student activist leaders in Bangkok."[80] The NSCT in Bangkok and the NSC in Chiang Mai organized protests and letter-writing campaigns to Parliament demanding that they take action to protect farmers' lives and apprehend the assassins.[81] A group of CMU professors issued a declaration calling on the police to work quickly to find the assassins, treat the farmers fairly, and not perceive them as agitators.[82] The Eastern Student Center (ESC) submitted a petition to the Ministry of Interior asking it to investigate the assassinations of the farmers and to arrest the assassins. The ESC viewed Intha's assassination as representing "a grave threat to the life, liberty, and rights of the people."[83] In its petition, the ESC stressed that farmers had peacefully petitioned and protested for justice, but had been ignored by the government. Even Prime Minister Kukrit Pramoj, who maintained that he could not intervene because the assassinations were the province of the police, urged them to hasten their investigation of the killings of the farmers following Intha's assassination.[84] Common to each demand was the hope that the police would identify the assassins. If the assassins were known and apprehended, perhaps the killings would cease.

Yet despite these urgings and admonitions, the police investigation into Intha's assassination began with denials of Intha's status as a farmer leader. One of the police investigators involved, the Chiang Mai provincial police commander,

Police Lieutenant General Thani Wiradecha, insisted on *evidence* that Intha was a farmer leader. He insisted on the need for "firm evidence that the dead person was the vice president of the Farmers' Federation of Thailand. You often say that the person who died was a farmer leader. But I haven't seen any evidence that these people were farmer leaders. If you have evidence, bring it to me."[85] What kind of *evidence* did Police Lieutenant General Thani want? If evidence was procured to his satisfaction, then he would "investigate it, and . . . have the police keep an eye on and watch over the farmer leaders. But the police can't keep vigil over them, because they have other citizens to watch over as well."[86] According to Therd Tharaninthorn, the *Thai Niu* reporter mentioned earlier, Intha was widely known throughout Chiang Mai. If Police Lieutenant General Thani had picked up a copy of *Thai Farmer*, he would have seen evidence that Intha Sribunruang was a leader and intellectual. If he had read *Thai Niu* or *Thin Thai*, the two major daily Chiang Mai papers, on almost any day between late 1974 and Intha's death in July 1975, he would have seen the name of Intha Sribunruang cited as an FFT leader. Yet perhaps nothing would have convinced Police Lieutenant General Thani that Intha Sribunruang was a leader of the people. By mid-1975, it was clear that a lot was at stake in doing so.

If the police recognized the assassinated leaders as such, they would also, by default, recognize the farmers' movement. Police Major General Suphak Vinin, commander of the Zone 5 Provincial Police, cited the illegality of the FFT as a reason to disregard Intha's status as the vice president of it as a factor in the investigation.[87] He suggested that many farmer activists had a history of antimonarchy sentiments and this may have angered their fellow villagers enough to kill them. In the specific case of Intha, Police Major General Suphak believed that "he was a radical whose activities and speeches might have caused conflict with rival political groups or endangered the interests of others."[88] In his comments, as well as those of many others, precisely what was meant by "interests" was left unspecified. Police Major General Suphak's mention of supposed antimonarchy sentiments compounded the void created by his reference to nonspecific "interests." To question his assertion would be to risk the charge of lèse-majesté.

Yet another police investigator, Nirandorn Witthayawuthakul, who was the deputy director general of the Chiang Mai Provincial Police, cited Intha's small shop as the reason for his assassination. He said, "Maybe it was a merchant. Because [Intha's] small-scale selling could have led to a conflict of interest with others."[89] However, Ruankham Sribunruang, Intha's wife, disputed this claim. She explained, "He wasn't a large merchant at all. He only sold a little bit, [and] we only saw a profit of 10–20 baht per day. How could that affect anyone's gains?"[90] In her view, his death was definitely a political killing. The Chiang Mai police seemed willing to consider every possible reason for Intha's killing other than his involvement in organizing his fellow farmers. Whether this resulted from honest confusion or machinations, the result was to focus attention away from the real dangers faced by farmer activists. In my assessment, the denial of the political nature of Intha's death further signals the importance of examining his work, as well as that of the FFT more broadly.

In addition to the various police denials and refusals to view Intha's assassination as related to his political activities, another disconcerting aspect of the investigation of his death was the reliance on false evidence. Shortly after his death, the police claimed to have found a letter written by Intha that shed light on his assassination. While the validity of the letter was never proven, in the crucial first days of the investigation the police insisted that its validity was beyond question. From the outset, I want to be very clear that what is at stake is not whether the police manufactured or planted the letter. They may have, as some alleged in this specific case and others commented about the assassinations more broadly.[91] However, other actors may have planted the letter, and the police may have been victims of their actions as well. What is of concern here, then, is the *use* of the letter by the police and its *effects* on the investigation and the farmers' movement.

On 4 August 1975, five days after Intha's assassination, a group of Chiang Mai provincial and regional police investigators went to visit his family. They gave the family a two-thousand-baht donation, as well as a thousand baht to make merit for Intha. The police also offered that if the family had any troubles, they would be more than happy to assist them. Then, during the same meeting, they showed Ruankham a signature on a piece of paper and asked her to certify that it was Intha's. This signature was on a letter that the police alleged Intha wrote and signed shortly before his death. Although the contents of the letter were made public and printed in *Baan Muang* newspaper on 8 August 1975, initially Police Lieutenant General Thani Wiradecha refused to show Ruankham anything other than the signature.[92]

When the police brought the letter to Ruankham, they claimed that it was found by a woman named Amporn Sirimuk, a fellow villager, two hours after the assassination. Amporn claimed to have taken it from a table in Intha's house before turning it in to the district officer. The letter was allegedly addressed to Prime Minister Kukrit Pramoj. In it, Intha supposedly wrote that he was prepared to break with the students because he had seen that they "only mislead and do not really do what they say."[93] In addition, Intha allegedly wrote that he planned to join the prime minister's Social Action Party (SAP) and would bring many FFT members with him as well. All of this was contingent on the prime minister allocating land to Intha's family personally.[94]

Ruankham refused to certify the signature as Intha's. She and her eldest son, Uthai, both said that although the signature was similar to Intha's, it was not his. Uthai brought out another document with Intha's signature on it to show the police the difference. Even further, Uthai noted that Intha always asked his advice about writing, since he had only completed grade 4. Intha had not consulted him about this letter, and Uthai felt certain that he would have done so had he been writing a letter to the prime minister.[95]

While the veracity of the letter was immediately disputed by student and FFT activists, and declared a fake by Police Director General Phoj by 7 August, there are four significant implications of the alleged letter. One, it offered an explanation for the assassination that simultaneously painted the students and farmers as a violent and divided group. Two, in so doing, it shifted the emphasis away from the possibility that state or parastate forces were behind the assassination. Three, the letter can be read as an attempt to discredit Intha as a leader of the FFT and the work he did fighting for the farmers and justice in Thai society. Four, and most potentially damaging, student groups reported that Uthai Sribunruang commented that shortly before his assassination, Intha had been approached by Asa Meksawan, the Chiang Mai governor. Asa allegedly offered Intha land and money if he left the FFT and stopped criticizing state policies and actions. Intha refused.[96] A few weeks later, he was dead.

The violence and profound disruption of the assassinations did not stop with the killing of the FFT leaders but continued to affect their families in a variety of ways following their deaths. When Intha died, his wife Ruankham was forty-one years old; she and Intha had been married for twenty-three years. After he died, she took sole responsibility for their whole family. Their livelihood became less secure. Ruankham was only able to make enough at the shop to feed the family from day to day.[97] And Ruankham had to deal not only with financial difficulty but with the continual denial of her husband's life.

This was sharply illustrated in an interview conducted months after Intha's assassination in which Ruankham offered another set of reasons why the letter allegedly found in her house after Intha's death was false. This time her reasons exceeded those of the mechanics of writing or signatures. Ruankham said that she did not know why the police or other state officials would want to produce, or validate, the letter. But she did say, "The letter alleges that Pho Luang Intha wanted to leave the Socialist Party. That isn't true. Because while we were together, everything I heard, was that Pho Intha was a very sincere person. And he was one person who unfailingly believed in the path of socialism."[98] Before his death, Intha worked closely with Inson Buakhiew, Dr. Bunsanong Punyodhayana, and other leaders of the Socialist Party of Thailand on shared goals of justice for farmers and workers.[99] She further explained, "It is impossible for sure that Pho Intha would turn to become a member of the SAP, since he didn't like the policy of the party and the various actions of the government that did not solve the problems and left the people dissatisfied, especially around issues of land rent control."[100] Given Intha's organizing and writing in *Thai Farmer*, it seems unlikely that he would have abandoned his alliances with students and the SPT to join the SAP.[101]

Most perplexing and troubling of the various Thai state responses to Intha's death was that of Asa Meksawan, the governor of Chiang Mai province.

Asa was particularly concerned with the assassination of Intha. On 1 August he went to the Saraphi district police station to urge the police to apprehend the assassin quickly. The same day he gave a thousand baht to make merit for Intha.[102] He attended Intha's funeral on 4 August 1975 and publicly said, "He was a good person, he was purposeful, when he spoke he knew what he was talking about."[103]

Yet the day after the funeral Asa held a press conference at the Chiang Mai Provincial Office to clarify his position vis-à-vis Intha. The day of the funeral, *Prachathipatai* newspaper reported that Asa had recently warned Intha of pending violence against the farmers at the hands of the Nawaphon. The article quoted Asa as telling Intha, "Presently over a hundred Nawaphon assassins are coming to take action. Be careful, Mr. Intha, take care of yourself."[104] Along with the Red Gaurs and the Village Scouts, the Nawaphon was a significant right-wing parastate group involved in several kinds of violence in the period between 1973 and 1976. When asked directly about the Nawaphon's role in the assassinations of the farmers, Wattana Kiewvimol, the founder, denied any involvement.[105] Today the assassinations of Intha and the FFT leaders continue to be attributed colloquially to the Nawaphon both by surviving activists from that period and by younger generations. Yet, as Jim Glassman notes, "Since much of the violence that occurred during the 1973 to 1976 period was unofficially sanctioned by state officials, there have rarely been revelations as to who was responsible, and thus it is difficult to establish precisely what activities might have been carried out by Nawaphon as opposed to other groups."[106]

At the press conference, Asa unequivocally denied that he had ever met with Intha to convey this warning. He claimed that he had only met Intha when he "led the farmers to the provincial office to petition for their living, for their mouths and stomachs. . . . [B]ut Mr. Intha Sribunruang never met individually with the provincial governor of Chiang Mai."[107] He clarified that his brief statements at Intha's funeral were his personal views, not those of the provincial government. Asa said that he felt very sorry about Intha's death, and uneasy.[108] Whether or not Asa did warn Intha about the possible violence at the hands of the Nawaphon, his denial is unsurprising given the reputation of the Nawaphon for killings and other violence. The news report did not reveal who, or what, caused Asa to call the press conference.

In the interview with *Chaturat* eleven days before his assassination, Intha cited the inability of the government to understand the material urgency of the work of the FFT. "As for the government," he said, "I think the government does not agree with the demands of the farmers about our livelihood. Every day the government eats the rice of the farmers. And then they turn around and destroy the farmers at every chance, overtly and covertly."[109] Asa Meksawan's unease over Intha's death can be read as prophetic of the violence that was yet to come.

Who Is Named, and Who Is Unnameable?

Out of all of the assassinations of farmer leaders, only in the case of Intha Sribunruang was an arrest made. Visooth Ruamchai, a twenty-four-year-old man from Sansai district in Chiang Mai province, was arrested on 10 August 1975 while walking near Tha Pae gate in Chiang Mai city.[110] Visooth was a seasoned criminal and had served time in prison in Phitsanulok on charges of accessory to murder and selling drugs. Although the gun was not recovered, a copy of a threatening letter and twenty thousand baht in cash was found on his person.[111] After initially denying that he killed Intha, Visooth confessed that he was paid five thousand baht to kill him.[112] When asked who paid him, Visooth claimed that it was the Committee for State Security (KGB).[113] Despite Visooth's claims of involvement from Moscow, the Chiang Mai police asserted that the forces behind the assassination were in Chiang Rai.[114]

Although the gun used to kill Intha was not recovered, the case against Visooth remained firm because he confessed and more than ten witnesses to the assassination identified him as the assassin.[115] In the period leading up to the court case, the primary witness, one of Intha's neighbors, was reportedly visited by Visooth's friends and asked how much money it would take for him to retract his identification of Visooth as the gunman. The witness refused to retract his identification, and on 22 October 1975, the first hearing in the case was held. Despite his earlier confession, Visooth denied that he killed Intha.[116] In the months that followed, under circumstances that remain unclear, the case against Visooth was dropped.

Intha's life and death offer evidence of how the 1974 LRCA, and the work of the FFT in a broad sense, reconfigured rural, and rural-urban, relations. These reconfigurations at once offered the promise of a brighter future for some segments of Thai society and spelled doom for others. Even if the opponents of the farmers were ultimately able to use extrajudicial means to silence or defeat farmers in land rent disputes, for example, farmers understood their right to dispute and had the tools and allies to legally do so. The extrajudicial actions of their opponents, landowning and otherwise, may be read as indicative of the success of the FFT's organizing to spread and use the 1974 LRCA.

In the face of state inaction to protect the farmers, the NSC sent over two hundred people to Chiang Mai to protect and support farmers in districts throughout Chiang Mai and Lamphun provinces.[117] Despite their work, harassment and assassination of the farmers continued. In late 1975 and 1976, the FFT largely disappeared from public sight and farmers and students took their struggles underground. The sharp polarization of Thai society in 1975 created a culture of impunity in which it was possible for those with power to kill their opponents without fear of censure or punishment. The assassinations were not only deadly, but untraceable.

At the very moment that the assassins were unnameable, progressive activists were too easily nameable. T., a former teacher and SPT activist, told me that he was afraid to go to the funerals of the assassinated FFT leaders in July and August 1975. T. recalled that he and others were afraid to go to the funerals because they suspected that there were members of Nawaphon and intelligence agents present. To attend was to mark oneself as a progressive, and therefore a future candidate for assassination. As a result, most of the funerals were only attended by the families of the assassinated people. In turn, T. explained, the opposing side was able to say "Look, this person wasn't important, wasn't beloved by the people." The polarized and contentious atmosphere made it impossible for people even to mourn and honor the dead properly. Like other forms of the political, counterrevolution is also personal.

5

A State in Disarray

Assassination is planned. Assassination is determined. There is no uncertainty; pure intention. Assassination axes jaggedly through the fabric of life, the bearable and borne, tears the assuaging progression of past into present and future. Murder strikes the lives corollary to an individual; assassination rips the life of a country, laying bare ganglia that civil institutions have been in the process of covering with flesh. Assassination is a gash.

Nadine Gordimer, *None to Accompany Me*

When fundamental premises of an order begin to erode, or simply begin to be exposed as fundamental premises, what reactive political formations emerge—and what anxieties, tensions, or binds do they carry?

Wendy Brown, *Politics out of History*

In *None to Accompany Me*, Nadine Gordimer's first postapartheid novel, political assassination signaled the lingering effects of a brutal state regime backed by a divided South African society. The end of the state policy of apartheid did not mean that everyone in the country—whether officially part of the ousted regime or simply its beneficiary—supported the end of white, European supremacy. Despite regime change, reactionary violence remained, to use Gordimer's language, in excess of the ability of either state or civil institutions to contain.[1] Similarly, neither the farmers themselves nor various Thai state actors were able to keep Intha Sribunruang and other FFT leaders safe in 1975. Not only were farmers assassinated in public view, but their assassins operated with impunity—whether due to a lack of ability (as they claimed) or a lack of will on the part of the Thai police.

Yet while assassination of young black leaders indicated the remaining effects of polarization and violence as a new, more just South African society was dawning, the assassination of Intha foretold the opposite in Thailand. His assassination marked the beginning of intensified counterrevolution, symptomized by a sharply divided society and a state in increasing disarray, marked by internal confusion and disorder, which often seeped into broad public view. In the weeks following Intha's death, a series of events sliced through the Thai nation. It began with the arrest of eight farmer leaders and one student leader under suspicious circumstances in Lamphun province on the day of Intha's funeral, 3 August 1975. When their arrests were met with protests calling for an explanation, various local and central state officials all denied ordering the arrests. After two weeks of widespread demonstrations and internal state conflict, the nine arrested activists were released.

Immediately, citizen opponents of the release launched their own protests. In short order, the police, initially threatening to strike over an unrelated issue, joined the protests of the release. Both the initial opponents of the release and the police cited the breakdown of the law into mob rule as the reason for their protests. The protests by the police climaxed in the sacking of Prime Minister Kukrit Pramoj's house in the early hours of 20 August 1975. Given their insistence that the breakdown of law was the raison d'être of their protests, the choice by the police to storm and loot the elected prime minister's house *while in uniform* raises serious questions about the exercise of power, authority, and influence.

It is not surprising that counterrevolution turned on the axis of law. What made the tenant farmers' struggle revolutionary was that they claimed the law as a tool that they could use to secure justice and improve their lives. Their actions as subjects—not only objects—of the law were deeply destabilizing to various segments of the Thai state and landholding elites. Counterrevolution aimed to reverse the new state of affairs. Yet while the events of August 1975 greatly damaged and ultimately interrupted the tenancy struggle, the transformations wrought by the farmers and students could not be fully undone. Instead, the at times bizarre forms of counterrevolution emphasized the changes that had taken place. During this series of events, nearly every Thai citizen experienced, as participant or witness, the muddling of the meaning of *law* itself.[2] If law is "both a system of meaning and an institutional structure backed by the political power of the state," then what happens when this system of meaning is in flux and the political power of the state is fragmented, perhaps beyond repair?[3] This crisis of flux—of politics and meaning—was signaled by the law itself becoming the subject of contention and struggle—evidenced by claims of various progressive, conservative, and state forces to follow the law, uphold the law, and restore the law. While the ostensible object of these calls was the text of the law, they often referenced additional, informal but ingrained, systems of meaning.

The simultaneous emptying and oversaturation of the meaning of law was accompanied by what I identify, informed by Philip Abrams, as the increasing disarray of the Thai state. In 1975–76, different parts of the Thai state continually acted to deny the claims of activists, obfuscated their own roles, and contradicted one another.[4] Although any state is always partially fragmented, as competing agencies and actors realign and compete for their visions of rule to be dominant, what made this moment significant is that this fragmentation was both a public act and appeared to be a strategy of governance. In other words, what if this striking disunity of the Thai state was not seen as a temporary aberration but rather as constitutive of the state and its violence(s)? How might this shift affect readings of the assassinations, the series of events they precipitated, and the 6 October 1976 massacre and what followed? The fragmented state in disarray and the emptying of the meaning of the law created the conditions for the boundary between law and extrajudicial violence to become very faint, if not to disappear altogether. A particular danger emerged when the violation of the law was claimed to be in the service of the restoration or protection of the law. This danger became deadly when it was the police—those officially charged with enforcing the law—who advocated its violation.

A Critical Theory and Practice against the State

Even as conservative pundits and some state officials castigated students for "creating chaos," and described assassinated farmers as "agitators," the Thai state itself was marked by contradiction, conflict, and real or stated failures to communicate among different officials, departments, and ministries. The state was a site, not only an actor, of struggle.[5] In particular, as I examined the assassination of Intha Sribunruang and the series of events that followed in its wake, the multiple voices and precise lack of coordination across various parts of the Thai state were striking.

The fragmented and weak nature of the Thai state contributed to creating the conditions under which activist leaders could be assassinated in broad daylight, their assassins never apprehended, and their colleagues arrested on trumped-up charges. In addition, the disunity (and at times, open hostility) among different state agencies helped create the opening for the emergence of a range of right-wing and parastate organizations. These organizations operated with varying degrees of closeness, official and otherwise, to various state officials and ministries. Without exception, they identified themselves as defenders of the Thai nation, Buddhist religion, and the monarchy.[6] At times the zeal to protect the nation erupted into direct calls for violence against their fellow citizens, as in the case of Phra Kittivuddho, a monk and Nawaphon member who claimed that "Killing communists is not demeritorious" in 1976.[7] As I explored earlier, how often this call translated into material violence is nearly impossible to ascertain. What can be posited, however, is that the official and unofficial relationships between parastate groups and various state officials and agencies bear some responsibility for the inability to answer this question.

The urgency with which I write in this chapter is derived largely from the continuing unnameability of the assassins of the farmers. Chief among my concerns is how to critically question and understand state roles in both the assassinations and the production of unnameability. In order to think about the various roles of different state actors and institutions, here I offer an analysis of the multiplicity of the state, which is usually masked by the day-to-day operations of rule. When day-to-day operations break down, and cannot be performed, the fiction of rule in the name of "the state" is made apparent. This makes the series of events in August 1975 an exemplary site at which to consider the disunity of the Thai state, as well as the broader, comparative implications. Before proceeding, therefore, I clarify what I mean by "the state."

Informed by Philip Abrams, I examine "the Thai state" as a collection of competing actors and agencies and their actions, as well as the ideas and actions that citizens, critics, and those actors and agencies attribute to it. To avoid mystifying the Thai state, whenever possible I name the *specific* state official, ministry, or defense agency to which I refer. While I have tried to do this throughout my analysis, at times I slipped into the shorthand "the Thai state," often because further specificity was not available. This should not be taken to indicate that the Thai state existed without fragmentation before August 1975, and then fragmented later, but rather that the always-ongoing process of state formation and fragmentation reached a particular crisis. Following Intha Sribunruang's assassination, there were many moments at which different offices, ministries, and defense factions took directly opposing (and often contradictory) positions in relation to one another. The choice to center my analysis of the Thai state on the assassinations and series of events that followed is intentional. Abrams privileges violence as a site at which the impossible unity of the state can be broken down analytically. Subjection is backed up by prisons, armies, immigration, and other disciplinary forces.[8] Connecting these entities with the state, then "silences protest, excuses force, and convinces almost all of us that the fate of the victims is just and necessary."[9] Refusing to slip into the catchall phrase "the state," and instead specifying a branch of the Provincial Police or a leader in the Ministry of Interior, therefore also prevents mystification. This is a key moment for a critical analysis of, and against, the state.

Not only is the moment of violence an exemplary time to parse the constituent elements of a state in disarray; it is also, to use Walter Benjamin's terms, a "moment of danger."[10] Abrams suggests that when the link between bodies of violence and the state is broken, transformative effects follow. When the link is broken, he argues, "*real hidden powers emerge. And when they do they are not the powers of the state but of armies of liberation or repression, foreign governments, guerilla movements, soviets, juntas, parties, classes.*"[11] In the context of mid-1975 Thailand, this list also includes individuals and factions within the police, army, and government ministries who acted in concert with right-wing parastate groups such as the Nawaphon, Red Gaurs, and Village Scouts.[12]

With this in mind, what was the nature of the relationships, official and unofficial, between state actors and often violent parastate groups? While the record of direct material or other support remains largely inaccessible, what kinds of violent parastate action against progressive activists may have been ignored, tolerated, or even encouraged by state actors?[13] Further, even within the context of the fragmentary state in disarray, there were limits to the dissent that individuals operating under the auspices of the Thai state could broach. What do these limits, and the penalties for crossing them, indicate about the nature of the constituent disunity of the state?

During the series of events following Intha's assassination that culminated in the sacking of Prime Minister Kukrit Pramoj's residence, representations of the police and Ministry of Interior emerge that indicate, at the very least, profound disunity. My account is drawn from Chiang Mai and Bangkok newspapers, as well as activist archival documents. In other words, my analysis of the Thai state in disarray is not based on an exclusive interview with a highly placed retired civil servant or other state insider. The most remarkable aspect of the fragmented Thai state was the public nature of the contradictions, tension, and sheer lack of coordination present. Every citizen was a witness.

The Arrests

Intha Sribunruang's prominence, as well as the assassinations that preceded his, catalyzed a mass mobilization of students, professors, farmers, and other people in the aftermath of his assassination. They called on the prime minister, the Ministry of Interior, and the police to arrest the assassins of the farmers and to prevent further assassinations of progressive activists.

Instead, on the day of his funeral, nine of Intha's colleagues were arrested on a range of charges covering two separate incidents in neighboring Lamphun province. The following individuals were arrested:

1. Bunma Ari (FFT president, Lamphun province)
2. Inkham Sinthornthong (FFT vice president, Lamphun province)
3. Intha Sriwongwan (FFT treasurer, Lamphun province)
4. Biew Daman (FFT member)
5. Khan Daman (FFT member)
6. La Manichai (FFT member)
7. Saengchu Khamsao (FFT member)
8. Oonruan Chaisak (FFT member)
9. Chatri Hutanuwat (Farmer Project activist and fourth-year medical student at CMU).[14]

The nine were initially held without bail at the Lamphun police station.[15] Bail was later set at thirty thousand baht per person.[16] From the beginning, the nine chose not to post bail as a critique of the illegitimacy of the arrests. Kriangkamol

Laophairoj, the secretary-general of the NSCT, sent a telegram to northern student leaders asking them not to bail out the nine.[17] Pradap Manurasada, the in-house FFT lawyer and legal educator, served as the lawyer for the nine.[18]

From the beginning the arrests were surrounded by irregularities, shifting stories, and unconfirmed rumors. For example, one Chiang Mai newspaper heralded the arrests with a headline reading "Big-Time Arrest of Agitators, Many Documents to Stir up Villagers Found."[19] These documents supposedly urged the masses to fight state officials. Among them was a collection of photocopied articles by Che Guevara on the situation and roles of young people in society.[20] The next day further details about the seized documents were forthcoming. They included a large number of books about communist China and posters that reportedly read: "Enemies of students: 1. feudal capitalists, high classes with special rights above ordinary citizens; 2. capitalists in the civil service who serve imperialism; 3. foreign imperialism of the United States of America and Japan."[21] Only one day later, the description of these documents grew more sinister and less precise: "documents inciting and spreading communism."[22] They were reportedly found in the houses of the farmers.[23] All of the documents were immediately seized as evidence. Although possession of these documents and books on their own was not yet banned by law, as it would be following 6 October 1976, here they were read as evidence suggestive of criminal behavior. The detailed reporting about the documents seems to indicate that mere possession was conceived as dangerous by the police.

Other reports suggest that the farmers may have been apprehended by the police under false pretenses. One villager who witnessed the arrests of farmer leaders in his village said that he heard police telling the farmers that they "want to take you into police custody because right now farmer leaders are being killed frequently. This is for [your] protection."[24] When the villager went to follow up at the police station, however, he was told that the farmers were being charged with crimes.

Comments made by the police director general, Phoj Phekanan, following the initial round of arrests raise additional questions about police intentions and actions. On 6 August, he said that additional farmers and students would be arrested because "the police have a namelist of a number of farmer and student activists who have 'committed crimes' on various occasions."[25] Although no further arrests were made at this time, the existence of a list of individuals who had supposedly committed crimes is troubling. If the crimes had already been committed, why would the police wait to make arrests? Who compiled these lists, and what criteria were used?

Examination of the crimes with which the nine activists were charged reveals a number of further irregularities. The eight farmers and one student were arrested on a range of charges covering two separate incidents. One set of charges alleged that farmer leaders had detained a mine owner and district officer in Mae Tha district in Lamphun, as well as engaged in "mobilizing the masses and encouraging them to disobey the law."[26] What actually happened is that, concerned with the effects of a coal mine on their water supply and crops, villagers held a protest at the offices of the Mae Wa antimony mine. When the mine was initially opened, the mining company promised to dispose of the harmful mine waste properly. However, it failed to do so and instead contaminated the villagers' water supply and destroyed their crops. In protest, six hundred villagers surrounded the mine and forced the workers to leave. When ten policemen came to the mine, the villagers disarmed them.[27] Following the demonstration, they held a meeting with the mine owner and the district officer that lasted deep into the night. The villagers refused to leave until the owner agreed to their demands, but they did not "detain" him or the district officer.[28] The incident took place on 12 May, but the arrest papers were not drawn up until 27 June.[29]

The second set of charges alleged that the farmers burned down a teak forest and engaged in "mobilizing the masses and encouraging them to disobey the law."[30] In this case, *one* tree was burned down, but there is a broader context. On 4 April 1975, an area of Lamphun province was designated a forest preservation area. As some of this area had been used for subsistence farming, the Ministry of Interior ruled that any land that had been used for subsistence could continue to be used as such. When government forestry officers planted a tree on this land, in contravention of this ruling, the farmers reacted by setting the tree on fire.[31] This incident occurred on 6 June, and the arrest papers were drawn up on 10 June.[32]

Many people found the temporal element of the arrests problematic. As one commentator in *Athipat*, the NSCT's newspaper, put it, if the arrest papers for both incidents were drawn up in June, why did no one take action until August, when members of the public were concerned with the issue of farmer assassinations?[33] This disagreement was echoed by some Thai state officials. The deputy communications minister, Anant Chaisaeng, said, "Personally I do not agree with such mass arrests. The crimes were committed three months ago. Why did police not make the arrest then?" He further asserted, "Right now is not the proper time to make such arrests because many farmer leaders have been killed."[34] Witnessing the delayed arrests, observers may have wondered if they, too, would be found retroactively suspect. The large number of police personnel involved and the coordination required to carry out the simultaneous raids to arrest the nine only compounded the injury resulting from the denials made by various police officials that they lacked sufficient resources to keep the farmer leaders safe.

Marut Bunnag, president of the Lawyers' Society of Thailand, criticized the length of time between the two incidents and the arrests as inappropriate. The accusation that the nine had "incited the masses" was of even greater concern to Marut. The farmers and student leaders were not criminals, he noted. If the government was going to bring the charge of inciting the masses, they "must have evidence that shows it clearly."[35] Marut argued that if they had told people to take up arms to topple the government, the charge could stand, but "[i]f they say that they want to change the government, then it cannot be considered treasonous.... Therefore, in line with the law, one should have the view that the police must find very clear evidence before proceeding."[36] Marut's observations give weight to the idea that at this time the distinction between criticism of the government and outright insurgency was becoming blurred. Critical discussion, and even thoughts, of dissent were becoming criminalized.

In addition, there was initial confusion about *who* ordered the arrests. Prime Minister Kukrit Pramoj immediately denied any involvement. Numerous high-ranking officials within the Ministry of Interior and the Department of Police, which is a division of the Ministry of Interior, denied being behind the arrests. Both the minister (Buntheng Thongsawat) and the deputy minister of interior (Chalor Wannaphut) claimed that the police ordered the arrests and they did not know about them ahead of time. The police director general (Police General Phoj Phekanan) claimed to know nothing about the arrest order. The Lamphun provincial police commander (Police Lieutenant General Sanan Narinsorasak) claimed that the deputy police director general (Police Lieutenant General Montchai Phunkhongchuen) ordered the Lamphun deputy provincial police commander (Police Major General Suthat Sukhumwat) to carry out the arrests; he himself claimed no involvement or knowledge. The Lamphun deputy commander, however, claimed that the order was given by the police director general, who, as you will remember, denied any knowledge. The deputy police director general, who also headed a special crime suppression division, initially claimed that the order came from the second deputy minister of interior (Bunlert Lertpreecha), with the cooperation of the deputy minister of interior.[37] However, as I noted at the beginning of the paragraph, the deputy minister of interior claimed that he did not know about the arrests ahead of time.

Yet, despite the confusion, one day after the arrests the deputy police director general–cum–head of the crime suppression division (Police Lieutenant General Montchai Phunkhongchuen) admitted to ordering the arrests.[38] The police director general did not know about them because the deputy police director general had acted in his capacity as the head of crime suppression, which was directly under the minister of interior, not within the Department of Police. Police Director General Phoj commented that the order could have come from within the Ministry of Interior itself, or from elsewhere. Commenting on Phoj's lack of prior knowledge of the planned arrests, one Chiang Mai newspaper noted, "There is a lot of criticism in many circles. Some say that in the Department of Police there was disagreement over the arrests of the suspects."[39] In this case, and given the state of confusion, it is worth reiterating that no one within the leadership of the Ministry of Interior claimed prior knowledge of the arrests. Given that the minister of interior and the deputy minister of interior denied involvement, Phoj's assertion of *elsewhere* seems likely. But where?

Although Phoj claimed initial ignorance about the arrests, he soon put the weight of his office behind them. When asked to explain the arrests of the nine in Lamphun, he said, "There's nothing that I need to clarify, because the evidence is already clear."[40] When a reporter pushed the question of evidence, the director said, "Eh, you don't have to worry. The evidence is really good."[41]

Those arrested offered a contrasting view on the issue of evidence. On 5 August 1975, *Chaturat* magazine interviewed three of the nine arrested. Despite Police Director General Phoj's insistence on the high quality of the evidence, Inkham Sinthornthong, who was one of the farmers arrested in connection to the events at the Mae Wa mine, said that he was not even present at the demonstration at the mine.[42] Bunma Ari, another farmer arrested in connection with the mine protests, was also not present. Expressing confusion at his arrest, Bunma commented, "We work for a living in the way of villagers, [and] we don't cause trouble for anybody."[43]

After those two brief statements, the jail officials took the two farmers back and let Chatri Hutanuwat, the sole student arrested, remain to continue talking to the *Chaturat* reporter.[44] Chatri explained that he began working with farmers in 1974. Before that he had been a typical university student and spent his free time having fun. But in 1974, he went to help families affected by a severe flood outside Chiang Mai city. While working, he met four farming children who had no rice to eat. Chatri decided that day to work with the farmers in their struggle for justice. He had done so up until the moment of his arrest.[45] In contrast to the confusion about who ordered the arrests and Police Director General Phoj's oblique references to evidence, Chatri and Bunma were strikingly clear in their objectives. In the context of the criminalization of dissenting action and thought, perhaps even the call for an ability to make a living and fill one's belly with rice was becoming seditious.

The Protests

Attempting to preempt protests around the arrests of the nine activists, on 7 August the Ministry of Interior issued a declaration in which it insisted that it was making progress on the assassinations. It cited this as difficult because in the four months between 13 April and 3 August, there had been nine assassinations of farmer leaders and over two hundred total murders.[46] In addition, in the same declaration the ministry insisted that the cases against the nine arrested activists were not connected to the assassinations.[47]

Their assertions rang hollow for many and came too late to prevent the growing protests. From the beginning, student leaders found claims of the lack of connection between the two sets of events unacceptable. Shortly after the arrests, the CMU Students' Organization issued a statement citing the long-standing struggle of the farmers and the injustice of their deaths. It criticized Prime Minister Kukrit Pramoj for not taking concrete action and closed by saying, "We want to express our opposition and condemnation of the actions without justice of the ruling classes, the cruelty of the landowners who conspire with the reactionary ruling classes, and ask for the support of the struggle of the farmers in every way."[48] Even here, as the students used radical language (inflammatory in the eyes of some), they were not urging anyone to violence.

The protests soon moved to the streets. On 5 August, approximately four hundred students met late into the night in the CMU Student Union building to develop a plan for further action.[49] They decided to go to Lamphun on the morning of 6 August to protest and visit the arrested activists.

On 6 August, approximately three hundred CMU students held an open debate in front of the Lamphun police station. They proclaimed, "The arrest is an arrest like that of an untamed ruler. There's no reason. Except that the Department of Police is contradicting itself."[50] The disarray and fragmentation of the Thai state not only reflects the division of departments and ministries but also reflects the rise of internal dissension. What is notable here is that this inter- and intraministry dissension did not lead to an immediate coup; another fourteen months passed before a coup created a sweeping change in the form and head of government. What kinds of violence at the hands of state actors—against other state actors and citizens—was made possible as this kind of tension was sustained?

The protestors carried banners criticizing the prime minister, the police, and the provincial governor. They used megaphones to proclaim their ideas in front of the Lamphun police station.[51] The protesting students had no way of knowing that in a few days the Department of Police would act in such a way as to make their internal contradictions starkly visible to the entire nation.

In the charged atmosphere of the time, not only were there critics of the arrests but also overt supporters of them. The students faced an immediate response to their protests from a group of supporters in Lamphun. Somboon Muangsawan, a Lamphun resident, went to observe the student protests and listen to the debate. He grew agitated and left the area in front of the police station. A short time later he returned with seven other men and three pickup trucks. They called themselves the Lamphun Province Farmer Agriculturalist Group (Klum Kasetakon Chao Na Changwat Lamphun). They watched the protesting students and then circled them in the trucks, shouting at them through megaphones. They accused the students of looking down on Lamphun people.[52] This accusation may seem odd, as the students had come to Lamphun to visit the arrested nine, eight of whom were farmers from Lamphun. Understood differently, their accusation may have been an attempt to undermine student-farmer solidarity and create hostility toward the students in the minds of other Lamphun people.

Somboon and his colleagues in the Lamphun Province Farmer Agriculturalist Group urged the Lamphun people present not to listen to the students and insisted that the arrests had been appropriate.[53] The situation grew tense, and some students wanted to leave. However, the counterprotestors soon left and no one was hurt.[54]

By 6 August, CMU was closed, and many students were boycotting classes at Thammasat and Ramkhamhaeng Universities, demanding the release of the nine.[55] Student unions at Chulalongkorn, Mahidol, and other universities called for students to protest; teachers' colleges were planning to shut down also.[56] By 7 August, all the universities in Bangkok except Kasetsart were closed.[57] In addition to the protests in the streets, many different groups issued declarations calling for the release of those arrested and action to stop the assassinations.[58]

Between 4 and 8 August, the number of protestors calling for the release of the nine grew to over ten thousand in Bangkok alone.[59] However, the centers of the protests, and the growing counterprotests, were Chiang Mai and Lamphun. On 7 August, at 3:00 p.m., approximately three thousand students massed inside the gates of CMU. At 4:30 the demonstrators left the campus and passed Suan Dok Hospital on their way to the Tha Pae gate in Chiang Mai city. The march was accompanied by vehicles using megaphones to broadcast their demands. Those marching held big banners and posters that decried the assassinations of the farmers and the arrests of the nine.

When the marchers arrived at Tha Pae, they were joined by approximately a thousand students from Chiang Mai Teachers' College. Theerachai Maruekhaphitak, the head of the political wing of the NSCT, as well as a CMU student and former NSC president, said that the protests had two purposes: to demand state action to stop the assassinations of the farmers and to demand the release of the nine arrested activists. The NSCT called for the state to investigate whether the arrests of the nine had been just. The mother of Chatri Hutanuwat, the arrested student among the nine, traveled to Chiang Mai from Bangkok to speak at the rally. Chatri himself sent a letter from jail, urging people to continue struggling and fighting. After midnight, the protest started to break up as students and other supporters returned home. By the morning all but twenty protestors had left.[60]

On 7 August, members of the Lamphun Province Farmer Agriculturalist Group issued a declaration in which they insisted that they loved peace, order, and quiet in Lamphun. They claimed that the majority of farmers in Lamphun did not agree with the protestors' demand that the nine be released; their claim was not backed up with numbers or other supporting evidence.[61] At this time there were also reports that important documents and valuables were being removed from the governor's residence and that the police were preparing to defend him.[62]

On 8 August, approximately one thousand students assembled again at Tha Pae and continued protesting for the release of the nine and a halt to the assassination of the farmers. While they were protesting, a bomb went off at the edge of the Tha Pae area. No one was hurt. A few seconds later, a second bomb went off. Five people were hurt by the second bomb and were taken to the hospital.

After the second bomb, a female student took the podium and challenged the opposition to set off another bomb. She insisted that she was ready to die. Then a third bomb went off very close to the podium. However, it did not explode completely, and the female student and many others in the packed area were not hurt. The bombs were later described as having been placed by a "hidden hand" (*mu mut*).[63] No arrests were made. At this time, demonstrations against the students were ongoing in neighboring Lamphun province.[64]

The protests reached a zenith on 12 August. Approximately three thousand people, comprised of CMU, Teachers' College, and other students from Chiang Mai; NSC activists; and representatives from the NSCT in Bangkok who had traveled north were massed at the provincial hall in downtown Chiang Mai.[65] The counterprotests reached a high point on 12 August as well. A group of approximately three hundred people calling themselves Young People of Chiang Mai (Klum Num Sao Chiang Mai), began protesting at 9:00 a.m. around the city. They claimed that the protesting students had "created chaos in Chiang Mai, which has been a tranquil and beautiful city for a long time, and has long-standing traditions and customs."[66] The reference to "traditions and customs" here is significant. The refrain is one frequently heard as part of conservative protests against change. But here the context begs the question of what traditions and customs the Young People of Chiang Mai viewed the NSCT and NSC as destroying, and themselves as protecting. At a time when the signifier *communist* had come to include almost anything even proximate to a criticism of (let alone a threat to) the status quo, perhaps the phrase "traditions and customs" had become equally empty.

The Young People of Chiang Mai further claimed that the students and farmers who were protesting were "destroying the tranquility and order in the homeland, and are inciting the people to devalue the sacredness of law, which is very inappropriate."[67] The sacredness at stake here was a claim to the role of landowners and right-wing actors to control the law and determine who became its subjects. Over the next weeks, the *law* came into increasing crisis. The claim of the members of the Young People raises the question of what they meant by *law*. The students and farmers they criticized protested the farmer assassinations and the arrests of the nine as *unjust*. Yet the Young People linked *law* to *order*. As they proceeded from an area close to the governor's house on the banks of the Ping River up to Tha Pae gate, where the other protestors were massed, they handed out fliers, carried posters, and waved the Thai flag.[68] When they arrived at Tha Pae, the massed students and farmers invited them to take the podium and speak. The Young People refused and instead used megaphones to criticize the students from the edge of the crowd.[69] While the signifiers *communist*, *law*, and *order* may have been in the process of being emptied (or perhaps overfilled), *student* was not. The Young People refused the identification of student, although some of them must have been enrolled in a secondary school, technical college, or university. Paradoxically, given their stated desire for peace and tranquility, by remaining at the edge of the crowd the Young People defiantly denied its possibility.

The Release

The charges against the nine arrested activists did not stick. At 2:00 p.m. on 14 August, the Lamphun provincial prosecutor called the provincial office to inform the governor that the charges against the nine individuals were being dropped due to lack of evidence. At 5:00, the regional prosecutor, the Lamphun and Chiang Mai provincial prosecutors, and the assistant provincial prosecutor for Lamphun (who was the official in direct charge of the case) went in person to the provincial hall to ask for their release. The nine appeared in court at 5:30. The judge read the dismissal of the charges. At 5:44, after being held for eleven days, the eight farmers and one student were set free.[70]

Immediately following their release, the nine went to Chiang Mai to speak at the protests that were continuing in front of the provincial hall. Over three thousand people were waiting to receive them.[71] When they arrived, they took the stage and thanked the people present for protesting and securing their release.[72] After their release, the NSCT sent an urgent telegram asking the nine to travel to Bangkok. The protestors refused to believe that the nine had been released until they saw concrete evidence of it. The nine traveled to Bangkok on 16 August and went to rallies at Thammasat University, Chulalongkorn University, and Sanam Luang.[73] At Sanam Luang, Chatri Hutanuwat cited his and the others' release as a victory for the people. He vowed to continue struggling for the rights of the farmers.[74] The events of the previous eleven days would make doing so, at least openly, difficult.

On the release of the nine, the NSCT met with Prime Minister Kukrit. He assured them in a written declaration that he was doing everything possible to find the assassins of the farmers.[75] Yet he also encouraged the students to stop protesting, "because it will instigate a reaction from another group."[76] On hearing Kukrit's statement, Thirayuth Bunmi, one of the thirteen people whose arrest precipitated the events of 14 October 1973 and onetime head of the NSCT, asked *what* precisely this unnamed group might be. Thirayuth suspected that it might be the powers of dictatorship.[77] Kukrit's reference to an unnamed group, as well as the attribution of the earlier bombs in Chiang Mai to a "hidden hand," contributed to creating an atmosphere of insecurity. Here, as with the case of the unnamed assassins of the FFT leaders, the logic of unnameability raises a question. Were they unnamed because their identities were literally unknown or because too much was at stake in revealing them?

While the students and farmers ceased their protests, this was not enough to prevent another group from reacting strongly to the arrests. Although it is impossible to know whether it was the group Prime Minister Kukrit was initially worried about, the counterprotestors who decried the release of the nine soon gave him cause for concern.

The Counterprotests

The day after the release of the eight farmers and one student, the counterprotestors took to the streets in new numbers and formations—in protest of the release. A group of over a thousand people calling themselves the Patriots of Lamphun (Klum Phitak Chat Lamphun) massed in front of the Lamphun provincial hall. Among the protestors were people from every occupation, including lawyers, farmers, and merchants.[78] They demanded an explanation for the release of the nine from the prime minister. If he did not respond, or they were not satisfied with his answer, they threatened to "resort to violent means to keep the law at work."[79] The growing number of counterprotestors engaged the law in an intriguing fashion. They claimed to be acting in order to uphold the sacredness of the law. Yet they actively broke the law in small ways and threatened to break it in dangerous and earth-shattering ways.

The Patriots of Lamphun began with conventional protest behavior, making speeches decrying the release of the nine and marching through Lamphun carrying posters criticizing the students. The group made four specific demands, calling on government officials to:

1. Examine and explain their actions (namely, the release of the nine)
2. Resign if they are unable to resolve the situation
3. Combine the country's three military forces [army, navy, air force] to assure the independence of the nation
4. Respond to the first three demands within twenty-four hours (i.e., by 16 August).[80]

For the Patriots of Lamphun, the release of the nine was an indication of the failure of Prime Minister Kukrit to govern. Their demands contained calls for both radical democracy and the return of a potentially authoritarian power in politics. They demanded that the state, by which they seemed to mean the prime minister (as it was unlikely that the career bureaucrats of the Ministry of Interior would resign), be accountable to them. Yet the Patriots were not willing to follow through on their call for power to the people: they also called for military action. When they tired of speeches, they projected three open-air films for the enjoyment of those present.[81] In the afternoon, they decided to take their protest of what they viewed as the devaluation of the law further—by actively violating the law.

In front of the provincial hall, a group of Patriots opened and drank bottles of unlicensed alcohol. Then they pulled out cards and began to gamble. Led by professional gamblers from Chiang Mai, Lamphun, and Lampang, approximately fifty people played Hi-Lo and other popular card games.[82] After they began playing, it started raining, and so they decided to take their gambling inside the provincial hall. As long as they remained outside, officials in Lamphun were willing to ignore their illegal actions. When they came inside, the Lamphun governor asked them to please stop breaking the law. The gamblers refused to stop and asserted that gambling was a small violation in comparison to the crimes of the nine released activists. When they refused to stop, the police arrested six of the gamblers.[83] They immediately posted bail, which totaled twenty thousand baht.[84] The bail was paid by Suwit Saenchai, a Lamphun lawyer who was himself one of the Patriots. Suwit claimed that he joined the protests because "the law is without sacredness" (*kotmai rai khwam saksit*).[85] Given that Suwit's fellow Patriots had violated the law as written, his claims demand reflection. As was the case with the protestors in Chiang Mai city a few days before, it is clear that the nature of the *law* at stake was not that written in the Criminal or Civil Code. What was losing sacredness was not the law as a set of guidelines marking what was and was not acceptable behavior for citizens but *control* of the law.

For some observers, the actions of the Lamphun protestors were an effective reflection of the crisis Thailand faced. One editorialist in Chiang Mai argued that those who gambled inside the provincial hall in Lamphun acted correctly because they showed that "when a group of individuals turns the law into something that is not the law, there will be a predicament like this. The actions of the citizens in front of the Lamphun provincial hall were an example and appropriate for the situation."[86] Yet another news report quoted an unnamed villager who also respected the logic of the protests. He or she commented, "When [the students and farmers] went against the law at the level of destroying the nation, the government released them. Why, then, [cannot] ordinary citizens . . . even gamble a little?"[87] By breaking the law, these two critics seemed to say, the Patriots of Lamphun illustrated the breakdown of the law that they believed was indicated by the release of the eight farmers and one student. But if we agree that the cases against the nine activists were marked by great irregularities and problems, and themselves indicated the fragility of the judicial system in Thailand, then the illegal gambling of the Patriots of Lamphun is cast in a vastly different light. They may then be seen as *contributing* to the breakdown of the law.

The Lamphun protestors did not receive a reply from the government by their deadline of 16 August. In response, on 17 August, five representatives of the Patriots of Lamphun planned to travel to Bangkok to meet with Prime Minister Kukrit in person. Claiming to act in his capacity as a private citizen, the Lamphun provincial governor offered to drive them to Bangkok himself. The protestors who remained in Lamphun were soon joined by the police. The police joined them not to arrest them or as adversaries but as members of the growing protests.[88]

The Police Protests

On 16 August 1975, the Provincial Police were threatening to strike over an unrelated issue.[89] On 17 August, 200 Lamphun police, in uniform, joined the protesting Patriots of Lamphun. In short order the protests grew in numbers, ferocity, and the magnitude of the threat they posed to open politics in Thailand. Throughout the day on 17 August, the initial 200 Lamphun police were joined by many additional civilians, as well as police from Nakhon Ratchasima, Nakhon Si Thammarat, Nakhon Sawan, Uthaithani, Singburi and Chainat provinces. Approximately 150 police walked off duty in neighboring Chiang Mai to join the protests. In the middle of the day, the protestors marched through Lamphun city carrying photographs of the king and posters calling for the restoration of the sacredness of the law. They sang police march music as they paraded through the city. When they arrived in front of the Lamphun provincial hall, they sang the national anthem. By the end of the day, over 2,000 police and civilians were massed in front of the provincial hall. Reports came over the police radio station indicating that more police were on their way from every region in the country.[90] The police were calling for an end to mob rule (*kot mu*) and the return of the law (*kot mai*).[91] Yet their decision to walk off the job can be read as a contribution to its breakdown—or perhaps a candid assessment of their own nonrole in its maintenance.

Various police entities responded differently to the protests. On 17 August, Police Lieutenant General Sanan Narinsorasak issued a circular asking the police to cease protesting, as he thought it would cause further unrest.[92] In a strategy reminiscent of the initial refusal of anyone to claim responsibility for ordering the arrests of the nine, Police Major Chan Khamwan claimed that no one was in charge of the protests. Yet at the same time, he also requested that all police present follow the rules. As the logical hosts (if not the leaders) of the protest, the Lamphun police collected between five and twenty baht per person to pay for food and to help offset the travel costs of police from other provinces.

By 18 August, there were over ten thousand police from around the country protesting in front of the Lamphun provincial hall.[93] As they massed in front of the provincial hall, they did so in orderly, straight lines. Among them were two hundred fully armed Border Patrol Police.[94] By this time, police were also protesting in Bangkok and other cities. On 18 August, Bangkok police officers issued a statement in support of the Lamphun protests and continuing protests throughout the kingdom.[95] By 18 August, police were threatening to use "force" if their demands were not met.[96] While it is easy to see this as dissonant thirty years later, the police did not see their actions as an example of the breakdown of the law. Instead, they cast themselves squarely as the protectors of the law. This indicates the severity of the crisis in Thailand at that moment. Thousands of police thought that by walking off the job (and in some places leaving police stations and prisons with either a skeleton staff or unprotected) and protesting in full uniform, they could protect the law.

While some citizens joined the police protests, many more felt the negative effects of police officers deserting their jobs. These effects were felt particularly acutely in neighboring Chiang Mai. Asa Meksawan, the governor, called on the Boy Scouts to take over the duties of the traffic police as they had all gone to join the protests in Lamphun.[97] Frustrated with the lack of experience of the Boy Scouts–cum–traffic police, many motorists yelled criticism at them. The Boy Scouts were harassed to such a degree that they wanted to cease working.[98] Individuals driving cars belonging to civil servants, identifiable due to their black license plates, were seen parking illegally and driving dangerously. In the absence of traffic police, the Chiang Mai city district education office called on people to join together to follow the law and, in so doing, protect the country.[99] Perhaps most alarming, on 18 August the police station was closed and there was no one guarding it. The deputy commander of the Chiang Mai Provincial Police went to the Lamphun protests to implore the Chiang Mai police to return to their jobs protecting the city.[100] His voice could barely be heard.

Throughout the protests, the police demanded that Prime Minister Kukrit meet with them in person to address their demands. Kukrit refused and maintained that they were under the administration of the minister of interior and should meet with him. The minister of interior told the police that the release of the nine was not theirs to question.[101] When they received the final word at 3:00 p.m. on 19 August that Prime Minister Kukrit would not meet with them, the police instructed those in the Lamphun provincial hall and the court to lock up their documents and vacate the buildings.[102] Using police radio, they instructed police across the country to abandon their posts. At 4:00, the crowd of twenty thousand police and civilian protestors burned puppets of Kukrit, Buntheng Thongsawat, and Aroon Issaraphakdi (the head of the Department of Prosecution).[103] The police protestors threatened to close the provincial hall and the roads in Lamphun and release all those being held in the prison.[104] Events in Bangkok that evening were to prove even more dramatic than those threatened in Lamphun.

Sacking the Prime Minister's House

Although the police protests were centered in Lamphun, over three thousand police and civilian supporters staged a solidarity protest at Sanam Luang in Bangkok on 19 August.[105] Like the protestors in Lamphun, they demanded an immediate response from Prime Minister Kukrit as to whether Thailand was going to be ruled by the law or by the mob.[106] When it became apparent that Kukrit was not going to respond to their demands, in late afternoon approximately two thousand of the police protestors moved the demonstration to his house in the Soi Suan Phlu area.

When they arrived at the prime minister's house, the police continued to demand that he meet with them. By they time they arrived, Kukrit had already left the house and was waiting at the local police station. Thirty policemen, wearing bulletproof vests and carrying batons and shotguns, had been sent to guard the house.[107] When he learned of the large number of police massed at his house, Kukrit agreed to meet with them. But he asked that they meet him at the police station rather than his house. The police refused. Instead, shortly after midnight, one hundred protesting and drunken police raided and looted the house. They stole French wine, brandy, and cigarettes, of which Kukrit was fond. They smashed televisions and radios. They destroyed antique furniture and threw it into the goldfish pond in the garden.[108] One report even noted that the police destroyed antique Buddha images.[109] While supposedly protesting mob rule, the police themselves acted like an out of control mob.

When he heard that his house had been attacked, Prime Minister Kukrit called an emergency Cabinet meeting. The Cabinet met until 3:30 a.m. on 20 August.[110] In response to the destruction of his house, Kukrit chose to "forgive" the protestors, citing the many members of his family who had been in the police force as the reason for his willingness to do so.[111] In an interview with *Siam Rat* newspaper, Kukrit explained that he did not criticize the police for protesting. Like ordinary people, he claimed, the police faced hardships and could choose to protest.[112] He felt that it would be impossible to prosecute specific policemen for their actions because determining who was responsible would be very difficult.[113] When asked if he planned to declare a state of emergency, he replied that he would not because only one house had been destroyed. However, he cautioned the police against further destruction: "It doesn't matter if [you] do this to the house of the prime minister. But [you] must not do it to the houses of other people, if [you] do, events will proceed irrevocably."[114] Kukrit asserted that the police, like any other group of citizens, could choose to protest. Of course. Yet during their five-day protest in Lamphun and Bangkok, the police chose to protest *as police*. In so doing, they limited the possibilities open to citizens who wished to dissent and protest.

The Meanings of Law

During the series of arrests, protests, and counterprotests that came in the wake of the assassination of Intha Sribunruang, many individuals and groups cited the *law* as central to their actions. Of these, most thought provoking is that the looting police claimed to demand the return of the law. Yet through their actions, they imposed the very mob rule that they decried. While their critics understood this point, the police themselves seemed to fail to understand. The words of the critics and the actions of the police are instructive here.

Before his release, Chatri Hutanuwat, the arrested CMU student, spoke from jail, saying, "I am not angry with the policemen who arrested me, [as] they were merely acting under orders from their bosses. . . . Their bosses . . . must be held responsible for this unconstitutional arrest. They took the *law* into their own hands and shamelessly claimed that they were just enforcing it."[115] For Chatri, the *law* was the power to rule and the agreement between citizens and rulers sanctifying that power. *Prachachat*, a progressive weekly, commented that the arrests indicated that "the government is creating a plan to change the current exercise of democratic rights by substituting mob rule for *law*"; here the presence of *law* also references the ability to protest and dissent.[116] When asked about the arrests on a radio program on 8 August, Prime Minister Kukrit said that "whoever broke the *law* must be prosecuted."[117] He explained that the arrests were ordered and carried out by local Provincial Police officers, "who based their actions on the *law* only."[118] Kukrit's comments seem to refer to the letter of the *law*. *Law* here refers at once to the printed legal code itself and the rights and possibilities represented by the equal and just enforcement of that code.

Voices inside and outside the state also linked analysis of the law to their criticism of the police protests. Kriangkamol Laophairoj, secretary-general of the NSCT, issued a statement arguing that the protest of the police in Lamphun was against the law. He contrasted the police protests with those that took place the week before at Thammasat University. The protests at Thammasat were legal because Article 43 of the Constitution allowed citizens to protest until they received an answer to their demands from the government. The police, Kriangkamol noted, could also protest, *as individual citizens*. However, protesting as police in uniform and armed with their weapons was against Article 166, numbers 1 and 2, of the Criminal Code. The violations carried a maximum penalty of ten years.[119] At this time, Buntheng Thongsawat, the minister of interior, also expressed concern that the police protests went against the code for civil servants, and joining them was therefore a punishable action.[120] Neither Kriangkamol nor Buntheng's concerns caused the police to cease protesting.

Even after Prime Minister Kukrit's house was ransacked in Bangkok, the police in Lamphun continued to protest for a few days. Rather than create mass chaos, they walked a fine balance between protest and threatening grave disorder. On 21 August, the assistant director of police, Police Lieutenant General Chamrat Mangkhlarat, visited the protests in Lamphun. On his arrival, the assembled police moved into formations of straight lines. He inspected the lines and noticed one policeman whose collar was not buttoned correctly. Chamrat attempted to correctly fasten the collar, but realized that the collar was awry because the policeman had a cluster of hand grenade pins dangling from his neck. Chamrat removed his hands while laughing nervously. He inquired into the health and happiness of this policeman and then proceeded with his inspection of the others assembled.[121] Had the police taken off their uniforms and acted as citizens, without conforming to *some* rules of police behavior, their protests would not have been so grave a threat.

After Kukrit's forgiveness, the police went back to work. Not only were they not punished, but Kukrit commented to the press of his smashed antiques, "I had been watching these things for so long, I began to get bored."[122] When the police invaded Kukrit's house in the early hours of 20 August 1975, they transgressed much more than the line separating the house from the street. The return of the police to work without sanction, coupled with the prime minister's easy dismissal of their actions, made the fragmentation of the Thai state a public event. Not only did Thai people witness the sacking of the prime minister's house, but they witnessed his decision not to challenge the police. If the police could do this to the prime minister with impunity, what could they *not* do to ordinary citizens? In this extremely divided and politically charged environment, what crimes might the police choose to ignore? Who would hold them, or the Ministry of Interior, or the army, or anyone else for that matter, responsible for their actions or inactions?

Rather than evaluating the series of events that followed in the wake of Intha Sribunruang's assassination as either a ploy or a mistake, I argue that we should treat it instead as an example of how rule is accomplished. I suggest that this kind of rule not be read as unusual, or peculiar to 1970s Thailand, but as an example of how harassment, the creation of chaos, and official dissimulation are typical strategies of the actors and institutions operating under the banner of "the state." A little over a year after Prime Minister Kukrit's antiques were smashed, the 6 October 1976 massacre demonstrated how some of the very worst rights violations could occur in the name of ending chaos and restoring law and order. The precise nature of *law* restored was one bereft of dissent.

Conclusion

Resuming Revolution?

I wish I were only speaking about the long-ago dead, about distant
memories, about old battles; I wish I were not speaking about now. But
unfortunately I speak of today. What was done to Caupolicán and that
unnamed Indian woman and their many brothers and sisters at the
dawn of Latin American history has been repeated in many other forms
throughout that history. Not only the multiplication of terror, but the
incessant forgetting of that terror. Yesterday is today.

Ariel Dorfman, Other Septembers, Many Americas

When the saktina scholars base their arguments on a single point—
namely, that *thai* means independent, and therefore the Thai never
had a slave system until a later period after they had contact with the
Khmer—can the scholars of the saktina chronicles, in the face of such
overwhelming historical and linguistic evidence as presented here in
point after point, continue to remain immobile like one-legged rabbits?

Somsamai Srisudravarna [Jit Phumisak],
The Real Face of Thai Feudalism Today

A semblance of open, parliamentary politics remained, at least in name, for over
a year until the 6 October 1976 massacre and coup returned Thailand to dictatorship. The intervening fourteen months between August 1975 and October 1976
were filled with mounting contention, polarization, and violence in the electoral,
as well as social and grassroots, political spheres. A variety of factors, including
conflict within the military and the growing political power of some military
factions, destabilized Prime Minister Kukrit's SAP-led coalition government so
severely that in January 1976 he called for new elections to be held on 14 April.

The April elections were incredibly violent, with more than thirty people killed during the course of the campaigning, including the SPT candidate for MP in Chiang Mai, Dr. Bunsanong Punyodhayana.[1] In the election, not only did Kukrit fail to be reelected, but his party lost as well. Instead, the Democrat Party won an overwhelming victory. Seni Pramoj, the head of the Democrat Party and Kukrit's older brother, became the new prime minister on 20 April 1976.

As electoral politics were reconfigured in late 1975 and 1976, those active in progressive politics adopted increasingly radical tactics as well. For some, this meant joining the CPT in the liberated areas or otherwise going underground. B., a former CMU activist, commented that while some went to the jungle out of commitment to the CPT's policies, many others fled out of either a desire to avoid arrest or murder or because the violence of the preceding months caused them to want to take up arms, by any means, against the Thai state. For others, this meant pushing parliamentary politics and public protest to its limits. Then the return of Thanom Kittikachorn, one of the dictators ousted during the events of 14 October 1973, catalyzed a series of events that culminated in the massacre of unarmed students by right-wing state and parastate actors at Thammasat University in Bangkok on 6 October 1976.

On 19 September 1976, Thanom Kittikachorn returned to Thailand and was ordained as a novice at Wat Boworniwet, a temple under heavy royal patronage in Bangkok. His return prompted concern among many progressives that a return to dictatorship was imminent. On 25 September, while posting fliers protesting the return of Thanom, two labor activists were captured and hung in Nakhon Pathom near Bangkok.[2] On 27 September, *Thai Rat* newspaper reported that the police were involved in the hanging of the two activists; on 4 October, someone bombed the *Thai Rat* office with an M79 grenade.[3] Also on 4 October, student activists reenacted the hanging in a skit as a critique of police violence.[4] Angered by the killings of the two labor activists and concerned that Thanom's return to Thailand might signal a possible coup, four to five thousand students and other activists massed inside the gates of Thammasat University.

On 5 October, *Dao Siam*, a right-wing Thai-language newspaper, reported that the skit about the murdered labor activists was actually a mock hanging of an effigy of the crown prince and accused the student activists of wanting to destroy the monarchy.[5] Right-wing forces circulated copies of the photograph and the newspaper article about the alleged mock hanging of the crown prince.[6] Throughout the evening of 5 October, military radio broadcasts called for the defense of "Nation, Religion, and King," the three pillars of Thai state nationalism that were promulgated during the reign of King Vajiravudh (Rama VI) and cited increasingly by right-wing elements throughout 1975 and 1976.[7]

Shortly after 2:00 a.m. on the morning of 6 October 1976, state and parastate forces, including Border Patrol Police, Village Scouts, and Red Gaurs, began a sustained period of violence against students and other activists inside Thammasat University that did not end until the declaration of martial law and the announcement of a new ruling body, the National Administrative Reform Council (NARC), at 6:00 p.m. on 6 October 1976.[8] The NARC reported that 3,059 people were arrested, 46 were killed, and over 180 were injured.[9] Unofficial estimates by the Chinese Benevolent Foundation, which carried the dead bodies outside the walls of Thammasat University and cremated them, put the number killed much higher.[10] The massacre showed the limit of parliamentary politics in Thailand at that moment and made flight to the jungle to join the CPT unavoidable for many.

Although there were also protests in Chiang Mai following the accusations of alleged lèse-majesté in early October 1976, the outcome of the events stands in stark contrast to the brutal violence in Bangkok. Beginning on 3 October, hundreds of students, farmers, and other people massed outside the Chiang Mai provincial building, decrying the return of Thanom and demonstrating in solidarity with those at Thammasat University in Bangkok. By 5 October, in response to reports of student protests on government radio stations, thousands of right-wing forces, including Red Gaurs, Nawaphon, and Village Scouts, were massed at Wat Chedi Luang, a few blocks from the provincial hall. The atmosphere between the two groups grew more and more heated. For a time the progressive activists massed at the provincial hall refused to end their protest. Finally the right-wing forces at Wat Chedi Luang announced that they would take decisive action to ensure that those protesting outside the provincial hall would disperse.

At 10:00 a.m. on 6 October, the Village Scouts sent ten representatives to meet with the progressive activists massed at the provincial hall. They gave the activists until noon to leave the area. At this time, student leaders became concerned about the possibility of imminent violence in Chiang Mai. Chaturon Chaisaeng, president of the CMU Students' Organization, decided to end the protest. The students and farmers massed at the provincial hall dispersed at 10:45. A massacre was averted in Chiang Mai. From the newspaper accounts of the massacre in Bangkok, as well as accounts from those present at the provincial building, it is unclear if activists in Chiang Mai knew about the violence in Bangkok when they dissolved their protest.[11]

A massacre was avoided by a margin of only five or ten minutes in the estimation of K., a former CMU activist who was present at the provincial building on 6 October. Like many other students and farmers, K. explained to me that she fled to the jungle to join the CPT directly from the provincial building. She was there with farmer colleagues, and she gave them money so that they could take *songthaeo* buses back to their villages.[12] For her, the decision to leave to join the CPT was immediate. She had worked with the Farmer Project since its inception and felt confident that her name was on a government blacklist.[13] If she stayed in the city, she was sure that she would be killed or arrested by state forces.[14] After leaving the provincial hall, she went to her dormitory at CMU and picked up a change of clothing. She abandoned all of her books, including many progressive and leftist books that she wishes she could recover now. On her way to meet the comrade who would take her to the liberated area controlled by the CPT, she traveled through nearby Lampang province to pass news of the events on to farmers she had worked with in the Farmer Project and to urge them to flee to the jungle as well.

Yet when the northern tenant farmers fled to the jungle, as many did, they did not flee to join the revolution. They fled because the revolution they had fomented in the streets, the rice fields, and the many spaces in between had been interrupted by counterrevolution. I have argued in this book that farmers became revolutionary not by taking up guns to destroy the Thai state but by joining hands with students and other allies to demand tenancy reform. The action of working for legal tenancy reform and then organizing village by village to make it real became transformative—and threatening—within a context in which poor, rural people were expected to neither use the law as their own nor to question the claims of landlords. The revolution was not the smashing of the state or the violent overthrow and expulsion of the landowners and capitalists from the countryside and the city. The revolution was made as farmers and students reimagined their lives and the possibility of a future, just Thai society, and then worked together to make this society. In the process, they transgressed the boundaries of class and space that separated them from each other. The individual lives of farmers and students changed as they learned from one another, and learned how to make political change together. This change became social—and was felt beyond their individual lives—when they demanded that landlords follow the terms of the 1974 LRCA. As farmers, students, and their allies launched the public campaign for state action to halt the assassinations of the farmer leaders in 1975, they invited all citizens to join them in solidarity. What began as the resurgence of a local struggle for changes in the land tenancy law defeated in 1951 became an attempt to reach and restructure Thai society as a whole, from margin to center. There was a sense in which, in Lenin's terms, the state was "shattered, broken to pieces," by the police protests and destruction of Prime Minister Kukrit's house in August 1975.[15] Yet this was the action of repressive counterrevolution, not revolution. The result was that the powers of the police, and the broader forces of extrajudiciality, were enhanced.

What made the tenant farmers' revolution so powerful was that their actions challenged the idea that the law was meant to be the province of only a small number of people. Their actions exposed the reality of the maxim "The class that writes the laws, certainly writes the laws for that class" (*chonchan dai khian kotmai ko nae sai phua chonchan nan*); the backlash against their actions indicated that this idea was meant to be lived, but kept invisible. By choosing the law, and not the AK-47, as their tool to challenge unjust tenancy practices, the northern farmers also surprised landlords and many Thai state actors. In prior years, landlords' control over the law had been so secure that they never imagined that farmers might use the law and certainly never imagined that farmers might use it *against* them. The reaction to the farmers' actions—born of surprise, fear, and loss of wealth both material and ontological—existed between one imagined and one unimaginable future.

What happens when one's worst dreams are eclipsed by something one never dreamed would come to pass? In the case of the tenancy struggle, the response was a series of assassinations in 1975 that were treated alternately as insignificant and impossible to solve by the authorities. Over thirty years later, the assassins have either died or are still roaming the cities and villages of Thailand. They have not, and will not, face a public hearing or prosecution of their crimes. They will remain unnamed. Wendy Brown writes that the goal of critique "is to set the times right again by discerning and repairing a tear in justice through practices that are themselves exemplary of the justice that has been rent."[16] While analytic work cannot hope to name the assassins of activists, perhaps what it can do is trace and name the conditions under which these things become unnameable and unspeakable. Similarly, scholars cannot resume the interrupted revolution, but we can track the conditions under which it may be resumed and continue to question *what* constitutes revolution. These are important tasks not only in the register of the unresolved recent past but also in the present. Nearly a decade into the twenty-first century, and over seventy-five years since the transition from absolute to constitutional monarchy in Thailand, poor, rural people are still fighting for a voice in their own rule and those who challenge the status quo still face the possibility of harassment, intimidation, and assassination.

Possible Futures, Acknowledged and Unacknowledged

Close your eyes. This is what will happen when the communist terrorists take over.

They will abrogate rights and take over the administration of the country. Landowners will be tried in sham courts. Communists will take this opportunity to destroy their opponents. Religious institutions will be dismantled. Monks' robes will be removed and Buddhist wisdom lost. The monarchy will be destroyed. Democracy will cease to exist, and along with it, political parties, Parliament, and the courts will disappear. Instead, the Communist Party will be the gangster controlling the land. Its words will be law.

The communists will use cruelty to secure power. They will burn villages to the ground, kill children in front of their parents, and rape wives in front of husbands. In the worldview of communists, these actions are lawful, moral, and humane. Freedom will be curtailed. There will be no freedom of speech or freedom of the press. People will be forced to work like animals, but not for themselves or for the nation. Only the communist leadership will benefit.

Happiness and warmth in families will disappear. All land and valuables will become the property of the state. The importance of ancestry will disappear. Thai identity will cease to matter. Children will spy on their parents. Life will be bereft of hope. We have nation, religion, king, rights, freedom, and family.

When that is gone, all that is left is being for oneself. The communists will take this. Loss will dominate. Life will lose all meaning. We will become slaves.[17]

This description is drawn from the middle of a volume written by Thanin Kraivichien about using the law to protect Thailand against the spread of communism. Thanin, who was appointed prime minister after the 6 October 1976 massacre and coup, was a prominent right-wing judge and legal thinker. He wrote prolifically about the dangers of communism, based on his research about life in China, Cuba, and Russia. When Thanin asked his readers to close their eyes and imagine what life would look like if Thailand became a communist nation, he painted a picture that was stark, terrifying, and full of emotion.

Thanin's account of the future was not unusual. While it might be easy to dismiss his claims as erroneous, the material fear of marauding, land-hungry communists was the felt experience of many elites, including those in the employ of the Thai state and private citizens. This fear motivated policy and gave a veneer of legitimacy to the violence used by Royal Thai Government forces and ISOC to suppress the CPT and any dissident action that could be conflated as communist. This vision of what would happen if revolution struck in Thailand could be publicly and officially acknowledged as damaging and in need of repression.

What could not be so easily named as dangerous was what might have happened if farmers had continued to act as subjects, not only objects, of the law. What could not be recognized as impossible was the idea of farmers, civil servants, and landowners sitting down to resolve disputes among themselves and come to an agreement about the price of land rent. What could not be imagined was landowners and farmers meeting on a shared, equal terrain. What could not be acknowledged as destabilizing was farmers speaking the truth about their lives, and rural relations more generally, and landlords and state officials listening with respect. To do so would have been to make public the exclusion present at the very core of "Thainess" that Thanin worried the communists would destroy. Close your eyes.

To Begin Again

Neither Thanin's vision of what would have happened if there was a communist transition in Thailand nor what might have happened if the farmers' revolution was not interrupted came to pass in Thailand. Instead, assassination and then massacre stopped the aboveground struggle on the terrain of law, and then many farmers either ceased struggling politically or joined the CPT. When the CPT dissolved in the early 1980s, the farmers who had survived came out of the jungle to continue struggling for rice and justice. The need to struggle has remained constant, as has the persistent silence around the assassinations of FFT leaders and the other events signaling the revolution that the farmers fomented.

The formation and interruption of the revolution fomented by tenant farmers who became subjects of the law in northern Thailand were the products of a set of historically contingent and unique circumstances. These circumstances—which were resonant with many other contexts across Asia and Latin America in the 1970s—included the dramatic end of dictatorship, an incredible sense of the possibility of a different future, and the brutal end to this sense of possibility with the return to dictatorship within the context of the internationalization of the Cold War. The return to dictatorship may be identified as counterrevolution in the sense described by Paolo Virno: a set of processes that "actively makes its own 'new order,' forging new mentalities, cultural habits, tastes, and customs—in short, a new common sense. It goes to the root of things, and works methodically."[18] Yet even as counterrevolution attempted to erase the voices and gains of the tenant farmers, it failed to do so completely.

Instead, legacies of the revolution they fomented survive in the forms of progressive activism and movements populated both by those who were part of the student and farmer movements and by those who were born later but were affected by the struggle. In a series of protests beginning in 1995, the Assembly of the Poor, a network of villager and people's organizations from across the country, united to fight dams, privatization, and the other ills of structural adjustment. During one continuous ninety-nine-day protest in 1997, they set up a "Village of the Poor" on the streets and sidewalks outside Government House in Bangkok, in order to "highlight the poor's exclusion from the places of authority and power" inside.[19] Landless farmers in northern Thailand, some of them former members of the FFT, have led land occupations in Lamphun and joined with landless farmers in Brazil and elsewhere to share knowledge and strategies. Between 2003 and 2005, a "study group" (*klum suksa*) was conceived by a Marxian activist in Chiang Mai. Every quarter, for two years, he organized weekends of lectures and progressive films on topics ranging from Che Guevara's life to the theory and practice of the Narodniks to the history of the FFT. Young farmer activists, nongovernmental organization workers, and the occasional foreign scholar activist (me) attended these weekends and shared ideas. These are only a few examples of how people continue to unite to creatively and courageously challenge oppression and change the shapes and sites of politics.

Yet in addition to legacies of the revolution created by farmers and students in the mid-1970s, legacies of its interruption also survive in continuing counterrevolution. When thinking about how the targeted killings of thirty-three farmer leaders were able to shut down a movement of over one million people, what might be identified as the repeated confluence of violence and unspeakability in Thailand offers one potential explanation. During the first government of former prime minister Thaksin Shinawatra (2001–5), eighteen human rights defenders were assassinated and one was disappeared; while speculation identifies a combination of state and private interests as behind the assassinations, prosecutions have been either slow or nonexistent.[20] For those who adopt a dissident position vis-à-vis powerful interests in Thailand, personal safety is a persistent concern. In late 2008, I asked a prominent human rights lawyer working on national security cases in southern Thailand if he was ever worried about being attacked or killed.[21] He responded that although he knew his phone and actions were monitored by the Special Branch (Santiban) and other security forces, he does not think about being killed. The people whose rights he works to defend are at much greater risk. The case of one of his former colleagues, Somchai Neelaphaichit, demonstrates acutely how violence remains unnamed and state perpetrators are not held to account in present-day Thailand.

Somchai was a lawyer who filed cases on behalf of five Muslim national security detainees in early 2004. They had been accused of having stolen three hundred guns from an army base and claimed that they were tortured during detention. Although torture continues to be used by some elements within the Thai military and police, Thailand has ratified the United Nations Convention against Torture, and torture is illegal under Thai law. Somchai was preparing to bring the allegations of torture before senior authorities. Then, on 12 March 2004, he disappeared. He was pulled from his car by five policemen on the outskirts of Bangkok. Evidence leaked to the media alleges that senior persons in the government were behind the disappearance, possibly those in the Department of Special Investigation, which fulfills a function within Thailand similar to that of the Federal Bureau of Investigation in the United States.

Angkhana Neelaphaichit, Somchai's wife, launched a highly public campaign to secure justice in the case of her husband's disappearance. After not receiving answers about her husband from the police or other state actors, in 2005 Angkhana brought the case to the attention of the United Nations Human Rights Commission in Geneva. Following concerted action by Somchai's family and human rights activists, five police officers from the Crime Suppression Division were arrested in April 2004 in connection to his disappearance: Police Major Ngern Thongsukand, Police Major Sinchai Nimpunyakampong, Police Sergeant Major Chaiweng Paduang, Police Sergeant Rundorn Sithiket, and Police Lieutenant Colonel Chadchai Liamsanguan. Somchai Neelaphaichit's body has not yet been recovered. Without a body, a murder trial cannot take place under Thai evidentiary rules. In the absence of Somchai's body, the five police officers were instead charged with robbery and coercion with the use of violence. In the course of the case proceedings, it came out that four of the five defendants had been involved in the arrests and interrogation of the five suspects who were tortured, on whose behalf Somchai was pressing the state. While there were multiple witnesses who watched Somchai being taken out of his car and placed into another vehicle by the defendants on 12 March 2004, they reported intimidation, and only one witness was willing to speak during the trial. In January 2006, the Bangkok Criminal Court ruled that Somchai Neelaphaijit had been disappeared, but that a lack of evidence made all other allegations, except coercion on the part of one of the defendants, impossible to prove. The robbery charge was dismissed because although there were three witnesses who saw Somchai being taken out of his car, there was not definitive evidence indicating that the five defendants intended to steal his car. Police Major Ngern Thongsukand was convicted of coercion with the use of violence and sentenced to three years in prison. Despite the conviction, Police Major Ngern remained out on bail while he appealed his case. The other four police officers returned to work. On 19 September 2008, Police Major Ngern disappeared following a mudslide. Since then, progress on the case has slowed to a standstill. As human rights groups have repeatedly indicated, Somchai's trial is extremely important for questions of impunity in Thailand since it is the first in which police officers have been tried in connection with a disappearance.[22]

In a chilling and ironic moment, as the Day of the Disappeared, 30 August, passed in 2009 without Somchai's abductors being held to account, the criminal justice system moved swiftly to close another case. On 28 August 2009, Darunee Charncherngsilpakul, also known as "Da Torpedo," was convicted and sentenced to eighteen years for allegedly committing lèse-majesté during speeches criticizing the royalist People's Alliance for Democracy (PAD) in July 2008.[23] The PAD was established in early 2006 by Sonthi Limthongkul as a network calling for the ouster of Prime Minister Thaksin Shinawatra and for greater adherence to the monarchy as a source of political guidance. The case against Darunee was one of a series of cases of alleged lèse-majesté that were prosecuted throughout late 2008 and 2009.[24] In the case against Darunee, as in many of the other cases, the precise content of her allegedly criminal speech remains unknown to the public. For the court to recite it, or the press to print it, would be to recommit the crime of lèse-majesté. The increase in these cases can be seen as part of the contention building in Thailand since the September 2006 coup that unseated Prime Minister Thaksin. If one were to cast the conflict in broad terms, it is a contest between those who are demanding a return to an ancien régime in which rule of the many by the few is the order of the day, and those who are demanding a new social contract in which all citizens participate in politics and governance. Within this context, the accusation of committing lèse-majesté as well as other censorship measures has been used to stifle dissent.

The reason why the disappearance of Somchai Neelaphaichit and the prosecution of Darunee Charncherngsilpakul are relevant to thinking about the violence that interrupted the tenancy struggle is not because either Somchai or Darunee carried out actions that might be seen as continuous with the tenant farmers' revolution. Instead, they are relevant because Somchai's and Darunee's lives, and Somchai's death, illustrate that in Thailand justice and the use of the law remain selective. The question of who can commit violence with impunity becomes more, not less, urgent as time passes without resolution of the assassinations of the FFT leaders. What citizens learn, year after year, is that alleged crimes against some will be prosecuted swiftly and vehemently and crimes against others will not even register as crimes. How many more activists will be killed? How many more killers will cease to be named or prosecuted?

So, then, what can scholars do in the face of repetitions of violence and a revolution that remains interrupted? If one is not to "continue to remain immobile like one-legged rabbits," in Jit Phumisak's evocative words, then where does one go?[25] I return to the premise with which I began, and suggest that what can be done is to continue to interrogate what constitutes revolution in the twenty-first century and to continually rethink moments that may have previously been deemed nonrevolutionary. In the case of Thailand, part of what historiographically signaled revolution was the disjuncture between the actions that tenant farmers took and the kind of violence they experienced. Writing about the United States and Chile after Salvador Allende was elected, Greg Grandin argues, "Washington's assault on Allende increased after it realized that he would not turn Chile into a Cuban-style Soviet satellite. . . . [T]he threat that *la via chilena* posed was that it provided an example of a popularly elected Marxist government that insisted it was possible to combine democratic pluralism and real socialism."[26] For those in power—both inside and far beyond Washington, DC—the greatest threat may not have been the communist one. Instead, radical democratic politics and the idea of justice for everyone— in Chile under Allende, in the groups spawned by liberation theology and consciousness-raising all across indigenous Latin America, and in the tenancy struggles of the FFT in Thailand, to name a few—were far more threatening. In addition to directly challenging the material privileges of those in power, these struggles exposed the ruse in the system and its lingering inequality.

Yet it is not enough to track revolution by means of the forms of counterrevolution. Instead, it is necessary to continue revising our—academic and activist—ideas about what constitutes revolution. In his book *Political Dictionary, Peoples' Edition*, written while he was a leftist political detainee in the 1950s but not published until the 1980s, Suphot Dantrakul defines *revolution* using the Thai word *patiwat*.[27] For Suphot, revolution is "change that rapidly excavates the roots of the evolution of society, both politically and economically, in order to reach a better state."[28] He does not mention the events of June 1932 in Thailand as either revolutionary or antithetical to revolution. He provides many examples of violent revolution, including the French and Russian revolutions. What he lacks an example for is precisely what he hopes the future will hold: a peaceful revolution. A peaceful revolution would take "the form of rule in which the people have extensive political rights and freedoms" and in which this is achieved without foreign imperialism and within a democracy.[29] Suphot's lack of examples of peaceful revolution may seem surprising, until one considers the violence with which the tenant farmers' struggle to act as full legal and national subjects in Thailand was interrupted in 1975. What other peaceful revolutions have been interrupted since the dawn of the Cold War and the end of it? Hegemony sometimes fractures in unexpected ways and places. The task before us now is to write and act in the service of imagining and engaging these revolutions and the better futures that they may hold.

Appendix

LEADERS OF THE FFT VICTIMIZED

BY VIOLENCE, 1974–1979

The information in this appendix is drawn from Nitirat Sapsomboon, ed., *The Path of Thai Farmers* (Bangkok: Mooniti Dek, 2542 [1999]), 155–60; and Kanoksak Kaewthep, *Analysis of the Farmers' Federation of Thailand: A Political Economy of the Modern Farmer* (Bangkok: Chulalongkorn University Social Research Institute, 2530 [1987]), 161–66. The numbers of those killed, injured, and disappeared may be higher, but the fear of negative consequences or further violence may have kept some family and community members connected to those targeted from reporting to the authorities their ties to the FFT or other dissenting entities. As is evident, the details known about leadership positions and places of death are uneven across the assassinations and injuries.

1. Mr. Sanit Sridej (นายสนิท ศรีเดช)
   Farmer representative
   Phitsanulok province
   Shot and killed on 31 March 1974
2. Mr. Methha (Luan) Lao-udom (นายเมตตา [ล้วน] เหล่าอุดม)
   Farmer representative
   Bang La Mung district, Chonburi province
   Shot and killed on 11 August 1974
3. Mr. Bunthing Srirat (นายบุญทิ้ง ศรีรัตน์)
   Farmer representative
   Shot and killed in October 1974
4. Mr. Bunma Somprasit (นายบุญมา สมประสิทธิ์)
   FFT committee member
   Ang Thong province
   Shot and killed in February 1975
5. Mr. Hieng Limmak (นายเฮียง ลิ้มมาก)
   Farmer representative
   Surin province
   Shot and killed on 5 April 1975

6. Mr. Aaj Thongtho (นายอาจ ธงโท)
   FFT committee member
   Baan Ton Thong district, Lamphun province
   Shot and killed on 10 April 1975
7. Mr. Prasert Chomomret (นายประเสริฐ โฉมอมฤต)
   FFT village president
   Hang Dong district, Chiang Mai province
   Shot and killed on 19 April 1975
8. Mr. Ngon Laowong (นายโหง่น ลาววงษ์)
   FFT village committee member
   Nong Wua Saw district, Udonthani province
   Strangled and beaten to death on 21 April 1975
9. Mr. Charoen Dangnok (นายเจริญ ดังนอก)
   FFT committee member
   Chomphuang district, Nakhon Ratchasima province
   Shot and injured in April 1975
10. Mr. Tawin (last name unknown) (นายถวิล ไม่ทราบนามสกุล)
    Farmer leader
    Taphanhin district, Phichit province
    Shot and killed in April 1975
11. Mr. Mongkhol Suknum (นายมงคล สุขหนุม)
    Farmer leader
    Nakhon Sawan province
    Shot and killed in May 1975
12. Mr. Bunsom Chandaeng (นายบุญสม จันแดง)
    FFT central committee member
    Sanpatong district, Chiang Mai province
    Shot and injured on 8 May 1975
13. Mr. Phad Muangmala (นายผัด เมืองมาหล้า)
    FFT district president
    Hang Chat district, Lampang province
    Shot and injured on 11 May 1975
14. Mr. Tawin Mungthanya (นายถวิล มุ่งธัญญา)
    Farmer representative
    Nakhon Ratchasima province
    Shot and killed on 26 May 1975
15. Mr. Phut Ponglangka (นายพุฒ ปงลังกา)
    Farmer leader
    Chiang Rai province
    Shot and killed on 22 June 1975
16. Mr. Kaew Pongsakham (นายแก้ว ปงซาคำ)
    Farmer leader

Chiang Rai province
Shot and killed on 22 June 1975

17. Mr. Cha Chakrawan (นายจา จักรวาล)
FFT village vice president
Mae Rim district, Chiang Mai province
Shot and killed on 3 July 1975

18. Mr. Bunchuay Direkchai (นายบุญช่วย ดิเรกชัย)
FFT district president
Fang district, Chiang Mai province
Shot and injured on 8 July 1975

19. Mr. Prasat Sirimuang (นายประสาท สิริม่วง)
Farmer representative
Surin province
Shot and killed on 8 July 1975

20. Mr. Buntha Yotha (นายบุญทา โยทา)
FFT committee member
Muang district, Lamphun province
Shot and killed on 18 July 1975

21. Mr. Klieng Mai-iam (นายเกลี้ยง ใหม่เอี่ยม)
FFT district vice president
Hang Chat district, Lampang province
Shot and killed on 22 July 1975

22. Mr. Intha Sribunruang (นายอินถา ศรีบุญเรือง)
FFT national vice president, FFT northern president
Saraphi district, Chiang Mai province
Shot and killed on 30 July 1975

23. Mr. Sawat Thatawan (นายสวัสดิ์ ตาถาวรรณ)
FFT village vice president
Doi Saket district, Chiang Mai province
Shot and killed on 3 August 1975

24. Mr. Mi Suanphlu (นายมี สวนพลู)
FFT committee member
Fang district, Chiang Mai province
Disappeared on 8 August 1975

25. Mr. Ta Kaewprasert (นายตา แก้วประเสริฐ)
FFT committee member
Fang district, Chiang Mai province
Disappeared on 8 August 1975

26. Mr. Ta Intadam (นายตา อินต๊ะคำ)
FFT committee member
Fang district, Chiang Mai province
Disappeared on 8 August 1975

27. Mr. Nuan Sitthisri (นายนวล สิทธิศรี)
    FFT member
    Mae Rim district, Chiang Mai province
    Shot on 11 August 1975
28. Mr. Phut Saikham (นายพุฒ ทรายดำ)
    Farmer leader
    Fang district, Chiang Mai province
    Shot and killed on 11 August 1975
29. Mr. Chuan Niemwira (นายช้วน เนียมวีระ)
    FFT committee member
    Uthong district, Suphanburi province
    Shot and killed on 12 August 1975
30. Mr. Sawaeng Chanthaphun (นายแสวง จันทาพูน)
    FFT village vice president
    Fang district, Chiang Mai province
    Shot and injured on 27 August 1975
31. Mr. Nuan Kawilo (นายนวล กาวิโล)
    Farmer leader
    Serm Ngam district, Lampang province
    Killed by a bomb on 12 October 1975
32. Mr. Mi Kawilo (นายมี กาวิโล)
    Farmer leader
    Serm Ngam district, Lampang province
    Injured by a bomb on 12 October 1975
33. Mr. Bunrat Chaiyen (นายบุญรัตน์ ใจเย็น)
    Farmer leader
    Serm Ngam district, Lampang province
    Shot and killed on 21 October 1975
34. Mr. Chanterm Kaewduangdee (นายจันเติม แก้วดวงดี)
    FFT village president
    Sanpatong district, Chiang Mai province
    Shot and injured on 5 December 1975
35. Mr. La Suphachan (นายลา สุภาจันทร์)
    FFT committee member
    Serm Ngam district, Lampang province
    Shot and killed on 12 December 1975
36. Mr. Pan Sunsai (นายปั้น สูญใส)
    FFT village vice president
    Chiang Dao district, Chiang Mai province
    Shot and injured on 20 March 1976
37. Mr. Kham Thamun (นายคำ ต๊ะมูล)
    Farmer leader
    Serm Ngam district, Lampang province

Shot and killed on 31 March 1976

38. Mr. Wong Munai (นายวงศ์ มูลอ้าย)
    Farmer representative
    Serm Ngam district, Lampang province
    Disappeared on 13 April 1976 and reported as dead by the NSC on
        19 May 1976

39. Mr. Phut Buawong (นายพุฒ บัววงศ์)
    Farmer representative
    Serm Ngam district, Lampang province
    Disappeared on 13 April 1976 and reported as dead by the NSC on
        19 May 1976

40. Mr. Song Kawilo (นายทรง กาวิโล)
    Farmer representative
    Serm Ngam district, Lampang province
    Disappeared on 13 April 1976 and reported as dead by the NSC on
        19 May 1976

41. Mr. Duangkham Pornhomdaeng (นายดวงคำ พรหมแดง)
    Farmer representative
    Wieng Pa Pao district, Chiang Rai province
    Shot and killed on 28 April 1976

42. Mr. Nuan Daotad (นายนวล ดาวตาด)
    FFT village president
    Doi Saket district, Chiang Mai province
    Shot and killed on 9 May 1976

43. Mr. Sithon Yodkantha (นายศรีธน ยอดกันทา)
    FFT northern region president
    Doi Saket district, Chiang Mai province
    Injured by a bomb on 17 July 1976

44. Mr. Chit Khonphetch (นายชิต คงเพชร)
    Farmer Leader
    Mae La Noi district, Mae Hong Son province
    Shot and killed on 18 August 1976

45. Mr. Sod Thani (นายทรอด ธานี)
    FFT northeastern region president, FFT national vice president
    Nong Bua Daeng district, Chaiyaphum province
    Shot and killed on 5 July 1978

46. Mr. Chamrat Muangyam (นายจำรัส ม่วงยาม)
    FFT eastern region president, FFT national president
    Baan Dan district, Rayong province
    Shot and killed on 21 July 1979

Notes

Preface

1. Adrienne Rich, *The Dream of a Common Language: Poems, 1974–1977* (New York: Norton, 1978), 17.
2. *Thai Rat*, 29 November 2517 [1974], 16.
3. Thongchai Winichakul, "Thongchai Winichakul on the Red 'Germs,'" *New Mandala*, 3 May 2010, http://asiapacific.anu.edu.au/newmandala/2010/05/03/thongchai-winichakul-on-the-red-germs/.
4. Rich, *The Dream of a Common Language*, 19.

Introduction

1. *Thai Niu*, 2 September 2517 [1974], 3.
2. *Thai Niu*, 3 September 2517 [1974], 3.
3. Ibid., 5.
4. Vladimir Ilyich Lenin, *State and Revolution* (New York: International Publishers, 1932), 89, emphasis in the original.
5. Greg Grandin, *The Last Colonial Massacre: Latin America in the Cold War* (Chicago: University of Chicago Press, 2004), 17.
6. Michael Walzer, "Intellectuals, Social Classes, and Revolutions," in *Democracy, Revolution, and History*, ed. Theda Skocpol (Ithaca, NY: Cornell University Press, 1998), 198.
7. James C. Scott, *Weapons of the Weak: Everyday Forms of Peasant Resistance* (New Haven, CT: Yale University Press, 1985), 29.
8. Kanoksak Kaewthep, *Analysis of the Farmers' Federation of Thailand: A Political Economy of the Modern Farmer* (Bangkok: Chulalongkorn University Social Research Institute, 2530 [1987]), 161–66.
9. Katherine Bowie, *Rituals of National Loyalty: An Anthropology of the State and the Village Scout Movement in Thailand* (New York: Columbia University Press, 1997), 155.
10. Cynthia Enloe, *The Curious Feminist: Searching for Women in a New Age of Empire* (Berkeley: University of California Press, 2004), 13.
11. Walter Benjamin, "Theses on the Philosophy of History," in *Illuminations: Essays and Reflections*, ed. Hannah Arendt, trans. Harry Zohn (New York: Schocken Books, 1968), 257.
12. Krirkkiat Phipatseritham, *Trends in Land Tenure and Security* (Bangkok: Thai University Research Association, 1979), 33; Krirkkiat Phipatseritham, "Land Problems and Assistance to Thai Farmers," *College of Commerce Journal* 1, no. 1 (2522 [1979]): 44–45.

165

13.   Pasuk Phongpaichit and Chris Baker, *Thailand: Economy and Politics*, 2nd ed. (Oxford: Oxford University Press, 2002), 451.

14.   Krirkkiat, *Trends in Land Tenure and Security*, 3.

15.   Regarding the Philippines, see Benedict J. Kerkvliet, *Everyday Politics in the Philippines: Class and Status Relations in a Central Luzon Village* (Oxford: Rowman and Littlefield, 2002). For China and Vietnam, see Benedict J. Tria Kerkvliet and Mark Selden, "Agrarian Transformations in China and Vietnam," *China Journal* 40 (July 1998): 37–58. For Brazil, see C. Daniel Dillman, "Land and Labor Practices in Brazil during the 1960s," *American Journal of Economics and Sociology* 35, no. 1 (1976): 49–70.

16.   1 *rai* equals 0.4 acres.

17.   Krirkkiat Phipatseritham, *Farmers and the Land: Reform or Revolution* (Bangkok: Duang Kamol, 2521 [1978]), 416.

18.   Krirkkiat Phipatseritham explains that between 1888 and 1914 ownership of land in the fertile Rangsit Plains in Pathumthani, a province now considered to be a suburb of Bangkok, was given to companies that excavated canals. The companies sold the land to investors, who then rented the land to tenant farmers. See Krirkkiat, *Trends in Land Tenure and Security*; and Witayakorn Chiengkul, *The Effects of Capitalist Penetration on the Transformation of the Agrarian Structure in the Central Region of Thailand (1960–1980)* (Bangkok: Chulalongkorn University Social Research Institute, 1983).

19.   David Wyatt, *Thailand: A Short History* (New Haven, CT: Yale University Press, 1984).

20.   National Statistical Office, *Statistical Yearbook of Thailand, 1976–1980* (Bangkok: Office of the Prime Minister, 1981), 5.

21.   Ibid., 62.

22.   Anan Ganjanapan, "The Partial Commercialization of Rice Production in Northern Thailand (1900–1981)" (PhD diss., Cornell University, 1984); Shigeharu Tanabe, "Ideological Practice in Peasant Rebellions: Siam at the Turn of the Twentieth Century," in *History and Peasant Consciousness in Southeast Asia*, ed. Shigeharu Tanabe and Andrew Turton (Osaka: National Museum of Ethnology), 75–110; Katherine Bowie, "Peasant Perspectives on the Political Economy of the Northern Thai Kingdom of Chiang Mai in the Nineteenth Century: Implications for the Understanding of Peasant Political Expression" (PhD diss., University of Chicago, 1988).

23.   Krirkkiat, *Farmers and the Land*, 416.

24.   Krirkkiat, *Trends in Land Tenure and Security*, 11.

25.   Carle C. Zimmerman, *Siam Rural Economic Survey, 1930–31* (Bangkok: Bangkok Times Press), 1931. Zimmerman used a very small sample size. He based his analysis of the entire country on data from forty villages spread across the four regions of the north, northeast, south, and center; analysis of each village was then based on data from fifty families in each village. His conclusions about the northern region were based on data from twelve villages, four of which were in Chiang Mai province (9).

26.   Ibid., 18.

27.   Michael Moerman, *Agricultural Change and Peasant Choice in a Thai Village* (Berkeley: University of California Press, 1968). Moerman notes an increase in land rent in a village in Chiang Rai province in 1960, from one-third to one-half of the harvest, and comments, "This high rent probably does not indicate a sudden increase in population; rather it is a culmination—based on the introduction of tractor agriculture—of the

accelerating demand for land that began about 1920, when the railroad from Bangkok first came to Lampang" (111–12).

28. Paul T. Cohen, "Problems of Tenancy and Landlessness in Northern Thailand," *Developing Economies* 21, no. 3 (1983): 247–48.

29. Krirkkiat, *Trends in Land Tenure and Security*, 32.

30. National Research Council of Thailand, *Socio-Political-Economic Analysis of Land Tenure for Agricultural Land Reform in Thailand: Comparative Study between Central and North Region, B.E. 2519* (Bangkok: Office of the Prime Minister, 2519 [1976]), 43.

31. The binds of blood did not necessarily prevent land disputes from becoming contentious or even litigious. For an analysis of how landownership disputes among siblings became litigious in Chiang Mai in May 1973, see David Engel, *Code and Custom in a Thai Provincial Court: The Interaction of Formal and Informal Systems of Justice* (Tucson: University of Arizona Press, 1978), 154–55.

32. Andrew Turton, "The Current Situation in the Thai Countryside," in *Thailand: Roots of Conflict*, ed. Andrew Turton, Jonathan Fast, and Malcolm Caldwell (Nottingham: Spokesman Press, 1978), 106.

33. Ibid.

34. Ibid., 115.

35. Ibid., 108.

36. Ibid., 113; David Morell and Chai-anan Samudavanija, *Political Conflict in Thailand: Reform, Reaction, and Revolution* (Cambridge: Oelgeschlager, Gunn and Hain, 1981), 210–11.

37. For an English translation of Pridi's economic plan, see Pridi Banomyong, *Pridi by Pridi: Selected Writings on Life, Politics, and Economy*, trans. Chris Baker and Pasuk Phongpaichit (Chiang Mai: Silkworm Books, 2000), 83–123.

38. Akira Suehiro, "Land Reform in Thailand: The Concept and Background of the Agricultural Land Reform Act of 1975," *Developing Economies* 19, no. 4 (1981): 314.

39. Ibid., 326.

40. Ibid., 327.

41. Cohen, "Problems of Tenancy and Landlessness in Northern Thailand," 261.

42. Suehiro, "Land Reform in Thailand," 338.

43. Ansil Ramsay, "The Limits of Land Reform in Thailand," *Journal of Developing Areas* 16, no. 2 (January 1982): 177.

44. Cohen, "Problems of Tenancy and Landlessness in Northern Thailand," 265; Suehiro, "Land Reform in Thailand," 343.

45. This summary is based on Charnvit Kasetsiri, *14 October* (Bangkok: Saithan Press, 2544 [2001]), especially Benedict Anderson's translation of Charnvit's account of the events on pages 183–215.

46. See my conclusion for information on numbers killed. For a detailed account of the events of this day, see Puey, "Violence and the Military Coup in Thailand"; and Charnvit Kasetsiri et al., *From 14 to 6 October* (Bangkok: Thammasat University Press, 2541 [1998]).

47. Important exceptions include Bowie, *Rituals of National Loyalty*, which is about the right-wing Village Scout movement; and Prajak Kongkirati, *And Now the Movement Emerges . . . Cultural Politics of Students and Intellectuals prior to 14 October* (Bangkok: Thammasat University Press, 2548 [2005]), which is about progressive cultural politics before 14 October 1973.

48. Thongchai Winichakul, "Remembering/Silencing the Traumatic Past: The Ambivalent Memories of the October 1976 Massacre in Bangkok," in *Cultural Crisis and Social Memory: Modernity and Identity in Thailand and Laos*, ed. Shigeharu Tanabe and Charles Keyes (Honolulu: University of Hawai'i Press, 2002), 243–86.

49. Royal Institute, *Royal Institute Dictionary* (Bangkok: Royal Institute, 2542 [1999]), 116.

50. This idea was prevalent in many of the early, foundational works on Thai politics, including Fred W. Riggs, *Thailand: The Modernization of a Bureaucratic Polity* (Honolulu: East-West Center Press, 1966); and David A. Wilson, *Politics in Thailand* (Ithaca, NY: Cornell University Press, 1967). State-focused work, such as Kullada Kesboonchu Mead, *The Rise and Decline of Thai Absolutism* (New York: Routledge Curzon, 2004), remains important. My intention here is not to devalue this work but instead to insist that work on Thai politics must go further. Across the fields of history, anthropology, and political science, there has been significant work on other forms and modalities of Thai politics, including Attachak Sattayanurak, *The "Third Hand" in Thai Political History* (Bangkok: Kobfai Publishing Project, 2549 [2006]), which is about the discourse of the "third hand," in Thai political life; and Michael Kelly Connors, *Democracy and National Identity in Thailand* (New York: Routledge Curzon, 2003), which addresses the cultural politics of democracy.

51. See Cynthia Enloe, *Bananas, Beaches, and Bases: Making Feminist Sense of International Politics* (Berkeley: University of California Press, 1990); Cynthia Enloe, *The Morning After: Sexual Politics at the End of the Cold War* (Berkeley: University of California Press, 1993); Cynthia Enloe, *Maneuvers: The International Politics of Militarizing Women's Lives* (Berkeley: University of California Press, 2000); and Enloe, *The Curious Feminist*.

52. Enloe, *The Curious Feminist*, 23.

53. Ibid.

54. In *Borderlands/La Frontera* (San Francisco: Aunt Lute, 1987), 109, Gloria Anzaldúa writes, "Nothing happens in the 'real' world unless it first happens in the images in our heads."

55. Antonio Gramsci, *Selections from the Prison Notebooks*, ed. and trans. Quintin Hoare and Geoffrey Nowell Smith (New York: International Publishers, 1971), 57–58.

56. Raymond Williams, *Keywords: A Vocabulary of Culture and Society* (New York: Oxford University Press, 1976), 145.

57. Ibid., 271.

58. Karl Marx and Friedrich Engels, *The Marx-Engels Reader*, ed. Robert C. Tucker (New York: Norton, 1972), 483.

59. Eugen Weber, "Revolution? Counterrevolution? What Revolution?" in *Fascism: A Reader's Guide*, ed. Walter Laqueur (Berkeley: University of California Press, 1976), 463.

60. Ibid., 447.

61. Pridi, *Pridi by Pridi*, 124–25.

62. For example, in *Thailand: A Short History*, historian David Wyatt commented, "The military coup that toppled the absolute monarchy on 24 June 1932, can in no sense of the word be accurately described as a revolution, save in its long-term implications" (234). In *Commodifying Marxism: The Formation of Modern Thai Radical Culture, 1927–1958* (Kyoto: Kyoto University Press, 2001), 34–35, Kasian Tejapira explained that

"the Siamese communists regarded the People's Party as self-styled, that is, fake 'people' and 'revolutionaries,' actually representing the bourgeoisie in alliance with some military leaders and disgruntled bureaucrats, who took power out of self-interest and conflict with the royalty rather than for the poor people who gained little benefit and no power from the whole revolutionary charade. . . . [T]he new regime was essentially a dictatorship that still served the interests of the monarchy, the rich, and the foreign imperialists as before, but which simply replaced one oppressor with many" (34–35).

63. Kasian, *Commodifying Marxism*, 197.

64. Ibid., 198.

65. Philip Corrigan and Derek Sayer, *The Great Arch: English State Formation as Cultural Revolution* (Oxford: Blackwell, 1985), 207.

66. Georges Bataille, *Erotism: Death and Sensuality* (San Francisco: City Lights Books, 1962), 63.

67. Mikhail Bakhtin, *Rabelais and His World*, trans. Helene Iswolsky (Cambridge, MA: MIT Press, 1968); Peter Stallybrass and Allon White, *The Poetics and Politics of Transgression* (Ithaca, NY: Cornell University Press, 1986), 17–18.

68. See J. K. Gibson-Graham, *The End of Capitalism (As We Knew It): A Feminist Critique of Political Economy* (Cambridge: Blackwell Publishers, 1996); J. K. Gibson-Graham, Stephen A. Resnick, and Richard D. Wolff, "Introduction: Class in a Poststructuralist Frame," in *Class and Its Others*, ed. J. K. Gibson-Graham, Stephen A. Resnick, and Richard D. Wolff (Minneapolis: University of Minnesota Press, 2000), 1–22; and J. K. Gibson-Graham, Stephen A. Resnick, and Richard D. Wolff, "Toward a Poststructuralist Political Economy," in *Re/Presenting Class: Essays in Postmodern Marxism*, ed. J. K. Gibson-Graham, Stephen A. Resnick, and Richard D. Wolff (Durham, NC: Duke University Press, 2001), 1–22.

69. Gibson-Graham, Resnick, and Wolff, "Introduction," 11.

70. Gibson-Graham, Resnick, and Wolff, "Toward a Poststructuralist Political Economy," 18–19.

71. In *The End of Capitalism (As We Knew It)*, J. K. Gibson-Graham writes, "We understand class processes as overdetermined, or constituted, by every other aspect of social life. By this we mean that we 'think' the existence of class and of particular class processes by initially presuming overdetermination rather than by positing a necessary or privileged association between exploitation and some set of social processes (such as control over the labor process or consciousness or struggle or ownership, to rename the familiar few). In this initial presumption, class is constituted at the intersection of all social dimensions or processes—economic, political, cultural, natural—and class processes themselves participate in constituting these other dimensions of social existence. This mutual constitution of social processes generates an unending sequence of surprises or contradictions. As the term 'process' is intended to suggest, class and other aspects of society are seen as existing in change and as continually undergoing novel and contradictory transformations" (55).

72. Akhil Gupta and James Ferguson, "Beyond 'Culture': Space, Identity, and the Politics of Difference," in *Culture, Power, Place: Explorations in Critical Anthropology*, ed. Akhil Gupta and James Ferguson (Durham, NC: Duke University Press, 1997), 33–34.

73. Bowie frames her dissertation, "Peasant Perspectives on the Political Economy of the Northern Thai Kingdom of Chiang Mai in the Nineteenth Century," with a critique of the inaccuracies and gaps in much earlier academic work about nineteenth-century

northern Thai history. She argues that many analyses falsely stress the self-sufficient economy of the peasants, the kindnesses of the lords, and the relative hegemony operative in the Chiang Mai kingdom. Her research shows these descriptions to be at once erroneous representations of peasant life and a dangerous mode of historiography. Bowie explains that when scholars have not found, or have missed, signs of "overt peasant political unrest," they have taken this to mean that peasants were content (16). The unquestioned idea of comfortable peasants who participate in a subsistence economy "has a political content. The characterization encourages a view of the past as idyllic, harmonious, and happy" (75). In contrast to these representations, Bowie draws on extensive oral history and archival research to offer a different picture of peasant-lord relations as dynamic and fraught with struggle. She argues against a subsistence economy by tracing rice shortages, hardship, famine, begging, and the differential economic positions of peasants in nineteenth-century Chiang Mai in the Lanna kingdom. Peasants were not satisfied with relations that left their bellies empty and the lords' full. Bowie further notes that "peasants were not content with lordly extraction, nor did the ruling lords have much legitimacy in their eyes" (21). Not only did the peasants view the lords as illegitimate, but Bowie's oral histories reveal that they perceived them as "arbitrary, capricious, petty, greedy, and even cruel figures of power and potential torment" (71).

74. In 1975, one of the two largest landowners in Chiang Mai province was a direct descendant of Jao Rajabutr, one of the sons of the last king of Lanna, Jao Kaew Nawarat. Morell and Chai-anan, *Political Conflict in Thailand*, 210.

75. Judith Butler's interpretation of Hegel's master-slave dialectic may be instructive here. In *The Psychic Life of Power: Theories in Subjection* (Stanford: Stanford University Press, 1997), she writes: "To disavow one's body, to render it 'Other' and then to establish the 'Other' as an effect of autonomy, is to produce one's body in such a way that the activity of its production—and its essential relation to the lord—is denied. This trick or ruse involves a double disavowal and an imperative that the 'Other' become complicit with this disavowal. In order not to be the body that the lord presumably is, and in order to have the bondsman posture as if the body that he is belongs to himself—and not be the orchestrated projection of the lord—there must be a certain kind of exchange, a bargain or deal, in which ruses are enacted and transacted. In effect, the imperative to the bondsman consists in the following formulation: you be my body for me, but do not let me know that the body you are is my body. An injunction and contract are here performed in such a way that the moves which guarantee the fulfillment of the injunction and the contract are immediately covered over and forgotten" (35). The farmers' organizing around land rent issues and the responses it provoked from landlords exposed the ruse.

76. Mary Beth Tierney-Tello, *Allegories of Transgression and Transformation: Experimental Fiction by Women Writing under Dictatorship* (Albany: State University of New York Press, 1996), 213.

77. Sally Merry, *Colonizing Hawai'i: The Cultural Power of Law* (Princeton, NJ: Princeton University Press, 2000), 17.

78. David Engel, "Litigation across Space and Time: Courts, Conflict, and Social Change," *Law and Society Review* 24, no. 2 (1990): 340.

79. Engel, *Code and Custom in a Thai Provincial Court*, 160.

80. Scott, *Weapons of the Weak*, 29.

81. E. P. Thompson, *Whigs and Hunters: The Origin of the Black Act* (London: Allen Lane, 1975), 259. For an assessment and rereading of the critiques of Thompson, see Daniel H. Cole, "'An Unqualified Human Good': E. P. Thompson and the Rule of Law," *Journal of Law and Society* 20, no. 2 (June 2001): 177–203.

82. Audre Lorde, *Sister Outsider* (Trumansburg, NY: Crossing Press, 1984), 112.

83. Gramsci, *The Prison Notebooks*, 367.

84. Ibid., 210, 276.

85. Ibid., 276, emphasis mine.

86. I made six trips to Thailand, comprising a total of twenty-nine months (May 2001, June–August 2002, December 2003–August 2005, September–October 2006, January 2008, and June–August 2008).

87. *Bangkok Post*, 9 October 1976, 3.

88. These volumes were Maxim Gorky, *Song of the Falcon* (Bangkok: Putuchon, 2518 [1975]); and Jit Phumisak, *With Blood and Life: Vietnamese Short Stories* (Bangkok: Chomrom Nangsu Saeng Thawan, 2519 [1976]).

89. Ann Laura Stoler, "[P]Refacing *Capitalism and Confrontation* in 1995," in *Capitalism and Confrontation in Sumatra's Plantation Belt, 1870–1979*, 2nd ed. (Ann Arbor: University of Michigan Press, 1995), viii.

90. In my initial request for a foreign researcher permit, I asked for access to the National Archives, the archives of the Ministry of Interior, and the archives of the Metropolitan Police Bureau. My application was returned to me with the admonition that my request for access to the Ministry of Interior and Metropolitan Police Bureau records from 1969 to 1979 was *inappropriate* as the records dealt with matters of national security. While I made my request as a foreign researcher, not a citizen, the tone of the response suggests the anxiety and concern surrounding the nondisclosure of records. Once my revised request was approved and I began my research, I was not surprised to learn that the index to public records in the Chiang Mai provincial archives abruptly stops in October 1976. When I asked about more recent records, the archival administrator cited the slowness of her subordinates in cataloging information. Whether it was the speed of the cataloguers or a more specious anxiety that prevented the release of the recent documents, they were not available.

91. At times laced with humor, but often deadly serious, on learning that I was from the United States, many people asked me directly if I worked for the Central Intelligence Agency or the National Security Agency. When I said no, the question of my political and class background arose. My frankness about my middle-class family background and my own history of human rights and labor activism satisfied most queries. Due to the history of U.S. involvement in Thailand, the question was not an unreasonable one.

92. Urvashi Butalia, *The Other Side of Silence: Voices from the Partition of India* (Durham, NC: Duke University Press, 2000), 278–79.

93. Azar Nafisi, *Reading Lolita in Tehran: A Memoir in Books* (New York: Random House, 2003), ix.

94. Craig Reynolds, *Thai Radical Discourse: The Real Face of Thai Feudalism Today* (Ithaca, NY: Cornell Southeast Asia Program, Cornell University, 1987), 14.

95. Paulo Freire, *The Pedagogy of the Oppressed*, trans. Myra Bergman Ramos (New York: Continuum, 1970).

Chapter 1. Breaking the Backbone of the Nation

1. The museum is located at 503/20 Nikommakkasan Road in the Ratchathewi district of Bangkok. Its online presence can be found at http://www.thailabourmuseum.org.

2. Tomas Larsson, "Capital to the Tiller? A Prehistory of the Commodification of Land in Thailand," Cornell Southeast Asia Program Brown Bag lecture, 8 February 2007.

3. *Bangkok Post*, 14 July 1951, 4.

4. For the full text of the law in Thai, see *Ratchakitchanubeksa*, 17 October 2493 [1950], book 67, part 56, 957–66. For the full text in English, see Translation and Secretarial Office, *Act Controlling the Hire of Paddy Land, B.E. 2493* (Thonburi: Translation and Secretarial Office, 1951).

5. As noted in the introduction, 1 *rai* equals 0.4 acres. Broadcasted rice is a process of planting in which rice is seeded into dry ground. When the rainy season begins, the seeds sprout. Transplanted rice is a process of planting in which seedlings are inserted into a level, already-wet paddy. Tze-Tzu Chang, "Rice," in *The Cambridge World History of Food*, ed. Kenneth F. Kiple and Kriemhild Coneé Ornelas (Cambridge: Cambridge University Press, 2000), 141, 143.

6. 1 *thang* equals 20 liters.

7. "Tea money" is another word for a bribe. In this context, some landowners demanded a small sum of money or labor from a tenant, over and above the rent, to secure the right to rent a particular plot of land.

8. Translation and Secretarial Office, *Act Controlling the Hire of Paddy Land, B.E. 2493*.

9. Central Thailand has typically had the highest percentage of tenancy nationally, often close to 40 percent of all cultivated land. Reasons include the rapid expansion of tenancy in the first part of the twentieth century, inheritance practices, and rapid development of capitalist practices, including extensive land-based lending by local moneylenders. Witayakorn Chiengkul, *The Effects of Capitalist Penetration on the Transformation of the Agrarian Structure in the Central Region of Thailand (1960–1980)* (Bangkok: Chulalongkorn University Social Research Institute, 1983), 109.

10. C.M. 1.2.2/3, Chiang Mai Provincial Government Documents, Provincial Administration Office, Laws and Orders, "Decree of 2493 B.E. Land Rent Control Act," 51.

11. Ibid., 56. In *Analysis of the Farmers' Federation of Thailand*, Kanoksak Kaewthep asserts that the second period of Phibun's rule, between 1948 and 1957, was marked by "reasonable political freedom" (56). Kanoksak cites the passage of the 1950 LRCA as one indication of this freedom. Although it is not addressed by Kanoksak, the actions taken by farmers in Saraphi district of Chiang Mai province in northern Thailand can also be read as an indication of this moment of slightly open politics. The precise nature of either what Kanoksak calls "reasonable political freedom" or what the farmers identify as "democracy" is difficult to ascertain. For an insightful assessment of Phibun's second term, see chapter 2 of Thak Chaloemtiarana, *Thailand: The Politics of Despotic Paternalism* (Bangkok: Social Science Research Association of Thailand, 1979). As I explain later, an analysis of the status of "democracy" in 1951 is outside the realm of my research. Instead I choose to understand democracy as it was articulated by the Saraphi farmers themselves.

12. David Wyatt, *Thailand: A Short History* (New Haven, CT: Yale University Press, 1984).

13. Pasuk Phongpaichit and Chris Baker, *Thailand: Economy and Politics*, 2nd ed. (Oxford: Oxford University Press, 2002), 119.

14. C.M. 1.2.2/3, "Decree of 2493 B.E. Land Rent Control Act," 48.

15. Even in the central region, the act has been criticized for its failure to effect change in farmers' lives. Kanoksak Kaewthep, in *Analysis of the Farmers' Federation of Thailand*, notes that it had no significant effect (43). Krirkkiat Phipatseritham, in *Farmers and the Land: Reform or Revolution* (Bangkok: Duang Kamol, 2521 [1978]), argues that, although the act was decreed, the government was not seriously committed to enforcing it and therefore its effects were limited (178). Andrew Turton, in "Poverty, Reform, and Class Struggle in Rural Thailand," in *Rural Poverty and Agrarian Reform*, ed. Steve Jones, P. C. Joshi, and Miguel Murmis (New Delhi: Allied Publishers [on behalf of Enda; Dakar, Senegal], 1982), argues that the act "was introduced mainly for political propaganda reasons and remained a dead letter. . . . [I]t did not provide any security of tenure, and introduced no powers of compulsory purchase" (29).

16. See Kanoksak Kaewthep, "Les transformations structurelles et les conflits de classes dans la société rurale thaïandaise d'après l'étude d'un cas: La Fédération de la Paysannerie Thaïlandaise" (PhD diss., Université Paris 7, 1984); Kanoksak Kaewthep, "The Political Economy of the Modern Thai Peasant Movement: The Case of the Farmers' Federation of Thailand (FFT), 1973–1976," in *Transnationalization, the State, and the People: The Case of Thailand* (Quezon City: Southeast Asian Perspectives Project, United Nations University, 1985); Kanoksak, *Analysis of the Farmers' Federation of Thailand*; Kanoksak Kaewthep, "Farmers Federation of Thailand (2517–2522) until the Assembly of the Poor (1995–): Continuity and Discontinuity," *Warasan Setthasat Karnmuang (Phua Chumchon)* 3 (2539 [1997]): 91–109; Kanoksak Kaewthep, "Thai Farmers' Struggles: Farmers' Federation of Thailand," in *The Path of Thai Farmers*, ed. Nitirat Sappayasomboon (Bangkok: Mooniti Dek, 2543 [1999]), 39–62; and Kanoksak Kaewthep, "Lessons from Thirty Years of the Farmers Movement and Protest in Thailand," *Fa Dieu Kan* 2, no. 4 (October–December 2548 [2004]): 88–111. For a review article addressing many themes in Kanoksak's work, see Pitch Pongsawat, "Political Economy of Agrarian Transformation and Peasant Movements in Contemporary Thailand: A Critical Observation," *Warasan Sangkhomsat* (Journal of Sociology, Chulalongkorn University) 32, no. 2 (2001): 1–73.

17. Kanoksak, *Analysis of the Farmers' Federation of Thailand*, 46.

18. Kanoksak, "The Political Economy of the Modern Thai Peasant Movement," 156–57.

19. Kanoksak, *Analysis of the Farmers' Federation of Thailand*, 46.

20. *Straits Times*, 6 September 1950, 8.

21. Ibid., 4 September 1950, 5.

22. *Bangkok Post*, 4 September 1950, 5.

23. Ibid.

24. Ibid., 8 September 1950, 1.

25. Ibid.

26. Ibid., 12 October 1951, 4.

27. For the proceedings of the conference, see Kenneth H. Parsons, Raymond J. Penn, and Philip M. Raup, eds., *Land Tenure: Proceedings of the International Conference*

on Land Tenure and Related Problems in World Agriculture, Held at Madison, Wisconsin, *1951* (Madison: University of Wisconsin Press, 1956).

28. *Bangkok Post*, 12 October 1951, 4.

29. Ranajit Guha, "On Some Aspects of the Historiography of Colonial India," in *Selected Subaltern Studies*, ed. Ranajit Guha and Gayatri Chakravorty Spivak (New York: Oxford University Press, 1988), 37–44; Ranajit Guha, "The Prose of Counter-Insurgency," in *Selected Subaltern Studies*, ed. Ranajit Guha and Gayatri Chakravorty Spivak (New York: Oxford University Press, 1988), 45–86.

30. Guha, "The Prose of Counter-Insurgency," 47.

31. Ibid.

32. Ibid., 46.

33. Ibid., 45.

34. Ibid., 46.

35. For accounts of various Thai rebellions, see Tej Bunnag, *Ro. So. 121 Rebellion* (Bangkok: Thai Watthana Phanit, 2524 [1981]); Wutthichai Munsin and Thammanit Worakorn, eds., *Peasant Rebellions* (Bangkok: Social Science Association of Thailand, 2525 [1982]); Chatthip Nartsupha, "The Ideology of 'Holy Men' Revolts in North East Thailand," in *History and Peasant Consciousness in South East Asia*, ed. Shigeharu Tanabe and Andrew Turton (Osaka: National Museum of Ethnology, 1984), 111–34; Shigeharu Tanabe, "Ideological Practice in Peasant Rebellions: Siam at the Turn of the Twentieth Century," in *History and Peasant Consciousness in Southeast Asia*, ed. Shigeharu Tanabe and Andrew Turton (Osaka: National Museum of Ethnology, 1984), 75–110; and Katherine Bowie, "Peasant Perspectives on the Political Economy of the Northern Thai Kingdom of Chiang Mai in the Nineteenth Century: Implications for the Understanding of Peasant Political Expression" (PhD diss., University of Chicago, 1988).

36. Although many Thai–foreign language dictionaries predated the *Royal Institute Dictionary* (Bangkok: Royal Institute, 2493 [1950]), including Edward Blair Michell's *A Siamese-English Dictionary for the Use of Students in Both Languages* (Bangkok, 1892) and Jean-Baptiste Palleqoix's *Siamese French English Dictionary* (Bangkok: Imprimerie de la Mission Catholique, 1896), here I am interested in analyzing the *Royal Institute Dictionary* as the official, Thai-Thai lexicon.

37. Siam was used until 1939, when the name of the country was changed to Thailand in one of the twelve *rathhaniyom*, or "state-isms," decreed by Field Marshal Phibunsongkhram. For full English translations of the twelve state-isms, see Thak Chaloemtiarana, ed., *Thai Politics: Extracts and Documents, 1932–1957* (Bangkok: Social Science Association of Thailand, 1978).

38. Royal Institute, *Royal Institute Dictionary* (Bangkok: Royal Institute, 2493 [1950]), kh.

39. Ibid.

40. A brief reference to some of the key actors involved is instructive here. Luang Wichitwathakan, described by David Wyatt as "the most prolific and ardent popularizer of the constitutional regime," personally recommended or approved all members of the institute. Wyatt, *Thailand*, 242. In Sulak Sivaraksa's assessment, the Royal Institute was one of the sites where Luang Wichitwathakan attempted to destroy "everything that the princes had created and preserved, starting with the word Siam . . . and the Royal Council, the last creation of Prince Damrong." Sulak Sivaraksa, *Siam in Crisis* (Bangkok: Santi Pracha Dhamma Institute, 1990), 50. See Saichon Sattayanurak, *The Changes in*

the Construction of "The Thai Nation" and "Thainess" by Luang Wichitwathakan (Bang-kok: Matichon, 2545 [2002]), for an illuminating discussion of Luang Wichitwathakan, nationalism, and Thainess. The first two presidents of the Royal Institute, Prince Wan Waithayakon and Phya Anuman Rajadhon, may be seen as standing in contrast to Luang Wichitwathakan, his support of Phibunsongkhram's efforts to "modernize" and "westernize" Siam, and his visions of exclusive "Thainess." Prince Wan, in particular, was very concerned with the creation of "Thai" words and the codification of the Thai lan-guage. A bilingual publication of his article "Coining Thai Words" is included in a com-memorative volume published on the 110th anniversary of his birth. See Munnithi Nara-thip Praphanphong-Worawan, ed., *Prince Wan Studies: 110th Anniversary of His Birth, 25 August 2001* (Bangkok: Munnithi Narathip Praphanphong-Worawan, 2544 [2001]). See Kasian Tejapira, *Commodifying Marxism: The Formation of Modern Thai Radical Culture, 1927–1958* (Kyoto: Kyoto University Press, 2001), 196–99, for Prince Wan's in-fluences on the creation of Thai words that could be used to talk about leftist and dis-sident politics. For accounts of Phya Anuman's life and work, see Sulak, *Siam in Crisis*; and Tej Bunnag and Michael Smithies, eds., *In Memoriam Phya Anuman Rajadhon: Contributions in Memory of the Late President of the Siam Society* (Bangkok: Siam Society, 1970). The Royal Institute itself has what Anthony Diller describes as a "plurality in its objectives" and has been under the purview of at least three different ministries since its inception, including the Prime Minister's Office, Ministry of Culture, and Ministry of Education. Anthony Diller, "What Makes Central Thai a National Language?" in *National Identity and Its Defenders, 1939–1989*, ed. Craig J. Reynolds, 2nd ed. (Chiang Mai: Silkworm Books, 2002), 87, 102n23.

41. Diller, "What Makes Central Thai a National Language?" 87.

42. For example, see Yot Pannasorn, *Student Dictionary* (Bangkok: Prasarnmit Press, 2543 [2000]).

43. Royal Institute, *Royal Institute Dictionary* (Bangkok: Royal Institute, 2525 [1982]); Royal Institute, *Royal Institute Dictionary* (Bangkok: Royal Institute, 2542 [1999]).

44. Royal Institute, *Royal Institute Dictionary* (Bangkok: Royal Institute 2542 [1999]), 34, emphasis mine.

45. Royal Institute, *Royal Institute Dictionary* (Bangkok: Royal Institute 2525 [1982]), 26.

46. *Prachathipatai*, 21 June 2494 [1951], 2.

47. Ibid.

48. Ibid.

49. Ibid.

50. Ibid.

51. Ibid.

52. *Prachathipatai*, 22 June 2494 [1951], 2. *Loranthus viscum* is a type of parasitic vine that destroys crops.

53. Ibid.

54. Ibid.

55. C.M. 1.2.2/3, "Decree of 2493 B.E. Land Rent Control Act," 59.

56. Ibid., 63.

57. Drawing on interviews with villagers in Satingpra district of Songkhla province in southern Thailand, Peter Vandergeest found that although the descendants of those

who had been wealthy prior to World War II spoke of the relationships with impoverished villagers in terms of charity and goodwill, those who were poor had a much different explanation. For the poor, rather than generosity, exchange and obligation were in place. He commented that the poor noted that they respected some of the wealthy, for "'we *had* to respect them. And we had to work in their fields for the rice.' They were clear that receiving food from the rich incurred an obligation to provide labour." Peter Vandergeest, "Gifts and Rights: Cautionary Notes on Community Self-Help in Thailand," *Development and Change* 22, no. 3 (1991), 435.

58. James C. Scott, "Patron-Client Politics and Political Change in Southeast Asia," *American Political Science Review* 66, no. 1 (March 1972): 7.

59. C.M. 1.2.2/3, "Decree of 2493 B.E. Land Rent Control Act," 55–56.

60. Ibid., 56. Rather than speculating on what constituted democracy in 1951 (and whether or not it was really democratic), here I choose to understand democracy as it is articulated by the Saraphi farmers themselves.

61. Ibid., 55–56.

62. Ibid., 66.

63. Ibid., 39; *Siam Rat*, 22 November 2494 [1951], 1.

64. C.M. 1.2.2/3, "Decree of 2493 B.E. Land Rent Control Act," 53.

65. Ann Laura Stoler, "Developing Historical Negatives: Race and the (Modernist) Visions of a Colonial State," in *From the Margins: Historical Anthropology and Its Futures*, ed. Brian Keith Axel (Durham, NC: Duke University Press, 2002), 157.

66. Ibid.

67. Twenty-two landowners were issued and delivered individual invitations to a meeting at the Chiang Mai provincial government building. The list of invitees, as well as information about who signed for each invitation, is contained in the archival file. Many of the invitees were from long-standing merchant and landholding families in Chiang Mai. For an illuminating history of capitalism in northern Thailand, see Plai-auw Chananont, "The Roles of Merchant Capitalists in the Expansion of Capitalism in Northern Thailand, 1921–1980" (MA thesis, Faculty of Economics, Chulalongkorn University, 2529 [1986]).

68. He even notes in his introduction to the meeting that in the opinion of some MPs, not enough farmer voices were being heard. This meeting was a strange solution. He commented, "We've heard from some MPs that the province only listens to landowners. We haven't listened to the voices of the tenant farmers. So our reporting of the facts is shaky. The Ministry of Interior has asked us to consider it again." C.M. 1.2.2/3, "Decree of 2493 B.E. Land Rent Control Act," 32.

69. Ibid.

70. Ibid., 33.

71. Ibid., 34.

72. Ibid., 38.

73. Ibid., 37.

74. Ibid., 36.

75. Ibid., 35.

76. Ibid. Humber was a brand of British bicycle that was later acquired by the Raleigh Bicycle Company.

77. To my great dismay, there is no archival record of the vehicles used by each

landowner to travel to the meeting. I can only speculate that Kraisri was driven in a car. The certainty would provide an interesting context for his statements.

78. C.M. 1.2.2/3, "Decree of 2493 B.E. Land Rent Control Act," 1–10.

79. Ibid., 5.

80. Karl Marx and Friedrich Engels, *The German Ideology* (New York: International Publishers, 1965), 61.

81. *Kittisak*, 7 September 2494 [1951], 3, 6.

82. Ibid.

83. Ibid., 6.

84. Ibid.

85. *Siam Rat*, 9 September 2494 [1951], 7.

86. Ibid.

87. Let me be clear. I am discussing the formulations of communism in circulation around the law and the farmers. I am not making a claim as to whether or not the law or the farmers *were* communist. There are various methodological problems, obstacles, and implications involved in making such a claim. Primary among these problems is the sheer lack of evidence or reference to Thai Communist Party (TCP) activity in the north in the early 1950s (the TCP was a precursor to the CPT). While Somsak Jeamteerasakul notes that at this time active organizing was taking place in the south and parts of the northeast, he makes no reference to the north. Somsak Jeamteerasakul, "The Communist Movement in Thailand" (PhD diss., Monash University, 1991). Jeffrey Race characterizes pre-1960 communist activity in the north as "rumor." Jeffrey Race, "The War in Northern Thailand," *Modern Asian Studies* 8, no. 1 (1974): 7–9.

88. James C. Scott, *Weapons of the Weak: Everyday Forms of Peasant Resistance* (New Haven, CT: Yale University Press, 1985).

89. Andrew Turton, "Limits of Ideological Domination and the Formation of Social Consciousness," in *History and Peasant Consciousness in Southeast Asia*, ed. Andrew Turton and Shigeharu Tanabe (Osaka: National Museum of Ethnology, 1984), 65–66.

90. Matichon, *Dictionary outside the Royal Institute* (Bangkok: Matichon Press, 2543 [2000]).

91. Matichon, *Matichon Dictionary* (Bangkok: Matichon Press, 2547 [2004]), 9, 10.

92. Ibid., 24, emphasis mine.

Chapter 2. From the Rice Fields to the Cities

1. Reynolds, *Thai Radical Discourse*, 26.

2. Andrew Turton, "Poverty, Reform, and Class Struggle in Rural Thailand," in *Rural Poverty and Agrarian Reform*, ed. Steve Jones, P. C. Joshi, and Miguel Murmis (New Delhi: Allied Publishers [on behalf of Enda; Dakar, Senegal], 1982), 28.

3. *Investor* 7, no. 8 (August 1975): 15, citing a 1974 survey of one district in Chiang Mai province, which "found that of 1,437 households, 37 were village landlords, 582 were owner occupiers, 338 were tenants and 531 were landless." Landless farmers were faced with the choice of either working as agricultural wage laborers or migrating to urban areas in search of other work.

4. Ibid., 7.

5. *Prachachat Weekly* 1, no. 48 (17 October 2517 [1974]): 31.

6. Hans Luther, *Peasants and State in Contemporary Thailand: From Regional Revolt to National Revolution?* (Hamburg: Institute fur Asienkunde, 1978), 74.

7. M. Ladd Thomas, *Political Violence in the Muslim Provinces of Southern Thailand*, Occasional Papers, no. 28 (Singapore: Institute of Southeast Asian Studies, 1975), 8, 25.

8. Witayakorn, *The Effects of Capitalist Penetration*, 98–99.

9. *Athipat*, 29 May–4 June 2517 [1974], 1, 16.

10. Sanam Luang is a large open space bordered by Thammasat University, the Grand Palace, and various government buildings near the Chao Phraya River in Bangkok. In addition to being a historical site of protests, Sanam Luang's proximity to Thammasat meant that the coordinating offices of the student organizations were nearby as well.

11. As an independent organization, the FFT stood in direct contrast to the numerous government-sponsored farmers' groups. Following a damaging flood in 1917, the first agricultural cooperative was established in 1919 as a cooperative credit society. National Food and Agriculture Organization Committee, *Thailand and Her Agricultural Problems* (Bangkok: Ministry of Agriculture, 1950), 90–91. Although some of these cooperatives were established in the early part of the twentieth century, the majority were established in the 1950s. In "Poverty, Reform, and Class Struggle in Rural Thailand," Andrew Turton notes that in 1973 "there were 1,076 cooperatives of various kinds in Thailand with 717,521 members and covering almost 20 percent of the farming families" (25). Turton also notes that the majority of these cooperatives were simply credit organizations and were inactive because of their own outstanding debts with the Bank for Agriculture and Agricultural Cooperatives. He critiques these cooperatives as dominated by local and wealthy elites, rife with corruption, and lacking the actual participation of their farmer-members.

12. Numerous licensed and unlicensed versions of *The Real Face of Thai Feudalism Today* have been published in Thai since 1957. As part of his *Thai Radical Discourse: The Real Face of Thai Feudalism Today*, Craig Reynolds completed an English translation of *The Real Face* and published it as part of his book about Jit and Thai historiography. In this chapter and throughout this book, I use and quote from Reynolds's translation, cited as Somsamai Srisudravarna, "The Real Face of Thai Saktina Today," trans. Craig Reynolds, in *Thai Radical Discourse: The Real Face of Thai Feudalism Today* (Ithaca, NY: Southeast Asia Program, Cornell University, 1987), 43–148. As Reynolds transliterates the Thai word for "feudal" (*sakdina*) as *saktina*, rather than translating it to "feudal," when quoting Reynolds' translation, I do as well. When not quoting Reynolds, I use the term *feudal*.

13. Reynolds, *Thai Radical Discourse*, 173.

14. Ibid., 13.

15. Ibid., 34.

16. Frantz Fanon, *The Wretched of the Earth*, trans. Cho Khiewphumphuang (Bangkok: Charoenwit Kanphim, 2517 [1974]); Paulo Freire, *Pedagogy of the Oppressed*, trans. Jiraporn Sirisupan (Bangkok: National Student Center of Thailand, 2517 [1974]); Paulo Freire, *Pedagogy of the Oppressed*, trans. Cho Khiewphumphuang (Bangkok: Federation of Independent Students of Thailand, 2517 [1974]); Mao Tse-tung, *President Mao Tse-tung's Speeches* (Bangkok: Sriphen Kanphim, 2518 [1975]); Vladimir Ilyich

Lenin, *State and Revolution* (Bangkok: United Front of Chulalongkorn University, 2518 [1975]).

17. Kulap Saipradit, who also wrote under the pen name Sriburapha, was born in 1905. He published many novels, essays, and other writings between the late 1920s and his death in 1973. By the late 1940s, he was writing on explicitly politically progressive topics. During the 1970s, his writings enjoyed renewed interest at the hands of intellectuals and came to be seen as early examples of "literature for life" (*wannakham phua chiwit*). For more information on Kulap's life and works, see Witayakorn Chiengkul, "Returning to Read the Novels of 'Sriburapha,'" *Sangkhomsat Parithat* 11, no. 7 (2516 [1973]): 69–72; Rungwit Suwannaphichon, *Sriburapha, a Great of Thai Literature* (Bangkok: Saengdao Press, 2532 [1989]); Benjamin Batson, "Kulab Saipradit and the 'War of Life,'" *Journal of the Siam Society* 69, nos. 1–2 (January–July 1981): 58–73; and David Smyth, "Siburapha: The Making of a Literary Reputation," in *Thai Constructions of Knowledge*, ed. Manas Chitkasem and Andrew Turton (London: School of Oriental and African Studies, University of London, 1991), 63–83. For an insightful analysis of the "literature for life" movement, see Chaisiri Samutwanit, *Thai Political Literature: 14 October 1973–6 October 1976* (Bangkok: Saithan, 2524 [1981]).

18. See Osamu Akagi, "Research Note and Data on 'Pocketbook' Publication in Thailand, 1973–1976," *South East Asian Studies* 16, no. 3 (December 1978): 473–523, for an annotated bibliography of many of the pocketbooks published during 1973–76.

19. Freire, *Pedagogy of the Oppressed*, trans. Ramos.

20. See Reynolds, *Thai Radical Discourse*, 34–35, for a rich analysis of the controversy surrounding the initial publication of *The Real Face*.

21. Somsamai, "The Real Face of Thai Saktina Today," 45.

22. Ibid.

23. Ibid., 47.

24. Ibid., 54.

25. Ibid., 59.

26. Ibid., 55.

27. Ibid.

28. Ibid.

29. Ibid.

30. Ibid., 59.

31. Reynolds, *Thai Radical Discourse*, 11.

32. Inson Buakiew, "Protesting Is the Best Strategy for Farmers and Workers," *Athipat* 2–8 October 2517 [1974]: 7.

33. Ibid.

34. Turton, "The Current Situation in the Thai Countryside," noted, "The documentation of the peasants movement 1974–1976 is still far from complete. Much information is contained in ephemeral publications of the time; in newspapers: including *Chao Na Thai, Prachachat, Prachathipatai, Athipat, The Nation, Bangkok Post*; and periodicals *Caturat, Prachachat Weekly, The Investor* (Bangkok)" (140n121). I second Turton's claims here. In the overview that follows, I draw primarily on *Thai Rat*, a centrist Bangkok daily; *Athipat*, the weekly newspaper of the NSCT; Kanoksak Kaewthep's extensive writing about the FFT (see chapter 1, note 16, for a list of these works); Nitirat Sapsomboon, ed., *The Path of Thai Farmers* (Bangkok: Mooniti Dek, 2542 [1999]), published on

the twenty-fifth anniversary of the establishment of the FFT; and chapter 8 ("Farmers and Modern Thai Politics") of Morell and Chai-anan, *Political Conflict in Thailand: Reform, Reaction, Revolution*, 205–33.

35. Nitirat Sapsomboon, "Beginnings and Life Histories of the Leaders of the Farmers' Federation of Thailand Movement," in Nitirat, *The Path of Thai Farmers*, 138.

36. The promulgation of a new, democratic constitution was one of the primary demands of the 14 October 1973 protests. However, the new constitution was not promulgated until 7 October 1974. Until then, the constitution of 15 December 1972 was used.

37. Office of the Juridical Council's Welfare Fund, *Constitution of the Kingdom, B.E.* (Bangkok: Office of the Juridical Council's Welfare Fund, 2515 [1972]), 8.

38. Thak Chaloemtiarana, *Thailand: The Politics of Despotic Paternalism* (Bangkok: Social Science Association of Thailand, 1979), 127.

39. Morell and Chai-anan, *Political Conflict in Thailand*, 215.

40. Ibid., 216.

41. Ibid., 215.

42. *Athipat*, 12–18 June 2517 [1974], 2.

43. *Thai Rat*, 27 June 2517 [1974], 2.

44. Nitirat, "Beginnings and Life Histories," 138; Kanoksak, "The Political Economy of the Modern Thai Peasant Movement," 160.

45. *Thai Rat*, 25 June 2517 [1974], 1.

46. Although the Thai word used here (*nai thun*) is often translated as "capitalist," as it is in this book, it also refers to creditors. At this time, one of the factors behind the growing landlessness was the seizure of land by creditors.

47. Nitirat, "Beginnings and Life Histories," 138.

48. Morell and Chai-anan, *Political Conflict in Thailand*, 217.

49. *Thai Rat*, 26 June 2517 [1974], 1.

50. *Thai Rat*, 27 June 2517 [1974], 1.

51. *Thai Rat*, 29 June 2517 [1974], 1.

52. Nitirat, "Beginnings and Life Histories," 138–39.

53. Morell and Chai-anan, *Political Conflict in Thailand*, 218.

54. The Land Reform Act was passed on 17 January 1975.

55. Morell and Chai-anan, *Political Conflict in Thailand*, 218.

56. Ibid.

57. Quoted in Nitirat, "Beginnings and Life Histories," 139.

58. *Athipat*, 4–10 September 2517 [1974], 2.

59. *Thai Niu*, 2 September 2517 [1974], 3.

60. *Thai Rat*, 20 November 2517 [1974], 1.

61. Nitirat, "Beginnings and Life Histories," 140; 1 *kwian* equals approximately 2,000 liters.

62. *Thai Rat*, 28 November 2517 [1974], 12.

63. Nitirat, "Beginnings and Life Histories," 140; *Thai Rat*, 30 November 2517 [1974], 1, 2, 16. One of the monks at Wat Dusidaram in Thonburi who joined the protests was removed from the temple. On 1 December 1974, students and monks marched to the temple to protest his removal. Kraiyudht Dhiratayakinant, ed., *Thailand—Profile 1975* (Bangkok: Voice of the Nation, 1975), 39.

64. Kanoksak, "The Political Economy of the Modern Thai Peasant Movement," 160.

65. A Noh. Soh. 3 certificate gives its holder the right to use land, but not to possess it per se.

66. Nitirat, "Beginnings and Life Histories," 140–41.

67. Morell and Chai-anan, *Political Conflict in Thailand*, 221.

68. *Thai Rat*, 28 November 2517 [1974], 12.

69. Nitirat, "Beginnings and Life Histories," 140.

70. Turton, "Poverty, Reform, and Class Struggle in Rural Thailand," 35.

71. Kanoksak, *Analysis of the Farmers' Federation of Thailand*, 87.

72. Ibid.

73. Victor Karunan, *If the Land Could Speak, It Would Speak for Us* (Hong Kong: Plough Publications, 1984), 47.

74. Andrew Turton et al., *Production, Power, and Participation in Rural Thailand. Experiences of Poor Farmers' Groups* (Geneva: United Nations Research Institute for Social Development, 1987), 38.

75. Turton, "Poverty, Reform, and Class Struggle in Rural Thailand," 34.

76. Ibid., 35.

77. Witayakorn, *The Effects of Capitalist Penetration*, 181.

78. Turton, "The Current Situation in the Thai Countryside," 122.

79. *Thai Niu*, 20 July 2517 [1974], 3.

80. *Thai Niu*, 21 June 2517 [1974], 3.

81. Ibid.

82. *Thai Niu*, 7 November 2517 [1974], 1.

83. Ibid.

84. *Thai Niu*, 9 November 2517 [1974], 3.

85. Ibid.

86. Ibid.

87. Ibid.

88. Ibid.

89. Ibid., 3, 10, emphasis mine.

90. *Prachathipatai*, 22 June 2494 [1951], 2.

91. *Thai Niu*, 16 November 2517 [1974], 3.

92. *Thai Niu*, 17 November 2517 [1974], 3, 11.

93. Ibid.

94. Ibid.

95. Ibid.

96. Translation and Secretarial Office, *Act Controlling the Hire of Paddy Land, B.E. 2493* (Thonburi: Translation and Secretarial Office, 1951), 1.

97. *Thai Niu*, 17 November 2517 [1974], 3, 11.

98. Ibid.

99. *Thai Rat*, 21 November 2517 [1974], 1.

100. Ibid., 16.

101. Ibid.

102. Nitirat, "Beginnings and Life Histories," 139.

103. *Thai Niu*, 23 November 2517 [1974], 1.

104. *Thai Rat*, 22 November 2517 [1974], 16.
105. *Thai Niu*, 23 November 2517 [1974], 1.
106. Ibid.
107. Ibid., 12.
108. *Thai Niu*, 26 November 2517 [1974], 3.
109. Ibid.
110. *Thai Niu*, 27 November 2517 [1974], 3.
111. *Thai Rat*, 29 November 2517 [1974], 16.
112. Ibid.
113. Turton, "Poverty, Reform, and Class Struggle in Rural Thailand," 35.
114. *Thai Rat*, 29 November 2517 [1974], 16.
115. *Ratchakitchanubeksa*, vol. 91, part 215, 16 December 2517 [1974], 591–607.
116. As noted earlier, 1 *thang* is the equivalent of 20 liters.
117. Included among these acts were the following: the tenant sublet the land to someone else without the landowners' knowledge, the tenant used the land for something other than agricultural purposes without the landowner's permission, the tenant caused degradation of the land, the tenant cultivated a banned crop, the tenant did not use the land for over one year, the tenant cultivated less than 75 percent of the land for two consecutive years, the tenant concealed the yield from the land in order to avoid paying the full amount of rent to the landowner, and the tenant did not follow the advice of local agricultural authorities or permitted the deterioration of the land such that the yield decreased by more than one-third of the usual yield.
118. Translation and Secretarial Office, *Act Controlling the Hire of Paddy Land, B.E. 2493*; *Ratchakitchanubeksa*, 16 December 2517 [1974], book 91, part 215, 591–607.
119. Royal Institute, *Royal Institute Dictionary* (Bangkok: Royal Institute, 2542 [1999]), 577.

Chapter 3. From the Classrooms to the Rice Fields

1. Nitirat, "Beginnings and Life Histories," 153–54.
2. See Tyrell Haberkorn, "At the Limits of Imagination: Ajarn Angun Malik and the Meanings of Politics," *Stance: The Thai Feminist Review* 1 (August 2007): 165–99, for an in-depth exploration of Ajarn Angun Malik's life and work as an early Thai feminist.
3. M., "Life Is Like a Dream, If It Is the Truth" (mimeograph, n.d.), n.p.
4. She used the English word *feminist* rather than the Thai translation *satri niyom*.
5. *Nong* means "younger (sister, brother)" in central Thai, and *phi* means "older (sister, brother)."
6. See Peter McLaren with Henry A. Giroux, "Radical Pedagogy as Cultural Politics: Beyond the Discourse of Critique and Anti-Utopianism," in Peter McLaren, *Critical Pedagogy and Predatory Culture: Oppositional Politics in a Postmodern Era* (New York: Routledge, 1995), 29–57.
7. Freire, *Pedagogy of the Oppressed*, trans. Ramos, 47.
8. As the identity "student" became increasingly charged in 1975 and early 1976, and as *student* became synonymous with *agitator* or *communist*, the presence of students in villages could place the villagers who lived there in danger—while students could leave at any time.

9. Thongchai Winichakul, "The Changing Landscape of the Past: New Histories in Thailand since 1973," *Journal of Southeast Asian Studies* 26, no. 1 (1995): 99.

10. Thanet Aphornsuvan, "The First Generation of Thai Students' Movement," in *Thai Student Movements, June 1932–14 October 1973*, ed. Witayakorn Chiengkul (Bangkok: Saithan, 2546 [2003]); Prajak, *And Now the Movement Emerges*.

11. Nisit Jirasophon was a student from southern Thailand who enrolled in the Faculty of Political Science at CMU in 1968. He was one of the editors of *Walanchathat* and active in many other publishing projects. Shortly after *Athipat*, the newspaper of the NSCT, was established following the 14 October 1973 movement, Nisit joined the staff in Bangkok. When he learned that there was no book about the farmers' struggles available in Thai, he organized the translation and printing of one of Mao Tse-tung's books. While on the train on his way to cover a story for *Athipat* in Nakorn Si Thammarat in early April 1975, Nisit was assassinated. See the special issue of *Athipat* (4–9 April 2518 [1975]) dedicated to his life and the circumstances of his death.

12. Young Men in the Flats at the Edge of the Mountain, ed., *His Name is Tongkwao: Writings of Young Men in the Flats at the Edge of the Mountain* (Chiang Mai: Chiang Mai University, 2513 [1970]). The campus of CMU backs up to a mountain, Doi Suthep.

13. Nidhi Eoseewong, "Introduction," in *His Name is Tongkwao: Writings of Young Men in the Flats at the Edge of the Mountain*, ed. Young Men in the Flats at the Edge of the Mountain (Chiang Mai: Chiang Mai University, 2513 [1970]), n.p.

14. Benedict Anderson, "Withdrawal Symptoms: Social and Cultural Aspects of the October 6 Coup," *Bulletin of Concerned Asian Scholars* 9, no. 3 (1977): 171, emphasis in original.

15. Thak Chaloemtiarana, "University Life," in *People of the New Generation*, ed. Thammasat Student Union (Bangkok: Thammasat University, 2518 [1975]), n.p.

16. "Universities and the Role They Should Fill in the Present Society" was published in *Athipat*, 12–18 June 2517 [1974]; and "Study for Life? Whose Life?" was published in *Prachachat Weekly* 1, no. 33 (4 July 2517 [1974]).

17. Louis Althusser, *Lenin and Philosophy and Other Essays*, trans. Ben Brewster (New York: Monthly Review Press, 1971); Freire, *Pedagogy of the Oppressed*, trans. Ramos.

18. Freire, *Pedagogy of the Oppressed*, trans. Jiraporn; Freire, *Pedagogy of the Oppressed*, trans. Cho.

19. "Who Does the Present System of Education Serve?" *Athipat*, 16–22 October 2517 [1974], 3.

20. Ibid.

21. Chaiyong Pornmuang, "Education and Democracy," *Prachachat Weekly* 1, no. 11 (31 January 2517 [1974]).

22. See Tejapira, *Commodifying Marxism*, for more information on Phin's life and the development of his and other CPT intellectuals' work.

23. Amnat Yuthiwiwat, *Education Revolution: Following the Path of Socialism* (Bangkok: Prachatham Press, 2519 [1976]), 1.

24. Ibid., n.p.

25. Niwet Tongkwao, "The Roles of Young People and Students in the Present Situation," in *The Struggle of the People Continues*, ed. Northern Student Center (Bangkok: Northern Student Center, Northeastern Student Center, Southern Student Center, 2517 [1974]), 1–7.

26. Ibid., 4–7.

27. Surachai, quoted in Thanet, "The First Generation of Thai Students' Movement," 78.

28. Komol Keemthong's life deserves far more attention than I can give it here. For more information on Komol's life and writing, see Komol Keemthong Foundation, *Reading Komol Keemthong* (Bangkok: Komol Keemthong Foundation, 2515 [1972]); Phra Santisuk Santhisukho, ed., *Remembering Komol* (Bangkok: Komol Keemthong Foundation, 2522 [1979]); Komol Keemthong, *Writings of Komol Keemthong* (Bangkok: Komol Keemthong Foundation, 2525 [1982]); Phot Kritkraiwan, ed., *Komol Keemthong: Philosophy and Resolution of Life* (Bangkok: Komol Keemthong Foundation, 2540 [1997]); and Pipob Thongchai, "The First Bricks and the Steps Forward," in Sem Pringpuangkaew, *Retracing the Path of an Idealistic Individual: From the Heart of Grandfather to All Idealistic Persons Working for the Commonpeople* (Bangkok: Komol Keemthong Foundation, 2001), 46–50.

29. John Value Dennis, "The Role of the Thai Student Movement in Rural Conflict, 1973–1976" (MS thesis, Cornell University, 1982), 47.

30. Kanoksak, "The Political Economy of the Modern Thai Peasant Movement," 166.

31. Volunteer Development Assembly, *Volunteer Development Assembly* (Chiang Mai: Chiang Mai University Students' Association, 2514 [1971]), n.p.

32. Ibid.

33. CMU Students' Association, quoted in Volunteer Development Assembly, *Volunteer Development Assembly*, n.p.

34. Mary Beth Mills, *Thai Women in the Global Labor Force: Consuming Desires, Contested Selves* (New Brunswick, NJ: Rutgers University Press, 1999), 10, 13.

35. Ibid., 59.

36. Yongyut, quoted in Volunteer Development Assembly, *Volunteer Development Assembly*, n.p.

37. For an insightful analysis of the mixed effects of the Green Revolution, see Harry Cleaver, "The Contradictions of the Green Revolution," *American Economic Review* 62, nos. 1–2 (1972): 177–86. For analyses of the Green Revolution in Thailand, see Pan Yotopoulos, *The Green Revolution in Thailand: With a Bang or with a Whimper?* (Stanford: Food Research Institute, Stanford University, 1975); and Guy Trébuil, "Pioneer Agriculture, Green Revolution, and Environmental Degradation in Thailand," in *Counting the Costs: Economic Growth and Environmental Change in Thailand*, ed. Jonathan Rigg (Singapore: Institute for Southeast Asian Studies, 1995), 67–89.

38. "The sacred hand," quoted in Volunteer Development Assembly, *Volunteer Development Assembly*, n.p., emphasis in original. My thanks to Thak Chaloemtiarana for help with translating this statement.

39. Bhumipol Adulyadej, quoted in Volunteer Development Assembly, *Volunteer Development Assembly*, n.p.

40. Mao Tse-tung, quoted in Volunteer Development Assembly, *Volunteer Development Assembly*, n.p.

41. Nancy Lin, *Reverberations: A New Translation of Complete Poems of Mao Tse-tung* (Hong Kong: Joint Publishing Company, 1980), 42.

42. Volunteer Development Assembly, *Volunteer Development Assembly*, n.p.

43. Although the editorial group was identified as belonging to the Department of Political Science in the Faculty of Social Sciences on the title page of the journal, during the April 2005 commemoration of Nisit Jirasophon's life, the independence of the journal from the faculty and the CMU administration was stressed.

44. Thanet Aphornsuvan, *Literature in Life, Life in Literature* (Bangkok: Samnak-phim Mingmit., 2539 [1996]), 41.

45. For a resonant discussion of risk and danger and the fears students at Thammasat felt in 1970 when they were printing the short book *Treatise* (*Khamphi*), see ibid., 33. The front cover featured a block print of Vladimir Lenin, and the students involved in printing it were concerned that either the print shop owner would refuse to print it or they would not be safe from the Special Branch police when they distributed it.

46. Indicating the reach and influence of *Walanchathat*, one of the former student activists present at the commemoration explained that, although he was from a younger generation than Nisit Jirasophon, and never met him, he read *Walanchathat* when he was a secondary school student at the CMU Demonstration School. He later went on to become an important student activist at CMU between 1974 and 1976.

47. The Thammasat University Center for Volunteer Development was founded in 1967. Between 1967 and 1973, its members took development camp trips to twenty-three places, including Chiang Rai and Narathiwat. Their work was extensively supported by Professor Puey Ungphakorn, the rector of Thammasat University between 1970 and 1976. See Thammasat University Volunteer Development Center, *Drops of Sweat and the Trace of a Smile* (Bangkok: Thammasat University Volunteer Development Center, 2516 [1973]), for photos, recollections, and self-critiques of the first six years of their action. Students at Mahidol University in Bangkok were also very active in rural development projects. For accounts of their activities, see Sanguan Nittayaramphong, ed., *Annals of the History of Mahidol for Democracy*, part 1, *Building the Movement* (Bangkok: Alpha Millennium Company, 2546 [2003]); Sanguan Nittayaramphong, ed., *Annals of the History of Mahidol for Democracy*, part 2, *Organizing the People, Dedicating Oneself to Ideals (14 October 1973–6 October 1976)* (Bangkok: Alpha Millennium Company, 2547 [2004]); and Sanguan Nittayaramphong, ed., *Annals of the History of Mahidol for Democracy*, part 3, *Reviving Hope, Building Strength, Looking to Serve Society (after 6 October 1976–1982)* (Bangkok: Ngandee Company, 2548 [2005]).

48. Morell and Chai-anan, *Political Conflict in Thailand*, 151.

49. Ibid., 152.

50. *Prachachat Weekly* 1, no. 21 (11 April 2517 [1974]), 12–13.

51. *Prachachat Weekly* 1, no. 24 (2 May 2517 [1974]), 12.

52. Ibid., 13.

53. Democracy Propagation Center, *Return to the Rural Areas Program* (Bangkok: Bureau of Universities, 2517 [1974]), 6.

54. Ibid., 6–7.

55. Ibid., 7–8.

56. Thanet Aphornsuvan, *Thai Society and Politics* (Bangkok: P. P. Press, 2521 [1978]), 117.

57. A gaur is a large wild ox. I discuss these right-wing groups in more detail in later chapters.

58. L.'s comment references the Ramkhamhaeng inscription, which dates from 1292 CE. The entire first verse reads:

> In the time of King Ramkhamhaeng the land of Sukhothai is thriving.
> There are fish in the water and rice in the fields.
> The lord of the realm does not levy tolls on his subjects.
> They are free to lead their cattle or ride their horses to engage in trade;
> Whoever wants to trade in horses, does so;
> Whoever wants to trade in silver or gold, does so.

The inscription is attributed to King Ramkhamhaeng and is used in many different ways. Perhaps most indicative of its continuing relevance are the critical reworkings of it by various activists. For example, during the May 2000 protests against the Asian Development Bank, antiprivatization activists printed posters and T-shirts with the following reinscription:

> There is a price on the water
> There are meters in the fields
> Whoever wants to market hospitals, does so
> Whoever wants to market universities, does so.

The authenticity of the inscription has been questioned. For an exhaustive treatment of various perspectives on the debate, see James R. Chamberlain, ed., *The Ram Khamhaeng Controversy: Collected Papers* (Bangkok: Siam Society, 1991).

59. For an analysis of the dangers of residual pesticides in Thailand, see Anat Thapinta and Paul F. Hudak, "Pesticide Use and Residual Occurrence in Thailand," *Environmental Monitoring and Assessment* 60, no. 1 (January 2000): 103–14.

60. For an introduction to these issues and the groups that were organizing in the north between 1985 and 2000, see Northern Farmers' Federation, *Voice of the Farmers* (Chiang Mai: Northern Farmers' Federation, 2543 [2001]).

61. The dangers and pitfalls of romanticizing resistance are well known. See Lila Abu-Lughod, "The Romance of Resistance: Tracing Transformations of Power through Bedouin Women," *American Ethnologist* 17, no. 1 (February 1990): 41–55. In my desire to celebrate the transformative effects and potential of the new alliances between farmers and students, I do not want to elide the inequalities between farmers and students and how they may have operated within the alliances. In refusing this elision, I am not discounting the significance of the alliances, or attempting to render them as ineffective in any way, but rather taking them as seriously and rigorously as I do the forms of violence that attempted to destroy them. In this sense, I am mindful of the careful critique made by Namhee Lee in her analysis of intellectual-worker alliances in South Korea in the 1970s and 1980s, in which she argued that "simply criticizing intellectuals alone is too easy and politically irresponsible. . . . One needs to interrogate the ways this type of criticism functions to limit or foreclose, however inadvertently, further discussion of political and social engagement." Namhee Lee, *The Making of Minjung: Democracy and the Politics of Representation in South Korea* (Ithaca, NY: Cornell University Press, 2007), 15.

62. C.M. 1.2.2/20, Chiang Mai Provincial Government Documents, Provincial Administration Office, Laws and Orders, "2517 Land Rent Control Act," n.p.

63. *Thai Niu*, 9 March 2518 [1975], 3.

64. C.M. 1.2.2/22, Chiang Mai Provincial Government Documents, Provincial Administration Office, Laws and Orders, "2517 B.E. Land Rent Control Act," n.p.

65. Turton, "Poverty, Reform, and Class Struggle in Rural Thailand," 36.

66. *Thai Niu*, 8 January 2518 [1975], 12.

67. Panrat Manurasada, "The Father That I Know," in *Courageous Lawyer of the People*, ed. Chanchai Songwonwong et al. (Bangkok: 179 Kanphim, 2537 [1994]), 127.

68. Sansern Sri-unruan, "Pradap Manurasada, Courageous Lawyer, Truthful Lawyer, One Quarter of My Experience," in *Courageous Lawyer of the People*, ed. Chanchai Songwonwong et al. (Bangkok: 179 Kanphim, 2537 [1994]), 61–62.

69. Turton et al., *Production, Power, and Participation in Rural Thailand*, 42.

70. Freire, *Pedagogy of the Oppressed*, trans. Jiraporn; Freire, *Pedagogy of the Oppressed*, trans. Cho.

71. While a comparison of the two translations might offer some insight into the tensions between the two student organizations, here I choose to temporarily elide the differences between them and celebrate the demand for Freire's ideas that they indicate. Nonetheless, I must do so cautiously; despite my excitement at learning of the two translations, I did not meet a former activist who had actually read the book at the time. Although many people mentioned having heard of the book, it was not cited by anyone I spoke with as having been important to their lives.

72. Cho Khiewphumphuang, the pen name of a Chulalongkorn University professor, also translated Everett Reimer's *School Is Dead* and Frantz Fanon's *Wretched of the Earth*. Everett Reimer, *School Is Dead*, trans. Cho Khiewphumphuang (Bangkok: San Siam, 2517 [1974]); Fanon, *The Wretched of the Earth*, trans. Cho.

73. Cho Khiewphumphuang, "Note to Readers," in Freire, *Pedagogy of the Oppressed*, trans. Cho, 196.

74. Somsamai, "The Real Face of Thai Saktina Today," 56.

75. This formulation belongs to Doreen Lee (personal communication, 8 May 2005). This recognition, she notes, is the site of risk and learning—as well as the home of errors.

Chapter 4. Violence and Its Denials

1. Slavoj Žižek, "Introduction: Between the Two Revolutions," in Vladimir Ilyich Lenin, *Revolution at the Gates: A Selection of Writings from February to October 1917*, ed. Slavoj Žižek (New York: Verso, 2002), 5.

2. Kanoksak, *Analysis of the Farmers' Federation of Thailand*, 161–66. These numbers reflect the assassinations, injuries, and disappearances that made it into the news at the time. See the appendix for a list of the names of those affected and dates of known events.

3. Morell and Chai-anan, *Political Conflict in Thailand*, 226.

4. Bowie, *Rituals of National Loyalty*, 155. Farmers were not the only group targeted during this period; students, workers, journalists, and Socialist Party members were also assassinated. See "Political Killings," *Prachachat Weekly* 3, no. 122 (18 March 2519 [1976]): 29–39, for biographies of different activists who were assassinated.

5. *Chaturat* 1, no. 6 (19 August 2518 [1975]): 35.

6. Benedict Anderson, "Murder and Progress in Modern Siam," *New Left Review* 181 (May–June 1990): 33–48.

7. *Thai Niu*, 8 January 2518 [1975], 12.

8. Michel Bruneau commented that landlord-tenant relations were constituted by dependency, which was "demonstrated by a form of pre-capitalist social relations, the patron-client relationship, a form which gives the whole a certain cohesion and veils the nascent antagonisms." Michel Bruneau, "Land Ownership and Tenure, Relations of Production, and Social Classes in the Rural Areas of Northern Thailand (1966–1976)," paper presented at the Thai-European Seminar on Social Change in Contemporary Thailand, University of Amsterdam, 28–30 May 1980, 20.

9. *Thai Niu*, 26 December 2517 [1974], 1, 12.

10. The third zone included Sanpatong, Hang Dong, Chomthong, Doi Tao, Hod, Mae Chaem, and Omkoi districts. Two MPs were to be elected from this zone. See Prachachat Daily, *Prachachat Presents the '75 Elections* (Bangkok: Samnakphim Prapansat, 2518 [1975]), 415.

11. C.M. 1.2.2/3, Chiang Mai Provincial Government Documents, Provincial Administration Office, Laws and Orders, "Decree of 2493 B.E. Land Rent Control Act," 37.

12. *Chaturat* 1, no. 6 (19 August 2518 [1975]): 34.

13. *Thin Thai*, 3 January 2518 [1975], 1, 10.

14. *Thin Thai*, 6 January 2518 [1975], 1, 10.

15. C.M. 1.2.2/3, "Decree of 2493 B.E. Land Rent Control Act," 38.

16. *Thin Thai*, 7 January 2518 [1975], 1, 10.

17. *Thai Niu*, 19 July 2518 [1975], 1, 12; *Chaturat* 1, no. 6 (19 August 2518 [1975]): 35.

18. *Sieng Chonabot*, 19 November 2518 [1975], 1.

19. *Sieng Chonabot*, 12 November 2518 [1975], 12.

20. *Kittisak*, 7 September 2494 [1951], 6.

21. While Saengkaew Waelayen, Eiakiew Chalermsuphakul, and Worasak Nimmanan offer a sense of the most acute responses to the LRCA, I want to note that they cannot be taken as representative of the entirety of the responses.

22. Dennis, "The Role of the Thai Student Movement in Rural Conflict," 65.

23. Ibid.

24. Bowie, "Peasant Perspectives."

25. Quoted in *Bangkok Post*, 8 May 1975, 1.

26. Quoted in *Bangkok Post*, 29 June 1975, 5.

27. Bowie, *Rituals of National Loyalty*, 55.

28. For example, the work of the FFT was described by one Chiang Mai daily newspaper as "bringing groups of farmers together for meetings in different places; it is agitation of the masses." *Thin Thai*, 2 August 2518 [1975], 12. For a similar example of the characterization of student organizing as such, see another Chiang Mai daily paper, *Thai Niu*, 9 July 2518 [1975], 1. These are only two of innumerable examples.

29. *Bangkok Post*, 11 June 1975, 3.

30. *Athipat*, 2–5 May 2518 [1975], 1, 12; *Athipat*, 6–8 May 2518 [1975], 1, 12.

31. *Bangkok Post*, 3 May 1975, 3. The complete list of demands is reproduced in appendix 7 of Kanoksak, *Analysis of the Farmers' Federation of Thailand*, 157–58.

32. *Bangkok Post*, 7 May 1975, 3.

33. Quoted in *Bangkok Post*, 8 May 1975, 1.

34. Turton et al., *Production, Power, and Participation in Rural Thailand*, 39–40.

35. Chatri Hutanuwat, a CMU student and one of the leaders of the Farmer Proj-

ect whose arrest I address in the next chapter, lived in a small house in the compound of Ajarn Angun Malik. While Ajarn Angun, Chatri, and other residents of the compound were at a protest, Chatri's house was burned down. See *Thai Niu*, 13 March 2518 [1975], 1, 12, for more details. For an account of the raid on a student-farmer house in Chiang Mai in May 1976, see Nitirat, *The Path of Thai Farmers*, 153–54.

36. Katherine Bowie and Brian Phelan, "Who's Killing the Farmers?" *Bangkok Post Sunday Magazine*, 17 August 1975, 5.

37. Kanoksak, "The Political Economy of the Modern Thai Peasant Movement," 162.

38. *Bangkok Post*, 11 July 1975, 1.

39. *Chaturat* 1, no. 6 (19 August 2518 [1975]): 37.

40. *Athipat*, 15–17 July 2518 [1975], 1.

41. *Bangkok Post*, 27 July 1975, 3.

42. *Siam Rat*, 1 August 2518 [1975], 16.

43. Quoted in *Voice of the Nation*, 5 August 1975, 8.

44. *Thin Thai*, 7 August 2518 [1975], 12.

45. Ibid.

46. *Thai Niu*, 8 August 2518 [1975], 3.

47. Ibid.

48. Ibid.

49. Ibid.

50. On hearing of Police General Phoj's statement, the NSCT responded by saying that the police *did* have a list of the leaders. The Ministry of Interior and Department of Police should have had lists of the leaders, as the Prime Minister's Office during the prior Sanya Thammasak regime had requested a list of FFT officials in late December 1974 in order "to facilitate cooperation in finding a solution to the worsening land problem." *Ampo* 7, no. 4 (October–December 1975): 47.

51. Bowie and Phelan, "Who's Killing the Farmers?" 6.

52. *Prachachat Weekly* 2, no. 92 (21 August 2518 [1975]): 10.

53. For an excellent analysis of *Yuthakot*, see Thak Chaloemtiarana, "Professionalism in the Modern Thai Army," paper presented at the Conference on Political Systems and Development, sponsored by the Indian Council of Social Science Research, Centre for the Study of Developing Societies, and the Centre for Policy Research, Delhi, February 1980. Thak analyzes the content of *Yuthakot* over the period 1947–77 in order to track changing attitudes in the Thai military. Of particular interest to my project here, he argues that by the middle of 1975 bold articles on social and political topics were appearing with increasing frequency in *Yuthakot*. He analyzes this as indicating a re-strengthening of the army's power. Many of the articles in the 1975–77 period, including the one by Major Worawut Kosonyutthasorn, which I discuss here, were harshly critical and dismissive of student, farmer, worker, and other dissenting groups.

54. Worawut Kosonyutthasorn, "Who Kills," *Yuthakot* 84, no. 1 (September 2518 [1975]): 41, emphasis mine.

55. Ibid.

56. Ibid.

57. Turton, "The Current Situation in the Thai Countryside," 123.

58. Thanet, *Thai Society and Politics*, 133.

59. Ibid.

60. Turton, "The Current Situation in the Thai Countryside," 123.

61. Ibid.

62. *Sieng Chonabot,* 7 October 2518 [1975], 4.

63. Turton, "The Current Situation in the Thai Countryside," 123. In considering the variety of leadership positions held by Intha during his life, Andrew Turton argues that we should take his life as an indication of the possibility of a progressive undercurrent in village politics: "What is of note is that his career contains all the elements which mark a man out for respect at the village level, with experience in religious, cultural, political, administrative and economic spheres. The fact that he had been an elected village headman (he resigned on becoming Vice-President) and elected head of a government sponsored farmers' group, should serve as a reminder that many progressive rural leaders gain experience in these ways and that not all such posts are held by rich peasants whose class interests would tend to align them with district officials and rural capitalists. Intha's experience and analysis of the critical situation of the majority of farmers led him beyond working within those structures and to seek more radical solutions" (123).

64. Intha Sribunruang, "Interview with *Chaturat* Magazine," *Chaturat* 1, no. 6 (19 August 2518 [1975]): 30.

65. *Prachachat,* 2 August 2518 [1975], 6.

66. Freire, *Pedagogy of the Oppressed,* trans. Ramos, 51.

67. Intha, "Interview with *Chaturat* Magazine," 29.

68. Ibid., 30.

69. Chai-anan Sanudavanija, "Farmers' Movement in Modern Thai Politics," paper presented at the Thai-European Seminar on Social Change in Contemporary Thailand, University of Amsterdam, 28–30 May 1980, 15.

70. Intha, "Interview with *Chaturat* Magazine," 30.

71. Quoted in Preecha and Chamrat, *The Path of Thai Farmers,* 108.

72. Ibid., 108–9.

73. Intha, "Interview with *Chaturat* Magazine," 30.

74. Anderson, "Withdrawal Symptoms," 19.

75. Lawrence Weschler, *A Miracle, a Universe: Settling Accounts with Torturers* (New York: Pantheon, 1990), 237.

76. Ibid.

77. Intha, "Interview with *Chaturat* Magazine," 30.

78. *Thai Niu,* 2 August 2518 [1975], 12.

79. *Thai Niu,* 1 August 2518 [1975], 1, 12.

80. *Bangkok Post,* 1 August 1975, 3.

81. *Daily Niu,* 2 August 2518 [1975], 1.

82. *Prachachat Weekly* 2, no. 90 (7 August 2518 [1975]): 10.

83. *Prachathipatai,* 2 August 2518 [1975], 3.

84. *Siam Rat,* 1 August 2518 [1975], 16; *Bangkok Post,* 2 August 1975, 1, 3.

85. *Prachathipatai,* 1 August 2518 [1975], 12.

86. Ibid.

87. It is true that the FFT did not undertake the arduous process of becoming an officially registered organization. However, responding to this concern, in *Thai Farmer* the FFT asserted: "That the establishment of the FFT is illegal is out of the question. For we peasants are acting according to our own freedom of association, clearly written in the constitution. We have, however, not applied for registration at a government office,

because we don't agree with the law specifying that people cannot form associations for achieving political ends. This law ignores us and aims to segregate us from participating in the politics of our own country." Quoted in Karunan, *If the Land Could Speak*, 48.

88. *Bangkok Post*, 2 August 1975, 3.

89. *Sieng Chonabot*, 13 September 2518 [1975], 8.

90. *Sieng Chonabot*, 7 October 2518 [1975], 4.

91. *Thai Niu*, 7 August 2518 [1975], 12; Turton, "The Current Situation in the Thai Countryside," 123.

92. *Voice of the Nation*, 5 August 1975, 1, 8; *Thai Niu*, 7 August 2518 [1975], 12.

93. *Thai Niu*, 7 August 2518 [1975], 12.

94. *Voice of the Nation*, 5 August 1975, 1, 8. The full text of the letter can be found in *Baan Muang*, 8 August 2518 [1975]. A typed reproduction can also be found in the Thammasat University Archives, T.U. B2/40, Communist Party of Thailand, Political Events Involving Students, Education Documents, "If the letter of Mr. Intha is fake, then we will know who is overseeing the killings of the farmers."

95. *Prachathipatai*, 5 August 2518 [1975], 1, 12; *Voice of the Nation*, 5 August 1975, 1, 8; *Thai Niu*, 7 August 2518 [1975], 1, 12.

96. T.U. B2/40, "If the letter of Mr. Intha is fake, then we will know who is overseeing the killings of the farmers."

97. *Sieng Chonabot*, 7 October 2518 [1975], 4.

98. Ibid., 4. *Pho* means "father," and *pho luang*, in this context, can be translated as "respected father." *Pho luang* is a title often used to indicate respect for an older male leader in a community.

99. The SPT was particularly strong in Chiang Mai. Inson Buakhiew was a party MP from Hang Dong district. In addition, Dr. Bunsanong Punyodhayana, who was a Cornell-educated sociologist and SPT candidate for MP in Chiang Mai in a by-election held when Thongdee Isarachiwin died in late 1975, was assassinated in early 1976. See Somporn Chanthachai, ed., *The People Must Be the Masters of the Land* (Bangkok: Rongphim Duan Tula, 2544 [2001]), published on the twenty-fifth anniversary of Dr. Bunsanong's death, for a collection of articles about the history and work of the SPT.

100. *Sieng Chonabot*, 7 October 2518 [1975], 4.

101. The SAP, led by then prime minister Kukrit Pramoj, is described by Robert Zimmerman as "center-right." Of it, Zimmerman writes, "Its leaders are constitutionalists and performance oriented technocrats (many former Democrat Party members) who recognize the weaknesses of the old bureaucratic polity and accept the need for fundamental but orderly restructuring of the political process. They reject 'socialism' as the answer to Thailand's problems, love their King and prefer a free, capitalist-oriented economic system with some socialistic welfare programs for the very poor in Thailand." Robert F. Zimmerman, "Thailand 1975: Transition to Constitutional Democracy Continues," *Asian Survey* 16, no. 2 (February 1976): 162.

102. *Thai Niu*, 2 August 2518 [1975], 12.

103. Quoted in Kanoksak, *Analysis of the Farmers' Federation of Thailand*, 167.

104. *Prachathipatai*, 4 August 2518 [1975], 2.

105. *Prachachat Weekly* 2, no. 93 (25 August 2518 [1975]): 3.

106. Jim Glassman, *Thailand at the Margins: Internationalization of the State and the Transformation of Labour* (New York: Oxford University Press, 2004), 69.

107. *Thai Niu*, 9 August 2518 [1975], 3.

108. Ibid.

109. Intha, "Interview with *Chaturat* Magazine," 30.

110. *Voice of the Nation*, 11 August 1975, 1.

111. *Thin Thai*, 12 August 2518 [1975], 1, 12.

112. *Voice of the Nation*, 12 August 1975, 1. Visooth was interrogated at the Karunyathep Center in Chiang Mai, which was a detention and reeducation center for suspected communists operated by the Internal Security Operations Command. Signaling further concerns, newspaper reports noted that he was interrogated using "secret methods" (*withi lap*). See, for example, *Thai Niu*, 13 August 2518 [1975], 12.

113. *Thai Niu*, 12 August 2518 [1975], 12. On hearing Visooth's assertion that the KGB was behind the assassination of Intha, the left-wing newspaper *Sieng Chonabot* printed an editorial refuting the claim. First, why would the KGB be interested in the struggle of the Thai farmers? How were Thai farmers' issues relevant to the Soviet Union? Second, if the KGB *did* want to destroy the power of the people, wouldn't working with the Thai government be a more effective strategy? Then *Sieng Chonabot* offered the theory that the U.S. Central Intelligence Agency (CIA) had hired the assassin and instructed him to say that he was hired by the KGB. *Sieng Chonabot*, 15 August 2518 [1975], 3. I suspect that those behind the assassinations were neither U.S. nor Soviet based but were rather more *national* in their locale.

114. *Thai Niu*, 13 August 2518 [1975], 12.

115. *Thai Niu*, 17 August 2518 [1975], 16.

116. *Thai Niu*, 23 October 2518 [1975], 16.

117. *Thai Niu*, 17 August 2518 [1975], 1, 16.

Chapter 5. A State in Disarray

1. For a critical account of the end of apartheid in South Africa, see Patti Waldmeir, *Anatomy of a Miracle: The End of Apartheid and the Birth of the New South Africa* (New Brunswick, NJ: Rutgers University Press, 1998). For analyses of life and violence in postapartheid South Africa, see Richard A. Wilson, *The Politics of Truth and Reconciliation in South Africa: Legitimizing the Post-apartheid State* (New York: Cambridge University Press, 2001); and Mark Shaw, *Crime and Policing in Post-apartheid South Africa: Transforming under Fire* (Bloomington: Indiana University Press, 2002).

2. Earlier scholars of Thailand have privileged law as a site of political, social, and historical change. In *Subject Siam: Family, Law, and Colonial Modernity in Thailand* (Chiang Mai: Silkworm Books, 2002), Tamara Loos argues that law was the vehicle through which the nation's rulers negotiated ideas and norms of gender and freedom with their subjects as well as competing powers. In *Code and Custom in a Thai Provincial Court*, David Engel traces the emergence of a new legal system under King Chulalongkorn as generative *and* representative of tensions between local and national spaces, secular and Buddhist conceptions, and ideas of tradition and modernity. In my work, I explore the law as a site of conflict and contention that is capable of illuminating the difficulties of transition from dictatorship to democracy, the existence of residual feudalism, and the violence existent behind the appearance of social and political stability.

3. Merry, *Colonizing Hawai'i*, 17.

4. Philip Abrams, "Notes on the Difficulty of Studying the State (1977)," *Journal of Historical Sociology* 1, no. 1 (March 1988): 58–89.

5. Bob Jessop, *State Theory: Putting the Capitalist State in Its Place* (University Park: Pennsylvania State University Press, 1990), 261.

6. Writing in a different context (that of neoliberal globalization in the mid-1990s), Gayatri Spivak noted, "Nationalism, like culture, is a moving base—a *socle mouvant* (to quote Foucault again)—of differences, as dangerous as it is powerful, always ahead or deferred by definitions, pro or contra, on which it relies. Against this, globality or postnationalist talk is a representation—both as *Darstellung* or theater and as *Vertretung* or delegation as functionary—of the financialization of the globe, or globalization. Fundamentalist nationalism arises in the loosened hyphen between nation and state as the latter is mortgaged further and further by the forces of financialisation, although the determinations are never clear." Gayatri Chakravorty Spivak, "Cultural Talks in the Hot Peace: Revisiting the 'Global Village,'" in *Cosmopolitics: Thinking and Feeling beyond the Nation*, ed. Pheng Cheah and Bruce Robbins (Minneapolis: University of Minnesota Press, 1998), 330.

7. Charles Keyes, "Political Crisis and Militant Buddhism in Contemporary Thailand," in *Religion and Legitimation of Power in Thailand, Laos, and Burma*, ed. Bardwell L. Smith (Chambersburg, PA: Anima Books, 1978), 153.

8. Abrams, "Notes on the Difficulty of Studying the State (1977)," 77.

9. Ibid.

10. The sixth thesis of Walter Benjamin's "Theses on the Philosophy of History" reads as follows: "To articulate the past historically does not mean to recognize it 'the way it really was' (Ranke). It means to seize hold of a memory as it flashes up at a moment of danger. Historical materialism wishes to retain that image of the past which unexpectedly appears to man singled out by history at a moment of danger. The danger affects both the content of the tradition and its receivers. The same threat hangs over both: that of becoming a tool of the ruling classes. In every era the attempt must be made anew to wrest tradition away from a conformism that is about to overpower it. The Messiah comes not only as the redeemer, he comes as the subduer of Antichrist. Only that historian will have the gift of fanning the spark of hope in the past who is firmly convinced that *even the dead* will not be safe from the enemy if he wins. And this enemy has not ceased to be victorious." Walter Benjamin, "Theses on the Philosophy of History," in *Illuminations: Essays and Reflections*, ed. Hannah Arendt, trans. Harry Zohn (New York: Schocken Books, 1968), 255.

11. Abrams, "Notes on the Difficulty of Studying the State (1977)," 77, emphasis mine.

12. What I hope is clear is that I am not interested in analyzing the workings of various Thai state and parastate entities as part of a bureaucratic whole. This is not because it is not relevant to my project, but only that I am choosing to put my emphasis elsewhere. Productive discussions of the Thai bureaucracy qua bureaucracy can be found in Riggs, *Thailand*; William J. Siffin, *The Thai Bureaucracy: Institutional Change and Development* (Honolulu: East-West Center Press, 1966); Chai-anan Samudavanija, *Thailand: State-Building, Democracy, and Globalization* (Bangkok: Institute of Public Policy Studies, 2002); and James Ockey, *Making Democracy: Leadership, Class, Gender, and Political Participation in Thailand* (Honolulu: University of Hawai'i Press, 2004).

13. As David Banisar noted in his survey of the state of freedom of information globally, Thailand's 1997 "People's Constitution" grants citizens the right to public information. The specific mechanism through which citizens can access public information

was further specified in Thailand in the 1997 Official Information Act (OIA). Under the two new instruments, all information was meant to become public after twenty years. A new office based in the Prime Minister's Office, the Office of the Official Information Commission, was created to handle citizen requests. However, as Banisar notes, both laws exclude information that might "jeopardize the Royal Institution"; this information cannot be released. Information "relating to the Royal Institution" will be released after seventy-five years. Finally, Banisar reports that "information that would jeopardize national security, international relations or national economic or financial security; cause the decline of the efficiency of law enforcement; disclose opinions and advice given internally; endanger the life of safety of any person; disclose medical or personal information which would unreasonably encroach upon the right of privacy; disclose information given by a person in confidence; [or affect] other cases prescribed by Royal Decree" can be held without release. The 1997 People's Constitution was destroyed with the 19 September 2006 coup, and subsequent constitutions have not addressed citizen access to government information. David Banisar, *The Freedominfo.org Global Survey: Freedom of Information and Access to Government Record Laws around the World* (New York: Open Society Institute, 2004), 85.

14. An additional person, Kanchana Yaiprasan, who was a first-year agriculture student at CMU, was also on the arrest lists. She could not be found.

15. *Thin Thai*, 6 August 2518 [1975], 12.

16. *Bangkok Post*, 7 August 1975, 1.

17. *Bangkok Post*, 5 August 1975, 1, 3.

18. *Thai Niu*, 5 August 2518 [1975], 12.

19. *Thai Niu*, 4 August 2518 [1975], 1.

20. Ibid., 12.

21. *Thai Niu*, 5 August 2518 [1975], 12.

22. *Thai Niu*, 6 August 2518 [1975], 1.

23. Ibid., 12.

24. *Prachathipatai*, 4 August 2518 [1975], 1.

25. *Bangkok Post*, 7 August 1975, 1.

26. *Voice of the Nation*, 4 August 1975, 8.

27. *Bangkok Post*, 15 May 1975, 5; Dennis, "The Role of the Thai Student Movement in Rural Conflict," 183.

28. Klum Bandit Phattana, *The Sickle* (Bangkok: Thai Karnphim, 2518 [1975]), 47.

29. Ibid., 49. Following the arrests of the eight farmers and one student, both the Chiang Mai University Students' Organization and the Faculty of Science at CMU conducted independent investigations of the mine and its effect on the villagers. The Students' Organization report can be found in *Thai Niu*, 16 August 2518 [1975], 3, 10. The Faculty of Science report can be found in *Thai Niu*, 17 August 2518 [1975], 3. The full text of the NSC declaration on the Mae Wa mine can be found in *Sieng Chonabot*, 13 August 2518 [1975], 4. In addition, the NSC and a group of health sciences students from the CMU faculties of medicine, dentistry, pharmacy, and medical technology compiled reports on the illegitimate nature of the arrests. For the NSC report, see (2) T.U. 2.14.3.3/5, Thammasat University Archives, Thammasat University Documents, Political Events, Unrest in August 2518, Subpoenaed as evidence (20 August 2518), "Facts Raised by the Northern Student Center," 8–9. For the report of the students in the health sciences faculties, see (2) T.U. 2.14.3.3/5, Thammasat University Archives, Tham-

masat University Documents, Political Events, Unrest in August 2518, Subpoenaed as evidence (20 August 2518), "Observations of members of the CMU Students' Organization," 19–21.

30. *Voice of the Nation*, 4 August 1975, 8.
31. Klum Bandit Phattana, *The Sickle*, 48.
32. Ibid., 47.
33. *Athipat*, 8–11 August 2518 [1975], 3.
34. *Bangkok Post*, 6 August 1975, 3.
35. *Siam Rat*, 6 August 2518 [1975], 1.
36. Ibid., 16.
37. *Prachachat Weekly*, 21 August 2518 [1975], 7.
38. *Voice of the Nation*, 5 August 1975, 1.
39. *Thin Thai*, 6 August 2518 [1975], 12.
40. *Thai Niu*, 8 August 2518 [1975], 3.
41. Ibid., 10.
42. *Chaturat* 1, no. 6 (19 August 2518 [1975]): 32.
43. Ibid.
44. When the reporter asked Police Lieutenant Major Sunthorn why the farmers were forced to return to their cells before Chatri, his response was strikingly class inflected. He commented that sometimes "[p]eople go to visit some people, like they visit normally, and it just makes them more stirred up and angrier." Ibid., 32–33. When the reporter then asked why it was acceptable to talk to Chatri, he answered, "[B]ecause we speak together and he understands" (33). *Understanding*, apparently, was the province of university students, not farmers.
45. Ibid., 32.
46. *Thin Thai*, 9 August 2518 [1975], 12.
47. Ibid. The full text of the declaration can be found on pages 3 and 10.
48. *Thai Niu*, 6 August 2518 [1975], 12.
49. *Thai Niu*, 7 August 2518 [1975], 1, 12.
50. Ibid., 12.
51. Ibid., 1, 12.
52. Ibid.
53. Ibid., 12.
54. Ibid., 1, 12.
55. *Bangkok Post*, 7 August 1975, 1.
56. Ibid.
57. *Bangkok Post*, 8 August 1975, 1.
58. Statements were issued by the Union for Civil Liberty (the group of thirteen that had been arrested for calling for a new constitution prior to 14 October 1973), the Thammasat University Faculty Assembly, the NSCT, Independent Students of Silpakorn University, the Northeastern Students' Association, the Labour Coordination Centre, the Standard Garment Workers, the Federation of Lawyers for Democracy, the People Who Love Justice group, the Vocational Students' Association of Thailand, a variety of groups from Bo Chang College, the FFT, the United Front against Dictatorship, the Society of Asian Students (via telegram), the Chulalongkorn University Faculty Assembly, the Ramkhamhaeng Students' Association, the Southern Vocational Association of Thailand, the Secondary Students' Association of Thailand, the United

Students of Samsen for the People, the Women of Ten Institutions Group, and the Mahidol University Students' Association. See (2) T.U. 2.14.3.3/5, Thammasat University Archives, Thammasat University Documents, Political Events, Unrest in August 2518, Subpoenaed as evidence (20 August 2518), "Various Declarations," 14–18.

59. *Voice of the Nation*, 8 August 1975, 1.

60. *Thai Niu*, 8 August 2518 [1975], 12.

61. Ibid.

62. Ibid.

63. *Thai Niu*, 10 August 2518 [1975], 12.

64. *Thai Niu*, 11 August 2518 [1975], 5. One unnamed Internal Security Operations Command (ISOC) officer accused the Soviet KGB and China of creating the unrest after the arrests of the nine. Apparently, the KGB was strongest in Bangkok and so was accused of being behind the unrest at Thammasat University; China, on the other hand, was considered to be strongest in the provinces. *Bangkok Post*, 9 August 1975, 3.

65. *Thai Niu*, 13 August 2518 [1975], 5.

66. *Thin Thai*, 13 August 2518 [1975], 12.

67. *Thai Niu*, 13 August 2518 [1975], 12.

68. *Thin Thai*, 13 August 2518 [1975], 12.

69. *Thai Niu*, 13 August 2518 [1975], 12.

70. *Thai Niu*, 16 August 2518 [1975], 12.

71. *Sieng Chonabot*, 16 August 2518 [1975], 8.

72. *Thai Niu*, 16 August 2518 [1975], 12; *Athipat*, 15–17 August 2518 [1975], 12.

73. *Thin Thai*, 17 August 2518 [1975], 12.

74. *Thai Niu*, 16 August 2518 [1975], 12.

75. *Athipat*, 15–17 August 2518 [1975], 12.

76. Ibid.

77. Ibid.

78. *Thin Thai*, 18 August 2518 [1975], 12.

79. *Voice of the Nation*, 16 August 1975, 3.

80. *Thai Niu*, 16 August 2518 [1975], 12.

81. *Bangkok Post*, 16 August 1975, 1.

82. *Thai Niu*, 16 August 2518 [1975], 12.

83. *Thin Thai*, 18 August 2518 [1975], 12.

84. *Sieng Chonabot*, 18 August 2518 [1975], 8.

85. *Thin Thai*, 17 August 2518 [1975], 12.

86. *Thin Thai*, 19 August 2518 [1975], 3.

87. *Thai Niu*, 16 August 2518 [1975], 12.

88. *Thin Thai*, 18 August 2516 [1975], 12. On the same day, 17 August, two hundred protestors in Saraphi district massed in front of the district office. One of the things they said was that students should be prohibited from coming to agitate in the district. If they came, the protestors warned, they would not take responsibility for their welfare.

89. Within the Department of Police in the Ministry of Interior, the Provincial Police and the Metropolitan Police (which covers the greater Bangkok area) are two separate divisions. In August 1975, there was a bill before Parliament that expanded those with investigative powers to include provincial governors, district officers, and assistant district officers, as well as the Provincial Police. At the first reading, the bill passed by a vote of 161 to 3. The bill was perceived by some as a slight against the Provincial Police,

since the Metropolitan Police still retained sole investigative power in Bangkok. The Provincial Police claimed that if the bill was not withdrawn, then "all the chiefs of provincial police stations will strike and demonstrate in Bangkok seven days before the bill is deliberated for its second reading. Low-ranking policeman will remain in office and carry out their routine work." *Bangkok Post*, 17 August 1975, 1. The sponsor of the bill cited corruption among the Provincial Police as the reason for its proposal; he explained, "I found injustice in my province when police officers monopolise investigations but I don't want to go into details." *Bangkok Post*, 18 August 1975, 3. While the sponsor's claim is legitimate, he failed to account for the near certain corruption practiced by some provincial governors, district officers, and assistant district officers.

90. *Thai Niu*, 18 August 2518 [1975], 16.

91. Ibid.

92. Ibid.

93. *Voice of the Nation*, 18 August 1975, 1.

94. *Bangkok Post*, 19 August 1975, 1.

95. *Voice of the Nation*, 19 August 1975, 3.

96. *Bangkok Post*, 19 August 1975, 1.

97. *Prachathipatai*, 20 August 2518 [1975], 12.

98. *Thin Thai*, 20 August 2518 [1975], 12.

99. Ibid.

100. *Thai Niu*, 19 August 2518 [1975], 16.

101. *Voice of the Nation*, 19 August 1975, 1.

102. Everyone except the deputy governor, Sant Manikhancha, left the Lamphun provincial hall. Sant continued to work as usual. *Thai Niu*, 21 August 2518 [1975], 15.

103. Ibid. The assistant prosecutor for Lamphun, who had just joined the protests, opposed the burning of the puppet of Aroon, who was his boss. The crowd did not alter its plans.

104. *Thai Niu*, 20 August 2518 [1975], 12.

105. *Thai Niu*, 21 August 2518 [1975], 16.

106. *Siam Rat*, 20 August 2518 [1975], 16.

107. *Bangkok Post*, 20 August 1975, 1.

108. *Voice of the Nation*, 20 August 1975, 1; *Far Eastern Economic Review*, 29 August 1975, 14.

109. *Siam Rat*, 20 August 2518 [1975], 16.

110. *Thai Niu*, 21 August 2518 [1975], 16.

111. *Voice of the Nation*, 21 August 1975, 4.

112. *Siam Rat*, 21 August 2518 [1975], 1.

113. Ibid., 16.

114. Ibid.

115. *Voice of the Nation*, 6 August 1975, 1, emphasis mine.

116. *Prachachat Weekly*, 21 August 2518 [1975], 7, emphasis mine.

117. *Voice of the Nation*, 9 August 1975, 1, emphasis mine.

118. *Voice of the Nation*, 14 August 1975, 1, emphasis mine.

119. *Athipat*, 19–21 August 2518 [1975], 1, 12.

120. Ibid.

121. *Thai Niu*, 22 August 2518 [1975], 16.

122. *Voice of the Nation*, 21 August 1975, 1.

Conclusion: Resuming Revolution?

1. Morell and Chai-anan, *Political Conflict in Thailand*, 262. For accounts of Dr. Bunsanong's life and work, see Carl A. Trocki, "Bunsanong Punyodyana: Thai Socialist and Scholar, 1936–1976," *Bulletin of Concerned Asian Scholars* 9, no. 3 (July–September 1977): 48–51; and Somporn, *The People Must Be the Masters of the Land*.

2. *Thai Rat*, 26 September 2519 [1976], 1.

3. Morell and Chai-anan, *Political Conflict in Thailand*, 273.

4. Puey Ungpakorn, "Violence and the Military Coup in Thailand," *Bulletin of Concerned Asian Scholars* 9, no. 3 (July–September 1977): 5.

5. Thongchai, "Remembering/Silencing the Traumatic Past," 249. Many people allege that *Dao Siam* and the *Bangkok Post*, which also printed an image, touched up the photograph. This remains contentious today. For an analysis, see Ji Ungpakorn and Suthachai Yimprasert, *The Crime of the State in the Crisis of Changes* (Bangkok: 6 October Fact-Finding Committee, 2544 [2001]).

6. Puey, "Violence and the Military Coup in Thailand," 5.

7. Bowie, *Rituals of National Loyalty*, 26, 48. For an analysis of the formation and dissemination of this kind of nationalism, see Craig Reynolds, ed., *National Identity and Its Defenders: Thailand, 1939–1989* (Clayton, Victoria, Australia: Centre of Southeast Asian Studies, Monash University, 1991).

8. For a detailed account of the events of this day, see Puey, "Violence and the Military Coup in Thailand"; and Charnvit et al., *From 14 to 6 October*.

9. Robert F. Zimmerman, *Reflections on the Collapse of Democracy in Thailand* (Singapore: Institute of Southeast Asian Studies, 1978), 58.

10. Puey, "Violence and the Military Coup in Thailand," 8.

11. *Thai Niu*, 7 October 2519 [1976], 1, 12; *Thin Thai*, 7 October 2519 [1976], 1, 12.

12. *Songthaeo* literally means "two rows." A *songthaeo* is a passenger vehicle with two rows of seats behind a cab.

13. As part of the right-wing backlash to the blossoming of progressive action during the period between October 1973 and October 1976, many Thai state agencies and departments kept lists of activists, critics, and people otherwise deemed undesirable. These lists were compiled by the police, military, and counterinsurgency agencies directly, as well as by civilians working for them in many different areas. One former CMU administrator commented to me that although he remained neutral during that period, among his colleagues there were both progressive activists and those who created blacklists. Further investigation of the blacklists and the ways in which they were used is urgent and necessary.

14. K.'s fear that she would be arrested if she did not flee to join the CPT after the coup was an astute one. On 13 October, the ruling NARC issued Order 22. In force until August 1979, Order 22 delineated nine categories of people deemed a "danger to society" subject to arbitrary, potentially infinite detention and "reeducation." Under Order 22, many people across Thailand underwent reeducation in order to become good citizens; this included acceptance of "democracy with the king as head of state" as the only legitimate form of government. *Ratchakitchanubeksa* (special edition), 13 October 2519 [1976], book 93, part 128, 1–5.

15. Lenin, *State and Revolution*, 25.

16. Wendy Brown, *Edgework: Critical Essays on Knowledge and Politics* (Princeton, NJ: Princeton University Press, 2005), 6.

17. Thanin Kraivichien, *Using the Law to Protect against the Communists* (Bangkok: Armed Forces Security Center, 2517 [1974]), 111–15.

18. Paolo Virno, "Do You Remember Counterrevolution?" in *Radical Thought in Italy: A Potential Politics*, ed. Paolo Virno and Michael Hardt (Minneapolis: University of Minnesota Press, 1996), 240.

19. Bruce Missingham, *The Assembly of the Poor in Thailand: From Local Struggles to National Protest Movement* (Chiang Mai: Silkworm Books, 2003), 140.

20. Fa Dieu Kan Editorial Collective, "Adorning the Earth," *Fa Dieu Kan* 2, no. 4 (October—December 2547 [2004]): 42–87; Tyrell Haberkorn, "Appendix 1: Collusion and Influence behind the Assassinations of Human Rights Defenders in Thailand," *article 2* 4, no. 2 (April 2005): 58–63. Assassination of activists was not the only persistent human rights violation emergent under Prime Minister Thaksin. In addition, in 2003, over 2,500 alleged drug offenders were extrajudicially killed in the so-called War on Drugs. Human Rights Watch, *Thailand, Not Enough Graves: The War on Drugs, HIV/ AIDS, and Violations of Human Rights* (New York: Human Rights Watch, 2004). In addition, the Krue Se mosque massacre and Tak Bai massacre both occurred during Thaksin's first term. In what has become known as simply "Krue Se," on 28 April 2004, clashes between state forces and Muslim militant men left 106 Muslims and 5 members of the state forces dead. What is clear is that while the militants did launch initial attacks on state forces in some locations, they were outnumbered and outarmed. Many of the militants were armed only with machetes, while the soldiers were well equipped with automatic weapons, grenades, and other hardware. Although the largest number of people were killed at the Krue Se mosque (32 men), there was fighting between Muslim men and Thai army forces in various locations in the south, including Saba Yoi district in Songkhla province and Krong Pinang district in Yala province. See *Fa Dieu Kan* 2, no. 3 (July–September 2547 [2004]), for commentaries on the Krue Se mosque massacre, as well as details about many of those who died. Eighty-five people died in the Tak Bai massacre on 25 October 2004. Seventy-eight of this number died when over 1,500 protestors were arrested and stacked, in horizontal layers, in trucks and transported to the Ingkayuthboriharn military base six hours away from the Tak Bai police station, where the protest took place. The 1,500 citizens were protesting what they believed was the unjust arrest of 6 villagers on charges of allegedly stealing guns from the local defense forces. At an event commemorating the two-year anniversary of the massacre, one survivor recalled that in his truck there were four layers of people; everyone on the bottom layer died.

21. The three southernmost provinces of Thailand—Yala, Pattani, and Narathiwat—along with four districts of Songkhla province, have been under martial law since January 2004 and emergency rule since July 2005. The reason given by the central Thai state for the suspension of ordinary rule is that there is a growing Islamic insurgency in southern Thailand. Since January 2004, an unknown number of people have been arrested for allegedly endangering national security. The provisions for a long period of pretrial, and precharge, detention possible under martial law and emergency rule mean that many of the cases have not yet been heard in court. In September 2008, the Accessing Justice and Legal Protection Project of the Cross Cultural Foundation reported

that there were 428 current national security detainees. Cross Cultural Foundation, *"Ayor Kunor Ikha, My Dad Was Busted": The Path to Justice for Families of Persons Held in Custody on Charges Related to Insurgencies in the Southern Border Provinces* (Bangkok: Cross Cultural Foundation, 2009). This does not account for those detained and released prior to September 2008, those who died during detention, and those being held arbitrarily in undisclosed locations.

22.   Angkhana Neelaphaichit, *Reading Between the Lines* (Bangkok: Working Group on Justice for Peace, 2009).

23.   *New York Times*, 29 August 2009, 1.

24.   See LM Watch (http://www.lmwatch.org) and Political Prisoners in Thailand (http://thaipoliticalprisoners.wordpress.com) for summaries and information related to each case.

25.   Somsamai, "The Real Face of Thai Saktina Today," 75.

26.   Grandin, *The Last Colonial Massacre*, 175.

27.   Suphot's choice to use *patiwat* is intriguing, given that in most places elsewhere in his writing he uses the more dissident *aphiwat*.

28.   Suphot Dantrakul, *Dictionary of Politics, Peoples' Edition* (Nonthaburi: Santhitham Press, 2528 [1985]), 257.

29.   Ibid., 260.

Bibliography

English-language Books and Journal Articles

Abrams, Philip. "Notes on the Difficulty of Studying the State (1977)." *Journal of Historical Sociology* 1, no. 1 (March 1988): 58–89.

Abu-Lughod, Lila. "The Romance of Resistance: Tracing Transformations of Power through Bedouin Women." *American Ethnologist* 17, no. 1 (February 1990): 41–55.

Althusser, Louis. *Lenin and Philosophy and Other Essays.* Trans. Ben Brewster. New York: Monthly Review Press, 1971.

Anan Ganjanapan. "The Partial Commercialization of Rice Production in Northern Thailand (1900–1981)." PhD diss., Cornell University, 1984.

Anat Thapinta and Paul F. Hudak. "Pesticide Use and Residual Occurrence in Thailand." *Environmental Monitoring and Assessment* 60, no. 1 (January 2000): 103–14.

Anderson, Benedict. "Murder and Progress in Modern Siam." *New Left Review* 181 (May–June 1990): 33–48.

———. "Withdrawal Symptoms: Social and Cultural Aspects of the October 6 Coup." *Bulletin of Concerned Asian Scholars* 9, no. 3 (1977): 13–30.

Angkhana Neelaphaichit. *Reading between the Lines.* Bangkok: Working Group on Justice for Peace, 2009.

Anzaldúa, Gloria. *Borderlands/La Frontera: The New Mestiza.* San Francisco: Aunt Lute, 1987.

Bakhtin, Mikhail. *Rabelais and His World.* Trans. Helene Iswolsky. Cambridge, MA: MIT Press, 1968.

Banisar, David. *The Freedominfo.org Global Survey: Freedom of Information and Access to Government Record Laws around the World.* New York: Open Society Institute, 2004.

Bataille, Georges. *Erotism: Death and Sensuality.* San Francisco: City Lights Books, 1962.

Batson, Benjamin. 1981. "Kulab Saipradit and the 'War of Life.'" *Journal of the Siam Society* 69, nos. 1–2 (January–July 1981): 58–73.

Benjamin, Walter. *Illuminations: Essays and Reflections.* Ed. Hannah Arendt. Trans. Harry Zohn. New York: Schocken Books, 1968.

———. "Theses on the Philosophy of History." In *Illuminations: Essays and Reflections,* ed. Hannah Arendt, trans. Harry Zohn. New York: Schocken Books, 1968.

Bowie, Katherine. "Peasant Perspectives on the Political Economy of the Northern Thai Kingdom of Chiang Mai in the Nineteenth Century: Implications for the Understanding of Peasant Political Expression." PhD diss., University of Chicago, 1988.

———. *Rituals of National Loyalty: An Anthropology of the State and the Village Scout Movement in Thailand.* New York: Columbia University Press, 1997.

Bowie, Katherine, and Brian Phelan. "Who's Killing the Farmers?" *Bangkok Post Sunday Magazine,* 17 August 1975, 5–7.

Brown, Wendy. *Edgework: Critical Essays on Knowledge and Politics.* Princeton, NJ: Princeton University Press, 2005.

———. *Politics Out of History.* Princeton, NJ: Princeton University Press, 2001.

Bruneau, Michel. "Land Ownership and Tenure, Relations of Production, and Social Classes in the Rural Areas of Northern Thailand (1966–1976)." Paper presented at the Thai-European Seminar on Social Change in Contemporary Thailand, University of Amsterdam, 28–30 May 1980.

Butalia, Urvashi. *The Other Side of Silence: Voices from the Partition of India.* Durham, NC: Duke University Press, 2000.

Butler, Judith. *The Psychic Life of Power: Theories in Subjection.* Stanford, CA: Stanford University Press, 1997.

Chai-anan Sanudavanija. "Farmers' Movement in Modern Thai Politics." Paper presented at the Thai-European Seminar on Social Change in Contemporary Thailand, University of Amsterdam, 28–30 May 1980.

———. *Thailand: State-Building, Democracy, and Globalization.* Bangkok: Institute of Public Policy Studies, 2002.

Chamberlain, James R., ed. *The Ram Khamhaeng Controversy: Collected Papers.* Bangkok: Siam Society, 1991.

Chang, Tze-Tzu. "Rice." In *The Cambridge World History of Food,* ed. Kenneth F. Kiple and Kriemhild Coneé Ornelas, 132–48. Cambridge: Cambridge University Press, 2000.

Chatterjee, Partha. *The Nation and Its Fragments: Colonial and Postcolonial Histories.* Princeton, NJ: Princeton University Press, 1993.

Chatthip Nartsupha. "The Ideology of 'Holy Men' Revolts in North East Thailand." In *History and Peasant Consciousness in South East Asia,* ed. Shigeharu Tanabe and Andrew Turton, 111–34. Osaka: National Museum of Ethnology, 1984.

Cleaver, Harry M. "The Contradictions of the Green Revolution." *American Economic Review* 62, nos. 1–2 (1972): 177–86.

Cohen, Paul T. "Problems of Tenancy and Landlessness in Northern Thailand." *Developing Economies* 21, no. 3 (1983): 244–66.

Cole, Daniel H. "'An Unqualified Human Good': E. P. Thompson and the Rule of Law." *Journal of Law and Society* 28, no. 2 (June 2001): 177–203.

Connors, Michael Kelly. *Democracy and National Identity in Thailand.* New York: RoutledgeCurzon, 2003.

Corrigan, Philip, and Derek Sayer. *The Great Arch: English State Formation as Cultural Revolution.* Oxford: Blackwell, 1985.

Cross Cultural Foundation. *"Ayor Kunor Ikha, My Dad Was Busted": The Path to Justice for Families of Persons Held in Custody on Charges Related to Insurgencies in the Southern Border Provinces.* Bangkok: Cross Cultural Foundation, 2009.

Dennis, John Value. "The Role of the Thai Student Movement in Rural Conflict, 1973–1976." MS thesis, Cornell University, 1982.

Diller, Anthony. "What Makes Central Thai a National Language?" In *National Identity and Its Defenders, 1939–1989*, ed. Craig J. Reynolds, 71–107. 2nd ed. Chiang Mai: Silkworm Books, 2002.

Dillman, C. Daniel. "Land and Labor Practices in Brazil during the 1960s." *American Journal of Economics and Sociology* 35, no. 1 (1976): 49–70.

Dorfman, Ariel. *Other Septembers, Many Americas: Selected Provocations, 1980–2004.* New York: Seven Stories Press, 2004.

Engel, David. *Code and Custom in a Thai Provincial Court: The Interaction of Formal and Informal Systems of Justice.* Tucson: University of Arizona Press, 1978.

———. "Litigation across Space and Time: Courts, Conflict, and Social Change." *Law and Society Review* 24, no. 2 (1990): 333–44.

Enloe, Cynthia. *Bananas, Beaches, and Bases: Making Feminist Sense of International Politics.* Berkeley: University of California Press, 1990.

———. *The Curious Feminist: Searching for Women in a New Age of Empire.* Berkeley: University of California Press, 2004.

———. *Maneuvers: The International Politics of Militarizing Women's Lives.* Berkeley: University of California Press, 2000.

———. *The Morning After: Sexual Politics at the End of the Cold War.* Berkeley: University of California Press, 1993.

Freire, Paulo. *Pedagogy of the Oppressed.* Trans. Myra Bergman Ramos. New York: Continuum, 1970.

Gibson-Graham, J. K. *The End of Capitalism (As We Knew It): A Feminist Critique of Political Economy.* Cambridge: Blackwell Publishers, 1996.

Gibson-Graham, J. K., Stephen A. Resnick, and Richard D. Wolff. "Introduction: Class in a Poststructuralist Frame." In *Class and Its Others*, ed. J. K. Gibson-Graham, Stephen A. Resnick, and Richard D. Wolff, 1–22. Minneapolis: University of Minnesota Press, 2000.

———. "Toward a Poststructuralist Political Economy." In *Re/Presenting Class: Essays in Postmodern Marxism*, ed. J. K. Gibson-Graham, Stephen A. Resnick, and Richard D. Wolff, 1–22. Durham, NC: Duke University Press, 2001.

Glassman, Jim. *Thailand at the Margins: Internationalization of the State and the Transformation of Labour.* New York: Oxford University Press, 2004.

Gordimer, Nadine. *None to Accompany Me.* New York: Farrar, Straus and Giroux, 1994.

Gramsci, Antonio. *Selections from the Prison Notebooks.* Ed. and trans. Quintin Hoare and Geoffrey Nowell Smith. New York: International Publishers, 1971.

Grandin, Greg. *The Last Colonial Massacre: Latin America in the Cold War.* Chicago: University of Chicago Press, 2004.

Guha, Ranajit. "On Some Aspects of the Historiography of Colonial India." In *Selected Subaltern Studies*, ed. Ranajit Guha and Gayatri Chakravorty Spivak, 37–44. New York: Oxford University Press, 1988.

———. "The Prose of Counter-Insurgency." In *Selected Subaltern Studies*, ed. Ranajit Guha and Gayatri Chakravorty Spivak, 45–86. New York: Oxford University Press, 1988.

Gupta, Akhil, and James Ferguson. 1997. "Beyond 'Culture': Space, Identity, and the Politics of Difference." In *Culture, Power, Place: Explorations in Critical Anthropology*, ed. Akhil Gupta and James Ferguson, 33–51. Durham, NC: Duke University Press, 1997.

Haberkorn, Tyrell. "Appendix 1: Collusion and Influence behind the Assassinations of Human Rights Defenders in Thailand." *article 2* 4, no. 2 (April 2005): 58–63.

———. "At the Limits of Imagination: Ajarn Angun Malik and the Meanings of Politics." *Stance: The Thai Feminist Review* 1 (August 2007): 165–99.

Human Rights Watch. *Thailand, Not Enough Graves: The War on Drugs, HIV/AIDS, and Violations of Human Rights.* New York: Human Rights Watch, 2004.

Jessop, Bob. *State Theory: Putting the Capitalist State in Its Place.* University Park: Pennsylvania State University Press, 1990.

Kanoksak Kaewthep. "Les transformations structurelles et les conflits de classes dans la société rurale thaïandaise d'après l'étude d'un cas: La Fédération de la Paysannerie Thaïlandaise." PhD diss., Université Paris 7, 1984.

———. "The Political Economy of the Modern Thai Peasant Movement: The Case of the Farmers' Federation of Thailand (FFT), 1973–1976." *In Transnationalization, the State, and the People: The Case of Thailand,* 141–85. Quezon City: Southeast Asian Perspectives Project, United Nations University, 1985.

Karunan, Victor. *If the Land Could Speak, It Would Speak for Us.* Hong Kong: Plough Publications, 1984.

Kasian Tejapira. *Commodifying Marxism: The Formation of Modern Thai Radical Culture, 1927–1958.* Kyoto: Kyoto University Press, 2001.

Kerkvliet, Benedict J. *Everyday Politics in the Philippines: Class and Status Relations in a Central Luzon Village.* Oxford: Rowman and Littlefield, 2002.

Kerkvliet, Benedict J. Tria, and Mark Selden. "Agrarian Transformations in China and Vietnam." *China Journal* 40 (July 1998): 37–58.

Keyes, Charles. "Political Crisis and Militant Buddhism in Contemporary Thailand." In *Religion and Legitimation of Power in Thailand, Laos, and Burma,* ed. Bardwell L. Smith, 147–64. Chambersburg, PA: Anima Books, 1978.

Kleinman, Arthur. "The Violences of Everyday Life: The Multiple Forms and Dynamics of Social Violence." In *Violence and Subjectivity,* ed. Veena Das, Arthur Kleinman, Mamphela Ramphele, and Pamela Reynolds, 226–41. Berkeley: University of California Press, 2000.

Kraiyudht Dhiratayakinant, ed. *Thailand—Profile 1975.* Bangkok: Voice of the Nation, 1975.

Krirkkiat Phipatseritham. *Trends in Land Tenure and Security.* Bangkok: Thai University Research Association, 1979.

Kullada Kesboonchu Mead. *The Rise and Decline of Thai Absolutism.* New York: RoutledgeCurzon, 2004.

Laclau, Ernesto. *New Reflections on the Revolution of Our Time.* New York: Verso, 1990.

Larsson, Tomas. "Capital to the Tiller? A Prehistory of the Commodification of Land in Thailand." Cornell Southeast Asia Program Brown Bag lecture, 8 February 2007.

Lee, Doreen. "Styling the Revolution: Masculinities, Youth, and Street Politics." Paper presented at the conference States of Transgression, Asia Research Institute, National University of Singapore, 24–26 May 2005.

Lee, Namhee. *The Making of Minjung: Democracy and the Politics of Representation in South Korea.* Ithaca, NY: Cornell University Press, 2007.

Lenin, Vladimir Ilyich. *State and Revolution.* New York: International Publishers, 1932.

———. *Revolution at the Gates: A Selection of Writings from February to October 1917.* Ed. Slavoj Žižek. New York: Verso, 2002.

Lin, Nancy. *Reverberations: A New Translation of Complete Poems of Mao Tse-tung.* Hong Kong: Joint Publishing Company, 1980.

Loos, Tamara. *Subject Siam: Family, Law, and Colonial Modernity in Thailand.* Chiang Mai: Silkworm Books, 2002.

Lorde, Audre. *Sister Outsider.* Trumansburg, NY: Crossing Press, 1984.

Luther, Hans. *Peasants and State in Contemporary Thailand: From Regional Revolt to National Revolution?* Hamburg: Institute fur Asienkunde, 1978.

Marx, Karl, and Friedrich Engels. *The German Ideology.* New York: International Publishers, 1965.

———. *The Marx-Engels Reader.* Edited by Robert C. Tucker. New York: Norton, 1972.

McLaren, Peter, with Henry A. Giroux. "Radical Pedagogy as Cultural Politics: Beyond the Discourse of Critique and Anti-Utopianism." In Peter McLaren, *Critical Pedagogy and Predatory Culture: Oppositional Politics in a Postmodern Era,* 29–57. New York: Routledge, 1995.

Merry, Sally. *Colonizing Hawai'i: The Cultural Power of Law.* Princeton, NJ: Princeton University Press, 2000.

Michell, Edward Blair. *A Siamese-English Dictionary for the Use of Students in Both Languages.* Bangkok, 1892.

Mills, Mary Beth. *Thai Women in the Global Labor Force: Consuming Desires, Contested Selves.* New Brunswick, NJ: Rutgers University Press, 1999.

Missingham, Bruce. *The Assembly of the Poor in Thailand: From Local Struggles to National Protest Movement.* Chiang Mai: Silkworm Books, 2003.

Moerman, Michael. *Agricultural Change and Peasant Choice in a Thai Village.* Berkeley: University of California Press, 1968.

Morell, David, and Chai-anan Samudavanija. *Political Conflict in Thailand: Reform, Reaction, Revolution.* Cambridge, MA: Oelgeschlager, Gunn and Hain, 1981.

Nafisi, Azar. *Reading Lolita in Tehran: A Memoir in Books.* New York: Random House, 2003.

National Food and Agriculture Organization Committee. *Thailand and Her Agricultural Problems.* Bangkok: Ministry of Agriculture, 1950.

National Statistical Office. *Statistical Yearbook of Thailand, 1976–1980.* Bangkok: Office of the Prime Minister, 1981.

Ockey, James. *Making Democracy: Leadership, Class, Gender, and Political Participation in Thailand.* Honolulu: University of Hawai'i Press, 2004.

Osamu Akagi. "Research Note and Data on 'Pocketbook' Publication in Thailand, 1973–1976." *South East Asian Studies* 16, no. 3 (December 1978): 473–523.

Palleqoix, Jean-Baptiste. *Siamese French English Dictionary.* Bangkok: Imprimerie de la Mission Catholique, 1896.

Parsons, Kenneth H., Raymond J. Penn, and Philip M. Raup, eds. *Land Tenure: Proceedings of the International Conference on Land Tenure and Related Problems in World Agriculture, Held at Madison, Wisconsin, 1951.* Madison: University of Wisconsin Press, 1956.

Pasuk Phongpaichit and Chris Baker. *Thailand: Economy and Politics.* 2nd ed. Oxford: Oxford University Press, 2002.

Pipob Thongchai. "The First Bricks and the Steps Forward." In *Retracing the Path of an Idealistic Individual: From the Heart of Grandfather to All Idealistic Persons Working for the Commonpeople*, ed. Sem Pringpuangkaew, 46–50. Bangkok: Komol Keemthong Foundation, 2001.

Pitch Pongsawat. "Political Economy of Agrarian Transformation and Peasant Movements in Contemporary Thailand: A Critical Observation." *Warasan Sangkhomsat* (Journal of Sociology, Chulalongkorn University) 32, no. 2 (2001): 1–73.

Pridi Banomyong. *Pridi by Pridi: Selected Writings on Life, Politics, and Economy*. Trans. Chris Baker and Pasuk Phongpaichit. Chiang Mai: Silkworm Books, 2000.

Puey Ungpakorn. "Violence and the Military Coup in Thailand." *Bulletin of Concerned Asian Scholars* 9, no. 3 (July–September 1977): 4–12.

Race, Jeffrey. "The War in Northern Thailand." *Modern Asian Studies* 8, no. 1 (1974): 85–112.

Ramsay, Ansil. "The Limits of Land Reform in Thailand." *Journal of Developing Areas* 16, no. 2 (January 1982): 173–96.

———. "Tenancy and Landlessness in Thailand: How Severe a Problem?" *Asian Survey* 22, no. 11 (November 1982): 1074–92.

Reynolds, Craig. *Thai Radical Discourse: The Real Face of Thai Feudalism Today*. Ithaca, NY: Southeast Asia Program, Cornell University, 1987.

Reynolds, Craig, ed. *National Identity and Its Defenders: Thailand, 1939–1989*. 2nd edition. Chiang Mai: Silkworm Books, 2002.

Rich, Adrienne. *The Dream of a Common Language: Poems, 1974–1977*. New York: Norton, 1978.

Riggs, Fred W. *Thailand: The Modernization of a Bureaucratic Polity*. Honolulu: East-West Center Press, 1966.

Scott, James C. "Patron-Client Politics and Political Change in Southeast Asia." *American Political Science Review* 66, no. 1 (March 1972): 91–113.

———. *Weapons of the Weak: Everyday Forms of Peasant Resistance*. New Haven, CT: Yale University Press, 1985.

Shaw, Mark. *Crime and Policing in Post-apartheid South Africa: Transforming under Fire*. Bloomington: Indiana University Press, 2002.

Siffin, William J. *Thai Bureaucracy: Institutional Change and Development*. Honolulu: East-West Center Press, 1966.

Smyth, David. "Siburapha: The Making of a Literary Reputation." In *Thai Constructions of Knowledge*, ed. Manas Chitkasem and Andrew Turton, 63–83. London: School of Oriental and African Studies, University of London, 1991.

Somsak Jeamteerasakul. "The Communist Movement in Thailand." PhD diss., Monash University, 1991.

Somsamai Srisudravarna. "The Real Face of Thai Saktina Today." Trans. Craig Reynolds. In *Thai Radical Discourse: The Real Face of Thai Feudalism Today*, ed. Craig Reynolds, 43–148. Ithaca, NY: Southeast Asia Program, Cornell University, 1987.

Spivak, Gayatri Chakravorty. "Cultural Talks in the Hot Peace: Revisiting the 'Global Village.'" In *Cosmopolitics: Thinking and Feeling beyond the Nation*, ed. Pheng Cheah and Bruce Robbins, 329–48. Minneapolis: University of Minnesota Press, 1998.

Stallybrass, Peter, and Allon White. *The Politics and Poetics of Transgression*. Ithaca, NY: Cornell University Press, 1986.

Stoler, Ann Laura. "Developing Historical Negatives: Race and the (Modernist) Visions of a Colonial State." In *From the Margins: Historical Anthropology and Its Futures*, ed. Brian Keith Axel, 156–85. Durham, NC: Duke University Press, 2002.

————. "[P]Refacing *Capitalism and Confrontation* in 1995." In *Capitalism and Confrontation in Sumatra's Plantation Belt, 1870–1979*, vii–xxxiv. 2nd ed. Ann Arbor: University of Michigan Press, 1995.

Suehiro, Akira. "Land Reform in Thailand: The Concept and Background of the Agricultural Land Reform Act of 1975." *Developing Economies* 19, no. 4 (1981): 314–47.

Sulak Sivaraksa. *Siam in Crisis.* Bangkok: Santi Pracha Dhamma Institute, 1990.

Tanabe, Shigeharu. "Ideological Practice in Peasant Rebellions: Siam at the Turn of the Twentieth Century." In *History and Peasant Consciousness in Southeast Asia*, ed. Shigeharu Tanabe and Andrew Turton, 75–110. Osaka: National Museum of Ethnology, 1984.

Tej Bunnag and Michael Smithies, eds. *In Memoriam Phya Anuman Rajadhon: Contributions in Memory of the Late President of the Siam Society.* Bangkok: Siam Society, 1970.

Thak Chaloemtiarana. "Professionalism in the Modern Thai Army." Paper presented at the conference Political Systems and Development, sponsored by the Indian Council of Social Science Research, Centre for the Study of Developing Societies, and the Centre for Policy Research, Delhi, February 1980.

————. *Thailand: The Politics of Despotic Paternalism.* Bangkok: Social Science Association of Thailand, 1979.

————, ed. *Thai Politics: Extracts and Documents, 1932–1957.* Bangkok: Social Science Association of Thailand, 1978.

Thomas, M. Ladd. *Political Violence in the Muslim Provinces of Southern Thailand.* ISEAS Occasional Papers 28. Singapore: Institute of Southeast Asian Studies, 1975.

Thompson, E. P. *The Poverty of Theory and Other Essays.* London: Monthly Review Press, 1978.

————. *Whigs and Hunters: The Origin of the Black Act.* London: Allen Lane, 1975.

Thongchai Winichakul. "The Changing Landscape of the Past: New Histories in Thailand since 1973." *Journal of Southeast Asian Studies* 26, no. 1 (1995): 99–120.

————. "Remembering/Silencing the Traumatic Past: The Ambivalent Memories of the October 1976 Massacre in Bangkok." In *Cultural Crisis and Social Memory: Modernity and Identity in Thailand and Laos*, ed. Shigeharu Tanabe and Charles Keyes, 243–86. Honolulu: University of Hawai'i Press, 2002.

————. "Thongchai Winichakul on the Red 'Germs.'" *New Mandala*, 3 May 2010. http://asiapacific.anu.edu.au/newmandala/2010/05/03/thongchai-winichakul-on-the-red-germs/.

Tierney-Tello, Mary Beth. *Allegories of Transgression and Transformation: Experimental Fiction by Women Writing under Dictatorship.* Albany: State University of New York Press, 1996.

Translation and Secretarial Office. *Act Controlling the Hire of Paddy Land, B.E. 2493.* Thonburi: Translation and Secretarial Office, 1951.

Trébuil, Guy. "Pioneer Agriculture, Green Revolution, and Environmental Degradation in Thailand." In *Counting the Costs: Economic Growth and Environmental Change in Thailand*, ed. Jonathan Rigg, 67–89. Singapore: Institute of Southeast Asian Studies, 1995.

Trocki, Carl A. "Bunsanong Punyodyana: Thai Socialist and Scholar, 1936–1976." *Bulletin of Concerned Asian Scholars* 9, no. 3 (July–September 1977): 48–51.

Turton, Andrew. "The Current Situation in the Thai Countryside." In *Thailand: Roots of Conflict*, ed. Andrew Turton, Jonathan Fast, and Malcolm Caldwell, 104–42. Nottingham: Spokesman Press, 1978.

———. "Limits of Ideological Domination and the Formation of Social Consciousness." In *History and Peasant Consciousness in Southeast Asia*, ed. Andrew Turton and Shigeharu Tanabe, 19–73. Osaka: National Museum of Ethnology, 1984.

———. "Poverty, Reform, and Class Struggle in Rural Thailand." In *Rural Poverty and Agrarian Reform*, ed. Steve Jones, P. C. Joshi, and Miguel Murmis, 20–45. New Delhi: Allied Publishers (on behalf of Enda; Dakar, Senegal), 1982.

Turton, Andrew, et al. *Production, Power, and Participation in Rural Thailand: Experiences of Poor Farmers' Groups*. Geneva: United Nations Research Institute for Social Development, 1987.

Vandergeest, Peter. "Gifts and Rights: Cautionary Notes on Community Self-Help in Thailand." *Development and Change* 22, no. 3 (1991): 421–43.

Virno, Paolo. "Do you Remember Counterrevolution?" In *Radical Thought in Italy: A Potential Politics*, ed. Paolo Virno and Michael Hardt, 241–59. Minneapolis: University of Minnesota Press, 1996.

Waldmeir, Patti. *Anatomy of a Miracle: The End of Apartheid and the Birth of the New South Africa*. New Brunswick, NJ: Rutgers University Press, 1998.

Walzer, Michael. "Intellectuals, Social Classes, and Revolutions." In *Democracy, Revolution, and History*, ed. Theda Skocpol, 127–42. Ithaca, NY: Cornell University Press, 1998.

Weber, Eugen. "Revolution? Counterrevolution? What Revolution?" In *Fascism: A Reader's Guide*, ed. Walter Laqueur, 435–68. Berkeley: University of California Press, 1976.

Weber, Max. *Economy and Society*. New York: Bedminster Press, 1968.

Weschler, Lawrence. *A Miracle, a Universe: Settling Accounts with Torturers*. New York: Pantheon, 1990.

Williams, Raymond. *Keywords: A Vocabulary of Culture and Society*. New York: Oxford University Press, 1976.

Wilson, David A. *Politics in Thailand*. Ithaca, NY: Cornell University Press, 1967.

Wilson, Richard A. *The Politics of Truth and Reconciliation in South Africa: Legitimizing the Post-apartheid State*. New York: Cambridge University Press, 2001.

Witayakorn Chiengkul. *The Effects of Capitalist Penetration on the Transformation of the Agrarian Structure in the Central Region of Thailand (1960–1980)*. Bangkok: Chulalongkorn University Social Research Institute, 1983.

Wyatt, David. *Thailand: A Short History*. New Haven, CT: Yale University Press, 1984.

Yotopoulos, Pan. *The Green Revolution in Thailand: With a Bang or with a Whimper?* Stanford: Food Research Institute, Stanford University, 1975.

Zimmerman, Carle C. *Siam Rural Economic Survey, 1930–31*. Bangkok: Bangkok Times Press, 1931.

Zimmerman, Robert F. *Reflections on the Collapse of Democracy in Thailand*. Singapore: Institute of Southeast Asian Studies, 1978.

———. "Thailand 1975: Transition to Constitutional Democracy Continues." *Asian Survey* 16, no. 2 (February 1976): 159–72.

Žižek, Slavoj. "Introduction: Between the Two Revolutions." In *Vladimir Ilyich Lenin, Revolution at the Gates: A Selection of Writings from February to October 1917*, ed. Slavoj Žižek, 1–14. New York: Verso, 2002.

Thai-Language Books and Journal Articles

อำนาจ ยุทธวิวัฒน์. *ปฏิวัติการศึกษา: ตามแนวทางสังคมนิยม.* กรุงเทพฯ: สำนักพิมพ์ประชาธรรม, ๒๕๑๙.
(Amnat Yuthiwiwat. *Education Revolution: Following the Path of Socialism.* Bangkok: Prachatham Press, 2519 [1976].)

อรรถจักร์ สัตยานุรักษ์. *"มือที่สาม" ในประวัติศาสตร์การเมืองไทย.* กรุงเทพฯ: โครงการจัดพิมพ์คบไฟ, ๒๕๔๙.
(Attachak Sattayanurak. *The "Third Hand" in Thai Political History.* Bangkok: Kobfai Publishing Project, 2549 [2006].)

ชัยสิริ สมุทวณิช. *วรรณกรรมการเมืองไทย: ๑๔ ตุลา—๖ ตุลา.* กรุงเทพฯ: สายธาร, ๑๕๒๔.
(Chaisiri Samutwanit. *Thai Political Literature: 14 October 1973–6 October 1976.* Bangkok: Saithan, 2524 [1981].)

ชัยวัฒน์ สุรวิชัย, บ. *เหตุเกิดที่ บ้าน นาทราย.* กรุงเทพฯ: โรงพิมพ์ จักรานุกูล, ๒๕๑๗.
(Chaiwat Suriwichai, ed. *The Events in Baan Na Sai.* Bangkok: Chakaranukun, 2517 [1974].)

ชาญวิทย์ เกษตรศิริ. *๑๔ ตุลา.* กรุงเทพฯ: สายธาร, ๒๕๔๔.
(Charnvit Kasetsiri. *14 October.* Bangkok: Saithan Press, 2544 [2001].)

ชาญวิทย์ เกษตรศิริ, บ. *จาก ๑๔ ถึง ๖ ตุลา.* กรุงเทพฯ: โรงพิมพ์มหาวิทยาลัยธรรมศาสตร์, ๒๕๔๑.
(Charnvit Kasetsiri et al. *From 14 to 6 October.* Bangkok: Thammasat University Press, 2541 [1998].)

ช. เขียวพุ่มพวง. "ถึงผู้อ่าน." ใน *การศึกษาสำหรับผู้ถูกกดขี่,* โดย เปาโล แฟรร์, แปลโดย ช. เขียวพุ่มพวง. กรุงเทพฯ: สหพันธ์นักศึกษาเสรีฯ, ๒๕๑๗.
(Cho Khiewphumphuang. "Note to Readers." In Paulo Freire, *Pedagogy of the Oppressed,* trans. Cho Khiewphumphuang. Bangkok: Federation of Independent Students of Thailand, 2517 [1974].)

ศูนย์ส่งเสริมการเผยแพร่ประชาธิปไตย. *โครงการกลับสู่ชนบท.* กรุงเทพฯ: ทบวงมหาวิทยาลัยของรัฐ, ๒๕๑๗.
(Democracy Propagation Center. *Return to the Rural Areas Program.* Bangkok: Bureau of Universities, 2517 [1974].)

กองบรรณาธิการฟ้าเดียวกัน. "ประดับไว้ในโลกา." *ฟ้าเดียวกัน* ๒. ๔[๒๕๖๗]: ๔๒–๘๗.
(Fa Dieu Kan Editorial Collective. "Adorning the Earth." *Fa Dieu Kan* 2 no. 4 (2547 [2004]): 42–87.)

เฟนอน, ฟรานทซ์. *โลกร้าว.* แปลโดย ช. เขียวพุ่มพวง. กรุงเทพฯ: เจริญวิทย์การพิมพ์, ๒๕๑๗.
(Fanon, Frantz. *The Wretched of the Earth.* Trans. Cho Khiewphumphuang. Bangkok: Charoenwit Kanphim, 2517 [1974].)

แฟรร์, เปาโว่โล. *คัมภีร์ของผู้ถูกกดขี่.* แปลโดย จิราภรณ์ ศิริสุพรรณ. กรุงเทพฯ: ศูนย์กลาง นิสิตนักศึกษาแห่งประเทศไทย, ๒๕๑๗.
(Freire, Paulo. *Pedagogy of the Oppressed.* Trans. Jiraporn Sirisupan. Bangkok: National Student Center of Thailand, 2517 [1974].)

แฟรร์, เปาโล. *การศึกษาสำหรับผู้ถูกกดขี่.* แปลโดย ช. เขียวพุ่มพวง. กรุงเทพฯ: สหพันธ์นักศึกษาเสรีฯ, ๒๕๑๗.
(Freire, Paulo. *Pedagogy of the Oppressed.* Trans. Cho Khiewphumphuang. Bangkok: Federation of Independent Students of Thailand, 2517 [1974].)

แมกซิม กอร์กี้. *เพลงพญาเหยี่ยว.* กรุงเทพฯ: ปุถุชน, ๒๕๑๘.

    (Gorky, Maksim. *Song of the Falcon.* Bangkok: Putuchon, 2518 [1975].)

อินสอน บัวเขียว. "เดินขบวน วิธีการที่ดีที่สุดสำหรับชาวนาและกรรมกร." *อธิปัตย์* ๒–๘
ตุลาคม ๒๕๑๗, ๗.

    (Inson Buakhiew. "Protesting Is the Best Strategy for Farmers and Workers."
        Athipat, 2–8 October 2517 [1974], 7.)

อินถา ศรีบุญเรือง. "บทสัมภาษณ์ด้วย 'จตุรัส.'" *จตุรัส* ๑.๖ (๑๙ สิงหาคม ๒๕๑๘):
๒๙–๓๒.

    (Intha Sribunruang. "Interview with *Chaturat* Magazine." *Chaturat* 1, no. 6 (19
        August 2518 [1975]): 29–32.)

ใจ อึ๊งภากรณ์ และ สุธาชัย ยิ้มประเสริฐ. *อาชญกรรมรัฐในวิกฤตการเปลี่ยนแปลง.*
กรุงเทพฯ: คณะกรรมการรับข้อมูลและสืบพยานเหตุการณ์ ๖ ตุลาคม ๒๕๑๙,
๒๕๔๔.

    (Ji Ungpakorn and Suthachai Yimprasert. *The Crime of the State in the Crisis of*
        Changes. Bangkok: 6 October Fact-Finding Committee, 2544 [2001].)

จิตร ภูมิศักดิ์. *ด้วยเลือดและชีวิต: รวมเรื่องสั้นเวียดนาม.* กรุงเทพฯ: ชมรมหนังสือแสงตะวัน,
๒๕๑๙.

    (Jit Phumisak. *With Blood and Life: Vietnamese Short Stories.* Bangkok: Chom-
        rom Nangsu Saeng Thawan, 2519 [1976].)

กนกศักดิ์ แก้วเทพ. *บทวิเคราะห์ สหพันธ์ชาวนาชาวไร่แห่งประเทศไทย:*
เศรษฐศาสตร์การเมืองว่าด้วยชาวนา ยุคใหม่. กรุงเทพฯ: สถาบันวิจัยสังคม
จุฬาลงกรณ์มหาวิทยาลัย, ๒๕๓๐.

    (Kanoksak Kaewthep. *Analysis of the Farmers' Federation of Thailand: A Political*
        Economy of the Modern Farmer. Bangkok: Chulalongkorn University Social
        Research Institute, 2530 [1987].)

กนกศักดิ์ แก้วเทพ. "สหพันธ์ชาวนาชาวไร่แห่งประเทศไทย (๒๕๑๗–๒๕๒๒)
ถึง สมัชชาคนจน (๒๕๓๘–): ความต่อเนื่องและความขัดต้น." *วารสาร*
เศรษฐศาสตร์การเมือง (เพื่อชุมชน) ๓ (๒๕๓๙): ๙๑–๑๐๙.

    (Kanoksak Kaewthep. "Farmers Federation of Thailand (2517–2522) until the
        Assembly of the Poor (1995–): Continuity and Discontinuity." *Warasan Set-*
        thasat Karnmuang (Phua Chumchon) 3 (2539 [1997]): 91–109.)

กนกศักดิ์ แก้วเทพ. "การต่อสู้ของชาวนาไทย: สหพันธ์ชาวนาชาวไร่แห่งประเทศ
ไทย." ใน *เส้นทางชาวนาไทย,* นิติรัตน์ ทรัพย์สมบูรณ์, บ., น. ๒๕–๖๓. กรุงเทพฯ:
มูลนิธิเด็ก, ๒๕๔๓.

    (Kanoksak Kaewthep. "Thai Farmers' Struggles: Farmers' Federation of Thai-
        land." In *The Path of Thai Farmers,* ed. Nitirat Sapsomboon, 25–63. Bang-
        kok: Mooniti Dek, 2543 [1999].)

กนกศักดิ์ แก้วเทพ. "บทเรียน ๓๐ ปี ของขบวนการเคลื่อนไหวทางสังคมของชาวนาชาวไร่
ไทย." *ฟ้าเดียวกัน* ๒.๔ (๒๕๔๘): ๘๘–๑๑๑.

    (Kanoksak Kaewthep. "Lessons from 30 Years of the Farmers' Movement
        and Protest in Thailand." *Fa Dieu Kan* 2, no. 4 (October–December 2548
        [2004]): 88–111.)

กลุ่มบัณฑิตพัฒนา. *แอก.* กรุงเทพฯ: ไทยการพิมพ์, ๒๕๑๘.

    (Klum Bandit Phattana. *The Sickle.* Bangkok: Thai Karnphim, 2518 [1975].)

โกมล คีมทอง. *ข้อเขียนของโกมล คีมทอง.* กรุงเทพฯ: มูลนิธิโกมล คีมทอง, ๒๕๒๕.

    (Komol Keemthong. *Writings of Komol Keemthong.* Bangkok: Komol Keem-
        thong Foundation, 2525 [1982].)

มูลนิธิโกมล คีมทอง. *อ่านโกมล คีมทอง.* กรุงเทพฯ: มูลนิธิโกมล คีมทอง, ๒๕๑๕.
    (Komol Keemthong Foundation. *Reading Komol Keemthong.* Bangkok: Komol
    Keemthong Foundation, 2515 [1972].)
เกริกเกียรติ พิพัฒน์เสรีธรรม. *ชาวนากับที่ดิน: ปฏิวัติหรือปฏิรูป.* กรุงเทพฯ: ดวงกมล,
    ๒๕๒๑.
    (Krirkkiat Phipatseritham. *Farmers and the Land: Reform or Revolution.* Bang-
    kok: Duang Kamol, 2521 [1978].)
เกริกเกียรติ พิพัฒน์เสรีธรรม. "ปัญหาที่ดินกับการช่วยเหลือชาวไร่ชาวนาไทย."
    วารสารวิทยาลัยการค้า ๑.๑ (๒๕๒๒): ๑–๖๒.
    (Krirkkiat Phipatseritham. "Land Problems and Assistance to Thai Farmers."
    College of Commerce Journal 1, no. 1 (2522 [1979]): 1–62.)
เลนิน, วลาดิมีร์ อิลยิช. *รัฐกับการปฏิวัติ.* กรุงเทพฯ: แนวหน้าจุฬา, ๒๕๑๘.
    (Lenin, Vladimir Ilyich. *State and Revolution.* Bangkok: United Front of Chu-
    lalongkorn University, 2518 [1975].)
ม. "ชีวิตดั่งฝัน หากมันคือความจริง." โรเนียว, ไร้ข้อมูลปีพิมพ์.
    (M. "Life Is Like a Dream, If It Is the Truth." Mimeograph, n.d.)
เหมาเจ๋อตง. *สุนทรพจน์ของประธานเหมาเจ๋อตง.* กรุงเทพฯ: ศรีเพ็ชร์การพิมพ์, ๒๕๑๘.
    (Mao Tse-tung. *President Mao Tse-tung's Speeches.* Bangkok: Sriphen Kanphim,
    2518 [1975].)
มติชน. *พจนานุกรมนอกราชบัณฑิตยฯ.* กรุงเทพฯ: สำนักพิมพ์มติชน, ๒๕๔๓.
    (Matichon. *Dictionary outside the Royal Institute.* Bangkok: Matichon Press, 2543
    [2000].)
มติชน. *พจนานุกรมฉบับมติชน.* กรุงเทพฯ: สำนักพิมพ์มติชน, ๒๕๔๗.
    (Matichon. *Matichon Dictionary.* Bangkok: Matichon Press, 2547 [2004].)
มูลนิธินราธิปประพันธ์พงศ์-วรวรรณ, บ. *วิทยทัศน์พระองค์วรวรรณฯ: ครบ ๑๑๐ ปี วันประสูติ*
    ๒๕ สิงหาคม ๒๕๔๔. กรุงเทพฯ: มูลนิธินราธิปประทันธ์พงศ์-วรวรรณ, ๒๕๔๔.
    (Munnithi Narathip Praphanphong-Worawan, ed. *Prince Wan Studies: 110th*
    Anniversary of His Birth, 25 August 2001. Bangkok: Munnithi Narathip
    Praphanphong-Worawan, 2544 [2001].)
สำนักงานวิจัยแห่งประเทศไทย. *การวิเคราะห์ผลงานด้าน เศรษฐกิจ สังคม และการเมือง*
    ของระบบการถือครองที่ดิน ทางด้านเกษตรกรรมเพื่อการปฏิรูปที่ดินในประเทศไทย.
    กรุงเทพฯ: สำนักงานนายกรัฐมนตรี, ๒๕๑๙.
    (National Research Council of Thailand. *Socio-Political-Economic Analysis of*
    Land Tenure for Agricultural Land Reform in Thailand: Comparative Study
    between Central and North Region, B.E. 2519. Bangkok: Office of the Prime
    Minister, 2519 [1976].)
ศูนย์กลางนักศึกษาแห่งประเทศไทย. *ขบวนการประชาชนตุลาคม ๒๕๑๖.* กรุงเทพฯ:
    ศูนย์กลาง นักศึกษาแห่งประเทศไทย, ๒๕๑๗.
    (National Student Center of Thailand. *Movement of the People, October 2516.*
    Bangkok: National Student Center of Thailand, 2517 [1974].)
นิธิ เอียวศรีวงศ์. "บทนำ." ใน *เจ้าชื่อทองกวาว: รวมผลงานของชาวหนุ่มที่ราบริมดอย,*
    ชาวหนุ่มที่ราบริมดอย, บ. เชียงใหม่: มหาวิทยาลัยเชียงใหม่, ๒๕๑๓.
    (Nidhi Eoseewong. "Introduction." In *His Name Is Tongkwao: Writings of Young*
    Men in the Flats at the Edge of the Mountain, ed. Young Men in the Flats
    at the Edge of the Mountain. Chiang Mai: Chiang Mai University, 2513
    [1970].)
นิติรัตน์ ทรัพย์สมบูรณ์. "ความเป็นมาและประวัติผู้นำ สหพันธ์ชาวนาชาวไร่แห่งประเทศ

ไทย." ใน *เส้นทาง ชาวนาไทย*, นิติรัตน์ ทรัพย์สมบูรณ์, บ., น. ๑๓๘–๑๕๔. กรุงเทพฯ: มูลนิธิเด็ก, ๒๕๔๒.

(Nitirat Sapsomboon. "Beginnings and Life Histories of the Leaders of the Farmers' Federation of Thailand Movement." In *The Path of Thai Farmers*, ed. Nitirat Sapsomboon, 138–54. Bangkok: Mooniti Dek, 2542 [1999].)

นิติรัตน์ ทรัพย์สมบูรณ์, บ. *เส้นทาง ชาวนาไทย*. กรุงเทพฯ: มูลนิธิเด็ก, ๒๕๔๒.

(Nitirat Sapsomboon, ed. *The Path of Thai Farmers*. Bangkok: Mooniti Dek, 2543 [1999].)

นิเวศน์ ทองกวาว. "บทบานเยาวชนนักศึกษาในปัจจุบัน." ใน *สู้ขบวนการณ์ประชาชน*, ศูนย์นักศึกษาภาคเหนือ, บ., น. ๑–๗. กรุงเทพฯ: ศูนย์นักศึกษาภาคเหนือ, ศูนย์นักศึกษาภาคอิสาน ศูนย์นักศึกษาภาคใต้, ๒๕๑๗.

(Niwet Tongkwao. "The Roles of Young People and Students in the Present Situation." In *The Struggle of the People Continues*, ed. Northern Student Center, 1–7. Bangkok: Northern Student Center, Northeastern Student Center, Southern Student Center, 2517 [1974].).)

สหพันธ์เกษตรกรภาคเหนือ. *เสียงเกษตรกร*. เชียงใหม่: สหพันธ์เกษตรกรภาคเหนือ, ๒๕๔๓.

(Northern Farmers' Federation. *Voice of the Farmers*. Chiang Mai: Northern Farmers' Federation, 2543 [2001].)

ปาลรัฐ มนูรัษฎา. "คุณพ่อที่ลูกรู้จัก." ใน *ทนายกล้าของประชาชน*, ชาญชัย สงวนวงศ์ ฯลฯ, บ., น. ๑๒๖–๑๒๗. กรุงเทพฯ: ๑๗๙ การพิมพ์, ๒๕๓๗.

(Panrat Manurasada. "The Father That I Know." In *Courageous Lawyer of the People*, ed. Chanchai Songwonwong et al., 126–27. Bangkok: 179 Kanphim, 2537 [1994].)

พจน์ กริชไกรวรรณ, บ. *โกมล คีมทอง: ปรัชญาและปณิธานแห่งชีวิต*. กรุงเทพฯ: มูลนิธิโกมล คีมทอง, ๒๕๔๐.

(Phot Kritkraiwan, ed. *Komol Keemthong: Philosophy and Resolution of Life*. Bangkok: Komol Keemthong Foundation, 2540 [1997].)

พระสันติสุข สนฺติสุโข, บ. *คิดถึงโกมล*. กรุงเทพฯ: มูลนิธิโกมล คีมทอง, ๒๕๒๒.

(Phra Santisuk Santhisukho, ed. *Remembering Komol*. Bangkok: Komol Keemthong Foundation, 2522 [1979].)

ปลายอ้อ ชนะนนท์. "บทบาทนายทุนพ่อค้าที่มีต่อการก่อและขยายตัวของทุนนิยม ภาคเหนือของ ประเทศไทย, พ.ศ. ๒๔๖๔–๒๕๒๓." วิทยานิพนธ์ปริญญาโท ภาควิชาเศรษฐศาสตร์ จุฬาลงกรณ์มหาวิทยาลัย, ๒๕๒๙.

(Plai-Auw Chananont. "The Roles of Merchant Capitalists in the Expansion of Capitalism in Northern Thailand, 1921–1980." MA thesis, Faculty of Economics, Chulalongkorn University, 2529 [1986].)

ประชาชาติรายวัน. *ประชาชาติเสนอเลือกตั้ง '๑๘*. กรุงเทพฯ: สำนักพิมพ์ประพันธ์สาส์น, ๒๕๑๘.

(Prachachat Daily. *Prachachat Presents the '75 Elections*. Bangkok: Samnakphim Prapansat, 2518 [1975].)

ประจักษ์ ก้องกีรติ. *และแล้วความเคลื่อนไหวก็ปรากฏ . . . การเมืองวัฒนธรรมของนักศึกษาและปัญญาชน ก่อน ๑๔ ตุลา*. กรุงเทพฯ: สำนักพิมพ์มหาวิทยาลัยธรรมศาสตร์, ๒๕๔๘.

(Prajak Kongkirati. *And Now the Movement Emerges . . . Cultural Politics of Students and Intellectuals prior to 14 October*. Bangkok: Thammasat University Press, 2548 [2005].)

ปรีชา เปี่ยมพงศ์สานต์ และ จำรัส ม่วงยาม. *ทางเดินของชาวนา.* กรุงเทพฯ: สำนักพิมพ์
ชาวบ้าน, ๒๕๒๒.
  (Preecha Phiamphongsan and Chamrat Muangyam. *The Path of Thai Farmers.*
  Bangkok: Samnakphim Chao Baan, 2522 [1979].)
รีมเมอร์, เอเวอเรท. *โรงเรียนตายแล้ว.* แปลโดย ช. เขียวพุ่มพวง. กรุงเทพฯ: สารสยาม,
๒๕๑๗.
  (Reimer, Everett. *School Is Dead.* Trans. Cho Khiewphumphuang. Bangkok: San
  Siam, 2517 [1974].)
ราชบัณฑิตยสถาน.พจนานุกรม ฉบับราชบัณฑิตยสถาน. กรุงเทพฯ: ราชบัณฑิตยสถาน,
๒๔๙๓.
  (Royal Institute. *Royal Institute Dictionary.* Bangkok: Royal Institute, 2493
  [1950].)
ราชบัณฑิตยสถาน. พจนานุกรม ฉบับราชบัณฑิตยสถาน. กรุงเทพฯ: ราชบัณฑิตยสถาน,
๒๕๒๕.
  (Royal Institute. *Royal Institute Dictionary.* Bangkok: Royal Institute, 2525
  [1982].)
ราชบัณฑิตยสถาน. พจนานุกรม ฉบับราชบัณฑิตยสถาน. กรุงเทพฯ: ราชบัณฑิตยสถาน,
๒๕๔๒.
  (Royal Institute. *Royal Institute Dictionary.* Bangkok: Royal Institute, 2542
  [1999].)
รุ่งวิทย์ สุวรรณอภิชน. *ศรีบูรพา ศรีแห่งวรรณกรรมไทย.* กรุงเทพฯ: สำนักพิมพ์แสงดาว,
๒๕๓๒.
  (Rungwit Suwannaphichon. *Sriburapha, a Great of Thai Literature.* Bangkok:
  Saengdao Press, 2532 [1989].)
สายชล สัตยานุรักษ์. *ความเปลี่ยนแปลงในการสร้าง "ชาติไทย" และ "ความเป็นไทย" โดย
หลวงวิจิตรวาทการ.* กรุงเทพฯ: มติชน, ๒๕๔๕.
  (Saichon Sattayanurak. *The Changes in the Construction of "The Thai Nation" and "Thainess" by Luang Wichitwathakan.* Bangkok: Matichon, 2545
  [2002].)
สงวน นิตยารัมภ์พงศ์, บ. *ปูมประวัติศาสตร์ มหิดลเพื่อประชาธิปไตย. ภาคที่ ๑,
ก่อเกิดขบวนการ.* กรุงเทพฯ: บริษัทอัลฟ่า มิเล็นเนียม, ๒๕๔๖.
  (Sanguan Nittayaramphong, ed. *Annals of the History of Mahidol for Democracy.*
  Part 1, *Building the Movement.* Bangkok: Alpha Millennium Company, 2546
  [2003].)
สงวน นิตยารัมภ์พงศ์, บ. *ปูมประวัติศาสตร์ มหิดลเพื่อประชาธิปไตย. ภาคที่ ๒,
ประสานประชาชน, อุทิศตนเพื่ออุดมการณ์ (๑๔ ตุลาคม ๒๕๑๖-๖ ตุลาคม ๒๕๑๙).*
กรุงเทพฯ: บริษัท อัลฟ่า มิเล็นเนียม, ๒๕๔๗.
  (Sanguan Nittayaramphong, ed. *Annals of the History of Mahidol for Democracy.*
  Part 2, *Organizing the People, Dedicating Oneself to Ideals (14 October 1973–6
  October 1976).* Bangkok: Alpha Millennium Company, 2547 [2004].)
สงวน นิตยารัมภ์พงศ์, บ. *ปูมประวัติศาสตร์ มหิดลเพื่อประชาธิปไตย. ภาคที่ ๓,
ฟื้นความหวัง, สร้างกำลังใจ, มุ่งรับใช้สังคม (หลัง ๖ ตุลาคม ๒๕๑๙–๒๕๒๕).*
กรุงเทพฯ: บริษัท งานดี, ๒๕๔๘.
  (Sanguan Nittayaramphong, ed. *Annals of the History of Mahidol for Democracy.*
  Part 3: *Reviving Hope, Building Strength, Looking to Serve Society (After 6 October 1976–1982).* Bangkok: Ngandee Company, 2548 [2005].)
สรรเสรญ ศรีอุ่นเรือน. "ประดับ มนุรัษฎา ทนายกล้า ทนายจริง เสี้ยวหนึ่งของชีวิตที่

ขัพเจ้าสัมผัส." ใน *ทนายกล้าของประชาชน*, ชาญชัย สงวนวงศ์ ฯลฯ, บ., น. ๖๑–๖๒.
กรุงเทพฯ: ๑๗๙ การพิมพ์, ๒๕๓๗.

   (Sansern Sri-unruan. "Pradap Manurasada, Courageous Lawyer, Truthful Lawyer, One Quarter of My Experience." In *Courageous Lawyer of the People*,
   ed. Chanchai Songwonwong et al., 61–62. Bangkok: 179 Kanphim, 2537
   [1994].)

สมพร จันทรชัย, บ. *ประชาชนต้องเป็นใหญ่ในแผ่นดิน*. กรุงเทพฯ: โรงพิมพ์เดือนตุลา,
๒๕๔๔.

   (Somporn Chanthachai, ed. *The People Must Be the Masters of the Land*. Bangkok: Rongphim Duan Tula, 2544 [2001].)

สุพจน์ ด่านตระกูล. *ปทานุกรมการเมือง ฉบับ ชาวบ้าน*. นนทบุรี: สำนักพิมพ์สันติธรรม,
๒๕๒๘.

   (Suphot Dantrakul. *Dictionary of Politics, Peoples' Edition*. Nonthaburi: Santhitham Press, 2528 [1985].)

เตช บุนนาค. *ขบถ ร.ศ. ๑๒๑*. กรุงเทพฯ: ไทยวัฒนาพานิช, ๒๕๒๔.

   (Tej Bunnag. *Ro. So. 121 Rebellion*. Bangkok: Thai Watthana Phanit, 2524
   [1981].)

ทักษ์ เฉลิมเตียรณ. "ชีวิตในมหาวิทยาลัย." ใน *คนรุ่นใหม่*, องค์การนักศึกษาธรรมศาสตร์,
บ. กรุงเทพฯ: มหาวิทยาลัยธรรมศาสตร์, ๒๕๑๘.

   (Thak Chaloemtiarana. "University Life." In *People of the New Generation*,
   ed. Thammasat Student Union. Bangkok: Thammasat University, 2518
   [1975].)

ทักษ์ เฉลิมเตียรณ. "กอ.รมน.: บทความเพื่อกล่อมผีคอมมิวนิสต์ให้ลับ." *วารสารธรรมศาสตร์*
๑๐.๒ (๒๕๒๔): ๑๐๗–๑๑๒.

   (Thak Chaloemtiarana. "ISOC: Lullaby for the Communist Specter." *Thammasat Journal* 10, no. 2 (2524 [1981]): 107–12.)

ศูนย์นักศึกษาอาษาพัฒนา มหาวิทยาลัยธรรมศาสตร์. *หยาดเหงื่อกับรอยยิ้ม*. กรุงเทพฯ:
ศูนย์นักศึกษา อาษาพัฒนามหาวิทยาลัยธรรมศาสตร์, ๒๕๑๖.

   (Thammasat University Volunteer Development Center. *Drops of Sweat and the
   Trace of a Smile*. Bangkok: Thammasat University Volunteer Development
   Center, 2516 [1973].)

ธเนศ อาภรณ์สุวรรณ. *สังคมและการเมืองไทย*. กรุงเทพฯ: สำนักพิมพ์ พี.พี., ๒๕๒๑.

   (Thanet Aphornsuvan. *Thai Society and Politics*. Bangkok: P. P. Press, 2521
   [1978].)

ธเนศ อาภรณ์สุวรรณ. *วรรณกรรมในชีวิต, ชีวิตในวรรณกรรม*. กรุงเทพฯ:
สำนักพิมพ์มิ่งมิตร, ๒๕๓๙.

   (Thanet Aphornsuvan. *Literature in Life, Life in Literature*. Bangkok: Samnakphim Mingmit, 2539 [1996].)

ธเนศ อาภรณ์สุวรรณ. "ความเคลื่อนไหวของนักศึกษาไทยในยุคแรก." ใน
ขบวนการนักศึกษาไทย จาก ๒๔๗๕–๑๔ ตุลาคม ๒๕๑๖, วิทยากร เชียงกูล, บ., น.
๑๑–๘๐. กรุงเทพฯ: สายธาร, ๒๕๔๖.

   (Thanet Aphornsuvan. "The First Generation of Thai Students' Movement." In
   Thai Student Movements, June 1932–14 October 1973, ed. Witayakorn Chiengkul, 11–80. Bangkok: Saithan, 2546 [2003].)

ธานินทร์ กรัยวิเชียร. *การใช้กฎหมายป้องกันคอมมิวนิสต์*. กรุงเทพฯ:
ศูนย์รักษาความปลอดภัย, กระทรวงกลาโหม, ๒๕๑๗.

   (Thanin Kraivichien. *Using the Law to Protect against the Communists*. Bangkok:
   Armed Forces Security Center, 2517 [1974].)

ชุมนุมอาสาพัฒนา. ชุมนุมอาสาพัฒนา. เชียงใหม่: สโมสรนักศึกษามหาวิทยาลัยเชียงใหม่,
๒๕๑๔.
    (Volunteer Development Assembly. *Volunteer Development Assembly.* Chiang
        Mai: Chiang Mai University Students' Association, 2514 [1971].)
วิทยากร เชียงกูล. "กลับไปอ่านนิยายของ 'ศรีบูรพา.'" *สังคมศาสตร์ ปริทัศน์.* ๑๑.๗
(๒๕๑๖): ๖๙–๗๒.
    (Witayakorn Chiengkul. "Returning to Read the Novels of 'Sriburapha.'" *Sang-*
        khomsat Parithat. 11, no. 7 (2516 [1973]): 69–72.)
วราวุธ โกศลยุทธศาร. "ใครฆ่า." *ยุทธโกษ* ๘๔.๑ (ก.ย. ๒๕๑๘): ๓๙–๔๔.
    (Worawut Kosonyutthasorn. "Who Kills." *Yuthakot* 84, no. 1 (September 2518
        [1975]): 39–44.)
วุฒิชัย มูลศิลป์ และ ธรรมนิตย์ วราภรณ์, บ. *กบฏชาวนา.* กรุงเทพฯ:
สมาคมสังคมศาสตร์แห่งประเทศไทย, ๒๕๒๕.
    (Wutthichai Munsin and Thammanit Worakorn, eds. *Peasant Rebellions.* Bang-
        kok: Social Science Association of Thailand, 2525 [1982].)
ยศ พนัสสรณ. *พจนานุกรมนักเรียน.* กรุงเทพฯ: สำนักพิมพ์ ประสานมิตร, ๒๕๔๓.
    (Yot Pannasorn. *Student Dictionary.* Bangkok: Prasarnmit Press, 2543 [2000].)
ชาวหนุ่มที่ราบริมดอย, บ. *เจ้าชื่อทองกวาว: รวมผลงานของชาวหนุ่มที่ราบริมดอย.*
เชียงใหม่: มหาวิทยาลัยเชียงใหม่, ๒๕๑๓.
    (Young Men in the Flats at the Edge of the Mountain, ed. *His Name is Tong-*
        kwao: Writings of Young Men in the Flats at the Edge of the Mountain. Chiang
        Mai: Chiang Mai University, 2513 [1970].)

Bilingual Book

สวัสดิการข้าราชการสำนักงานคณะกรรมการกฤษฎีกา.
    ธรรมนูณการปกครองราชอาณาจักร พุทธศักราช ๒๕๑๕. กรุงเทพฯ: สวัสดิการ
    ข้าราชการสำนักงานคณะกรรมการกฤษฎีกา, ๒๕๑๕.
    (Office of the Juridical Council's Welfare Fund. *Constitution of the Kingdom, B.E.*
        2515. Bangkok: Office of the Juridical Council's Welfare Fund, 2515 [1972].)

English-Language Periodicals

Ampo
Bangkok Post
Far Eastern Economic Review
Investor
Nation
New York Times
Straits Times
Voice of the Nation

Thai-Language Periodicals

Athipat (อธิปัตย์)
Baan Muang (บ้านเมือง)
Chaturat (จตุรัส)
Daily Niu (เดลินิวส์)

Fa Dieu Kan (ฟ้าเดียวกัน)
Kittisak (เกียรติศักดิ์)
Prachachat (ประชาชาติ)
Prachachat Weekly (ประชาชาติรายสัปดาห์)
Prachathipatai (ประชาธิปไตย)
Ratchakitchanubeksa (ราชกิจจานุเบกษา)
Sajja (สัจจา)
Siam Rat (สยามรัฐ)
Sieng Chonabot (เสียงชนบท)
Su Sarn Muanchon (สื่อสารมวลชน)
Thai Niu (ไทนิวส์)
Thai Rat (ไทยรัฐ)
Thin Thai (ถิ่นไทย)
Walanchathat (วลัญชทัศน์)
Yuthakot (ยุทธโกษ)

Thai-Language Archival Sources

ช.ม. ๑.๒.๒/๓. เอกสารจังหวัดเชียงใหม่. สำนักงานปกครองจังหวัด. ประกาศ, พระราชบัญญัติ. "การประกาศใช้พระราชบัญญาติ ควบคุมการเช่านา พ.ศ. ๒๔๙๓."
  (C.M. 1.2.2/3. Chiang Mai Provincial Government Documents. Provincial Administration Office. Laws and Orders. "Decree of 2493 B.E. Land Rent Control Act.")
ช.ม. ๑.๒.๒/๒๐. เอกสารจังหวัดเชียงใหม่. สำนักงานปกครองจังหวัด. ประกาศ, พระราชบัญญัติ. "พระราชบัญญาติ ควบคุมการเช่านา ปี ๒๕๑๗."
  (C.M. 1.2.2/20. Chiang Mai Provincial Government Documents. Provincial Administration Office. Laws and Orders. "2517 Land Rent Control Act.")
ช.ม. ๑.๒.๒/๒๒. เอกสารจังหวัดเชียงใหม่. สำนักงานปกครองจังหวัด. ประกาศ, พระราชบัญญัติ. "พระราชบัญญาติ ควบคุมการเช่านา พ.ศ. ๒๕๑๗."
  (C.M. 1.2.2/22. Chiang Mai Provincial Government Documents. Provincial Administration Office. Laws and Orders. "2517 B.E. Land Rent Control Act.")
(๒) มธ. 2.14.3.3/5, หน้า 8–9. หอจดหมายเหตุธรรมศาสตร์. เอกสารมหาวิทยาลัยธรรมศาสตร์. เหตุการณ์ทางการเมือง. เหตุการณ์ไม่สงบสิงหาคม 2518. รับหมายศาลเป็นพยาน (20 ส.ค. 2518). "ข้อเทจจริงที่ศูนย์กลางนักศึกษาภาคเหนือลงมา."
  ((2) T.U. 2.14.3.3/5, pages 8–9. Thammasat University Archives. Thammasat University Documents. Political Events. Unrest in August 2518. Subpoenaed as evidence (20 August 2518). "Facts Raised by the Northern Student Center.")
(๒) มธ. 2.14.3.3/5, หน้า 19–21. หอจดหมายเหตุธรรมศาสตร์. เอกสารมหาวิทยาลัยธรรมศาสตร์. เหตุการณ์ทางการเมือง. เหตุการณ์ไม่สงบสิงหาคม 2518. รับหมายศาลเป็นพยาน (20 ส.ค. 2518). "คำชี้แจงจากสมาชิกกองค์การนักศึกษาเชียงใหม่."
  ((2) T.U. 2.14.3.3/5, pages 19–21. Thammasat University Archives. Thammasat University Documents. Political Events. Unrest in August 2518. Subpoenaed as evidence (20 August 2518). "Observations of members of the CMU Students' Organization.")
(๒) มธ. 2.14.3.3/5, หน้า 14–18. หอจดหมายเหตุธรรมศาสตร์. เอกสารมหาวิทยาลัยธรรมศาสตร์.

เหตุการณ์ทางการเมือง. เหตุการณ์ไม่สงบสิงหาคม 2518. รับหมายศาลเป็นพยาน (20 ส.ค. 2518). "แถลงการณ์ต่างๆ."

((2) T.U. 2.14.3.3/5, pages 14–18. Thammasat University Archives. Thammasat University Documents. Political Events. Unrest in August 2518. Subpoenaed as evidence (20 August 2518). "Various Declarations.")

มธ. B2/40. หอจดหมายเหตุธรรมศาสตร. พรรคคอมมิวนิสต์แห่งประเทศไทย. เหตุการณ์ทางการเมืองที่เกี่ยวข้อง กับนักศึกษา. เอกสารการศึกษา. "ถ้าจดหมายของนายอินถาปลอม เราจะรู้ว่าใครบ้างมอง การฆ่าผู้นำชาวนา."

(T.U. B2/40. Thammasat University Archives. Communist Party of Thailand. Political Events Involving Students. Education Documents. "If the letter of Mr. Intha is fake, then we will know who is overseeing the killings of the farmers.")

Index

Abrams, Philip, 130–31, 132

absolute monarchy: kings and, 7, 8, 150, 192n2; revolution of 1932 and, xi, 17, 30, 32, 43–44, 168n62; Siam and, 32, 38, 174n37, 174n40. *See also* feudalism; government of Thailand; lords; peasants

activists. *See* farmer activists; students/student activists; teacher activists; *specific activists*; *specific organizations*

Ajarn Angun, 81, 83, 97, 189n35

alliances, 18, 58, 82, 113

Anderson, Benedict, 86, 120–21

Angkhana Neelaphaichit, 156

Angun Malik, 81, 83, 97, 189n35

Anzaldúa, Gloria, 168n54

arrests. *See under* farmer activists; students/student activists

Article 17, 60–64

Asa Meksawan, 72–73, 100–101, 115, 125–26, 145

assassinations, ix–x, 114, 150, 155, 187n4. *See also* assassinations of farmer activists/leaders

assassinations of farmer activists/leaders: accountability for, 22, 107, 115, 122, 133, 141, 153; Article 17 and, 61; calls for end to, 107, 122, 133; contradictory responses to, 117, 125–26, 189n50, 189n53; denial of political subjectivity of leaders and, 115–17, 122–24; denials of, 115–16, 117, 189n50, 189n53; of FFT leaders, ix–x, 22, 106, 114, 117–22, 148, 161, 187n2; hegemony crisis and, 21–22, 153; landlords' role in, 22, 27, 106, 114, 121; military's denials of, 117, 189n53; named/unnamed assassins and, 6, 106, 114–15, 127–28, 137, 153, 155, 192nn112–13; parastate forces' role in, 22–23, 27; personal aspect of, 28, 107, 125, 128; police investigations into, 115–16, 122–26, 134, 136–37, 189n50;

revolution interrupted and, 23, 106; scholarship and, 153; state officials' (in)actions/responses to, 107, 115–17, 125–26, 189n50, 189n53; statistics of, 106, 122, 159–63, 187n2; student activists and, ix–x, 115, 121, 122; theories about, 114, 120, 123–24. *See also* assassinations

Assembly of the Poor, 155

Athipat (newspaper), 24, 61, 87, 88, 115, 135, 183n11

Bangkok: activists' protests in, xi, 19, 22, 72–73, 107, 139, 196n64; 14 October 1973 movement and, 12; police protests in, 144, 145–46; space transgression by activists in, xi, 19, 22. *See also* National Student Center of Thailand (NSCT); Sanam Luang; Thammasat University; urban protests by farmer activists

Bank for Agriculture and Cooperatives, 63, 67, 178n11

Bataille, Georges, 18

Benjamin, Walter, 7, 132, 193n10

Bhumipol (king), 12, 13, 93

blacklists, 151, 198n13

Bowie, Katherine, 20, 112, 114, 169n73

broadcasted rice practice, 31, 72, 172n5

Brown, Wendy, 129, 153

Buddhism, 27, 56, 66, 131, 150, 153, 180n63, 193n6

Bumbam, Mister (pseud.), 39–42, 44, 45, 71

Bunsanong Punyodhayana, 125, 150, 191n99

Buntheng Thongsawat, 112, 116, 136, 145, 147

Butalia, Urvashi, 25

Butler, Judith, 170n75

capitalists: overview, 3, 79–80; farmers and, 46–47, 79–80, 109, 114, 120, 121; landlords

capitalists (*continued*)
and, 46–47, 79–80, 109, 121; processes and, 14, 18–19
central Thailand, 32, 44, 45, 100, 171n9, 173n15
Chai-anan Samudavanija, 61, 64–65, 67
Chaiyong Pronmung, 88
Chatri Hutanuwat, 133, 137, 139, 141, 146–47, 188n35, 195n44
Chatterjee, Partha, 29
Chiang Mai city: location of, 9; NSC and, 88, 122, 139, 194n29; protests in, 70–74, 139–41, 143, 145, 151; Tha Pae gate, 70, 127, 139–40; violence against activists and, 114, 151, 188n35. *See also* Chiang Mai University (CMU); Northern Student Center (NSC)
Chiang Mai province, 5, 8–9, 20, 32, 170n73; elections and, 109–10, 188n10; 14 October 1973 movement and, 12; LRCA of 1974 and, 77, 78, 100–101, 107–8; map of, 2; protection for farmer activists and, 127; provincial government and, 125, 126; sedition accusations against farmer activists and, 112–13; SPT and, 191n99; statistics about, 8, 9, 170n74; tenancy and, 8–10, 32, 53–54, 167n31. *See also* contention over LRCA of 1950; rural activism by students; *specific districts*; *specific farmer activists*; *specific organizations*
Chiang Mai Teachers' College, 18, 139, 140
Chiang Mai University (CMU): publications, 24, 93–94, 183n11, 185n43, 185nn45–46, 185n46; student activists and, 94, 139, 151, 185n45, 194n29, 198n13; Students' Association, 90–91; Students' Organization, 137–38, 151, 194n29; teacher activists and, 18, 81, 83, 97, 139, 140, 189n35; VDA and, 85, 90–95. *See also* rural activism by students
Chiang Rai province, 92, 127, 166n27, 185n47. *See also* rural activism by students
China: communism and, 35, 36, 134, 154, 196n64; Mao Tse-tung and, 12, 16, 35, 48, 56, 93, 109, 183n11
Cho Khiewphumphuang (pseud.), 103, 187n72
Chulalongkorn (king), 7, 8, 192n2
Chulalongkorn University, 89, 96, 139, 141, 187n72
Chumphon Lohachalah, 69, 115–16

class/class boundaries: contention over LRCA of 1950 and, 48, 49–50; farmer activists and, 5, 18–19, 50, 82–84, 86, 119–21, 152, 195n44; 14 October 1973 movement and, 12, 18; LRCA of 1974 and, 50; Marxism and, 18; middle class and, 86, 103; process and, 18–19, 169n71; student activists and, 18–19, 82–84, 86, 103, 119–21, 152, 195n44
CMU (Chiang Mai University). *See* Chiang Mai University (CMU)
Cold War, 4–6, 8, 26, 29, 155, 158
Committee to Investigate the Problems of Indebted Farmers, 60–66, 71
Communist Party of Thailand (CPT), 4, 6, 12, 99, 103, 154, 177n87; farmer activists and, 99, 152, 154; liberated areas and, 4, 150, 151–52; student activists and, 21, 99, 150, 151–52, 198n14
communists/communist movements: China and, 35, 36, 134, 154, 196n64; communist, use of term, 140; counterinsurgency and, 4, 35–37, 40, 61, 69; farmer activists and, ix, 29, 99, 152, 154; fears of spread of, 6, 12, 30, 35–37, 48–50, 98, 107, 112–13, 123, 153–54, 177n87, 188n28; imagined future and, 153–54; revolution and, 4–5, 15–16, 17, 30, 168n62; revolution interrupted and, 17; student activists and, ix, 21, 95, 99, 150, 151–52, 198n14. *See also* Communist Party of Thailand (CPT); counterrevolution; Marxism; socialists
conservative forces, 22, 59, 65, 69–72, 121, 130, 131, 140
Constitution(s), 60–64, 180n36
constitutional monarchy: decrees for LRCA of 1950 and, 19, 27, 30, 32–33; kings and, 12, 13, 17, 93; Land Reform Act of 1975 and, 11, 180n54; military relations with monarch and, 4, 56; PAD and, 157; People's Party and, 10, 17, 32, 169n62; Royal Institute and, 38, 174n40; SAP and, 125, 191n101; social justice and, xi, 19, 58; tenancy practices and, 11, 17, 30, 32, 55, 59, 80, 150; threat of assassinations to, 107; transition to, xi, 17, 30, 32, 43–44, 168n62. *See also* legal system/law(s); nationalism

contention over LRCA of 1950, 26–27, 29–30; class boundaries and, 48, 49–50; counterinsurgency and, 35–37, 40; CPT and, 30, 103; decrees and, 27, 32; farmers as backbone of the nation and, 39–40; landlord-tenant relations and, 31, 33, 43, 71, 76–79; land rent rates and, 31–34, 107–8, 172n7; land rent relief and, 19, 30, 31; legacy of transition to constitutional monarchy and, 30, 32; LRCA of 1950 described, 30, 31, 172n5; material conditions/loss for landowners and, 30, 32–33, 46; meetings with landlords and, 32, 42, 45–46, 48, 176nn67–68, 176n77; noneventfulness of, as basis for analysis, 44–45; nonimplementation of LRCA of 1950 and, 44–45; patron/landowner-client/tenant relations and, 30, 33, 49; peasants as agents of politics and, 36–37; political consciousness of farmers and, 33–34, 41–42, 45; political rights of farmers and, 30, 32–33, 39–43, 48, 172n11; poverty/hunger of farmers and, 19, 32–33, 45–47, 50, 110; portrayal of tenant farmers as capitalists, 46–47; as praxis, 37, 57; prevention of decree and, 19, 27, 32, 45, 71, 109; protests by farmers and, xi, 73–74; reevaluation of decree and, 44–48, 176nn67–68. *See also* farmer activists; Saraphi district farmers
Corrigan, Philip, 17
counterinsurgency, and communism, 4, 35–37, 40, 61, 69
counterprotests. *See* counterrevolution
counterrevolution, 27–28, 128, 130, 154–55, 196n89; as interruption of revolution, 18, 21–23, 130, 152; in Lamphun province, 130, 138–39, 140, 142–43; law/control of law issues and, 22, 28, 130–31, 133, 140–46, 152; police actions and, 22, 28, 130, 131, 133, 145–46, 152; police protests in support of, 130, 143–48, 152, 197nn102–3; state officials' reactions to police actions and, 146–48; symptoms of, 28, 106, 130; transformations and, 22, 130. *See also* assassinations of farmer activists/leaders; revolution interrupted; state disunity
coups. *See under* government of Thailand

CPT (Communist Party of Thailand). *See* Communist Party of Thailand (CPT)

"danger to society" detainees, ix–x, 92n112, 198n14
Darunee Charncherngsilpakul ("Da Torpedo"), 157
democratic politics. *See* political rights
Democrat Party, 109, 110, 150, 191n101
Dennis, John, 89, 111
Department of Police (police): arrests/charges against Lamphun activists and, 130, 133–37, 194n29, 195n44; assassination of farmers investigations by, 115–16, 122–26, 134, 136–37, 189n50; Border Patrol Police, 144, 150–51; communism's spread by activists, and fears of, 123; contradictions among, 133, 138; counterrevolution and, 22, 28, 130, 131, 133, 143–48, 152, 197nn102–3; denial of political subjectivity and, 116, 123; "disappeared" perpetrators trials and, 156–57; false evidence and, 124–25; liberated area investigations by, 4; massacre of 6 October 1976 and, ix; police protests and, 130, 143–48, 147, 152, 197nn102–3; sedition accusations made by, 123; tensions between divisions of, 144, 196n89; unnamed groups used as governance strategy and, 123. *See also* Ministry of Interior
Department of Special Investigations, 156
dictatorships, xii, 10, 12, 17, 53, 60, 92, 93, 149, 150, 155, 168n62
Diller, Anthony, 38, 175n40
disappear/"disappeared," 6, 106, 155, 156–57, 159, 161, 163, 187n2
Doi Saket district, 42, 43, 56, 79, 109
Dorfman, Ariel, 149

elections, 109–10, 149–50, 188n10, 191n99, 191n101
elite. *See* landlords; state officials; *specific state departments and ministries*
Engel, David, 21, 192n2
Engels, Friedrich, 15–16, 47. *See also* Marxism
Enloe, Cynthia, 6–7, 14
equality/inequality issues, 20, 86–87, 154, 186n61

farmer activists, ix–xi, 6–7, 127, 155, 179n74; assassinations of, ix–x, 6, 22, 106, 114, 159–63, 187n2; class boundaries and, 5, 18, 152, 195n44; communism and, ix, 29, 99, 152, 154; CPT membership and, 99, 152, 154; disappeared, 6, 106, 159–63, 187n2; Farmer Project and, 18, 81–82, 84–85, 90, 99, 101–4, 133, 151–52; fear of communism being spread by, 6, 12, 30, 35–37, 48–50, 98, 107, 112–13, 123, 177n87, 188n28; 14 October 1973 movement and, 12, 84; imagined future and, 98–99; injured, 106, 159–63, 187n2; liberated areas and, 4, 6, 65; political consciousness of, 59–60; political subjectivity of, 19, 21, 38, 80, 106, 115–19, 121–24, 152–53; reconciliation Thai-style and, x; revolution interrupted and, 16, 18, 22, 158; sedition accusations against, 112–13; social justice and, x, 3; teacher support for, 81, 97; "three links" alliance and, 18, 113; transformations and, 13, 17–18, 22, 84. *See also* assassinations of farmer activists/leaders; contention over LRCA of 1950; counterrevolution; farmers; state disunity; tenancy; urban protests by farmer activists; violence; *specific activists*; *specific organizations*; *specific provinces*

Farmer Project (Khrongkan Chao Na), 18, 81–82, 84–85, 90, 99, 101–4, 133, 151–52

farmers: as backbone of the nation, 10, 37–39, 48, 51–52; capitalists and, 46–47, 79–80, 109, 114, 120, 121; as counterinsurgency tool, 4, 35–37, 40, 61, 69; feudalism and, 7, 9, 11, 55–59, 79, 149; land issues and, 7, 41, 54, 155, 177n3; patron-client relations and, 9, 20, 22–23, 30, 44; political consciousness of, 33–34, 41–42, 45; as political objects, 13, 21, 39–42, 130; typology of, 40–41, 44; as wage laborers, 29, 41, 68, 172n7, 177n3. *See also* farmer activists; peasants; poverty/hunger of farmers; tenancy; *specific districts*; *specific organizations*

Farmers' Federation of Thailand (FFT): overview, xi, 6, 22, 55, 67–68, 127, 178n11; assassination of activists and, ix–x, 6, 98, 106, 107, 114, 115, 122, 187n2; assassination of leaders and, 106, 114, 117–22, 148, 159–63,

161; capitalists and, 114, 120; denials of importance of assassinations, 115, 117; Farmer Project alliance with, 82; imagined future and, 98, 186n58; landlords' conflicts with, 114; as legal political organization, 115, 117, 123, 190n87; legal rights education campaign and, 101; in northern provinces, 5, 69, 82, 101; NSCT and, 115; political consciousness of farmers and, 33–34; poverty/hunger of farmers and, 126; protests by, 66–67, 107, 113–14; silence of marginalized people and, xi–xii; state response to activism and, 66–67; statistics on, 68, 69; student-farmer relations as dangerous and, 102–3; violence against, 24, 99, 113–14. *See also* Intha Sribunruang; *specific FFT leaders and members*

farmers' legal actions: class boundaries and, 5; landlord-tenant relations and, 20, 22, 152–53; lawyers and, 5, 110; legal rights and, 7–8, 15, 20, 101–2, 152, 154; LRCA of 1974 and, 5–6, 15, 50, 58, 107–9, 110–11; political education and, 85, 95–97, 100–103, 118–19, 155; revolution interrupted and, 5, 6, 20–21; violence and, 6, 107–11

farmer-student relations. *See* rural activism by students; student-farmer relations

Federation of Independent Students of Thailand (FIST), 63, 103

feminism, 14, 182n4. *See also* women

feudalism, 7, 9, 11, 55–59, 79, 149. *See also* absolute monarchy; farmers; peasants

FFT (Farmers' Federation of Thailand). *See* Farmers' Federation of Thailand (FFT)

14 October 1973 movement, 3, 4, 11–13, 17, 18, 21–22, 180n36, 198n13

freedom of information, 194n13

Freire, Paolo, 27, 56–57, 84, 87, 103, 118, 187n71

gendering categories, 83, 95, 192n2. *See also* women

Gibson-Graham, J. K., 19, 169n71

Glassman, Jim, 126

Gordimer, Nadine, 129

government of Thailand: 1932 coup, 17, 30, 32, 43–44, 168n62; October 1958 coup, 53; 17 November 1971 coup, 92–94; October

1974 coup, 106; 19 September 2006 coup, xii, 157, 194n17; administrative divisions, map of, 2; cooperatives for farmers and, 178n11; CPT and, 12; dictatorships and, xii, 10, 12, 17, 53, 60, 92, 93, 149, 150, 155, 168n62; hegemony resistance/production and, 14–15, 17; history of Thailand and, 32, 38, 174n37; implementation of responses from, 61–62, 64; landlord-tenant-nation relations and, 119; Ministry of Agriculture and Cooperatives, 42, 71, 100; NARC and, 151, 198n14; Order 22, 198n14; power of, xi–xii, 12, 14–15, 17; responses to demands by farmers from, 60–62, 63–64, 66–67, 74–76; rural development programs and, 85, 90, 95–97; silence of marginalized people and, xi–xii, 14; 6 October 1976 coup, xi, 4, 6, 10, 12, 53, 60, 92, 149, 150; unnamed groups used as strategy by, 123, 141–42. *See also* absolute monarchy; constitutional monarchy; dictatorships; legal system/ law(s); parastate forces; right-wing forces; state disunity; state officials

Gramsci, Antonio, 14–15, 21–22
Grandin, Greg, 4–5, 158
Guevara, Che, 103, 134
Guha, Ranajit, 36–37

Hasawut Withitwichaikul, 107
hegemony, 14–15, 17, 21–22, 153, 170n73
human rights activists, 155
hunger/poverty of farmers. *See* poverty/hunger of farmers
Hutasingh, Prakob, 4, 63, 65, 75

inequality/equality issues, 20, 86–87, 154, 186n61
Inson Buakiew, 59–60, 69, 110, 125, 199n99
Internal Security Operations Command (ISOC), 154, 196n64
Intha Sribunruang: activism and, 118, 119, 190n63; assassination of, 106, 114, 117–22, 148, 161; assassination theories and, 120; biographical information about, 68, 117–18, 121, 125, 133; contradictory responses to assassination of, 125–26; denial of political subjectivity of farmer activists and, 116,

122–24, 123; false evidence in investigating death of, 124–25; ideology of, 119, 120, 126; implementation of LRCA of 1974 and, 28, 118–19; military denials of responsibility for assassinating activist leaders and, 117; named/unnamed assassins and, 106, 114, 127; pedagogy of solidarity and, 118; police investigations into assassination of, 122–26; as political subject, 115, 117–19, 123; provincial government, and role of, 126; Ruankham and, 28, 117, 121, 123, 125; social justice and, 119–20. *See also* Farmers' Federation of Thailand (FFT)
Islam, 156–57, 199n20

Jit Phumisak (pseud. Somsamai Srisudra-varna), 27, 55–59, 75, 79, 82, 103, 149, 158, 178n12
journalists, 12, 187n4
justice. *See* social justice

Kanoksak Kaewthep, 33–34, 51, 90, 114, 159, 172n11, 173n15, 187n2
Kasian Tejapira, 17, 168n62
KGB (Committee for State Security, USSR), 127, 192n113, 196n64
Komol Keemthong, 89, 94
Kriangkamol Laophairoj, 133–34, 147
Krirkkiat Phipatseritham, 8, 166n18
Krue Se mosque massacre, 199n20. *See also* Muslims
Kukrit Pramoj: arrest of activists from Lumphon province and, 133, 137; assassi-nation of farmer activists and, 113, 115, 122, 141; on fears of communism, 112; police counterrevolutionary actions and, 22, 28, 130, 131, 133, 145–46; on police protests, 145, 147, 148; SAP and, 149, 191n101; using specter of unnamed group as warning to activists, 141–42
Kulap Saipradit (pseud. Sriburapha), 56, 82, 179n17

Lampang province, 9, 27, 82, 83, 91, 167n27
Lamphun province, 9, 54; arrests/charges against activists from, 130, 133–37, 194n29, 195n44; counterrevolution in, 130, 138–39,

Lamphun province (*continued*)
140, 142–43; FFT and, 5, 69, 82, 101;
imagined future and, 159; LRCA of 1950
decree and, 55, 70–74, 107–8; LRCA of
1974 implementation tensions and, 107–8;
police protests in, 144–45, 147, 197nn102–3;
protection for farmer activists and, 127;
protests in, 138, 139, 140; rural activism by
students in, 27, 82; state response to activists and, 67, 73, 75–76
Lamphun Province Farmer Agriculturalist Group (Klum Kasetakon Chao Na
Changwat Lamphun), 138–39
landlords, 18, 26; and accusations of sedition
against activists, 107, 112–13; assassinations
of farmers and, 22, 27, 106, 114, 121; attempt
by, to halt progressive social transformation, 22; capitalists and, 46–47, 79–80, 109,
121; decrees for LRCA of 1950 and, 19, 27,
32, 45, 71, 109; and fear of communism, 6,
12, 30, 35–37, 48–50, 98, 107, 112–13, 177n87,
188n28; feudalism and, 7, 9, 11, 55–59, 79,
149 (*see also* absolute monarchy; farmers;
peasants); land issues and, 9–10, 166n27,
167n31, 170n74, 180n54; legal rights and,
19, 20, 154; LRCA of 1974 and, 5–6, 19–20;
material conditions/loss and, 30, 32–33,
46, 190n63; moral code of, 20, 23, 33, 112;
ontological struggle between farmers and,
20, 30, 32–33, 37, 47, 50, 79–80, 153, 170n75;
political subjectivity and, 80, 152–53;
power of, 9, 20, 21, 98, 103; social justice
and, 39–42; 22. *See also* landlord-tenant
relations; right-wing forces
landlord-tenant relations, 9, 10, 13; contention over LRCA of 1950 and, 31, 33, 43,
71, 76–79; farmers' legal actions and, 20,
152–53; hegemony crisis and, 22, 153, 154;
legal rights education campaign and,
101–2; LRCA of 1974 and, 5–6, 15, 19–20,
21, 76–78, 107–11, 120, 188n21; myths about,
20, 169nn73–74; patron-client relations
and, 9, 20, 22–23, 30, 44, 55; political
transformation and, 10, 17–18; symptoms
of crisis and, 22; transgression of, 18,
152; violence and, 107–12, 120, 121, 188n8,
188n21. *See also* tenancy

Land Reform Act of 1975, 11, 180n54
Land Rent Control Act of 1950 (LRCA of
1950), 30, 31, 172n5; central Thailand and,
32, 173n15; decrees for, 19, 27, 30, 32–33;
Lamphun province and, 55, 70–74, 107–8;
landlord-tenant relations and, 31, 33, 43, 71,
76–79; land rent rates and, 9, 44, 71, 76–78,
77, 100–101, 107–8; Ministry of Interior
and, 31–32, 42–45, 47. *See also* contention
over LRCA of 1950
Land Rent Control Act of 1974 (LRCA of
1974), 21, 30, 55, 76–78, 182n117; activism and, 5–6, 15, 50, 68, 113; Chiang Mai
province and, 77, 78, 100–101, 107–8; CPT
and, 21, 30, 98; implementation of, 5–6,
28, 100–101, 107–11, 118–19, 120, 188n21;
landlord-tenant relations and, 5–6, 15,
19–20, 76–78, 107–11, 120, 188n21; land
rent rates and, 76–78, 98, 100, 107–8; land
rent relief and, 19–20, 28, 100; LRCA of
1950 compared with, 76–78. *See also* Intha
Sribunruang; rural activism by students;
urban protests by farmer activists
land rent relief, 19–20, 28, 30–31, 55, 100. *See
also* contention over LRCA of 1950; Land
Rent Control Act of 1974 (LRCA of 1974)
land tenancy. *See* tenancy
language. *See* linguistics
Lanna kingdom, 8–9, 20, 32, 170n73
law(s)/legal system. *See* legal system/law(s)
lawyers, 5, 101, 102, 110, 155–57, 156–57
Lawyers' Society of Thailand (Lawyers' Association of Thailand), 67, 74, 135–36
leftist politics, xviii, 23, 24, 151–53, 158, 175n40
legal system/law(s), 3, 20–21; Codes and, 10,
143, 147; control of law issues and, 22,
28, 130–31, 133, 140–46, 152; extrajudicial
violence/law boundary and, 22, 28, 130,
131, 133, 145–48, 152, 156, 192n2; legal rights
and, 7–8, 15, 19, 20, 101–2, 152, 154, 194n13;
prosecution of assassins and, 106, 137,
157; protests and, 147; as state power, 21,
146–47, 192n2; use of, against spread of
communism, 153–54
Lenin, V. I., 4, 12, 16, 56, 88, 152, 185n45
liberated areas (autonomous zones), 4, 6, 65,
150, 151–52

liberation process, 21, 84, 87, 121
liberation theology movements, 16, 27, 56–57, 84, 87, 103, 118, 187n71
linguistics: language of Thailand and, 13, 38, 174n40; *Matichon Dictionary of the Thai Language* and, 17, 51–52; "revolution" defined, 17, 158, 200n27; *Royal Institute Dictionary* and, 13, 17, 35, 38–40, 45, 51–52, 174n36
Lorde, Audre, 21
lords, 9, 11, 20, 170n73. *See also* landlords

Mae Wa mine, 135, 137, 194n29
Mao Tse-tung, 12, 16, 35, 48, 56, 93, 109, 183n11
Marut Bunnag, 74, 135–36
Marxism, 4, 14–18, 21, 47, 88, 155. *See also* communists/communist movements; socialists
material conditions/loss, 30, 32–33, 46, 190n63. *See also* poverty/hunger of farmers
Matichon Dictionary of the Thai Language, 17, 51–52
Mengrai (king), 8
Merry, Sally, 20–21
Metropolitan Police, 171n90, 196n89
military forces, ix, 4, 27, 56, 94, 117, 149–50, 185n45, 189n53, 199n20
Mills, Mary Beth, 91
Ministry of Agriculture and Cooperatives, 42, 71, 100
Ministry of Interior, 31–32, 42–45, 47, 100, 110, 133, 135, 137, 148, 171n90, 176n68, 196n89. *See also* Department of Police (police); *specific state officials*
monk/nun activism, 66, 131, 180n63
Morell, David, 61, 64–65, 67
Muslims, 156–57, 199n20

Nafisi, Azar, 25–26
Narong Kittikachorn, 10, 12
National Administrative Reform Council (NARC), 151, 198n14
nationalism: Buddhism and, 27, 56, 131, 150, 153, 193n6; farmers and, 39, 41; military forces and, 27, 56, 150; right-wing forces and, 131, 193n6; sedition accusations and, 112–13, 123, 150, 157, 198n5
national security detainees, 156–57

National Student Center of Thailand (NSCT): on arrests/release of Lamphun activists, 139, 141, 195n58; on assassinations, 115, 122, 140, 141, 189n50; *Athipat*, 24, 61, 87, 88, 115, 135, 183n11; ideology of, 103, 113, 147; student activism and, 11–12, 68, 133–34, 147
Nawaphon, 98, 126, 128, 131, 132, 151
New Left, 17–18, 94
Nidhi Eoseewong, 86
Nisit Jirasophon, 85, 94, 183n11, 185n43, 185n46
Niwet Tongkwao (pseud.), 88
Northeastern Student Center, 88, 195n58
Northern Farmers' Federation, 117
Northern Student Center (NSC), 88, 122, 139, 194n29
northern Thailand. *See specific cities; specific provinces*
NSCT (National Student Center of Thailand). *See* National Student Center of Thailand (NSCT)

Order 22, 198n14

parastate forces, 12, 22–23, 27, 98, 126, 128, 131–32, 150–51, 157, 193n6. *See also* right-wing forces; state officials
Patriots of Lamphun (Klum Phitak Chat Lamphun), 142–44
patron-client relations, 9, 20, 22–23, 30, 44, 55. *See also* landlord-tenant relations
peasants, 9, 20, 34, 36–37, 58, 114, 170n73. *See also* farmers
pedagogy of solidarity, 27, 84–85, 97–99, 103
People for Democracy Group (PDG), 63
People's Alliance for Democracy (PAD), 157
People's Constitution, 194n17
People's Party, 10, 17, 32, 169n62
Phao Sriyanond, 53
Phelan, Brian, 114
Phibun Songkhram, 10, 31, 44, 53, 174n37, 175n40
Phin Bua-on (pseud. Amnat Yutthawiwat), 88
Phinit Jarusombat, 67–68
Phoj Phekanan, 116, 125, 134, 136–37, 189n50
Ping River basin, 8, 32, 54, 107
polarization, 12, 127–28, 130, 149–50, 191n99
police. *See* Department of Police

political rights, 13–14, 149, 168n50, 168n54;
agency and, 34, 36–37; capitalism as process, 18–19; farmer activists' education and,
85, 95–97, 100–103, 118–19, 155; of farmers,
30, 32–33, 39–44, 48, 172n11, 176n60; imagined future and, 14, 168n54; object role of
farmers and, 21, 130; political consciousness and, 33–34, 41–42, 45, 59–60, 85–89,
95–96; "political" defined, 100; poverty,
and exclusion from, xi, 84, 155; socialists
and, 15–16; subjectivity and, 19, 21, 38, 58,
80, 106, 115–19, 121–24, 152–53, 157. *See also*
power; social justice
politics: definition of, 13–14, 168n50, 168n54;
elections, 109–10, 149–50, 188n10, 191n99,
191n101. *See also* government of Thailand;
political rights; *and specific individuals and
organizations*
poverty, of citizens, xi, 84, 155
poverty/hunger of farmers, xi, 8, 11, 13; contention over LRCA of 1950 and, 19, 32–33,
45–47, 50, 110, 126; transformations and, 5,
27; urban protests by farmer activists, 69–70
power: of government, xi–xii, 12, 14–15, 17; of
landlords, 9, 20, 21, 103; landlord-tenant
relations and, 11, 18, 20, 22–23, 45, 78–79,
120; laws as political state, 21, 130, 146–47,
192n2; within military forces, 94, 149,
185n45
Pradap Manurasada, 102, 110, 134
Prajak Kongkirati, 85
Prakob Hutasingh, 4, 63, 65, 75
Praphat Jarusathien, 10, 12, 92, 93
Pridi Banomyong, 10, 17
progress (economic), xi, 91
progressives/progressive activists. *See* farmer
activists; students/student activists; *specific
activists*; *specific organizations*
Provincial Police, 132, 144–45, 147, 196n89

radical actions, 16, 60, 73, 78–79, 113, 142, 153,
158, 190n63
Ramkhamhaeng (king), 186n58
Ramkhamhaeng University, 139, 195n58
Rangsit Plains, 8, 166n18
Real Face of Thai Feudalism Today, The (Som-
samai), 27, 55–59, 103, 149, 178n12

reconciliation, "Thai-style," x
Red Gaurs, 98, 126, 132, 150–51, 185n57
reeducation program, ix, 92n112, 198n14
religion. *See specific religions*
research methodology, 23–26, 171n86,
171nn90–91
Return to Rural Areas Program, 85, 90, 95–97.
See also Volunteer Development Assembly
(VDA)
revolution: communism and, 4–5, 15–16, 17,
30, 168n62; definition of, 3, 15–16, 17, 158,
200n27; 14 October 1973 movement as,
12–13; imagined/reimagined future and,
10, 14, 16, 17, 28, 152, 158, 168n54; legacies of
1932, 17, 30, 32, 43–44, 168n62; legal system
and, 21; peaceful, 158
revolution interrupted, 4–7, 16, 28, 153; assassinations and, 23, 106; communism and, 17;
counterrevolution and, 18, 21–23, 130, 152;
farmer activists and, 16, 18, 22, 158; transformations and, 5, 7, 17–18. *See also* Department of Police; farmer activists; farmers;
parastate forces; right-wing forces; state
officials; students/student activists
rice, 10, 31, 36, 54, 71, 72, 126, 172n5
Rich, Adrienne, xi, xii
right-wing forces: assassination of farmers
and, 22–23, 27; elites and, 98, 131; named/
unnamed assassins and, 106; nationalism
and, 131, 193n6; revolution interrupted
and, 22; sedition accusations made by, 150,
198n5; violence against activists and, 12,
98, 99, 106, 120–21, 126, 131, 140, 150–51.
*See also specific right-wing individuals and
organizations*
Royal Institute, 38, 174n40
Royal Institute Dictionary, 13, 17, 35, 38–40, 45,
51–52, 174n36
Ruankham Sribunruang, 117, 121, 123, 124, 125
rural activism by students, 27, 81–85, 103–4, 137;
class status of students and, 82–83, 86;
contention over land rent rates and, 98,
100–101, 186n58; critiques of rural development projects and, 92–93; democratic
politics of students and, 95–96; Farmer
Project and, 18, 81–82, 84–85, 90, 99, 101–4,
133, 151–52; gendering categories and,

83, 95; imagined future and, 82–84; legal rights education and, 101–2; pedagogy of solidarity and, 84, 97–99, 103, 187n71; political consciousness/education of students and, 85–89, 95–96, 102, 103; as praxis, 84, 88; radicalization of education and, 84–85; rural development projects and, 82, 89–90, 91; rural students and, 86; student-farmer relations as dangerous for farmers and, 85, 101–3, 104, 113–14, 182n8, 185n45, 186n61, 187n75, 188n35; student-farmer relations as familial and, 99; student-farmer tensions and, 99, 186n61, 187n71; students as revolutionary subjects and, 88; teachers and, 83, 86–87; VDA and, 85, 90–95; youth-rural people links and, 82, 89–90. *See also* student-farmer relations; students/ student activists

rural development projects, 82, 89–90, 91–92. *See also specific development projects*

rural relations of power. *See* landlord-tenant relations

Sanam Luang: police protests in, 145; urban protests by farmer activists and, 11, 55, 60, 62–63, 65–67, 74, 79, 84, 101, 113, 178n10; workers' activism and, 63

Sanan Narinsorasak, 113, 136, 144

Sanya Thammasak, 4, 12, 60, 79, 95, 189n50

Saraphi district farmers, 34, 35, 50; denial of poverty/hunger among, 46, 110; farmers as backbone of the nation and, 37–39, 51–52; feudalism analysis and, 57, 79; imagined future of, 50–51; on legacy of 1932 revolution, 43–44; LRCA of 1950 decree and, 32, 42–44, 45, 48, 109; LRCA of 1974 implementation tensions and, 101; political rights of, 32, 34, 38, 43–44, 118, 172n11, 176n60, 190n63

Sarit Thanarat, 53, 55, 60, 61

Sayer, Derek, 17

Scott, James, 5, 21, 43, 51

sedition accusations (lèse-majesté), 107, 112–13, 123, 150, 157, 198n5

Siam (later Thailand), 32, 38, 174n37, 174n40. *See also* government of Thailand; lords

silence of marginalized people, xi–xii, 12, 14, 19. *See also* social justice

Sithon Yodkantha, 114

6 October 1976 massacre, ix–x, 11–12, 23, 98–99, 150–51. *See also* 14 October 1973 movement; Thammasat University

Social Action Party (SAP), 124, 125, 149, 191n101

socialists, 12, 15–16, 18, 56, 82, 87, 88. *See also* Marxism

social justice, x, 18, 58, 149; constitutional monarchy and, xi, 19, 58; contention over LRCA of 1950 and, 44, 149; equality/in-equality issues and, 20, 86–87, 154, 186n61; farmer activists and, x, 3, 18, 20, 58, 119–20; 14 October 1973 movement and, 12, 18; imagined future and, 10, 14, 16, 17, 168n54; silence of marginalized people and, xi–xii, 12, 14, 19; social and political transformation and, 5, 27, 84; student activists and, x, 18; tenancy and, 10. *See also* poverty/ hunger of farmers; power

Somchai Neelaphaichit, 156–57

southern provinces, 8, 54, 89, 155–56, 175n57, 199n21

Southern Student Center, 88

space: farmer activists and, xi, 19, 68; state officials and, 13, 18; students/student activists and, xi, 13, 19, 22, 68; transgressions of, xi, 5–6, 18, 19, 22, 152, 155

Special Branch police (Santiban), 94, 97, 156, 185n45

SPT (Socialist Party of Thailand), 59, 110, 125, 128, 187n4, 191n99, 191n101

Stallybrass, Peter, 18

state disunity, 28, 129–31, 148; arrests/charges against Lamphun activists and, 130, 133–37, 194n29, 195n44; contradictions among state officials and, 133, 138; as governance strategy, 130, 131–33, 141–42, 144; internal state conflicts and, 130, 138; protests about arrests of Lamphun activists and, 130, 137–41, 195n58, 196n64; as public event, 130, 133, 148; release of activists from Lamphun province and, 141–42; right-wing forces and, 131; state described, 133; state/parastate relations and, 131, 133–34, 193nn12–13; state response

state disunity (*continued*)
　　to police protests and, 145, 147, 148; un-
　　nameable groups creating insecurity and,
　　141–42; violence/state link and, 133, 148,
　　193n10. *See also* counterrevolution; govern-
　　ment of Thailand
state officials: assassinations, and (in)actions/
　　responses by, 107, 115–17, 125–26, 189n50,
　　189n53; blacklists and, 151, 198n13; capital-
　　ists and, 3; and fear of communism, 6, 12,
　　30, 35–37, 48–50, 107, 112–13, 177n87, 188n28;
　　and fear of farmers as political subjects,
　　152–53; hegemony crisis and, 22; LRCA
　　of 1974 implementations and, 5–6, 110;
　　military relations with, 4; parastate forces'
　　relations with, 131, 157; politics/law and,
　　130; relations of, with farmers, 18; research
　　methodology and, 26; sedition accusations
　　against activists and, 107, 112–13; silence
　　of marginalized people and, xi–xii; space
　　issues and, 13, 18. *See also* parastate forces;
　　specific political leaders; specific state officials
Stoler, Ann Laura, 24, 45
student-farmer relations: class boundaries
　　and, 18–19, 82–84, 86, 119–20, 121, 152;
　　as dangerous for farmers, 85, 99, 101–3,
　　104, 113, 182n8, 185n45, 186n61, 187n75; as
　　familial, 99; inequalities and, 186n61; in
　　Lamphun province, 138; landlord-tenant
　　relations and, 18; NSCT on, 113; reimag-
　　ined future and, 105–6, 152; research
　　methodology and, 24, 26; Return to Rural
　　Areas Program and, 85, 90, 95–97; rural
　　development projects and, 82, 89–90;
　　tensions and, 99, 186n61; transformations
　　and, 152; transgression of space and, 5–6,
　　18, 19, 152; VDA and, 85, 90–95. *See also*
　　Farmer Project (Khrongkan Chao Na);
　　rural activism by students
Students' Association/Organization, 90–91,
　　137–38, 194n29
students/student activists, ix–x; arrests of, 130,
　　133–37, 139, 141, 146–47, 188n35, 194n29,
　　195n44; assassinations of farmer activists
　　and, ix–x, 115, 121, 122; class boundaries
　　and, 19, 82–84, 86, 103, 119–20, 195n44;
　　communism and, 21, 99, 150, 151–52,

198n14; elites' fears of communism's
　　spread by, 112–13, 188n28; 14 October 1973
　　movement and, 12, 22; imagined future
　　and, 99; in Lamphun province, 27, 82;
　　legacies of, 155; legal system and, 18, 147;
　　political consciousness of, 85–89, 95–96;
　　protests about arrests of Lamphun and,
　　130, 137–41, 195n58, 196n64; publications
　　of, 85, 94; reconciliation "Thai-style" and,
　　x; right-wing forces and, 98; sedition ac-
　　cusations against, 150, 198n5; social justice
　　and, x, 18; space issues and, xi, 13, 19, 22, 68;
　　teacher support for, 81, 83, 189n35; "three
　　links" alliance and, 18, 113; transformation
　　and, 17–18, 105; transgressions by, xi, 18, 19,
　　22; urban protests by farmer activists and,
　　66, 180n63; violence against, ix–x, 11–12,
　　23, 98–99, 114, 150–51, 187n4, 188n35. *See
　　also* rural activism by students
subjectivity. *See under* political rights
Suphot Dantrakul, 158, 200n27
symptoms of crisis, 22–23, 27, 106

Tak Bai massacre, 199n20
teacher activists, ix, 84, 122; at CMU, 18, 81, 83,
　　97, 139, 140, 189n35; equality/inequality
　　issues and, 86–87; 14 October 1973 move-
　　ment and, 22, 84
tenancy, 5, 7–11, 29; Chiang Mai province and,
　　8–9, 32, 53–54; land issues and, 9–10, 11,
　　119, 166n27, 167n31, 180n54; politics of, 7–8,
　　13, 14–15; poverty/hunger of farmers and,
　　13; reimagined future and, 10; statistics
　　on, 8, 32, 166n18. *See also* landlord-tenant
　　relations
tenant farmers. *See* farmers; tenancy
Thailand (formerly Siam): central, 32, 44, 45,
　　100, 171n9, 173n15; history of, 32, 38, 174n37.
　　See also absolute monarchy; constitutional
　　monarchy; government of Thailand;
　　specific cities; specific provinces
Thainess, 154, 175n40
Thak Chaloemtiarana, 86–87, 88, 189n53
Thaksin Shinawatra, 155, 157, 199n20
Thammasak, Sanya, 4, 12, 60, 79, 189n50
Thammasat University: massacre of 6 October
　　1976 and, ix–x, 11–12, 23, 98–99, 150–51;

protest actions and, 139, 150, 196n64; pub-
lications at, 23, 85; Students' Association,
86–87. *See also* 14 October 1973 movement
Thanet Aphornsuvan, 85, 89, 97
Thanin Kraivichien, 154, 175n40
Thani Wiradecha, 123, 124
Thanom Kittikachorn, 10, 12, 53, 60, 92, 93,
150, 151
Tha Pae gate, 70, 127, 139–40. *See also* Chiang
Mai city
Theerachai Maruekhaphitak, 139
Therd Tharaninthorn, 116, 132
Thirayuth Bunmi, 11, 141
Thompson, E. P., 3, 21
Thongchai Winichakul, ix–x, 12
Thongdee Isarachiwin, 32, 43–45, 47–49,
191n99
"three links" (*sam prasan*) alliance, 18, 113
Tierney-Tello, Mary Beth, 20
transformation(s), social and political: activists
and, 13, 17–18, 21, 22, 84, 105; counterrevolution and, 22, 130; landlord-tenant relations and, 10, 17–18, 22, 78–79; Marxism
as basis for, 17–18; parastate forces and, 22;
processes of, 7, 16; revolution interrupted
and, 5, 7, 17–18; social justice and, 5, 27, 84;
student-farmer relations and, 152; transgressions as foundation for, 18, 105–6, 152
transgression(s), 18, 111; class boundaries,
18–19, 121, 152; farmer activists', 18, 20,
152; landlords' moral code, 20, 23, 33, 112;
landlord-tenant relations, 18, 20, 22–23,
152; of space, xi, 5–6, 18, 19, 22, 152, 155; state
officials and, 18, 47; student-farmer relations, 18–19, 105–6, 121, 152; transformations built on, 18, 105–6, 152; by women, 20
transplanted rice practice, 31, 72, 172n5
Turton, Andrew, 51, 68, 102–3, 113, 178n11,
190n63

Udom Bunprasop, 45–48
United Nations, 36, 156
urban protests by farmer activists, 27, 53–56,
58–59, 152; actions by farmers and, 60,
62, 65–67, 75, 107, 179n34; Article 17 and,
60–64; in Bangkok, xi, 19, 22, 72–73, 107,
139, 196n64; chaos accusations against pro-

testers and, 59, 63, 64–65; in Chiang Mai
city, 70–74; feudalism analysis and, 55–59;
imagined future and, 70; implementation
of state's response to demands of farmers
and, 61–62, 64; landlord-tenant transformations and, 78–79; legal debates and, 71,
72, 74; LRCA of 1950 and, 72–76; LRCA
of 1974 and, 55, 62–63; NSCT and, 63;
pedagogy of solidarity and, 84–85; political consciousness of farmers and, 59–60;
political subjectivity of farmers and, 65,
68, 69, 70, 80; poverty/hunger of farmers
and, 69–70; publications, 55, 56–57; radical actions and, 60, 73, 78–79; at Sanam
Luang, 11, 55, 60, 62–63, 65–67, 74, 79, 84,
101, 113, 178n10; social justice and, 58; space
issues and, xi, 19, 68; state's response to
demands by farmers and, 60–62, 63–64,
66–67, 74–75, 75–76; student activists and,
66, 180n63; threats against/made by farmers and, 3–4, 6, 65, 75. *See also* Land Rent
Control Act of 1974 (LRCA of 1974)

Vajiravudh (King Rama VI), 150
Village Scouts, 126, 132, 150–51
violence, 27–28, 105–7, 127–28, 156; against
activists, 114, 120–21, 151, 188n35; Article
17 and, 61; against citizens, 12, 156, 187n4;
elections and, 149–50, 191n99; 14 October
1973 movement and, 12; landlord-tenant
relations and, 11, 107–12, 120, 121, 188n8,
188n21; law/extrajudicial violence boundary and, 22, 28, 130, 131, 133, 145–48, 152,
156, 192n2; peaceful protests against, 107,
122; portrayal of landlords as capitalists
and, 109, 121; protest actions and, 107,
113–14, 122; sedition accusations against
activists and, 107, 112–13; social justice
and, 7, 149; state intimidation and, 98, 126,
128, 131, 132, 151; statistics on, 106, 187n2;
student-farmer relations and, 18, 105–6,
111–12, 121; as symptoms of crisis, 28, 106;
violent backlash of right-wing forces, 12,
17, 21–22, 106–7, 111, 152, 198n13. *See also*
assassinations of farmer activists/leaders;
counterrevolution; right-wing forces; state
disunity

Visooth Ruamchai, 127, 150–51, 192nn112–13
Volunteer Development Assembly (VDA), 85, 90–95. *See also* Return to Rural Areas Program
volunteer development camps, 89

Walanchathat (publication), 24, 93–94, 183n11, 185n43, 185nn45–46
Walzer, Michael, 5
Weber, Eugen, 16
Weschler, Lawrence, 121
White, Allon, 18
Williams, Raymond, 15
women, xi, 14, 20, 82, 83, 182n4
Women's Group, 82, 83, 182n4
Worasak Nimmanan, 46, 109–12

Worawut Kosonyutthasorn, 117, 189n53
workers, 12, 22, 29; alliances with, 18, 58, 113; chaos accusations against, 64–65; farmers as wage laborers, 29, 41, 68, 172n7, 177n3; in mines, 135; protests by, 63, 66, 150, 187n4, 195n58; sedition accusations against, 113; transformations and, 84
Wyatt, David, 168n62, 174n40

Yongyut Sujjavanich, 91
Young People of Chiang Mai (Klum Num Sao Chiang Mai), 140–41

Zimmerman, Carle C., 9, 166n25
Žižek, Slovaj, 106

NEW PERSPECTIVES IN
SOUTHEAST ASIAN STUDIES

The Burma Delta: Economic Development and Social Change on an Asian Rice Frontier, 1852–1941
Michael Adas

From Rebellion to Riots: Collective Violence on Indonesian Borneo
Jamie S. Davidson

The Floracrats: State-Sponsored Science and the Failure of the Enlightenment in Indonesia
Andrew Goss

Revolution Interrupted: Farmers, Students, Law, and Violence in Northern Thailand
Tyrell Haberkorn

Amazons of the Huk Rebellion: Gender, Sex, and Revolution in the Philippines
Vina A. Lanzona

Policing America's Empire: The United States, the Philippines, and the Rise of the Surveillance State
Alfred W. McCoy

An Anarchy of Families: State and Family in the Philippines
Edited by Alfred W. McCoy

The Hispanization of the Philippines: Spanish Aims and Filipino Responses, 1565–1700
John Leddy Phelan

Pretext for Mass Murder: The September 30th Movement and Suharto's Coup d'État in Indonesia
John Roosa

The Social World of Batavia: Europeans and Eurasians in Colonial Indonesia,
    second edition
Jean Gelman Taylor

Việt Nam: Borderless Histories
Edited by Nhung Tuyet Tran and Anthony Reid

Modern Noise, Fluid Genres: Popular Music in Indonesia, 1997–2001
Jeremy Wallach